A HISTORY OF
THE KING'S FLIGHT
AND
THE QUEEN'S FLIGHT
1936 – 1995

A history of
The King's Flight
and
The Queen's Flight
1936-1995

First edition, published in 2003 by

WOODFIELD PUBLISHING
Bognor Regis, West Sussex PO21 5EL
United Kingdom
www.woodfieldpublishing.com

ISBN 1-903953-32-4

The Queen's Flight Association website is at
tqfa-kittyhawk.org.uk

CONTENTS

FOREWORD

by Air Vice-Marshal Sir John Severne, KCVO, OBE, AFC, DL.
Captain, The Queen's Flight, 27ᵗʰ January 1982 – 13ᵗʰ January 1989

It all seems a very long time since my days as Equerry to HRH The Duke of Edinburgh and my early introduction to travel with The Queen's Flight. I would at that time have been greatly surprised should anyone have suggested that one day I would be Captain of The Queen's Flight.

I had already retired from the service about eighteen months before when the Captaincy of The Queen's Flight came my way in January 1982. Thereafter followed a most interesting and rewarding seven years serving with men and women of the Royal Air Force who were dedicated to the task of Royal Flying. Their story is told in the pages of this book, a compilation of personal accounts, odd experiences and of how the flight operated. It tells stories of individuals and their view of things, from airman to Air Vice-Marshal all are included.

The book covers the full story from the formation of The King's Flight in 1936 until the disbandment of The Queen's Flight in 1995. It is a compilation from many sources within The Queen's Flight Association and it is to the secretary of the Association, Squadron Leader Brian Sowerby, LVO, RAF (Ret'd), that thanks must go for his hard and unrelenting work without which it could not have been produced.

It is a good account of the inside of royal flying from the hangar floor upwards and truly reflects the various facets of life on 'The Flight'.

EDITOR'S COMMENTS

This history was written by members of The Queen's Flight prior to its disbandment in 1995 and by members of The Queen's Flight Association since that date. The book is intended to be used as a reference document and as a tribute to all past members for their achievements.

Much encouragement was given to me by the Committee of The Queen's Flight Association in the preparation of this book and I pay particular tribute to Sydney (Jack) Frost, RVM, and to Neil Davies, RVM, for their time and effort they put into ensuring that the copyright of this book will remain the property of The Queen's Flight Association.

We wish to thank the many people whose efforts and assistance brought together much of the information and illustration material that forms the basis of this book. We are particularly grateful for the gracious permission of Her Majesty The Queen for the use of material from The Royal Archives; to Octopus Publishing for the reversion of rights to The Queen's Flight Association of the book 'The Queen's Flight – Fifty Years of Royal Flying'; to Robert Taylor and The Military Gallery, Bath for their kind permission to use the painting 'The Queen's Flight by Robert Taylor' as a cover for this book; to the Air Historical Branch of the Ministry of Defence; The Royal Air Force Museum; Unpublished Royal Air Force Journals; Images of The Flight Collection, Flight International and the Museum of Royal Flying, Royal Air Force, Northolt.

Every effort has been made to trace the copyright holder of material used and I apologise if it has not been possible to do so. The author accepts no liability as to the accuracy of content or detailed statements of various contributors. Whilst every effort has been made to provide an honest report on the life and work of Royal Flying on The King's Flight and The Queen's Flight, any item included as a personal anecdote of a past member is taken in the spirit in which it has been written.

Brian Sowerby
Secretary, TQFA
March 2003

1. Pre-Flight ~ Royal Flying 1917-1936

Three Kings in Royal Air Force Uniform
Edward VIII, George V, and George VI at RAF Northolt on 6th July 1935

The Queen's Flight, disbanded in 1995, was descended from the personal flying unit established by His Royal Highness The Prince of Wales at Northolt in 1929, which subsequently became The King's Flight in 1936. However, Royal Flights and Royal Aircraft go back much further than The King's Flight, for the history of Royal Flying can be traced to the summer of 1917.

The Prince of Wales was the first member of The Royal Family to fly when he was taken up in France during the First World War. On the 24th July 1917 he wrote to his father, King George V: "It was so kind of you to give me leave to fly, which permission I took advantage of last Tuesday (exactly a week ago) and had ½ hour in the air above Abeele and Cassel with General Longcroft (GOC 5th Bde RFC) in a 'R.E.8'. He is considered one of the best pilots in France but of course he is no longer allowed to fly over the lines tho' he has done very well in the air earlier in the war. I must say I enjoyed my first trip very much indeed as such flying is really extraordinarily safe nowadays. But it was a hazy evening and clouds were low so that we couldn't go above 3,000 ft. I shall wait for a clear evening before I go up again, tho' of course nowhere near the line or within range of AA guns. But it makes all the difference having been up and knowing what it is like in the air." He next flew on the 16th September 1918 with Captain W.G. Barker in a Bristol Fighter of No. 139 Squadron when he visited the Italian Front.

In the meantime Prince Albert was taken up on the 4th March 1918 for his first flight by Lieutenant R.E.C. Peirse, later to become Air Chief Marshal Sir Richard Peirse, KCB, DSO, AFC (whose son became a Deputy Captain of The Queen's Flight 1969-72) at the RN Air Station, Sleaford (Cranwell), where Prince Albert was serving as a Naval Officer. "It was a curious sensation and one which takes a lot of getting used to," he wrote to his mother, Queen Mary, the following day. In March 1919 he took a flying course under the instruction of Lieutenant W.A. Coryton (later Air Chief Marshal Sir Alec Coryton, KCB, KBE, MVO, DFC) at Wadden Lane, Croydon, the site that was later absorbed into Croydon Airport. Two Avro 504s from the Air Council Communications Squadron were allocated for the course. He received his wings as a certified pilot on 31st July 1919 and his permanent commission as a Squadron Leader was gazetted the following day. He was thus the first member of the Royal Family to become a fully qualified pilot and is the only British Sovereign to have achieved this distinction.

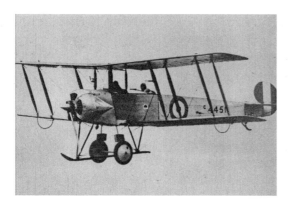

Prince Albert gained his wings flying an Avro 504J, C4451, the first aircraft allocated specifically for a Royal task.

The 504J was developed as a trainer from the 504A fighting machine and was used as the RFC and RAF training schools.

These activities were short lived however, for after the war The Prince of Wales again met Barker, now a Major with the VC, and flew with him in a Sopwith Dove. Barker, still recovering from wounds received on the Western front, piloted with one arm in a sling, and when the King heard of the risks involved, he advised his sons not to fly again.

THE FIRST 'ROYAL FLIGHT'

It took some years for King George V's attitude to change, and it was not until 1928 that The Prince of Wales again took up flying seriously, although in the meantime he had patronised some of the early airline services to the Continent. On 27th April 1928, the Prince flew for 30 minutes at Northolt in a Bristol Fighter of No. 24 Squadron, piloted by Flying Officer G.C. Stemp, and two weeks later that unit's establishment was increased by the addition of a Bristol Fighter annotated 'for Special Service', this being a temporary allocation pending delivery of two specially equipped Westland Wapiti 1A's. The first official conveyance of a member of the Royal Family by air came on 27th May 1928, when Flight Lieutenant J.S. Don flew The Prince of Wales from Scarborough to Bircham Newton in a Bristol Fighter.

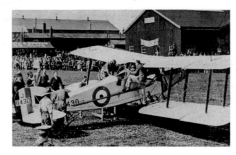

Bristol F2B Fighter J8430 was the first aircraft officially allocated for Royal engagements.

It had a modified rear cockpit with a windscreen and was fitted with Handley Page slats in the upper wing leading edge.

Held by No. 24 (Communications) Squadron, it was finished in standard RAF aluminium dope with the Squadron's red chevron emblem on the fin.

FLT LT EDWARD FIELDEN APPOINTED PERSONAL PILOT TO HRH THE PRINCE OF WALES:

Two Wapiti's, J9095 and J9096, arrived at Northolt in June 1928, and were soon in demand for a variety of VIP's, even though their 'VIP' fit still included an open cockpit rather than an enclosed cabin.

Wapiti J9095 in standard service finish.

Overall aluminium dope with dark green upper decking.

The Prince made a number of journeys in J9095, flown by Don, but his interests in flying was soon such that in September 1929 he forsook the Wapiti's and bought an aeroplane of his own, a De Havilland Gipsy Moth, G-AALG, which was finished in the red and blue colours of the Brigade of Guards, colours which have now become traditional in one form or another for Royal Aircraft.

DH60M Gipsy Moth G-AALG

Owned by the Prince of Wales from 1929 until 1933.

He arranged for Don to teach him to fly and on 17th November 1929, after some 30 hours dual (most of it cross country) the Prince flew a short solo sortie at Northolt in Gipsy Moth G-AAKV. However, by this time it was becoming increasingly difficult to carry out his No. 24 Squadron duties as well as overseeing the operation of the Prince's private aeroplane, and it was suggested that the Prince should appoint his own personal pilot. This he did, choosing for the task Flight Lieutenant E.H. Fielden (the late Air Vice Marshal Sir Edward Fielden, GCVO, CB, DFC, AFC) who had recently been transferred to the Reserve of Royal Air Force Officers; Fielden took full charge of the Prince's private aeroplane, which was kept at Northolt. He flew it at all times and was responsible for its maintenance. The Wapiti J9095 continued to be used occasionally, and three RAF pilots, headed by Squadron Leader Don, were authorised to fly it carrying The Prince of Wales and other members of the Royal Family.

In 1930, The Prince of Wales bought another DG60 Gipsy Moth, G-ABCW, to supplement G-AALG, and when this new addition suffered an unspecified mishap on 18th July 1930, it was quickly replaced by a third Gipsy Moth, G-ABDB. A further purchase was a cabin monoplane, DH80A Puss Moth G-ABBS. The Prince continued to call on No. 24 Squadron to fly him on some official visits, and for this the Wapiti's were replaced in 1930 by Fairey 111F's: K1115 (the Royal Aircraft) and J9061. The Prince sought every opportunity to indulge his love of flying, using a variety of aircraft and flying boats, and in 1931 he hired a Westland Wessex for his holiday in France, gaining first hand experience of operating a large multi-engined aeroplane.

DH60M Gipsy Moth G-AALG.

With the latest in cockpit luxury, pneumatic upholstery. It was fully dual-control equipped and the Prince learned to fly in this aircraft, tutored by Squadron Leader Don, with the permission of the King.

For Royal Flying, however, Don flew the aircraft. On 16th November 1929, Don made a forced landing in G-AALG; the axle was broken in this, the first Royal flying accident, but neither Don nor the Prince was hurt. G-AALG was finished, as were all the Prince's privately owned aircraft, in the red and blue colours of the Brigade of Guards, with whom the Prince had served during the Great War.

DH80A Puss Moth G-ABBS. The Prince of Wales' first cabin monoplane.

His other DH30A, G-ABFV, was sent, crated aboard HMS Eagle, to South America for his 1931 Royal tour.

"THE ROYAL FLIGHT" – HENDON

In 1931, The Prince of Wales' private aircraft had moved from Northolt to Hendon. Since the Prince held the RAF rank of an Air Chief Marshal, the aircraft were housed in the Display Hangar "under the same conditions which permitted serving officers to maintain private aeroplanes". Servicing, inspection and maintenance remained the responsibility of Flight Lieutenant Fielden, although the aircraft were in every way the property of The Prince of Wales – albeit registered in Fielden's name. Since they had the numerical strength of a Royal Air Force Flight – they soon became known collectively as "The Royal Flight". This title was quite unofficial, for such a unit was not to be established for a further six years, but the style "The Prince of Wales's Hangar" was in semi-official use by 1932.

In 1930 the first Royal entries in the King's Cup Air Race took place when Prince George (later to become The Duke of Kent) entered a DH Hawk Moth (G-AAUZ) flown by Flight Lieutenant Fielden and The Prince of Wales entered a Hawker Tomtit (G-AALL) flown by Squadron Leader Don; Fielden came seventh and Don eighteenth.

Tomtit G-AALL, loaned to The Prince of Wales for the 1930 King's Cup Air Race.

From 1931 onwards The Prince of Wales relied less and less on RAF aircraft and used his private aeroplanes, chiefly the Puss Moth, on almost all occasions. The original Puss Moth, G-ABBS, had been replaced in turn during 1931 by a third Puss Moth, G-ABNN which set the style followed on all but one of The Prince's subsequent aircraft, that of having the last two registration letters the same. The fourth and final Puss Moth, G-ABRR, was obtained in September 1931.

In 1931 The Prince of Wales carried out a tour of South America using Puss Moth G-ABFV, which had been shipped out in HMS Eagle. During this tour, on 9th April, HRH carried out the first Royal deck landing when he flew on to the deck of HMS Eagle in a Fairey 111F off the coast of Rio de Janeiro. His brother Prince George who was flying in the Puss Moth with Edward Fielden witnessed this event from the air.

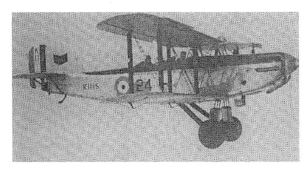

K1115, was one of the original two specially-fitted Fairey 111F's operated by No.24 Squadron

When in December 1932, G-ABNN gave way to a slightly larger Fox Moth G-ACDD; the fleet comprised three generations of the de Havilland Moth family – two DH60 Gipsy Moths, One DH80 Puss Moth, and a DH83 Fox Moth.

DH83 Fox Moth G-ACDD, procured in exchange for the smaller Puss Moth G-ABNN in December 1932.

It was also finished in the Brigade of Guards' colours – red and blue, with a silver cheat line – and followed the practice on Royal aircraft of having the two last letters of the registration the same.

Meanwhile, in 1932, a special aircraft was built for Fielden to race in The King's Cup Air Race. Although the aircraft, a Comper Swift, remained the property of The Comper Aircraft Company Ltd., and its engine belonged to de Havillands, it was commissioned and entered for the race by The Prince of Wales, was painted in his colours, and registered G-ABWW. Edward Fielden flew the Swift to second place in the 1932 King's Cup at a speed of 155.75 mph, also putting up the fastest time in the London to Newcastle Air Race later in the year; despite these successes, a Royal entry was not repeated until 1959, when a Turbulent, entered by HRH The Duke of Edinburgh and flown by his Equerry, Squadron Leader John Severne, flew in the National Air Races.

Comper Swift G-ABWW

The original Gipsy Moth, G-AALG, was sold in February 1933 and shortly afterwards Fox Moth G-ACDD was replaced by the similar G-ABXS. The association with the De Havilland Company was a strong one, but for his next aircraft The Prince of Wales bought elsewhere. Late in 1932 the Prince, in consultation with Fielden reviewed his aircraft requirements, as the existing machines were too small to carry more than an ADC and valet. His experience of the Wessex and the larger Imperial Airways aircraft had been invaluable, and on 15th May 1933 Fielden took delivery of a twin-engined Vickers Viastra X, G-ACCC, which was the first aircraft specifically ordered and built for a member of the Royal Family.

Vickers Viastra X
G-ACCC delivered on
15th May 1933

In the event, the Viastra was little used, although it did make several trips to the Continent, and in fact its replacement had been mooted before it was actually delivered to Hendon! The replacement was another de Havilland machine. The Gipsy Moth G-ABDB, Puss Moth G-ABRR and Fox Moth G-ABXS being part exchanged for a new DH84 Dragon, G-ACGG, which was delivered on 12th June 1933. One notable flight in this aircraft was when The Prince of Wales flew from Smiths Lawn to Cranwell to open the new College Hall building on 11th October 1934.

HRH The Prince of Wales arriving at Brooklands in DH84 Dragon, G-ACGG.

'Mouse' Fielding stepping from the aircraft with Tom Jenkins the Engineer standing under the wing.

The Dragon proved popular and successful, and remained with the fleet until February 1935, when it was sold to Mr R. Shuttleworth, the founder of the Shuttleworth Collection of historic aeroplanes and motor cars. The Viastra too was sold, in March 1935, having flown less than 10 hours in the previous year, and for a short time the Prince was without an aircraft of his own. However, orders had been placed with de Havillands, and a pair of DH89 Dragon Rapides were soon delivered, G-ACTT on 27th April 1935 and G-ADDD on 8th June. An extensive flying programme had been envisaged for the summer of 1935, in connection with King George V's Jubilee Celebrations, but once again there was found to be insufficient work for two aeroplanes, and by October 1935, G-ACTT was being offered for sale, having flown only 51 hours.

THE FIRST BRITISH MONARCH TO FLY

When George V died on 20th January 1936, The Prince of Wales became King Edward VIII. He had to attend the Accession Council in London the following day and Edward Fielden flew The King and The Duke of York from Bircham Newton to Hendon in the Rapide, G-ADDD, which was the only aircraft now operated by The King. Since neither King George V nor Queen Mary ever flew, this was the first occasion that a British Monarch had taken to the air.

2. The King's Flight 1936-1952

As a Marshal of the Royal Air Force, HM The King was entitled to a communications type aircraft for use on official occasions, and so the Air Ministry agreed to meet the cost of any replacement for his Dragon Rapide and, from 1st April 1936, to finance the support of the royal aircraft. This led in June to the institution of The King's Flight and, on July 21st, it formed officially at Hendon. On the same day Flight Lieutenant Edward Fielden was nominated as an Equerry in Waiting with the appointment of Captain of The King's Flight. Fielden was promoted to Wing Commander, and the two civilian ground engineers, T. Jenkins and R.T. Hussey, were given appropriate RAF NCO status; the fourth member of the Flight was Mr. Peskett, the Captain's secretary.

Rapide G-ADDD

The single Dragon Rapide, G-ADDD, of the new King's Flight was fairly extensively used and in the latter half of 1936 it made 61 flights, of which twelve were with HM The King and fourteen with his brothers, The Dukes of York, Gloucester and Kent. During this time, Wing Commander Fielden collected data on a wide range of aircraft (including the Bristol Bombay, the Bristol 143 – the forerunner of the Blenheim – and the Lockheed Super Electra, from which the Hudson was developed) with a view to replacing the Dragon Rapide, but before the survey was complete King Edward abdicated in favour of The Duke of York on 11 December 1936. The new King retained Wing Commander Fielden's services as Captain of The King's Flight, but for the moment the Flight was without aircraft. Since the Dragon Rapide, G-ADDD, was the personal property of the former King (and as such it was sold in May 1937).

King Edward VIII arriving in Rapide G-ADDD at RAF Mildenhall on 8th July 1936 to review the Handley Page Heyfords of Nos. 39 and 99 Squadrons and the Hawker Hinds of No. 40 Squadron.

G-ADDD was sold after a total of 194 hours in Royal service to Western Airways Ltd for £3,345

The search for a new aircraft was now urgent. Early in 1937, interest centred on the Airspeed Envoy, and although Edward Fielden considered it too small for the requirements of The King's Flight, it was the most suitable replacement available, and it had the advantage that a military version was to enter RAF service as the Oxford. Accordingly, in March 1937, Air Ministry Specification No. 6/37 was drawn up to cover "the Airspeed Envoy 111 aircraft for The King's Flight, and to define certain special requirements which are necessary." This was the first official specification to be made for a royal aircraft, and the aeroplane that emerged, G-AEXX, was the first royal aircraft to be financed from public funds. It is noteworthy that the Envoy had to meet the military requirements of the Air Ministry Directorates of Technical Development and Aeronautical Inspection, as well as satisfying the British Civil Airworthiness Requirements (and, in addition being fully satisfactory to The Captain of The King's Flight). These multiple standards have been applied to all subsequent peacetime aircraft of The King's Flight and The Queen's Flight.

The Airspeed Envoy III G-AEXX was the first publicly-funded Royal Aircraft.

Finished in blue and red with silver wings the Envoy underwent flight testing at A & AEE Martlesham Heath between April and May 1937.

After the Envoy had passed its service acceptance trials at Martlesham Heath, Wing Commander Fielden collected it from the Airspeed works at Portsmouth on 7th May 1937 and flew it to Hendon, where it was officially allotted to No. 24 (Communications) Squadron, for use by The King's Flight. The Air Ministry had suggested that, since the Envoy was to be maintained from Service sources, the servicing crew should be put into uniform and the aircraft should become a military one, bearing the serial number L7270. These measures Wing Commander Fielden forestalled for as long as possible, and the aircraft retained its civil registration, G-AEXX throughout its service on The Flight.

HM King George VI leaving the cabin of the Airspeed Envoy III, whose door was positioned conveniently over the wing.

Meanwhile, as ever, Edward Fielden was on the lookout for a larger and potentially safer aeroplane for the King, and in 1938 suggested the de Havilland Flamingo, a medium range civil airliner which, as the Hertfordshire, was to be ordered for the RAF. As war became imminent, however, it was decided that the King should have an aircraft with defensive armament, and the choice fell on the Lockheed Hudson, descendant of the Super Electra Airliner.

On 4th August 1939, therefore, Hudson N7263 arrived at Hendon to replace the Envoy, which in any case had become too small to accommodate comfortably the number of passengers and the amount of luggage now required. The Envoy had operated satisfactorily for more than two years, the only incident being late in its King's Flight career when, in July 1939, a wheel bogged down on take-off from Aberdeen, with The Duke of Kent on board, and considerable damage was done. The Envoy was then returned to its ostensible owners, No.24 Squadron, now at Northolt, at last bearing its military serial number, L7270.

HRH The Duke of Kent leaving Lockheed Hudson N7263. The Hudson met the need for a larger aircraft, with armament, the Boulton Paul turret equipped with twin .303 inch Brownings.

The Hudson, officially known as the Hudson (Long Range), had been extensively modified internally, both to improve passenger comfort and to provide fuel tankage for a range of 3,000 miles, which was now an official requirement. The aircraft retained its Boulton Paul turret with twin .303 Browning machine guns, and relinquished the now traditional red, blue and silver paint scheme in favour of standard RAF camouflage, with no distinctive marking other than its serial number. Fielden did not particularly like the Hudson, pointing out that it could carry but one passenger over the target range, and proposed that the Flight should acquire the two de Havilland Albatross prototypes, G-AEVV and G-AEVW. This proposal was not taken up, however, and Hudson N7263 was used by The King during the first two years of the war, being replaced for a month early in 1940, due to unserviceability by a standard transport Hudson, N7364 of No. 24 Squadron.

MOVE TO RAF BENSON

Meanwhile, on the outbreak of war, it was suggested that The King's Flight should be transferred from Hendon, which was both busy and vulnerable, and be rehoused outside the London area. Wing Commander Fielden proposed a move to Smith's Lawn, in Windsor Great Park, from where he had flown many times in the early days with The Prince of Wales, but this move was not approved by the Air Ministry and, in September 1939, the Flight made its new home at Benson, Oxfordshire, as a lodger unit of No.12 OTU and sharing 'A' Hangar with the Battles of 287 Squadron. In March 1940, the strength of The Flight was increased by the attachment of a Percival Q6, P5634, from Northolt for the use of AOC-in-C Bomber Command.

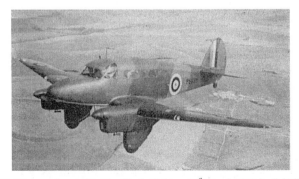

Percival Q6 P5634 was allocated to The King's Flight on 15th March 1940 for light liaison duties. It was subsequently used by the C-in-C Bomber Command and was re-allocated to RAF Halton on 25th May 1942 after The King's Flight was disbanded.

During 1940, Wing Commander Fielden represented to the Air Ministry that a small communications type aircraft was necessary to speed up collection of spares, etc., from depots around the country, even suggesting the acquisition of the captured Messerschmidt Me109, G-AFRN, held in Farnborough, but not surprisingly this plan was turned down and eventually the Flight was brought to its peak wartime strength of four aircraft by the allotment of an Avro Tutor, K6120. This tutor was used for all liaison work and was often flown by one of the 207 Squadron pilots, Flight Lieutenant N. Wheeler, (later ACM Sir Neil Wheeler GCB, CBE, DSO, DFC, AFC) who assisted Wing Commander Fielding on an unofficial basis between April and July 1940.

Avro Tutor K6120 was on the strength of The King's Flight from 1940 until the Flight disbanded.

It is the only King's or Queen's Flight aircraft of which no photograph is known to exist.

In September of that year came the delivery of the latest royal aircraft, a deluxe version of the de Havilland DH95 Flamingo. This aircraft was initially given the serial number R2766, but as it was considered that a civil registration might facilitate the aeroplane's passage through neutral countries in the event of an emergency, it was registered as G-AGCC, although retaining its RAF roundels and camouflage. The aircraft was fitted out to deluxe standards, with two cabins and repositioned windows.

DH 95 Flamingo R2766

DH 95 Flamingo G-AGCC (ex-R2766)

THE KING'S FLIGHT DISBANDS TO BE ABSORBED BY NO. 161 SQUADRON

The aircraft of The King's Flight saw little use in 1941, particularly as the unarmed Flamingo would have required a fighter escort, and in any case, being an unfamiliar aircraft, it could have been in some danger from the home defence. The King was concerned at the difficulties of operating the Flamingo and felt that his aircraft could be put to better use in normal service, and so The King's Flight was disbanded as a separate unit. The Flamingo, having reverted to the serial number R2766, was first to go and followed the Envoy to No. 24 Squadron at Northolt in February 1941; the Tutor was reallocated to No. 22 MU at Silloth but crashed en-route, and in May 1942 the Percival Q6 went to Halton. The Flight was officially absorbed by No. 161 Squadron at Newmarket on 14th February 1942, with Wing Commander Fielden commanding the new Squadron, but retaining his appointment as The Captain of The King's Flight. The Flight personnel gradually dispersed and finally, in June, the Royal Hudson N7263 joined Edward Fielden on No. 161 Squadron at Tempsford; this aircraft continued to be flown on Special Duties Operations throughout the war. As a Group Captain, Edward Fielden became Tempsford's Station Commander.

With the disbandment of The King's Flight, arrangements for Royal flying reverted to No. 24 Squadron, still operating as a VIP transport unit from Northolt. Under their aegis came the two longest Royal flights thus far, when King George VI flew from Northolt to Tripoli and back in June 1943, (amusingly described in Air Vice-Marshal Tony Dudgeon's book *Wings over North Africa*) and from Northolt to Naples and return in July and August 1944, both flights being made in the Prime Minister's personal Avro York, LV633 "Ascalon". In mid-1944, No. 24 Squadron changed roles to become a transport support unit flying Dakotas, and it was planned that the Metropolitan Communications Squadron, recently formed at Hendon, would assume responsibility for such Royal flights as were necessary. However, the King had been impressed by a flight in a Dakota during his visit to Italy, and it was decided to allot one for future Royal flights. Dakota MkIV, KN386 was selected for the King, and it joined No. 24 Squadron at Hendon in June 1945. The aircraft was used extensively during the summer of 1945, but after that the King had little occasion to fly for many months, and KN386 reverted to general VIP duties, so that once again there was no specific aircraft allotted for Royal flying.

Late in 1945, it was represented to the King that, in coming years, Royal travel by air over long distances would become as natural as travel by car over short distances, so in early 1946 the King formally approved the reconstitution of The King's Flight, confirming Edward Fielden, now an Air Commodore, in the appointment of Captain of The King's Flight. As his deputy and RAF Officer Commanding of the Flight, Fielden selected a New Zealander, Wing Commander W. (Bill) Tacon, DSO, DFC, AFC.

Air Commodore Fielden with Wing Commander Bill Tacon

THE KING'S FLIGHT REFORMS

The King's Flight officially reformed on 1st May 1946 at Royal Air Force Station, Benson, and it was hoped that it would be manned and equipped to establishment by 1st August in preparation for the forthcoming Royal Visit to the Union of South Africa. The intended aircraft establishment was one Avro York (VVIP) and three Vickers Vikings (one for the King, One for The Queen and one for the ground crew) but by mid-May the York proposal had been dropped in favour of a fourth Viking in freighter/workshop fit. It was hoped that the normal passenger aircraft would be available by July (for crew training and route proving) and the other three special aircraft by November; to this end BEA were persuaded to give up two of their early places on the production line, being recompensed by aircraft of the standard RAF order. In the event, the first of the special order, the normal passenger aircraft VL245, was collected from Wisley on 11th August 1946.

Another early addition to the establishment was a de Havilland Dominie, RL951, which was collected from Dumfries on 15th July 1946 and was used for communication purposes until it was written off in an accident at Mount Farm, just north of Benson, on 11th November 1946, fortunately with no injury to the crew.

ARRIVAL OF THE VIKINGS – THE SOUTH AFRICAN TOUR

Two standard Vikings were delivered to Benson to help in working up the Flight. The remainder of the special Vikings soon followed, all arriving by January 1947.

HM The King's Vickers Viking VL246

A Royal Arrival.

The Vickers Viking aircraft arrival in South Africa, 1947.

By February the fleet of four special aircraft had established their base for the Royal Tour at Brooklyn Air Base, near Cape Town. The Vikings performed faultlessly during the long tour, carrying The King and The Queen, together with the two Princesses, to various parts of the Union and to North and South Rhodesia, flying 160,000 miles without incident. In February 1947, Flight Sergeant Lowe of the South African Air Force had painted The King's cypher on to the Vikings. This is thought to be the first time the cipher appeared on our aircraft; the basic design has never changed since then.

The King's Crew

'John' Reid (left) with The King's Crew.

Dennis Fawkes (Navigator), Bill Tacon (Captain & OC The King's Flight), Alan Lee (Co-Pilot) and Lofty Reed (Signaller).

The Royal Saloon – Vickers Viking 1947 Interior of the workshop Vickers Viking 1947

On 21st April 1947 at Government House, Cape Town, on the occasion of the 21st birthday of Princess Elizabeth, Air Commodore Fielden presented Her Royal Highness with a diamond wings brooch on behalf of all members of The King's Flight.

After their return to Benson the Vikings were regularly used for a number of years on Royal visits, giving largely trouble-free service except for one mishap. On 12th September 1947, whilst the Royal Family were in residence at Balmoral, VL245 took off from Aberdeen for Benson after the daily official mail delivery, developed engine trouble (a runaway propeller) and forced landed in a field, demolishing a stone wall in the process. Considerable repairs were required and the aircraft never returned to King's Flight service, being replaced in July 1948 by two standard RAF Vikings, experience having shown that ideally five Vikings were required for long tours such as the previous visit to South Africa and the projected trip to Australia and New Zealand.

THE FIRST HELICOPTERS

Although they proved unfortunate for the Vikings, the mail deliveries during the summer of 1947 had been helpful in giving The King's Flight its first experience of helicopter operations. Two

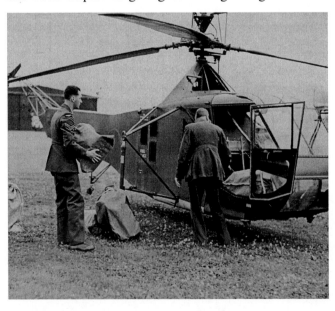

Hoverfly Mk.1's were borrowed from the Royal Navy in August and flown to Aberdeen Dyce Airport, whence they were asked to shuttle the mail to Balmoral and back. One of these aircraft suffered an engine failure on 16th August and was replaced, but otherwise the exercise was successful, and was repeated the following year, again with aircraft borrowed from the Royal Navy.

This was to be the last such exercise however, for in 1949 the source of Hoverfly Mk. 1's dried up and at the time there were no other suitable helicopters. These experimental flights had been useful in assessing the value of helicopters to The King's Flight, as well as giving the Scottish public a glimpse of such machines at Battle of Britain displays at Dyce and Edinburgh Turnhouse Airports. Furthermore, the Post Office found the October 1947 King's Flight report extremely useful in their evaluation of helicopters for mail delivery.

Meanwhile, the Vikings had been used extensively in November 1947 for flights in connection with the wedding of Princess Elizabeth and Prince Philip, and although little used by The King and The Queen, they made many official flights with other members of the Royal Family in the next few years, and on several occasions they were used by Princess Elizabeth to fly to Malta. The Avro York proposal reappeared briefly in 1948 and in fact The King's Flight borrowed one example, MW140 (which had been The Duke of Gloucester's aeroplane "Endeavour" in 1945), from Bassingbourn in January 1948 for two proving flights to Ceylon. The exercise was not repeated however, and the Flight continued to use the shorter range Viking.

THE FIRST CIVIL CHARTERS 1951

When Princess Elizabeth and Prince Philip flew to Montreal on 8th October 1951, it was the first ever crossing of the Atlantic by air by a member of the Royal Family. The aircraft was the BAOC Stratocruiser "Canopus"; captained by O.P Jones, the famous Imperial Airways pioneer. On 31st January 1952 HRH Princess Elizabeth and The Duke of Edinburgh flew out of London airport in BOAC Argonaut Atlanta – a Canadair C-4 – to begin a tour of East Africa. While the Royal couple were in East Africa, the King died. The Argonaut conveyed HM Queen Elizabeth II and The Duke of Edinburgh from Entebbe to England on 7th February 1952, where she was met by bare-headed Winston Churchill and Clement Attlee.

HM Queen Elizabeth II arriving back in England – 7th February 1952.

The King's Flight 1951

3.   The Queen's Flight 1952-1960

1952

When HM The Queen acceded to the throne on 6th February 1952, The King's Flight was still operating the Vikings, although the pressure of work was by now much less than in previous years. This led to the suggestion that, on the grounds of efficiency and economy, The King's Flight should cease to exist and that the task of Royal flying should be carried out by BEA, BOAC and the RAF, as appropriate, co-ordinated by the Air Equerry with a small staff. A committee, comprising senior officials of the Royal Household, the Treasury, the Air Ministry and the Ministry of Civil Aviation was formed to discuss the suggestion, and the outcome was a system which, with some amendments, has operated ever since; The King's Flight, renamed The Queen's Flight on 1st August 1952, would continue as before. And the Ministry of Civil Aviation would arrange the provision of civil aircraft when those of The Queen's Flight were unsuitable for a particular task. Air Commodore Edward Fielden was confirmed in his appointment as Captain of The Queen's Flight, and at this time the Officer Commanding was Wing Commander R.C.E. Scott, AFC.

A Queen's Flight Viking being serviced in the hangar

THE DUKE OF EDINBURGH LEARNS TO FLY

In May 1952, whilst these discussions were in progress, Prince Philip decided to take a course of flying instruction. He felt strongly that he should be taught to fly by the RAF, and so a small flying unit was set up at White Waltham under the aegis of Home Command. Prince Philip was instructed by Flight Lieutenant Caryl Gordon, initially in de Havilland Chipmunk T Mk. 10, WP861, and progress was such that on 20th December 1952, he made his first solo flight in another Chipmunk T10, WP912.

Two DH Chipmunk T10's were allocated to The Queen's Flight, WP912 and WP861, for Prince Philip's primary flying training.

They were based at White Waltham.

He then graduated onto the Harvard using FX459 for both training and cross country (communications) flying. North American Harvards FX459 and KF729 were allocated for his flying tuition at White Waltham. The Duke of Edinburgh won his wings in exactly the same manner as any other ab initio student pilot. The Chief of Air Staff, Air Chief Marshal Sir William Dickson, presented him with his wings at Buckingham Palace on 8th May 1953,

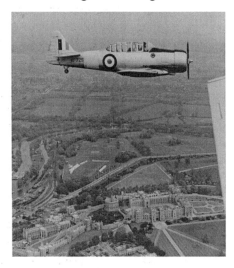

The Duke of Edinburgh flying Harvard XF729 over Windsor Castle.

It is the only Harvard to have borne five-star insignia, denoting a Marshal of the Royal Air Force.

The logical progression was to a twin-engined trainer and several aircraft of this type were evaluated for the task, including the Oxford and the Anson. Oxford 4204 was used from April to June 1953 when de Havilland Devon VP961 arrived at White Waltham, where for several years it saw regular use for training and communication flights. However it was soon found that the Devon was not big enough to carry more than a few staff and their baggage, and so an order was placed for a larger four engined de Havilland Heron, to be designated Prince Philip's personal aircraft.

1953-1954

VISCOUNTS CONSIDERED TO REPLACE THE VIKINGS

In the meantime, with the future role of The Queen's Flight assured, Fielden, by now Air Commodore Sir Edward Fielden, KCVO, CB, DFC, AFC, suggested that by 1953 the time was right to examine the question of re-equipping The Queen's Flight with modern aircraft, for although the Vikings had given most satisfactory service for six years there was no doubt that they were of obsolescent design. Sir Edward felt that once the new Heron arrived to fulfil Prince Philip's engagements and to fly other members of the Royal Family to smaller, less developed airfields, and with two Whirlwind helicopters to carry out short range tasks, the work which the five Vikings had done over the years could now be undertaken by two Vickers Viscounts. (In fact, only four of the Vikings were operating at this stage. The workshop aircraft, which had undergone a major servicing in May 1950, had flown only four hours before being placed on trestles with the wings and engines removed and was eventually to be reassembled and sold in November 1953).

The Duke of Edinburgh in the pilot's seat of his personal DH Heron C3, XH375, which replaced a Viking of The Queen's Flight in mid-1955.

It was equipped to carry three crew and six passengers and had a very comprehensive radio suite.

It was powered by four DH Gipsy Queen 30 Mk. 2 engines with DH two-blade constant-speed airscrews.

By December 1953, The Queen had agreed to the carriage in The Queen's Flight aircraft of certain Government Ministers and Service Chiefs of Staff. Air Commodore Fielden was now putting forward, to replace the obsolescent Vikings, a firm requirement for one de Havilland Heron Series II as Prince Philip's personal aircraft, to be introduced in March 1954; one Vickers Viscount in VIP fit, to be delivered in June 1954; and two Viscounts to VVIP specification, to be ready by August 1954 and March 1955. Throughout the Spring of 1954, during which time the Vikings were operating temporarily from Northolt whilst the Benson hangar was being renovated, discussions were held with Vickers-Armstrong Ltd at Weybridge, and although there was nothing official about these discussions, the company issued drawings of the proposed aircraft fits, and built a floor-line mock-up of the VVIP version. In fact, Vickers went so far as to earmark places on the Viscount production line, but eventually these were surrendered due to lack of a firm order. Air Commodore Fielden altered his requirements to suit the ever-changing work load and climate of Air Ministry opinion, and in December 1954, having secured Prince Philip's agreement to his Heron being used by other members of the Royal Family, (subject to his own overriding requirement), he suggested that one Viscount could possibly do the work of all the Vikings.

HM The Queen and HRH The Duke of Edinburgh arriving at Enugu, Nigeria. 6th February 1956.

Although it was The Duke of Edinburgh's personal aeroplane, Heron XH375 was used extensively for Royal Flying at home and overseas.

It was in natural metal finish overall, with an Edinburgh green cheat line.

Ultimately, in June 1955, he was to revise his requirements again to two Viscounts, the previous six months having shown a marked increase in flying tasks, but by this time the Air Council had agreed on a single Viscount plan, and had approached the Treasury for approval to purchase a Viscount 700D. The eventual establishment of The Queen's Flight would then have been one Viscount 700D, one Viking VVIP, one Heron and two Westland Whirlwind Mk.2 helicopters. However, even this much-pruned request was turned down by the Treasury, and eventually the whole Viscount project fell through.

THE FIRST ROYAL HELICOPTER FLIGHTS

HRH Prince Philip was the first member of the Royal Family to fly in a helicopter when he flew several sorties in a civil Dragonfly belonging to Westlands (G-AKTW temporarily registered as XD649 and flown by Squadron Leader Ron Gellatly) on an official visit to Germany between 18th and 20th March 1953.

The need for helicopters for Royal Flights was nevertheless becoming increasingly obvious and a visit by HRH The Princess Margaret to several Army units in Germany in July 1954 was planned to be done by helicopter within Germany. The Queen's Flight still had no helicopters of its own, so the newly formed Central Flying School Helicopter Unit of 3 Dragonflies was borrowed for the occasion, the Princess being flown by the Unit Commander, Flight Lieutenant J.R. Dowling, in a Dragonfly HC4 (XF261) specially modified for VVIP carriage. The other two Dragonflies carried the entourage. The weather was foul throughout the visit; only one flight was made with the Princess when she took off to fly from Costedt to Sennelager on July 14th, but low cloud and rain prevented completion of the flight and all three helicopters returned to Sennelager. However, the practice of Royal helicopter flying had been established. In the same month, agreement in principle was given for The Queen's Flight to operate two VVIP helicopters and, in September 1954, the Flight received its own first passenger carrying helicopter – the VVIP modified Dragonfly XF261 on extended loan from the Central Flying School Helicopter Unit at South Cerney. The pilot, Flight Lieutenant A.J. Lee, late of The King's Flight as a Viking Pilot in 1946 and a Hoverfly pilot in 1947, was detached from the Central Flying School to fly it – a temporary aircraft allocation which remained for more than four years. Immediately on arrival at Benson on 6th September 1954, it was used to fly Prince Philip from Buckingham Palace to Shinfield (Reading).

Picture left: HM The Queen Mother leaving Westland Dragonfly HC4 XF261 which was on loan to The Queen's Flight from the Central Flying School (Helicopter Division) between September 1954 and August 1958. It was the first helicopter to be permanently established as part of the Flight.

Picture right: A Viking, Duke of Edinburgh's Heron and a Dragonfly in The Queen's Flight Hangar.

1955

Other early users of helicopters were The Duke and Duchess of Gloucester, The Queen Mother and Princess Margaret, but it was Prince Philip who became the champion of the helicopter, soon taking a flying course and in 1955 qualifying as a helicopter pilot under the tutelage of Lieutenant Commander M. H. Simpson, the Chief Flying Instructor on No. 705 Squadron, Royal Navy at Gosport. Prince Philip also continued his fixed wing flying, at first in Percival Provost WV679 and Devon VP961 and, after its delivery on 18th May 1955, in his personal de Havilland Heron C3, XH 375. The latter, like the Devon, departed from the usual Queen's Flight Colours in that it had an overall polished silver finish with a cheat line along the fuselage in Edinburgh green. In July 1955, in order to rationalise the arrangements for Royal Flights, it was decided to transfer the Devon and the Heron from White Waltham to Benson, whence The Queen's Flight would supervise all future communications flights by Prince Philip, although his instructional flying from White Waltham would remain a Home Command responsibility.

Having qualified as a helicopter pilot under the auspices of the Royal Navy, Prince Philip continued to use the Naval Whirlwind Mk.22 for official visits, and this lead was followed by other members of the Royal Family until eventually Royal helicopter flying was carried out solely in the Naval Whirlwinds, although the flights were planned and organised by The Queen's Flight. The Dragonfly was used for route and landing site reconnaissance, communications work and pilot continuation training, for a Queen's Flight pilot always accompanied the naval helicopter on Royal Flights. In October 1955, a draft Standard of Preparation was issued, covering two Westland Whirlwind Mk.2's for The Queen's Flight, and by that December the Air Council had firmly recommended the establishment of a Whirlwind in The Queen's Flight by the following Spring to give The Queen's Flight pilots intensive flying practice before delivery of the VIP helicopters some two to three months later. However, this proved highly optimistic, for although Whirlwind Mk.2 XJ432 was used by The Queen's Flight in May and June 1956, it was clear by that time that the Pratt and Whitney-engined Mk.2's would be unsuitable for Royal flying, particularly as modifications to the emergency power control systems might take as long as 18 months to complete. Air Commodore Fielden was asked to consider two Bristol Sycamores instead. Having already turned down this proposal once, he now countered it by asking for the redeployment of the Naval Whirlwind Mk.22, WV219, to The Queen's Flight, complete with a Naval maintenance crew and the current pilot, Lieutenant Commander R. Turpin. This suggestion came to naught, however, and The Queen's Flight was faced with operating the Dragonfly on its own for the foreseeable future.

1956-1957

HERONS REPLACE THE VIKINGS

The introduction of helicopters into The Queen's Flight had been marked by long delays, but the provision of replacements for the Vikings took even longer. By the end of 1955 it was clear that The Queen's Flight was unlikely ever to get the Viscount, and Air Commodore Fielden turned elsewhere. The Bristol Britannia was considered briefly but it was felt that it would suffer the same fate as the Viscount, with similar delays, and so in April 1956 a firm order was placed for two more de Havilland Herons, this time to C4 standard. It took two years for these aircraft to materialise, for again there were problems in agreeing a Standard of Preparation. Edward Fielden had envisaged the new aircraft as being virtual copies of Prince Philip's Heron, but the Treasury were not prepared to pay the price of such a standard, and a compromise had to be reached. Meanwhile The Queen's Flight continued to operate four Vikings, one Heron C3, one Devon and one Dragonfly although the bulk of the Royal flying was done by Vikings VL233 and VL246 and the Heron.

FIRST VISIT BY A REIGNING MONARCH

In September 1956, Wing Commander D.F. Hyland-Smith, DFC, AFC, took over as Officer Commanding, and in November 1956 Group Captain A.D. Mitchell, DFC, AFC, was appointed to the new post of Deputy Captain of The Queen's Flight. Also in November, HM The Queen reviewed the Flight and its personnel at Benson, the first such visit by a reigning monarch although The Queen, as Princess Elizabeth, had visited the Flight in July 1949 and had previously inspected a representative detachment at Moreton Vallance in May 1955, whilst The Queen Mother had visited the hangar at Benson in 1953.

In November 1956, the Air Council decided that the policy of establishing Whirlwind helicopters on The Queen's Flight should be reconsidered when a firm estimate for the Mk. 5 (with the Alvis Leonides Major engine) could be provided against an agreed Standard of Preparation. A draft form of this Standard of Preparation was issued in February 1957, but a whole year went by with interminable discussions and bickering on minor differences of furnishings, radio and engineering fitments, and general finish before the draft was agreed by all the interested parties – not that this was significant for by this time the Leonides Major had run into serious development problems and it was likely that delivery of the first aircraft would take at least another year after placing of a contract. Meanwhile the Naval Whirlwind, now flown by Lieutenant Commander E.C. Spreadbury, carried out most of the Royal Flights whilst the Dragonfly continued to operate from Benson; in August 1956 the Dragonfly carried out the first of what were to become annual flights, delivering Royal Mail to HM Yacht Britannia cruising off the Western Isles with the Royal Family on board.

FAREWELL TO THE VIKINGS

The year 1958 was one of change for The Queen's Flight. The last special flight in a Viking took place on 22nd April and shortly afterwards the three remaining Vikings left the Flight, eventually to be sold to Tradair. The two new Herons were collected from Hawarden on 16th April and were soon in use on special flights, XM295 on 1st May and XM296 on 7th May. The aircrews quickly worked up sufficient experience to enable them to embark on a major tour, by The Duke and Duchess of Gloucester to Ethiopia, British Somaliland and Aden in November 1958, and whereas in their later years the Vikings had been largely confined to Europe, it was soon to become commonplace to see the Herons in almost every part of the world.

de Havilland Heron C4

Operating normally in pairs, because of limited pay-load and baggage capacity (although due to the amount of work, the Devon was pressed into service on occasion) the Herons undertook tours of Kenya, Uganda, Nigeria and Ghana in 1959 and Rhodesia, Nyasaland and Nigeria in 1960, as well as coping with an ever increasing workload within the United Kingdom and on the Continent.

In July 1958 a contract for the VVIP Whirlwinds (now known as Mk. 8's) had at last been placed with Westlands, delivery being expected the following Spring, and a Mk. 4 aircraft was collected from Aston Down at the end of the month for crew training. The faithful Dragonfly, XF261, was returned to South Cerney in August 1958, but again the change proved somewhat premature in terms of crew training, for in January 1959 the Leonides Major was still giving trouble and the first engine had not even arrived at Westlands. Despite these delays, Air Commodore Fielden continued to press for the establishment of two helicopter crews on The Queen's Flight. In 1954, a meeting of senior RAF, Naval and Military representatives had agreed that one of the eventual crew vacancies should be filled alternately by Naval and Military officers since Naval and Military helicopter resources were greater than those of the RAF, which might have been unduly strained by the provision of two crews for The Queen's Flight. Air Commodore Fielden now felt that, as the Naval authorities had been so helpful with previous helicopter trips, and as in any case the Army had no Whirlwind qualified pilots, the Admiralty should be invited to appoint a naval helicopter pilot to join The Queen's Flight when the VVIP helicopters were delivered. Lieutenant R.M. (Ron) Kerr, who had taken over the Naval Whirlwind flying from Lieutenant Commander Spreadbury was selected to fill this post, a post incidentally which is still filled by a naval pilot. Lieutenant Kerr eventually joined the Flight in January 1960, and subsequently transferred to the Royal Air Force, remained until 1976 as Prince Philip's personal helicopter pilot.

A Second Deputy Captain is appointed

In January 1959, Wing Commander Hyland-Smith relinquished command of the Flight to Wing Commander H.G. Currell who in turn handed over in July 1959 to Wing Commander R.G. Wakeford, OBE, AFC. In the same month Group Captain T.N. Stack, AFC, became Deputy Captain in place of Group Captain A.D. Mitchell, who was to leave that October; such was the increase in workload, however, that a second Deputy Captain was needed, and in April 1960 Group Captain J. Wallace, DSO, DFC, AFC, was posted to this appointment.

The Leonides Major engine continued to give trouble and by June 1959, all the Naval Whirlwind Mk. 7's, from which The Queen's Flight's machines were derived, had been grounded for modification. A new series of trials were started at Culdrose in July 1959, the successful outcome of which resulted in the Mk. 8's receiving their Release to Service in October 1959 by which time, however, Air Commodore Fielden was showing interest in the Gnome gas-turbine powered version of the Whirlwind. The first of the new aircraft, XN126, was collected from Boscombe Down on 1st October and the second, XN127, from Yeovil on 5th November. The Mk. 4, was soon disposed of, and there followed a short period of crew training and working up before the helicopters were successfully introduced to Royal flying on 23rd February 1960, with a flight by The Duchess of Kent from Kensington Palace to Papworth – almost four years after the originally projected date of introduction

Whirlwind HCC8 XN127

This helicopter served on The Queen's Flight from 5th November 1959 to 25th May 1964.

Prince Philip Flies a Single-Seater

On 24th October 1959, HRH The Duke of Edinburgh carried out a short flight from White Waltham in Turbulent G-APNZ; this is the only occasion that any member of The Royal Family has flown a single-seater aircraft. He also entered this aircraft in the National Air Races of 1959, 1960 and 1961, the aircraft being flown by his Equerry, Squadron Leader John Severne.

The Duke of Edinburgh's Equerry, Squadron Leader John Severne, swings the propeller of Rollason
Turbulent G-APNZ at White Waltham on 24th October 1959.

(Air Vice-Marshal Sir John Severne, KCVO OBE AFC was The Captain of The Queen's Flight from
January 1982 to January 1989).

John Severne won the King's Cup in 1960 (at a speed of 109 mph – nearly 50 mph slower than the speed achieved by Flight Lieutenant Fielden in 1932!) and became National Air Racing Champion. The aircraft was painted in Prince Philip's colours and was flown in the races with HRH's badge on the side of the aircraft. Prince Philip's interest at that time in general aviation and sporting flying gave great encouragement to the movement, particularly when in 1959 he accepted honorary membership of the Tiger Club.

4. The Queen's Flight 1960-1973

1960

A Chipmunk joins the Flight in Fluorescent Red

A new arrival in 1960 was a de Havilland Chipmunk T10, WP903, which was collected from Silloth in September and was painted overall fluorescent red.

By this time the Herons too were painted fluorescent red, because patches of Day-Glo were appearing on many RAF aircraft as a flight safety measure, and it was considered that aircraft of The Queen's Flight should be similarly treated. The Herons lost their traditional finish of polished silver trimmed with red and blue, although the basic colours were retained by the addition of a Royal Blue line along the fuselage (Prince Philip's aircraft in fact retained its Edinburgh green line). The Chipmunk was originally intended for use by Prince Philip, but was subsequently used to teach The Duke of Kent, Prince Michael and Prince William to fly. By this time it was clear that a fourth Heron would be required to cope with the ever increasing demand for Royal Flights, and with surprisingly little discussion it was agreed at the end of 1960 to place an order with Hawker Siddeley. To make way for the new Heron, the Devon was phased out and flown to the MU at Shawbury in October 1960.

1961

Before the fourth Heron could be completed, however, came the tour of India and Pakistan and the State Visit to Nepal and Iran. It was found that the Herons had insufficient carrying capacity for the mountainous regions of Nepal, and the new Handley Page Herald had therefore been suggested as the most suitable aircraft. However, the Herald was relatively untried at that time and recourse was finally made to the Dakota. Two machines were used, KN645 which had once been the personal transport of Field Marshal Lord Montgomery, and KN452 which had previously been used by the Air Officer Commanding, Malta. Both aircraft were re-furbished for the tour, and two very experienced crews were selected to fly them. The crews arrived at The Queen's Flight at much the same time as the new Officer Commanding, Wing Commander D.L. Attlee. The Dakotas performed well in Nepal, as did the two Mk4 Herons which were used during the Indian and Pakistan parts of this very long tour; but inevitably, when the aircraft returned to Benson the Dakotas and their crews were dispersed to their parent units.

The Fourth Heron

The delivery of the fourth Heron on 16th June 1961, came just in time, for the existing aircraft, were beginning to wilt under the volume of work. Since the Indian visit the other Mk.4's had been on tour again with The Duke of Kent to Sierra Leone, and by the end of the year all four Herons had been overseas together – three of them on the tour of Ghana, Sierra Leone and The Gambia, the State Visit to Liberia, and continuing to Tanganyika for the Independence celebrations with Prince Philip. The fourth Heron was in the Far East with Princess Alexandra. 1961 saw the highest number of hours flown by the Flight (2,678.50 hours).

KITTY ONE CREW ARRESTED

On 9th July 1961 during the proving flight to West Africa for The Queen's forthcoming visit in November, Kitty One and his crew were arrested at Gao, in the newly independent Republic of Mali. On taxying in for a correctly authorised refuelling stop, the aircraft was surrounded by armed Mali police and subsequently locked in a hangar. Meantime the runway and taxyway had been blocked by barrels to prevent an escape. After much haggling, with neither side being able to speak adequately the other's language, Kitty One was permitted to leave the following morning. This is thought to be the first occasion a Royal aircraft and crew have been arrested. (The incident is described in Chapter Ten).

1962

SIR EDWARD FIELDEN RETIRES

On 1st January 1962, Air Commodore Edward Fielden retired from The Queen's Flight and was promoted to Air Vice-Marshal and appointed Senior Air Equerry to The Queen; a short biography is covered in another Chapter. He was succeeded on 21st March as Captain of The Queen's Flight by Air Commodore A.D. Mitchell, CVO, DFC, AFC, a previous Deputy Captain, and in June Group Captain P.W.D. Heal was appointed as a third Deputy Captain. There were fewer overseas tours in 1962 than had been the rule in recent years, although the Herons made their first appearance in North America, when two were used during Prince Philip's visit to Canada, and at the end of the year the two original Mk.4's made their way to Uganda with The Duke and Duchess of Kent for the Independence celebrations.

HERONS TO BE REPLACED BY THE ANDOVERS

In May 1962 came the first mention of finding replacements for the Herons. Although they had given excellent service, they had in some ways always been ill suited to the task they had to perform. Their range and payload were limited, especially when Prince Philip's aircraft was involved, due to the extra equipment it carried. Consequently two, and sometimes three Herons were required to support an overseas tour. On occasions, being limited in altitude, the Herons had to divert around high ground, and in any case their unpressurised cabins made for a less comfortable ride than was desirable for passengers who had to be on top form immediately upon arrival at their destination. These arguments were put to a working party, chaired by The Queen's Private Secretary, Sir Michael Adeane, and included senior officials of the Treasury and Air Ministry. The working party considered that another important factor weighing against the Herons was the prestige value of a large and more modern aircraft (in 1958, The Queen had been advised against using the Herons for a State Visit to The Netherlands for just that reason) and after some deliberation, and consideration of the Handley Page Herald, the Hawker Siddeley HS125, HS126, HS748 and the British Aircraft Corporation BAC 1-11, it was proposed that two of the Herons should be replaced by HS748's. It was pointed out that this move would involve little capital expenditure, since The Queen's Flight would use two of the 748's ordered by the RAF as the Andover CC Mk.2.

1963

Replacement of the helicopters was also considered, but for the time being, work continued with the Whirlwind Mk.8's and the Herons, which in 1963 carried out tours of Cyprus and Jordan with The Duke and Duchess of Gloucester, and Sudan.

Group Captain Heal retired in February 1963 and his place was taken by Group Captain P.E. Vaughan-Fowler, DSO, DFC, AFC, who became the only Deputy Captain when Group Captain Wallace left in August. July 1963 saw Wing Commander Attlee hand over as Officer Commanding to Wing Commander A.W. (Tony) Ringer, AFC, who was to remain with the Flight for some five years.

ANDOVERS AND WHIRLWIND MK.12'S ARRIVE

The general RAF changeover from piston-engined Whirlwinds to the Gnome-engined HAR Mk.10 was reflected on The Queen's Flight by the arrival on 26th March 1964 of a Whirlwind HCC Mk.12, the first of two VVIP versions of the HAR 10 specially ordered for the Flight. 1964 was to be a year of change for the Flight, for the Andover proposal had been agreed and on 31st March, pilot conversion started on a civil HS748, G-ARAY, loaned by the makers. Prince Philip soon started his own conversion, and on 1st May G-ARAY was used for the first time on a communications sortie, taking Prince Philip from Cardiff to London. G-ARAY was used for nine other communications flights before the first Andover, XS790, was handed over to Wing Commander Tony Ringer at the Hawker Siddeley Avro Division factory at Woodford on 10th July.

By this time the second HCC MK.12 Whirlwind had arrived, the two Mk.8's being retired and eventually modified to HAR 10 standard, and the Chipmunk had been returned to the MU.

HRH Prince Philip in the cockpit of the Gnome-engined Whirlwind HCC12. XR486.

The HCC12 was the VVIP version of the standard Whirlwind HAR10

Air Commodore Mitchell retired on 1st August 1964, and the new Captain of The Queen's Flight, Air Commodore J.H.L. Blount, DFC, arrived just in time to see the re-equipment completed when, on 7th August, Wing Commander Ringer collected the second Andover. For a short time The Queen's Flight had eight aircraft on charge – two Andovers, four Herons and two Whirlwinds.

A typical scene at RAF Benson in the mid-60's, with a Westland Whirlwind HCC12, a DH Heron C4 and an Andover CC2. The Andover CC2 is shown in the original finish of white upper fuselage, red wings and tail surfaces, blue cheat line and natural metal lower fuselage and engine nacelles

This state of affairs was short lived, however, for in September the original Heron, Prince Philip's personal Mk.3, left the Flight after nine years service and 3,560 flying hours. XM295 followed the Mk.3 in January 1965, having logged 3,710 flying hours, and the Flight settled down for the next few years with its established six aeroplanes (two Andovers, two Herons and two Whirlwinds).
With the advent of the Andovers, the remaining Herons were relegated to service within the United Kingdom and Europe. The Andovers were introduced to overseas flights on Prince Philip's tour of Mexico and the Caribbean in October 1964.

THE FIRST ROYAL HELICOPTER FLIGHT TO A WARSHIP AT SEA

On the 20th May Lieutenant Commander MacLean flew HRH The Duchess of Gloucester (Princess Alice) in a Whirlwind from Buckingham Palace to the Cruiser HMS London off Portsmouth.

1965

In February 1965 both Andover aircraft were used on the State Visit to Ethiopia, and the Sudan, and one aircraft on a tour of Saudi Arabia, India, Nepal, Singapore and Borneo with Prince Philip. Such was the amount of work that no aeroplane was available when The Duke and Duchess of Kent visited the Gambia in February 1965 for the independence celebrations of Britain's last African colony; consequently, Their Royal Highnesses flew in a Royal Air Force Britannia. One Andover returned to Africa in March 1965 on a tour of Uganda with Princess Margaret, and in November of that year to North America, again with Princess Margaret on a tour of the United States.

Andover Aircrew c.1965. The Officer Commanding, Wing Commander Anthony Ringer, AFC, is fifth from the left.

1966

1966 came in with XS790 on its way to the Far East again, this time on a tour with The Duke and Duchess of Gloucester.

XS789 returned to Canada and the United States with Prince Philip in March, and in May the Flight had to borrow Andover CC2 XS794 from the Metropolitan Communications Squadron to carry out special flights whilst XS790 was in the Caribbean with The Duke and Duchess of Kent for the Independence celebrations of British Guiana. These overseas journeys were but a tip of the iceberg, however, for the Andover, Herons and Whirlwinds were employed on an ever-increasing number of Royal and special flights within Europe.

TRH's The Duke and Duchess of Gloucester pictured with the crew of Andover XS790 in Kuala Lumpur on 17th January 1966 during their tour of Malaysia.

The aircraft commodore is Group Captain Vaughan-Fowler.

Group Captain J.L. Gilbert, DFC, had been appointed to the vacant Deputy Captain post in January 1966, and at the end of the year Group Captain A.R. Gordon-Cumming joined him, taking over from Group Captain Vaughan-Fowler, who had held the appointment for almost four years.

THE FIRST ROYAL HELICOPTER DECK LANDING ON AN AIRCRAFT CARRIER

On the 20th September HM Queen Elizabeth The Queen Mother made the first Royal helicopter flight onto an aircraft carrier at sea; flying from her residence at Birkhall in Whirlwind XR986, piloted by Lieutenant Commander MacLean, RN, she landed on HMS Ark Royal off Aberdeen. Her Majesty trailed a scarf from the partly opened door during a farewell flypast, a gesture which delighted the entire ships company drawn up on the flight deck.

1967

XS 794 was borrowed again in June 1967, and was used for several Royal and special flights whilst the Flight's Andovers were overseas, One in Canada with The Queen and the other visiting the Pacific, taking The Duke and Duchess of Kent to Tonga to represent The Queen at the Coronation of the King. (This tour was the longest yet undertaken by the Flight, the aircraft flying 165 hours in 5 weeks).

THE WESSEX IS CHOSEN TO REPLACE THE WHIRLWIND

In the middle of 1967, negotiations were under way for the replacement of the Whirlwind HCC12 helicopters. The twin-engined Wessex had been in general service use for some time and a VVIP version was planned for The Queen's Flight; in fact, a standard Wessex HC2 had already been used by the Flight when XT673 was borrowed from No. 72 Squadron in July 1967 to fly Prince Philip to the North Sea oil rig "Sea Quest".

THE WHIRLWINDS ARE GROUNDED

In December 1967 the third Andover CC2, XS793 was ferried to Benson from Aden, where it had been used by the Commander-in-Chief. The technicians began a long period of servicing to make it ready for Royal flying because it had suffered a very heavy landing in Aden and much repair work was necessary. The Flight at the same time prepared to give up its two remaining Herons. However this was overshadowed, as were all other considerations, by the tragic accident of 7th December 1967. Whirlwind XR487 was en-route to Yeovil, where a meeting was to be held to discuss the

VVIP Wessex, when the main rotor shaft snapped and the helicopter crashed at Brightwalton, Berkshire. The accident resulted in the deaths of the passengers, Air Commodore J.H.L. Blount, DFC, The Captain of The Queen's Flight, and Squadron Leader M.W. Hermon, the Flight's Engineering Officer, and also the crew, Squadron Leader J.H. (John) Liversedge, DFC, AFC and Flight Lieutenant R. (Ron) Fisher. All Whirlwind helicopters throughout the services were grounded pending the report of the Board of Enquiry into the accident, and The Queen's Flight was not to fly another Royal helicopter sortie until the end of March 1968.

Andover, Herons and Whirlwind in the hangar

1968

Group Captain Gordon-Cumming took over as acting Captain of The Queen's Flight following the accident, for Group Captain Gilbert was due to leave the Flight, and in February 1968 Wing Commander M.J. (Mike) Rayson took over as Officer Commanding from Wing Commander Tony Ringer. On 15th February 1968, Air Commodore A.L. (Archie) Winskill, CBE, DFC, was appointed Captain of The Queen's Flight, and the second Deputy Captain's post was filled in March 1968 by Group Captain B.A. Primavesi.

A standard Whirlwind HAR10 was collected from Odiham on 31st January 1968 as a temporary replacement for the crashed HCC12, but it was not cleared for use by the Royal Family, and when helicopter passenger flying was restarted in March, XR486 was used for all Royal Flights.

On 26th May 1968, the third Andover, XS793, commenced operational flying, having been virtually rebuilt by the Flight's excellent technicians in the previous six months. This was the signal for the retirements of the Herons, and XR391, which had completed 1,820 flying hours in its seven years on the Flight, was flown to No. 27 MU at Shawbury on 17th June 1968; the last Heron Royal Flight took place on 25th June 1968, and shortly afterwards XM296 was delivered to the MU at Leconfield, having completed 4,310 flying hours in its ten years of Royal service.

HRH THE PRINCE OF WALES LEARNS TO FLY

July 1968 also saw the return to the Flight of the red painted Chipmunk T10, WP903, which was allocated for the flying instruction of HRH The Prince of Wales.

On 31st July Squadron Leader P.G. Pinney gave The Prince of Wales the first air experience flight of a syllabus which was to continue, interspersed with his university studies, for three years, and which would use the RAF airfields at Bassingbourn, Benson, Oakington, Tangmere, West Raynham and White Waltham, as well as (during his term at the University College of Wales at Aberystwyth) the RAE airfield at Aberporth. The first milestone of this syllabus was reached on 14th January 1969, when The Prince of Wales flew solo for the first time at Bassingbourn.

HRH The Prince of Wales, having passed his preliminary flying badge, photographed with The Captain of The Queen's Flight, Air Commodore Archie Winskill, his Instructor, Squadron Leader Philip Pinney, and his 'Chipmunk Team' at RAF Tangmere 2nd August 1969

ARRIVAL OF THE WESSEX

Meanwhile, in June 1968, The Queen's Flight had again borrowed a Wessex HC2, when XT672 of No.72 Squadron was used by Prince Philip for a Duke of Edinburgh's Award Scheme tour of South Wales and the Midlands. In December 1968 the Flight acquired its own Wessex HC2, XV726 being collected from Wroughton for crew training in preparation for the re-equipment programme scheduled for 1969. Although, like the Whirlwind Mk.10, this Wessex was not intended for Royal flying, it was in fact so used quite extensively, particularly when the Whirlwinds were again grounded following an accident to an RAF Mk.10. The first of the VVIP helicopters, was collected from Yeovil on 25th June 1969, and was in Royal use only two days later to fly The Duke and Duchess of Kent from Maidstone to Coppins. The target date for the introduction of the Wessex HCC4's had been 1st July and the second aeroplane was handed over to Air Commodore Winskill on the appointed day. By this time the first was operating at Caernarvon in connection with the Investiture of The Prince of Wales, and his subsequent tour of the Principality.

After the delivery of the Wessex the Whirlwinds were phased out and the last one was flown to No. 15 MU at Wroughton on 23rd July. It had been intended to keep the Mk.2 Wessex for some time, as it was invaluable for crew training and reconnaissance flights, but it did not last long and was collected by an Odiham crew on 5th August for use on No.72 Squadron.

XV732 and XV733, the two Westland Wessex HCC4s allocated to The Queen's Flight, were taken on charge on 25th June and 11th July 1969 respectively. They provided a very cost and time-effective means of transport for members of the Royal Family.

1969

1968 had seen few overseas tours, although those that had taken place had been long ones (Prince Philip to Australia and to The Olympic Games in Mexico, and the State Visit to Brazil and Chile). In 1969 however, the Andovers were used on a number of tours, including the State Visit to Austria and visits by other members of the Royal Family to Australia and the Pacific, Canada, The United States, Ethiopia, Singapore, Cambodia, Thailand, Iran, Swaziland and Malagasy. September, for instance, was a gruelling month, with three major tours in progress as well as a proving flight to Canada. Andover XS790, having completed a three week visit to the Pacific, landed at Singapore where a Base 2 inspection was carried out by personnel specially flown out from Benson and a fresh crew then took it on for a tour of Cambodia, Thailand and Iran.

On 2nd April 1969, The Queen's Flight was honoured by a visit from HM Queen Elizabeth The Queen Mother and The Prince of Wales, the first Royal Visit since that of Princess Margaret and Lord Snowdon in 1966. The Flight also received well deserved publicity during 1969 and 1970 when unpublished Royal Air Force journals produced a series of articles on "A History of Royal Flights" starting with the first flight of the then Prince of Wales in 1917.

FIRST QUEEN'S FLIGHT HELICOPTER TO AN OIL RIG

HRH The Princess Anne was the first member of The Royal Family to fly in a Queen's Flight helicopter to an oil rig when she visited the Amaco 'B' in XV732 on 28th October.

TEN AIRCRAFT AND SIX TYPES

In October 1969, Group Captain Gordon-Cumming retired from the RAF and was replaced as Deputy Captain by Group Captain R.C.F. Peirse, who arrived just in time to oversee The Prince of Wales' graduation from the Chipmunk to a twin-engined trainer. A Basset CC1 was allotted in June 1969, and The Queen's Flight was brought to its greatest ever aircraft strength, briefly operating ten aircraft of six different types.

The Chipmunk was eventually returned to No.27 MU at Shawbury on 9th October 1969, having been used by The Prince of Wales for 101 flights, culminating in the award of his Private Pilot's Licence in March 1969 and his RAF Preliminary Flying Badge on 2nd August 1969.

Beagle Basset CC1 XS770 was allocated to The Queen's Flight on 27th June 1969 for The Prince of Wales' twin-engined flying instruction. After the Prince began his Cranwell course it was retained to train The Duke of Kent at Leuchars, then at Benson. It was re-allocated to No. 32 Squadron on 16th September 1971.

Award of Wings to HRH The Prince of Wales

The Prince of Wales continued his flying training on the Basset, flying solo for the first time at Oakington on 6th February 1970 (although accompanied by his Queen's Flight Navigator) and used the machine more and more for communications flying throughout 1970 and 1971, the latter including trips to Paris and to Bad Soellingen in Germany. The Prince of Wales' penultimate Basset flight was on 8th March 1971, when as a RAF Flight Lieutenant, he flew from Benson to Cranwell to join the first Graduate Entry at the RAF College and to complete his flying training under the auspices of Training Command with over 100 hours flying in Jet Provost Mk.5's XW322 and XW323. The Prince of Wales graduated from the RAF College on 20th August 1971, and was presented with his RAF wings by The Chief of the Air Staff, Air Chief Marshal Sir Denis Spotswood.

Wing Commander Mike Rayson left The Queen's Flight in May 1970, handing over as Officer Commanding to Wing Commander D.M. (Des) Divers, LVO, who had previously served on the unit as Prince Philip's personal pilot. During Wing Commander Divers' period of command came two auspicious occasions for the Flight; the visit by HRH The Princess Anne on 13th October 1970, and the inspection by HM The Queen and Prince Philip on 19th April 1971, during which The Prince of Wales and Prince Andrew also made brief visits. There were few long overseas tours in 1970 and 1971, but Andovers visited The United States, Canada, Mexico with Prince Philip in March 1970, Nepal with Prince Richard in the same month, Yugoslavia with Princess Margaret in June 1970, Canada again with Prince Philip and East Africa with The Prince of Wales and Princess Anne (where a television film was made for the programme Blue Peter) both in February 1971.

Prince Philip also travelled by Andover during October to the celebrations in Perseopolis, Iran, of the 2000th year of the Peacock Throne. However, during this time the Flight was kept busy within the United Kingdom and Europe and in January 1971 again had to borrow Andover CC2 XS794. The helicopters in particular were worked almost to capacity in 1970, so much so that requests were made – without success – for the return of a Wessex HC2 for crew training and proving flights, and to take the pressure off the HCC4's. The helicopters continued the now traditional delivery of mail to HM Yacht Britannia off Western Scotland, and whilst operating from Stornoway during this exercise in August 1970 the crew of XV732 was called on to fly a doctor to the German trawler Skagerak. This exploit in high seas and heavy weather earned a Queen's Commendation for the Crew Chief, Chief Technician S.A. (Jack) Frost (later elected Chairman of The Queen's Flight Association in May 2000). On 14th July 1971 General Idi Amin was flown from Heathrow to Turnhouse in an Andover.

The Basset continued in use as a training aircraft for some time after The Prince of Wales had started his Cranwell course, being used to train The Duke of Kent, initially at Leuchars and later at Benson. This exercise finished in August 1971, which coincided with Group Captain M.A. D'Arcy taking over from Group Captain Primavesi as Deputy Captain, and the following month the Basset was transferred to No. 32 Squadron at Northolt, leaving The Queen's Flight with the aircraft which were to serve unchanged for almost fifteen years: Andover CC2's XS789, XS790 and XS793, and Wessex HCC4's XV732 and XV733.

The BAC 1-11 is considered

During 1971 the BAC 1-11, which was first mooted for The Queen's Flight in 1962, was considered as a replacement for the Andovers. However it was not until 1977 that the matter was to be seriously raised again.

Both the Andovers and Wessex were very busy during 1972 although the only tours were The Queen's State Visit to Thailand Malaysia in February and Prince Philip's visit to Kenya in March. XV732 went on the most distant helicopter overseas flight so far undertaken (in October) to Yugoslavia for The Queen's State Visit. Unfortunately poor weather prevented the task from being carried out.

THE DEATH OF THE DUKE OF WINDSOR

In May the sad news was received that The Duke of Windsor had died. As the founder of The Prince of Wales' Flight and later, as Edward VIII, the founder of The King's Flight, it was appropriate that on 31st May his body was flown home from France to Royal Air Force Benson, the home of The Queen's Flight, and was laid in state in the Station Church.

A NEW ANDOVER COLOUR SCHEME

For some time the Andovers had shown signs of corrosion in the "Alclad" skin of the exposed aluminium underbody. This was discovered to have been caused by continual polishing. To overcome this a number of new paint schemes were submitted to The Queen who selected an all-white polyurethane finish. This was applied to XS790 in April.

Andover CC2 XS790

Group Captain B. D'Iongh succeeded Group Captain Peirse as Deputy Captain in February 1972 and Wing Commander D.W. (Dave) Parsons took over as Officer Commanding from Wing Commander Divers in October. The Flight had recently been able to return to the hangar after the completion of repairs to the floor and the laying of a new Armalux surface. This work took up much of 1972 during which time the Flight operated from the nearby C hangar.

During May, Squadron Leader T.A. (Jacko) Jackson, MVO, AFC, and Squadron Leader P.G. (Phil) Fearn, MVO, flew their last Royal Flight after eleven years and 400 Royal Flights crewed together on Herons and Andovers; appropriately this was with Her Majesty The Queen. Both officers completed over 500 Royal Flights during their tours on The Queen's Flight. By 1972 other officers who had completed over 500 Royal Flights were: Squadron Leader Ron Kerr, AFC, Prince Philip's personal helicopter pilot (who was the first to reach this figure on 4th July 1969); Squadron Leader Ralph Lee, MVO, DFC; Squadron Leader R.E. (Reg) Mitchie, MBE and Squadron Leader H.G. (Fred) Sealey, Prince Philip's personal fixed wing navigator.

HRH Prince William's Funeral

Further sad news was to come on 28th August 1972 when it was learnt that HRH Prince William of Gloucester had been killed when his Piper Cherokee had struck a tree at the start of the Goodyear Trophy Air Race. Six Andover flights carried eleven members of the Royal Family to his funeral. Prince William had been due to visit the Middle East in September with The Queen's Flight.

1973

The Oil Crisis

1972 and 1973 saw an unusually high turnover of engineering manpower, some 30%. This and the national oil crisis coincided with the second and third busiest years on record, both Wessex and Andover Royal Flights and the overall flying hours for both types reached a new peak. The oil crisis did however cause the Flight to lose 24 Royal and 3 Special Flights in December and did continue to have a marked effect on The Queen's Flight, but within two years the steady upward trend in the number of Royal Flights, in both fixed and rotary wing aircraft, was to continue. During this busy period the only change to the appearance of the aircraft was the replacement of the military insignia by the Union Flag on the fins of the Andovers in December 1973.

XS790's Record Tour

In March and April 1973 Prince Philip toured Australia in connection with his Award Scheme. In the December Princess Anne toured Mexico, Columbia and Ecuador, this tour was combined with her honeymoon after her marriage to Captain Mark Phillips. The Queen and Prince Philip toured Australia and New Zealand during October and November. On the latter tour XS790 was away from Benson for 75 days, completed Royal Flights in Thailand and Burma with The Duke and Duchess of Kent, and proving flights to the Solomon Islands, New Hebrides, Papua New Guinea and Indonesia. The whole task involved three crews, the aircraft flew 223 hours and 10 minutes and the period of operation away from base was the longest ever undertaken. Other visits in 1973 were made by members of the Royal Family to Ethiopia, Russia, Bulgaria and Germany.

Three Royal Visits

In the early part of 1973 the Flight was honoured by three Royal visits; Princess Alexandra on 20th March, HRH The Princess Margaret with Viscount Linley and Lady Sarah Armstrong Jones on 18th April and then, on 26th April, Prince Philip accompanied by Prince Andrew and Prince Edward paid an informal visit. In the midst of these visits Chief Technician B.A. (Brian) Johnson, BEM, who was posted to the Flight on 8th February 1954, retired from the Service on 2nd April 1973 after more than 19 years; this was believed to be the longest period of service spent by an individual on the Flight. In March Group Captain D.L. (Eddie) Edmunds, AFC, took over as Deputy Captain from Group Captain D'Iongh. These events were crowned in June when Air Commodore Archie Winskill was made a Commander of The Royal Victorian Order in The Queen's Birthday Honours List.

During 1973 the Megadata system was installed in The Queen's Flight Operations Room. This facility provided a direct line to airports throughout the world and so, for the first time The Queen's Flight was able to operate independently of No. 38 Group for operational communications.

A Queen's Flight magazine was launched during October; this was the first time that such a venture had been undertaken. However it was not to prove successful, and the second issue, published in January 1974 was to be the last.

Royal Mail Delivery - August 1970 – The Queen's Flight Style

Wessex XV732 on approach to HM Yacht Britannia. Pilot: Lieutenant Commander John Hedges, RN; Navigator: Squadron Leader Ralph Lee, RAF; Crew Chief: Chief Technician Jack Frost; Winch Operator: Flight Sergeant John Reeson. Note the safety boat is manned and ready.

John Reeson giving Jack Frost a helping hand over the edge of the cabin.

During the Royal Tour of the Western Islands in August 1970 by HM The Queen in HM Yacht Britannia the Royal Mail was delivered by Wessex XV732, flown by Lieutenant Commander John Hedges, RN. HM Yacht was travelling forward at a speed somewhere between 5 and 10 knots. The helicopter had to travel sideways at the same speed whilst the Crew Chief made the delivery of the mail and collected the return mail. Keen observers will note that the Crew Chief was improperly dressed – no black-soled shoes allowed on the deck of HM Yacht Britannia!

5. The Queen's Flight 1974-1982

1974

The effect of the oil crisis continued to cut deeply into the operations of the Flight in 1974, many trips being undertaken by civil airlines. Not long returned from the Royal Tour of Australia, The Queen, accompanied by Prince Philip undertook an arduous tour in the Pacific for the Independence Celebrations of Papua New Guinea in February. She also visited the Solomon Islands together with Princess Anne, who was continuing her honeymoon. Whilst The Queen then returned to the United Kingdom for the general election, the Andover flew to Malaysia with Lord Mountbatten, before repositioning at Bali to continue with The Queen's tour of Indonesia. There were also Andover visits by Prince Philip to Canada and the USA, and by Princess Alexandra to Poland and Berlin; this was the first Royal visit to Poland since the end of World War II.

In July 1974 Group Captain D'Arcy was succeeded as Deputy Captain by Group Captain J.D. (Don) Spottiswood, AFC, who in 1976 also became the first Deputy Captain to hold the office of Station Commander RAF Benson. The Flight was honoured to receive a Royal Visit from The Duke and Duchess of Kent on 15th October.

1975

The Flight carried Royal visitors to the USA, Canada, Holland, Saudi Arabia and Morocco during 1975. In addition Prince Philip toured the Caribbean and Central American Republics in March, visited Poland for the World Driving Championships in August, and Spain for the Coronation of King Juan Carlos in November. HM Queen Elizabeth The Queen Mother toured the Channel Islands by Wessex and in October The Queen's visit to Nigeria was cancelled due to political unrest and a delicate political situation also caused the cancellation of The Prince of Wales's visit to India scheduled for November; after cancellation again in 1979 the trip eventually took place in November 1980.

Wing Commander Stan Hitchen, AFC, succeeded Wing Commander Dave Parsons as Officer Commanding The Queen's Flight on 21st October 1975 and Warrant Officer R.F. (Ron) Tooke, MBE, RVM, BEM, retired from the Service after 18 ½ years on the Flight, which is believed to be the second longest period of service on the Flight after Chief Technician Brian Johnson. Lengthy periods of service although unusual, are by no means unknown on The Queen's Flight.

1976

The start of 1976 was marked by a visit to the Flight by The Duke of Gloucester on 30th January; this was to be the first of several notable occasions that year. Now on his second tour flying helicopters on the Unit, Squadron Leader Ralph Lee, MVO, DFC achieved 1,000 Royal Flights and 5000 hours on the Flight when he carried Princess Alice Duchess of Gloucester in June. Squadron Leader Jim Millar, DFC, became the seventh officer to reach a total of 500 Royal Flights. Shortly afterwards on 5th July The Duke of Kent became the first member of the Royal Family since Princess Anne in 1969 to be flown in a Queen's Flight helicopter to an oil rig, the Forties Field. (Prince Philip had previously flown with the Flight in a Wessex borrowed from No. 72 Squadron to an oil rig in 1967). The mail runs carried out by the Wessex to HMY Britannia were to cease after the hot summer of 1976 when the RN helicopter attached to Britannia's escort took over the task.

Wessex XV733 at Balmoral

Although there were few overseas trips for the Andovers in 1976, all three aircraft were heavily involved in The Queen's State Visit to Luxembourg in November. One surprising aspect of Andover flying was that more hours were flown in one calendar month (237.15 in October) than ever before, beating the previous total set in November 1973.

THE AIRCRAFT ARE RETRIMMED

During the year the Wessex was retrimmed internally and the Andover Royal Compartment was completely re-designed and refitted by the Interior Furnishings Section of the Flight. A start was made on the rationalisation of the Andover servicing schedules; the amended schedules being subsequently introduced on XS790 in June 1977.

In December Group Captain R.A. (Richard) Millar, OBE, ADC, MRAeS, MBIM, took over as Deputy Captain and as Station Commander from Group Captain Don Spottiswood.

1977

THE SILVER JUBILEE

Her Majesty The Queen's Silver Jubilee Year was an interesting and busy year for the Flight. The Wessex workload had been increasing by approximately 10% per annum since the fuel crisis of 1973 and Jubilee Year was to prove the busiest yet; in June and July there were 70 Royal and Special Flights. The Wessex were involved with the European Foreign Minister's Conference at Leeds Castle in May. For the first time the Wessex flew in Northern Ireland carrying The Duke of Gloucester in February, followed in March by Princess Anne's visit to the Province. On 10th August The Queen made her first helicopter flight when she flew in XV732 from HMS Fife (escort to the Royal Yacht) to Hillsborough Castle; she later returned to HMS Fife in XV733. The next day Her Majesty flew in XV733 from HMS Fife to Coleraine and returned in the same aircraft.

Wessex HCC Mk4 XV732 passes a familiar landmark.

It was fitting that both Squadron Leader Jim Millar, DFC, and Squadron Leader Ralph Lee, MVO, DFC, who between them had over 24 years service and 1700 Royal Flights, should carry The Queen on her first helicopter trip as they were due to leave the Flight in October. They also received Her Majesty's Silver Jubilee Medal in June together with 48 other members of the Flight. Also in June ten airmen from the Flight were honoured to visit Buckingham Palace to see The Queen presented with her Silver Jubilee presents to which the Flight had contributed. As The Prince of Wales was flying increasingly more in the Wessex it was decided that Squadron Leader A. Gutteridge, who had replaced Squadron Leader Millar, should become The Prince of Wales' personal helicopter pilot.

The Andovers had an even busier year with The Queen's Silver Jubilee tour of Fiji and Papua New Guinea in February with the aircraft (XS789) returning with Prince Philip through Afghanistan in March having been away eight weeks. Royal visits with the Andover were also made to the Oman, Ghana, Ivory Coast, Nigeria, Canada and Jamaica. Two Andovers carrying HM The Queen and HRH The Prince of Wales and a Wessex carrying HM Queen Elizabeth The Queen Mother were involved at Finningley on 29th July for The Queen's Review of The Royal Air Force. Chief Technician Roger Harris, Crew Chief, on the Andover carrying The Queen, was completing his 500th Royal Flight.

The Queen's Review coincided with the publication of an article on the Flight by the Royal Air Force News, and a booklet by Flight Magazine entitled 'Royal Wings Through Five Reigns' whilst two weeks earlier on 11th July, the Flight had been honoured by a visit from Her Majesty Queen Elizabeth The Queen Mother.

The BAC 1-11 was again being considered as a replacement for the Andover and work which was begun in late 1977 on revising the 1971 specifications was completed in early 1978. The rationalisation of servicing schedules successfully introduced with the Andover in 1977 was extended to the Wessex during the same year and introduced in April 1978 commencing with XV733.

1978

1978 saw the 10th Anniversary of Air Commodore Archie Winskill's arrival as Captain of The Queen's Flight. A party was held to celebrate that Anniversary on 15th February. The Andovers visited Canada, Hungary, Yugoslavia, Puerto Rico, Egypt and the Sudan. The Duke and Duchess of Gloucester also made visits to Northern Ireland. On The Queen's visit to Germany in May all three Andovers were involved. The Duke and Duchess of Gloucester were present for the Independence ceremonies of the Solomon Islands, and The Prince of Wales carried out a tour of Brazil and Venezuela. The Prince of Wales also made his first trip to an oil rig in a Wessex in February when he visited the Claymore/Piper field. Later, on 4th July he honoured the Flight with an official visit, his first since 1969.

The Wessex tasking continued to increase reaching a peak in 1978, when a third Navigator was posted in. Notable trips were to Leeds Castle in Kent carrying the Israeli, Egyptian and American delegates to the Middle East peace talks in July and the second Queen's Flight helicopter task to an aircraft carrier at sea. Again the flight was with HM Queen Elizabeth The Queen Mother from her residence at Birkhall to HMS Ark Royal steaming in the Moray Firth. The Navigator on this trip, Flight Lieutenant D.J. (Derek) James, had the previous month been the eighth officer of the Flight to attain a total of 500 Royal Flights.

Group Captain D.L. Edmunds, AFC, ADC, left the Flight and retired from the Service in March 1978, handing over as Deputy Captain after five years to Group Captain D.St.J. Homer, MVO. Group Captain K.J. Goodwin, CBE, AFC, succeeded Group Captain Richard Miller as Deputy Captain in December. Group Captain Homer taking over as Station Commander.

1979

In 1979 HM The Queen travelled to Denmark and France with the Flight. She also flew to the Gulf States in February where she was the first female Royal Visitor to be received as Head of State, and later to Africa in July and August. During this tour she visited all countries bordering Rhodesia and opened the Commonwealth Conference in Lusaka. Prince Philip visited Moscow in March and Princess Anne attended the Independence celebrations of the Gilbert Islands in July. The Prince of Wales' visit to India, reorganised after the cancellation of his visit in 1975, was again called off.

Following the tragic death of Lord Mountbatten and the injuries to his family in August, Lord Brabourne was airlifted from Aldergrove to Northolt, together with his family, on 10th September in XS793 which was fitted for the casualty evacuation (casevac) role – the first time such a role had been undertaken by The Queen's Flight.

PRINCE ANDREW BEGINS HIS FLYING CAREER

In April Prince Andrew completed his Royal Naval Pilot Grading under the auspices of The Queen's Flight in Chipmunk T10 WP904; his instructor was Lieutenant Commander A.McK. Sinclair, MBE, RN. Whilst on 30th July The Prince of Wales took to the air in a privately owned Tiger Moth G-ADIA during an informal visit to the Flight.

During 1979 Squadron Leader G.H. (Geoff) Williams, Prince Philip's personal fixed wing pilot, and Squadron Leader Derek Lovett, personal fixed wing pilot to The Prince of Wales, joined the small band of officers who have achieved 500 Royal Flights. Wing Commander Stan Hitchen left the Flight in December 1979 after 4 years, handing over as Officer Commanding to Wing Commander E.T.I. (Eric) King. Also in December, Group Captain Anthony Mumford, OBE, ADC, became Deputy Captain in place of Group Captain Ken Goodwin who was promoted on posting.

1980

1980 started on a high note with the award of a Knighthood in the New Year's Honours List to the Captain of The Queen's Flight, Air Commodore Sir Archie Winskill, KCVO, CBE, DFC*, AE, MRAeS. He received his accolade from The Queen at a private audience on 20th February 1980, 12 years, almost to the day, since he was appointed as Captain of The Queen's Flight.

PRINCE PHILIP FLIES THE 1-11

Work had been resumed on the BAC 1-11 project at the end of 1979 when the concept was changed from a short to a medium range aircraft with a special modification to increase its range to 2,400 miles. This work was completed early in 1980 and in April Prince Philip made a series of flights from Benson in a BAC 1-11 of British Aerospace, G-ASYD.

ROYAL VISIT TO THE FLIGHT AND PRINCE EDWARD TAKES UP GLIDING

HRH The Prince of Wales made an informal visit to the Flight in March in the course of which he was presented by the Captain with a memento to commemorate His Royal Highness's 1,000 flying hours. Prince Edward, following in his brother's footsteps, took to the air at Benson, and attained his Gliding Proficiency Certificate in July in a Sedburgh Glider XN151. Earlier in April, Squadron Leader W.B. (Brian) Sowerby, MVO, became the latest member of the Flight to attain a total of 500 Royal Flights.

The Andovers visited the USA, Canada and Thailand and carried The Prince of Wales on a tour of India (which had twice previously been cancelled in 1975 and 1979) and Nepal. The Wessex operated for the first time in France, flying The Prince of Wales, and also flew The Duke of Gloucester to the Murchison Oil Rig on 30th September 1980. This was the most northerly platform at that time and is the first occasion that an oil rig has been inaugurated by a member of the Royal Family.

1981

In January 1981 Group Captain J.F.B. (Jeremy) Jones succeeded Group Captain D.St.J. Homer as Deputy Captain, and Group Captain Anthony Mumford took over as Station Commander from Group Captain Homer.

THE PRINCE OF WALES DINES WITH THE QUEEN'S FLIGHT.

HRH The Prince of Wales was guest of honour at a dinner held in the Officer's Mess on 18th February 1981 at which Flight members from all ranks were present. Shortly afterwards, the engagement of His Royal Highness to Lady Diana Spencer was announced and on 27th March Lady Diana made her first journey with the Flight in a Wessex accompanying The Prince of Wales to Cheltenham.

In March, whilst continuing his Sea King training, Prince Andrew spent three days based with the Flight and on 6th April Prince Philip honoured the Flight during a brief visit for continuation training by participating in a group photograph of all members.

AWARD OF WINGS TO HRH THE PRINCE ANDREW

HRH The Duke of Edinburgh presented Prince Andrew with his pilot's wings at 705 Naval Air Squadron on 2nd April, at the end of No. 93 course.

A RECORD

The flying commitment built up steadily during 1981 and April, June and September were the busiest ever respective months. On 2nd June all aircraft of the Flight flew on task and achieved 14

Royal Flights in one day which is believed to be a record, while in September the combined aircraft hours were the highest flown since the arrival of the Wessex in 1969.

The Andovers achieved their busiest ever four-month period between September and December during which time Princess Margaret visited Swaziland, The Duke of Kent toured West Africa, Princess Anne flew in India and Nepal, and The Duke of Gloucester toured the Philippines, Indonesia, Malaysia, Burma and Thailand. Earlier in the year The Duke of Kent had visited the United Arab Emirates and Prince Philip had flown to Egypt and the Gulf.

The wedding of The Prince of Wales and Lady Diana Spencer took place on 29th July 1981. Twelve members of the Flight were privileged to attend the wedding, to act as ushers and to form part of the step lining contingent at Westminster Abbey. On 1st August, The Prince and Princess were flown from Southampton to Gibraltar on their honeymoon by Squadron Leader Derek Lovett on what was his last flight in the Royal Air Force after 9 years on the Flight.

During the year the helicopters assisted Thames Television in their production of a documentary programme on Princess Anne and in the summer months flew Prince Philip on the Silver Jubilee Tour of his award scheme and operated twice in Northern Ireland. In June the Wessex achieved the highest number of hours ever recorded. In the course of 1981, Squadron Leader David Hurley, AFC, and Flight Lieutenant M.I.S. (Ian) Anderson joined those who have achieved 500 Royal Flights and SAC L. Hodgetts became the first aircraftman to be invited to attend a function at Buckingham Palace.

SIR ARCHIE WINSKILL RETIRES

The year ended on a sad note when the Captain, Sir Archie Winskill made his last flight before retirement; appropriately this was with Prince Philip, The Prince and Princess of Wales, Princess Anne and Prince Edward. The fourth Captain of The Queen's Flight, Sir Archie was appointed on 15th February 1968, and his tenure of office of almost 14 years was exceeded only by Sir Edward Fielden. He was succeeded on 27th January 1982 by Air Vice-Marshal John de M. Severne, LVO, OBE, AFC, a former Equerry to The Duke of Edinburgh.

1982

In March 1982, The Prince Andrew completed a short conversion course on to the Wessex 4 with Flight Lieutenant Hugh Northey. However, Naval duty in the Falklands prevented him flying further with the Flight during the year.

THE INAUGURATION OF THE QUEEN'S FLIGHT ASSOCIATION

The newly formed Queen's Flight Association celebrated its formation with an Inaugural Dinner on 7th May 1982 at which Sir Archie Winskill was elected President. On 25th June The Prince of Wales had been the first member of the Royal Family to make a helicopter flight from British to foreign soil when he flew to Port Antifer, France and on 11th July he flew on to the SS Canberra in Southampton Water to welcome home returning servicemen from the Falklands. On 17th September The Queen flew from Lee-on-Solent to Aberdeen in an Andover after welcoming home Prince Andrew in HMS Invincible. A number of other sorties were flown throughout the summer with the Royal Family to meet the homecoming ships and aircraft of the Task Force.

The helicopters again operated in Northern Ireland and also flew HM Queen Elizabeth The Queen Mother and Princess Margaret in Germany in July.

During June, Sergeant Alan Hogan became the first helicopter crew chief to attain 500 Royal Flights, and his final total of 565 hours after 4 years is the highest reached by any crew chief on the Flight. Other members of the unit to reach 500 Royal Flights during the year were Squadron Leader M. J. (Mike) Hawes LVO, Squadron Leader B.J. (Brian) Crawford, MVO and Squadron Leader D.J. (David) Rowe, LVO.

Prince William's First Flight

On 17th August HRH Prince William of Wales flew for the first time with the Flight from Kemble to Aberdeen with his parents and Prince Philip.

During 1982 the modification programme to fit a dual radio compass system to the Andover, and the two year programme cosmetically to refurbish the Andover Flight Deck were completed. The Wessex cockpit was similarly refurbished in 1981. During August a revised Andover servicing was introduced, the basic servicing periodicity being changed from a flying to a calendar base. British Aerospace/Teleflex Morse presented the Flight with improved 1st pilot and co-pilot seats for the Andover.

The Andovers again experienced a busy year. After the tour by Prince Philip early in 1982 to Saudi Arabia and the Indian sub-continent, a tour of Central Africa was cancelled by The Duke of Gloucester due to illness although the Andover had already pre-positioned, and a tour of Peru by Princess Anne had to be cancelled because of the Falklands War, but in August XS793 toured the Pacific and Far East on a recce diverting on its homeward leg to Africa to carry Prince Michael of Kent to the funeral of the King of Swaziland.

Kitty Four Crew Arrested

Shortly after the cessation of hostilities in the Lebanon, Princess Anne (President of the Save the Children Fund) visited Beirut while returning from her tour of Southern and East Africa at the end of the year. On a proving flight during this tour Squadron Leader G.H. (Graham) Laurie, his crew and aircraft were held on the ground for some hours on 18th October 1982, by Zimbabwean troops at Aberdeen Two airfield, in circumstances remarkably similar to Kitty One's incident 21 years earlier in Mali. Further explanation of this detention is revealed by Graham Laurie in Chapter 10.

Prince Philip toured the United States for three weeks from mid October and XS793 visited the Caribbean, Mexico, the USA and Canada at the end of the year.

The year's flying statistics show that in July the total Wessex and Andover flights were the highest ever recorded for one month including 121 Royal stages, while there were 8 Andover tours during the year totalling nearly 650 hours, again a record.

On 14th September and 4th November visits were made to British Aerospace and Westland's respectively to view and fly the BAe 146 airliner and the W30 helicopter, both possible future replacements for the Flight. On 17th December, Wing Commander B.P. (Brian) Synott took over as Officer Commanding from Wing Commander Eric King.

The BAe 146 is Chosen

1982 was very satisfactorily rounded off on 22nd December when Mr. John Knott, the Secretary of State for Defence, announced in the House that the RAF would purchase two 146 BAe 146's in the spring of 1983 and, subject to a satisfactory two year proving period, The Queen's Flight would subsequently re-equip with the extended version of the aircraft.

Njombe, Tanzania – March 1984

Andover XS793 being repositioned after being dug out of hole on a high altitude grass strip at Njombe in Tanzania.
The aircraft had started to sink as soon as HRH The Prince of Wales had left the aircraft.

6. The Queen's Flight 1983-1988

1983

PRINCESS ALEXANDRA VISITS THE QUEEN'S FLIGHT

On 13th January 1983 HRH Princess Alexandra returned to The Queen's Flight after ten years when she made a tour of the hangar and later informally met families of the Flight members.

The following day Group Captain R.B. (Dickie) Duckett, AFC, took over as Station Commander Benson and as Deputy Captain from Group Captain Anthony Mumford, OBE, ADC.

HRH Prince William, who in August 1982 had flown for the first time, travelled on his first journey as principal passenger with the Flight when on 4th March his parents disembarked at Glasgow to fulfil public engagements and the infant Prince travelled on to Aberdeen.

THE PRINCE OF WALES – PATRON OF THE QUEEN'S FLIGHT ASSOCIATION

HRH The Prince of Wales was invited in the spring to become Patron of The Queen's Flight Association, a position which he accepted on 6th June 1983.

FLYING ACHIEVEMENTS

When XV732 reached 5,000 flying hours on 16th March 1983 the helicopters attained a milestone, for it raised to over 10,000 the total hours flown by the two Wessex since their introduction to the Flight in 1969. Further milestones were reached when Andover XS789 reached a total of 10,000 hours on 24th May, the same total being achieved by XS790 five days later.

The use of The Queen's Flight helicopters since their introduction to Royal Flying in 1960 has continually increased as shown by three particular events during 1983; Squadron Leader Derek James, on 24th May, became the second Flight member to reach a total of 1,000 Royal Flights. He reached this figure in 8 years, whilst Squadron Leader Ralph Lee MVO, DFC, took 16 years; in July the helicopters flew 135.05 hours, the highest figure yet for a calendar month, surpassing the previous highest of June 1981; and, on 16th November, Flight Lieutenant A.R. (Tony) Bennett joined the number of those who have achieved 500 Royal Flights.

In periods of high work load the reliability of the machines and the expertise of the members of the Flight is well illustrated by the fact that, due to servicing and modification work, only one helicopter was available for Royal flying for the 9 month period between 13th August 1982 and 11th May 1983, with the exception of one week in October.

HRH The Princess Margaret arriving on board HMS Illustrious on 30th March 1983.

PRINCE PHILIP FLIES THE WESTLAND W30

On 28th February, HRH The Duke of Edinburgh flew in a W30 in California when he visited the USA with The Queen. On 9th May The Duke of Edinburgh again flew a W30 from Llantrissant to Cardiff and on to Buckingham Palace.

BAe 146 IN ROYAL AIR FORCE COLOURS

Group Captain Duckett represented the Captain of The Queen's Flight at Hatfield on 6th June when the Royal Air Force took over the first BAe 146 for evaluation. The aircraft later flew Group Captain Duckett to Benson where it was met by Flight members.

Her Majesty The Queen viewed the aircraft on 3rd November at RAF Marham. Earlier, members of the Flight were able to fly in the BAe 146 on a sortie from RAF Benson.

The Andovers continued to be busy during 1983, flying tours earlier in the year to Saudi Arabia, Jordan, Pakistan, Zambia, Zimbabwe, Turkey, Egypt and Canada.

In October The Duke of Edinburgh carried out a tour of the Far East, and in November he used an Andover on a number of occasions when he accompanied Her Majesty The Queen on their tour of Kenya, Bangladesh and India.

1984

BAe 146 FOR THE QUEEN'S FLIGHT

1984 arrived with the confirmation that the evaluation of the BAe 146 at Brize Norton had been successful and that The Queen's Flight was to be re-equipped with two BAe 146 aircraft in 1986. It was also confirmed that, due to the present and projected tasking, one Andover would remain to maintain a total of three fixed wing aircraft.

The first 146 for the Flight, ZE700, entered the production track at Hatfield on 30th January, followed by ZE701 on 9th June. ZE700 made its maiden flight to Hawarden on 25th November where it remained for completion of the interior fit. The BAe 146 contract was signed on 27th November.

THE BUSIEST YEAR TO DATE

The present workload was confirmed in no uncertain terms with record achievements throughout the year. The Andovers flew their highest ever number of hours (1837.50) surpassing the previous highest of 1973. The fifteen tours and 855.25 hours – both records – to the far corners of the world contributed in no small measure to this total.

The Wessex also were busy, flying the second highest number of hours (858.50) in their fifteen years service on the Flight. The combined aircraft total hours flown was the highest ever (2696.10), as were the combined number of Royal, Special and VVIP Flights, which, at 784, surpassed the previous highest of 1978.

Princess Anne for the first time became the most prolific user of the Flight, including in her year strenuous tours of West Africa and the Indian sub continent in her capacity as President of The Save the Children Fund. Princess Anne's tour of India was cut short due to the assassination of Mrs Ghandi whilst the Andover was at Delhi.

THE QUEEN FLIES BY HELICOPTER IN FRANCE

The Wessex ventured overseas more than in previous years, including flying The Prince of Wales to France on 5th June, only the second time that a helicopter has carried a member of the Royal Family from British to foreign soil.

The following day, 6th June, Her Majesty The Queen and The Duke of Edinburgh flew four sectors in Wessex XV732 during their visit to Normandy to commemorate the 40th Anniversary of the D-Day Landings by the Allied Forces. This was only the second occasion that The Queen has flown in a helicopter and the first overseas.

Sergeant Mick Brown, crew chief on this day, achieved an unprecedented distinction by flying all the entitled members of The Royal Family during a 5-week period.

HER MAJESTY VISITS THE QUEEN'S FLIGHT

It was perhaps appropriate that during this eventful year the Flight should have been honoured with a visit by The Queen, her first since 1971. On 6th April Her Majesty, accompanied by HRH The Duke of Edinburgh, was greeted on her arrival at The Queen's Flight by Prince Edward who had arrived earlier in a Bulldog aircraft from RAF Abingdon where he completed a course to achieve his Preliminary Flying Badge.

AUDIENCE WITH THE QUEEN

Another notable departure was that of Warrant Officer Ken Broddle, RAF Police. Mr Broddle left the Flight after 8 years service and over 500 Royal Flights, the first policeman to reach this total. After his last flight, he was granted a private audience with The Queen at Buckingham Palace, the first member of the Flight to receive this honour.

PRINCE WILLIAM'S FIRST HELICOPTER FLIGHT

Prince William of Wales flew for the first time in a helicopter when he accompanied The Prince of Wales on a short trip from the family home at Highgrove on 26th October.

A month earlier The Duke of Kent undertook some flying training at the Flight in a Piper Seminole owned by British Aerospace.

1985

AN EVEN BUSIER YEAR

The total number of flying hours was down on the previous year, but the combined number of Royal, Special and VVIP Flights at a total of 893 surpassed the record high total of the previous year by 14%.

The Wessex flew their highest ever number of hours (915.10).

In January the 'Megadata' equipment, which was installed in Operations in 1973, was replaced by 'Telemate'. This new equipment greatly enhanced the Flights capability to communicate worldwide using OFTS and SITA. In November, a 'Jet Plan' Terminal was installed in Operations in preparation for the introduction of the BAe 146.

FLYING ACHIEVEMENTS

Squadron Leader Geoffrey Williams, The Duke of Edinburgh's personal pilot, became the first fixed wing pilot to achieve 1,000 Royal Flights.

Squadron Leader Ian Anderson, The Duke of Edinburgh's personal fixed wing navigator, achieved a total of 10,000 flying hours.

Squadron Leader Brian Sowerby, The Prince of Wales' personal navigator, became the first fixed wing navigator to achieve 1,000 Royal Flights, at the same time having flown 5,000 hours on Andovers. He left the Flight in November after thirteen years.

Squadron Leader David Hurley, The Duke of Edinburgh's personal helicopter pilot, became the first helicopter pilot to achieve 1,000 Royal Flights.

Andover XS793 reached its 10,000 flying hours since production.

CHANGE OF DEPUTY CAPTAIN

Group Captain A.M. (Marcus) Wills, OBE succeeded Group Captain R.B. Duckett, AFC, in February as Station Commander Royal Air Force Benson and as Deputy Captain of The Queen's Flight.

HRH THE PRINCESS ANNE'S TOUR OF INDIA

In February, Princess Anne continued her tour of India in connection with The Save the Children Fund, which had had to be curtailed the previous year. In addition to this tour another ten were flown covering West Africa, Canada, Egypt, Algeria, Tunisia, The Caribbean, Madagascar, Tanzania, Mozambique, Zambia and Sudan, involving nearly four hundred hours flying.

HELICOPTERS' BUSIEST YEAR

The Wessex flew a total of 452 Royal, Special and VVIP Flights, three of which involved flights to oil rigs; The Prince of Wales to Forties Bravo, The Princess of Wales to Forties Charlie and The Duchess of Kent to Beatrice Alpha.

Tasks involved flying The Duke of Edinburgh in Germany, The Duchess of Kent in the Channel Islands, The Prince and Princess of Wales touring the Western Islands and Princess Anne out to the island of St. Kilda.

In April, Life President Hastings Banda of Malawi flew in XV733 from Holyrood Palace to Balmoral and return.

HELICOPTER SUPPORT

After nearly eighteen years of service the Helicopter Support vehicles (HSV) were replaced by new vehicles, purpose built to provide full helicopter support facilities.

During the year the HSV achieved record mileage and almost doubled their refuelling of the Wessex.

The first task with the new HSV took place in May in support of a flight by The Duke of Kent to Mitcheldean.

During the month of May, The Duke of Kent undertook some further refresher flying training at The Queen's Flight in a Piper Seminole owned by British Aerospace.

TWO ROYAL VISITS

On 21st March, Princess Anne visited the Flight, when she toured the hangar, lunched with Officers and their ladies in the Officer's Mess, and later informally met the families of the Flight in the hangar.

On 25th November, The Princess of Wales paid her first visit to The Queen's Flight to see the day-to-day operations, lunching in The Queen's Flight and talking to families.

HM Yacht Britannia

The Queen's Flight has always had excellent relations with the crew of HM Yacht Britannia, meeting up in many remote areas of the world and many very long standing friendships have been forged throughout the years. The annual sports day, which were fought out on a home and away basis with the trophy usually being won by the home team, was another occasion when friendships were forged and renewed whilst a copious amount of refreshment was being consumed. A very much sort after 'perk' was a bunk on HM Yacht Britannia sailing from Aberdeen to Portsmouth every year after the Royal Family had been positioned at Balmoral for their summer holiday. Some 'Yachties' were flown south by the Flight to make accommodation available on the Yacht. A very memorable occasion for the lucky ones!

The 1965 contingent aboard HM Yacht Britannia.

1986

Introduction of the BAe 146

On 23rd April the logbook of BAe 146 ZE700, designated BAe 146 CC Mk.2, was handed over to the Captain of The Queen's Flight, by Sir Austin Pearce, Chairman of British Aerospace, at a ceremony at Hatfield. At the same time Sir Austin presented the Captain with a painting by Robert Taylor depicting 50 years of Royal flying. After converting our first crews to ZE700 at Hatfield, the aircraft was delivered to the Flight on 6th May, followed by ZE701 on 9th July; the first official Royal Flight with the new aircraft being carried out when The Duke and Duchess of York were flown to the Azores for their honeymoon, although The Duke of Edinburgh had flown the aircraft earlier during his conversion.

The Duke of Edinburgh carried out a period of BAe 146 simulator training in June, with flying training the following month and after a period of continuation training at Marham on the 14th July had flown the aircraft from Marham to Gatwick which in reality was the first Royal flight beating the honeymooners who flew on the 23rd July. The Prince of Wales converted to the BAe 146 in November.

With the introduction of the new aircraft, the Flight reallocated two of the Andovers to No. 32 Squadron at RAF Northolt; XS789 on 20th June, followed by XS793 on 1st October.

During the construction of the BAe 146's there had been considerable discussion on the colour scheme. BAe advised against having a red fin and rudder because the large area would make the aircraft appear tail heavy. The BAe 146 therefore first entered service with a white fin and rudder. What had not been appreciated during the construction phase was that the red colour on the wings is hardly seen when the aircraft is on the ground due to the anhedral and the silver leading edges. Consequently, after the aircraft were delivered, there were universal comments that more red needed to be seen. After much discussion with Buckingham Palace and BAe on the precise colour scheme, the first BAe 146 was repainted with a red fin and rudder in August 1986.

BAe 146 overhead RAF Benson.

THE QUEEN MOTHER VISITS THE QUEEN'S FLIGHT

On 7th May Her Majesty Queen Elizabeth The Queen Mother paid an informal visit to the Flight, it being most appropriate that she should be the first member of The Royal Family to see the new BAe 146, which had been delivered the previous day.

50TH ANNIVERSARY OF THE FORMATION OF THE KING'S FLIGHT

On the 26th June 1986, HM The Queen and The Duke of Edinburgh, accompanied by The Prince Edward, attended a reception at St. James's Palace to celebrate the 50th Anniversary of the formation of The King's Flight. The Prince and Princess of Wales, The Princess Margaret, Princess Alice, The Duke and Duchess of Gloucester and The Duke and Duchess of Kent were also present.

Her Majesty and Their Royal Highnesses were received upon arrival by the Captain of The Queen's Flight before being presented to VIP Guests in the Council Chamber, where the 50th Anniversary painting, presented by British Aerospace, was on display.

Thereafter Members of The Royal Family were conducted through the State Rooms meeting Members of the Flight, Members of The Queen's Flight Association, invited guests and their ladies. A total of about 700 were present.

On departure the Captain presented Her Majesty and other Members of The Royal Family with the book 'The Queen's Flight, Fifty Years of Royal Flying', the publication of which had been planned to coincide with the Anniversary. In addition, to mark the Anniversary, all Members of The Royal Family presented the Flight with signed portraits.

WEDDING OF HRH THE PRINCE ANDREW

Six members of the Flight and their wives attended the wedding of Prince Andrew (created on the same day HRH The Duke of York) to Miss Sarah Ferguson at Westminster Abbey on 23rd July. The Duke and Duchess of York were flown in Wessex XV732 from Chelsea Hospital to Heathrow where they boarded the BAe 146, ZE701 for the flight to the Azores at the start of their honeymoon.

FIRST ROYAL TOUR IN A BAE 146 AND THE FIRST ROYAL TOUR OF CHINA

HRH The Prince of Wales flew to Boston and Chicago from the 2nd to 6th September 1986. Graham Laurie (Kitty 4) was the aircraft Captain with David Gale (Kitty 8) as the Co-Pilot. The aircraft routed Aberdeen, Reykjavik, Gander, Boston, Chicago/Midway, Goose Bay, Reykjavik and back to Aberdeen.

David Gale (Kitty Eight) was the aircraft Captain in ZE701 taking The Duke of Kent on his tour of Tanzania, Botswana and Zimbabwe from 26th September to 6th October. This was the first Royal Tour flown in the new aircraft. The aircraft positioned to Mombasa via Rome, Cairo, and Khartoum. A Royal flight from Mombasa to Gabarone was followed by a proving flight to Maun, a small strip near the Okavango. The runway was made out of coral which was very sharp and shredded the aircraft tyres. A complete set of main wheel tyres had to be sent out from Benson.

The next Royal stage was Gaberone to Maun and the crew then took time out to fly to a safari camp in the Okavango by small aircraft and had a three day, five star camping/safari holiday. They saw elephants, giraffe, zebra, monkeys, buffalo and hippos. Back to work and Royal flights Maun-Victoria Falls-Harare. Permission was given for the aircraft to fly low over the Falls on departure for Harare. The aircraft returned to Benson via Nairobi, Cairo and Rome.

HM The Queen and HRH The Duke of Edinburgh were to carry out a State Visit to China in October 1986 flying from Shanghai to Xian and Kunming and then on to Canton. It was decided that the internal flying would be carried out by BAe 146 as would some internal flying by HRH The Duke of Edinburgh. Consequently a proving flight was arranged during the August 'break' to be flown by the Kitty 3 crew with Graham Laurie (Kitty 4) as a second captain.

Squadron Leader Ian Anderson reports that the aircraft departed Benson on 4th August with night stops at Bahrain, Bombay and Phuket before arriving in Hong Kong on 7th August and the following day carried out some local flying to familiarise the crew with the Hong Kong approaches before they flew into China directly to Beijing (formerly known as Peking).

The first problem – there were no route maps published in English for the routes that were to be flown. Two China Airlines crew were allocated to fly with the aircraft. One was a radio operator who spoke good English and the other was a navigator who didn't speak any! The navigator carried a rather grubby notebook in which were hand written frequencies of various beacons the crew would have to use. He also had route-maps annotated only with Chinese symbols, which the radio man said they could look at but not take away. Anyway the route was flown from Beijing to Nanchang, Cheng Du, Canton and back to Hong Kong. This was at the time before China had opened to tourists and some of the accommodation was a little strange. At Nanchang the crew stayed in a Russian built guesthouse that was very basic. Imagine their surprise when they were presented with a bill which was even more expensive then the Harbour View Holiday Inn where they had stayed in Hong Kong! The Defence Attaché from the British Embassy travelling with the crew was able with his language capability to establish that the rate was determined by the fact they were 'rich' Westerners and could afford it. The two Chinese Crew members were charged nothing.

From Hong Kong the route home was Bangkok, Muscat and Cairo to get back to Benson on 17th August. To have carried out the first major route prover in the BAe 146 in less than two weeks was a considerable achievement. Unfortunately the Royal Tour was not so incident free.

The Royal Tour in BAe 146, ZE700, started on September 30th when the Kitty 3 crew picked up HRH The Duke of Edinburgh in Perugia, Italy where they had left him a few days earlier. From there they went via Luxor, Muscat, Madras, Phuket and Bali to Alice Springs in Australia. Then it was off to Sydney for a few days before leaving Oz via Port Moresby and Guam to Tokyo. After five days in Tokyo they flew to Beijing where they handed over the aircraft to the Kitty 1 crew (Wing Commander Mike Schofield) who had arrived there on the British Airways flight that had brought HM The Queen to China. The Kitty 3 crew were then left to suffer the hardships of Hong Kong for the next eleven days whilst Kitty 1 flew HM The Queen and HRH The Duke of Edinburgh around China.

After HM's tour was completed the Kitty 3 crew took the aircraft over again to take Prince Philip on a WWF tour of China involving visits to Nanchang, Simao, Cheng Du and Kunming. The visit to Chend Du got off to a bad start as far as the crew were concerned with the Chinese Authorities insisting that they stayed in another ghastly guest house. However, the crew won the battle and got into the same hotel that they had stayed in on the proving flight. This was the hotel which had two Chinese restaurants, one for Chinese residents and the other for foreigners in which the food was identical but cost ten times the price in the one for the locals. The other thing one remembers about that hotel was the wake-up call which consisted of a girl shouting through the phone "Get up!"

Prince Philip's reason for visiting Cheng Du was to see the Panda reserve in the mountains. The crew were taken to the local zoo where they saw more Pandas than HRH including a newly born baby!

On to Kunming for the last visit of the tour where Don Gordon reported that there was some metal wearing off the blades of one of the engines. Kunming was not the sort of place to let HRH be stuck so they proceeded with the itinerary via Simeo and Canton to Hong Kong where they reported the findings back to Benson. Consultation with the manufacturers resulted in the decision that an engine change was needed so HRH was booked on a commercial flight home and the crew awaited a new engine and a team from the Flight to change it. To obtain a new engine the OC (Mike Schofield) had to use his own credit card to guarantee payment! The engine and team duly arrived in Hong Kong after some problems getting a suitable commercial freighter to transport it. The team worked overnight and after an airtest on 4th November they flew home.

This major tour only five months of receiving the BAe 146 on the Flight and for the engineers to carry out the first engine change overnight down route were excellent achievements.

Kitty Eight (David Gale) in ZE701 flew The Duke and Duchess of Kent on a tour of India during November. The aircraft left Benson on the 9th and positioned to Bombay via Rome, Cairo, Bahrain and Seeb. A proving flight was flown to Goa before the first Royal Flights Bombay to Goa and return to Bombay. TRH's were then flown to Delhi via Udaipur. Further proving flights were then flown to Gwalior and Agra. Royal Flights were then flown Delhi – Gwalior – Delhi – Agra – Delhi.

On arrival in Delhi on 13th November, a small amount of smoke was seen coming out of the back of one of the engines. An oil seal had failed and replacement required the back part of the engine to be removed in order for the replacement to be installed. However, the parts were only available from the USA! The parts were sent via Concorde to London Heathrow; meanwhile the Flight engineers were having visas prepared expeditiously by the Indian Embassy in London (a process that normally takes a week or more). The parts and engineers boarded the same flight from Heathrow to Delhi and the team worked through the night to replace the part. The aircraft was ready to go one hour before scheduled departure on 15th November.

During the tour, the crew were able to visit the Taj Mahal and stay in the Lake Palace Hotel, previously a Maharaja's Palace on an island in the middle of a lake in Udaipur.

FLYING ACHIEVEMENTS

On 4th November The Duchess of York, who was undergoing flying instruction in a Piper Warrior G-BLVL, flew solo from Benson. She is the first lady member of The Royal Family to learn to fly.

Squadron Leader David Hurley, The Duke of Edinburgh's personal helicopter pilot, achieved 10,000 flying hours, 7,800 being in helicopters.

Squadron Leader Ian Anderson and Squadron Leader Brian Crawford, The Duke of Edinburgh's personal fixed wing and helicopter navigators respectively, joined those members achieving 1,000 Royal Flight.

Squadron Leader Graham Laurie, The Prince of Wales' personal fixed wing pilot, and Flight Lieutenant Richard Stanton achieved 500 Royal Flights.

1987

This was the first full year of operation of the two BAe 146 aircraft, during which there has been a record number of 20 overseas Royal Tours, which also involved the Andover and Wessex. The five aircraft completed a record total of 989 Royal, Special and VIP flights during the year. It is hoped that this steady annual increase over the years can be levelled off as the Flight is now operating at full stretch.

THE QUEEN'S FLIGHT MUSEUM

The Duchess of Gloucester paid an informal visit to the Flight on the 10th March, during which she officially opened The Queen's Flight Museum, as well as seeing the day to day operations and meeting the families of Flight members.

FLYING TRAINING FOR THE DUCHESS OF YORK

The Duchess of York completed her fixed wing flying training in a Piper Warrior, G-BLVL, being awarded her Private Pilots Licence in January. To mark the occasion The Duchess was presented with a model of a Piper Warrior on behalf of CSE Kidlington and The Queen's Flight. Later in the year she carried out helicopter flying training in a Bell Jet Ranger, G-DOFY, going solo in October and receiving the helicopter endorsement to her Private Pilots Licence in December.

CHANGE OF DEPUTY CAPTAIN

Group Captain P.G. Pinney, LVO, ADC, succeeded Group Captain A.M. (Marcus) Wills, OBE, ADC, in October as Station Commander of Royal Air Force Benson and Deputy Captain of The Queen's Flight. Group Captain Pinney is a former member of the Flight having been responsible for the flying training of The Prince of Wales on the Chipmunk and the Basset.

FLYING ACHIEVEMENTS

Squadron Leader Derek James, personal helicopter navigator to The Prince of Wales, became the first member of the Flight to achieve 1,500 Royal Flights, taking just over twelve years to do so.

Squadron Leader D.J. (David) Rowe, Andover Captain, joined the ranks of members achieving 1,000 Royal Flights.

Master Air Loadmaster P.R. (Peter) Stokes, Chief Technician T.M. (Terry) Fry, fixed wing crew chief, Sergeants T.J. (Tom) Griffiths and S.J. (Steve) Giles, Air Stewards, joined those members who have achieved 500 Royal Flights.

Squadron Leader D.W. (David) Gale became the first RAF pilot to achieve 1,000 hours on the BAe 146.

In August the two BAe 146 aircraft were flown in formation over Windsor Castle for a photographic session; the result becoming the December entry of the 1988 Royal Air Force Calendar.

The Wessex helicopters landed on both HMS Ark Royal and HMS Illustrious.

The first category II ILS approach (100 ft cloud base, 400m visibility) on a Royal Flight was carried out in January by Squadron Leader David Gale flying BAe 146 ZE700 with The Duchess of Gloucester whilst landing at Manchester Airport. By a remarkable co-incidence, this occurred the day after the crew qualified for Category II approaches on the simulator at Hatfield.

A Record Number of Tours

A record number of overseas tours were carried out by the Flight's aircraft during the year.

The Duke of Edinburgh visited the Caribbean, United States, Canada and Sweden.

The Prince and Princess of Wales visited Portugal, France, Spain and Germany, with The Prince also visiting Belgium, which included meeting personnel involved with The Herald of Free Enterprise Ferry disaster at Zeebrugge.

The Princess Royal visited Cyprus, the Persian Gulf States, Brazil, Korea, Singapore, Burma, Thailand, and in visiting Laos became the first member of The Royal Family to do so.

Kitty Eight (David Gale) and his crew in BAe 146, ZE701, flew the aircraft for HRH The Princess Margaret's visit to China. The aircraft left Northolt on 6th May with Viscount Linley and Lady Sarah Armstrong-Jones on board and flew to Hong Kong via Rome, Cairo, Bahrain, Seeb, Bombay, Calcutta and Bangkok. Proving Flights were carried out from Hong Kong to Beijing, Xian, Guilin and Shanghai. The aircraft couldn't land in Canton due to bad weather, so diverted back to Hong Kong.

Royal Flights with HRH and her two children were flown Hong Kong – Beijing – Xian – Guilin – Shanghai – Canton – Hong Kong. The dust in the air was so thick in Beijing that the aeroplane was covered in a thick layer of dust, including half an inch or so in the door tracks. The crew bought feather dusters with long handles to whip the dust off the outside of the aircraft just before the arrival of the passengers.

The crew were able to do some sightseeing themselves. In Beijing they saw the Great Wall, the Ming Tombs, the Forbidden City and Tiananmen Square. In Xian the Terra Cotta Army of Qin Shi Huang and in Guilin the massive underground caves and enjoyed a 5-hour boat trip with a banquet on the River Li.

The aircraft returned to Northolt with their outbound passengers via Bangkok, Calcutta, Bombay, Seeb, Bahrain, Cairo and Rome arriving on 31st May.

The Duke of Gloucester visited Saudi Arabia, Bangladesh, Indonesia and Hong Kong.

The Duke of Kent visited Indonesia, Thailand, Greece, Spain and accompanied by The Duchess visited Sierra Leone.

Princess Alexandra visited Pakistan and Cyprus.

The Queen accompanied by The Duke of Edinburgh, Queen Elizabeth The Queen Mother and The Princess Royal visited Berlin at different times during the 750th Anniversary of the city.

The Duke of York, The Princess Royal, Princess Alice and Princess Alexandra visited Northern Ireland during the year.

The Duke and Duchess of Kent visited Spain.

The hope of a "levelling off" mentioned last year was in fact achieved. However there were several months when one or other of the aircraft were off line for lengthy servicing and one BAe 146 away over a lengthy period.

Still Some Firsts

BAe 146, ZE701, became the first jet aircraft to land at Dounreay when The Prince of Wales made a visit in April.

Squadron Leader Bob King (Kitty 6) carried out the Flight's first helicopter night deck landing when flying The Duke of York to join Royal Fleet Auxiliary Engadine off Start Point.

Her Majesty The Queen, accompanied by The Duke of Edinburgh, was flown to Madrid in ZE700, for the first Royal Visit to Spain by a British Monarch.

Princess Beatrice of York flew for the first time with the Flight, flying with her parents from Royal Air Force Northolt to Royal Air Force Kinloss in August.

The Flight's Most Frequent Passenger

HRH The Princess Royal continues to be the most prolific user of the Flight, breaking all previous records for both fixed wing and rotary wing with a total of 230 flights (97 fixed and 133 rotary wing).

During the year HRH became the first member of The Royal Family to visit Uganda since 1965, during her African tour to Uganda, Mozambique and Somalia in connection with The Save the Children Fund. The aircraft departed Benson on 20th February and positioned to Nairobi via Rome, Cairo, and Djibouti. Royal Flights flown were Nairobi – Entebbe – Quelimane – Maputo – Quelimane – Mogadishu – Galcaio – Hargeisha – Jeddah – Athens and back to Lyneham arriving on 4th March.

This was the first RAF aircraft to visit Uganda since Idi Amin was overthrown. Human skulls with bullet holes were being sold on many street corners. In Entebbe, the aircraft was parked next to the terminal where the Israelis had raided the airfield. Rocket marks and bullet holes could still be seen all over the building.

In September The Princess Royal was flown to Seoul from Hong Kong in BAe 146 ZE701 to attend the Olympic Games. A proving flight was flown to Pusan and on 23rd September HRH was flown from Seoul to Pusan and return and on 2nd October HRH was flown back from Seoul to Hong Kong. The aircraft returned to Benson via Chiang Mai, Calcutta, Bombay, Cairo and Rome arriving back on 5th October. The crew were given tickets to any event they wished to see throughout the Games and also had access to the Olympic Village where all the athletes were staying. A very memorable tour without much flying.

The Queen's Flight Provides Disaster Aid

Whilst flying The Prince and Princess of Wales to Aberdeen, the BAe 146 was used to carry vital equipment for use by plastic surgeons operating on people seriously injured in the Piper Alpha oil rig disaster.

Tours

Not such a busy year for tours, only ten being carried out to the Caribbean, Pakistan, Middle East, Far East, Central and South America, Spain, USA and Africa. The tour to Central and South America by The Duke of Edinburgh being the most comprehensive involving almost 73 hours and 33 flights.

During the year HM Queen Elizabeth The Queen Mother, The Princess Royal, The Duke and Duchess of York, The Prince Edward and The Duchess of Kent visited Northern Ireland.

CHANGE OF OFFICER COMMANDING

Wing Commander Mike Schofield, Officer Commanding since October 1984, was succeeded in the post on 26th November by Wing Commander N.E.L. (Nigel) Beresford. On 29th November Wing Commander Schofield was granted an Audience with Her Majesty The Queen, during which he was invested with the insignia of a Lieutenant in the Royal Victorian Order.

GUILD OF AIR PILOTS AND NAVIGATORS

The Queen's Flight was privileged to become affiliated to the Guild of Air Pilots and Navigators.

THE QUEEN'S FLIGHT ASSOCIATION HONORARY MEMBERS

At the Annual General meeting this year it was decided to add two more Honorary members to the Association Roll. Air Chief Marshal Sir Neil Wheeler, GCB, CBE, DSO, DFC*, AFC, FRAeS, and Mr A.F.N. Taylor, Bristol Siddley Representative in the Viking aircraft days, were elected.

FLYING ACHIEVEMENTS

The Wessex had their busiest April and November since their introduction to the Flight. In April, with mainly one aircraft and one task cancelled due to snow, a total of 98 hours 45 minutes were flown carrying out 178 Royal, Special and VVIP tasks. In November, 89 hours and 10 minutes were flown carrying out 148 tasks.

In March 1988 Squadron Leader Mike Hawes, the Flight's Adjutant, achieved 1,000 Royal Flights.

Squadron Leader D.L. (Denis) Mooney, helicopter navigator, achieved 500 Royal Flights.

During the year the Kings of Norway, Sweden and Jordan, The Queens of The Hellenes and Denmark, President Mitterand and Chancellor Kohl were flown in aircraft of the Flight.

THE CAPTAIN IS AWARDED KNIGHTHOOD

In December the Captain, Air Vice Marshal John Severne, CVO, OBE, AFC, was granted an Audience with Her Majesty The Queen prior to relinquishing his appointment as Captain of The Queen's Flight early next year.

During his Audience Her Majesty conferred the accolade of Knighthood upon the Captain and invested him with the insignia of a Knight Commander of the Royal Victorian Order.

7. The Queen's Flight 1989-1995

1989

ALL CHANGE AT THE TOP

Air Commodore The Hon T.C. (Tim) Elworthy, CBE, succeeded Air Vice-Marshal Sir John Severne, KCVO, OBE, AFC, as Captain of The Queen's Flight on 14th January 1989.

Air Vice-Marshal Sir John Severne (right) handing over to Air Commodore The Hon. Tim Elworthy.

Group Captain M.V.P.H. (Mike) Harrington, ADC, BA, FBIM, succeeded Group Captain J.F.B. (Jeremy) Jones, CVO, ADC, as Deputy Captain of The Queen's Flight on 19th May.

Group Captain D.H.A. (David) Greenway, OBE, ADC, succeeded Group Captain P.G. Pinney, LVO, ADC, as Station Commander of Royal Air Force Benson and Deputy Captain of The Queen's Flight on 17th November.

THIRD BAE 146

In October it was announced that a third BAe 146-100 is to be purchased for The Queen's Flight to replace the Andover, with delivery anticipated in one year.

FLYING ACHIEVEMENTS

Despite only one Wessex being available for tasking during almost 6 months of the year due to engineering requirements, there was a 17% increase in the number of Royal, Special and VVIP Flights.

The BAe 146's had their busiest April, September and November since their introduction to the Flight. The Wessex had its busiest month in June beating the previous highest in 1967 by an hour.

Two more aircrew achieved a total of 1,500 Royal Flights. Squadron Leader G.H. (Geoffrey) Williams, LVO, Flight Commander Fixed Wing and Personal Pilot to HRH The Duke of Edinburgh, after 16 years, and Squadron Leader B.J. (Brian) Crawford, MVO, a Wessex navigator, after 12 years.

Squadron Leader R.F. (Bob) King, Flight Commander Wessex and Personal Pilot to HRH The Duke of Edinburgh, and Sergeant A.R. (André) Bird, Wessex Crew Chief, joined those members who have achieved 500 Royal Flights.

TOURS

The total number of tours for 1989 was ten, the same number as last year. Among them HRH The Prince Edward visited Moscow for three days, and HRH Princess Alexandra toured the Caribbean to inspect the damage caused by Hurricane Hugo.

During the year HRH The Princess Royal, TRH The Duke and Duchess of Gloucester and TRH The Duke and Duchess of Kent visited Northern Ireland. One visit by The Duke of Gloucester was in connection with the Memorial Service for victims of the British Midland aircraft disaster on the M1 motorway.

HRH The Princess Royal continues to be the greatest user of The Queen's Flight aircraft, including 177 Wessex flights, the highest ever utilisation by one Member of The Royal Family.

A proving flight in BAe 146, ZE 700, to South America was flown from 4th to 19th July to prepare for a visit to South America by HRH The Princess Royal in late August, early September. The flight was notable because the aircraft was taken into La Paz and Potosi which were both 13,300 ft. above sea level. The aircraft had to be specially modified to permit this so that the oxygen masks wouldn't drop automatically. Also the BAe 146 was not certified and had not been tested above 8,000 ft, so the crew had to interpolate and dramatically reduce the projected performance.

Potosi was a 6,000 ft long strip in the middle of a valley, surrounded by steep terrain. The proving flight to Potosi was done in a turbo-charged twin-prop aircraft operated by the Bolivian Air Force, as no jets had never before landed there. It was calculated that, if all the aircraft spares, catering, baggage etc., was removed from the aircraft, and took minimum crew, fuel and passengers, it was just possible to get in and out of the airfield. It was planned that on the Royal tour it would fly into Potosi at minimum weight, fly 10 minutes to Sucre and wait for the Royal party to finish their business, fly 10 minutes back into Potosi to pick them up, and then back to Sucre to refuel. An engine would be kept running during the stops at Potosi because the altitude was too high for an engine start from the APU.

The aircraft left Benson on 29th August for HRH's Tour to Central and South America routing via Lajes – St. John's – Bermuda – San Juan. Royal Flights were flown from San Juan – Belize – Tegucigalpa – San Pedro – Tegucigalpa – Quito – Shellmera – Quito – La Paz – Potosi. Empty legs were then flown Potosi – Sucre – Potosi. Royal Flights were then flown Potosi – Sucre – Santa Cruz – Trinidad – La Paz – Quito – Grand Cayman to Miami. The aircraft returned empty to Benson via Orlando – Dulles – Gander and Reykjavik arriving on 16th September.

President Ershad of Bangladesh was flown in the Andover, The President of Nigeria in the Wessex and Prime Minister Benazir Bhutto of Pakistan in the BAe 146.

IN MEMORIAM

Group Captain and Mrs J.F.B. Jones were both tragically killed in a road accident near Benson on 19th May 1989, shortly after Group Captain Jones had handed over to his successor as DC1. Group Captain Jones had been appointed to be a Commander of the Royal Victorian Order in the 1989 Birthday Honours List.

Their funeral was held in the Station Church at RAF Benson on 3rd June and was attended by representatives from The Royal Family as well as by family, friends and colleagues.

Not quite as busy this year. Tasking was affected by the vagaries of the weather at certain times of the year, and by HRH The Prince of Wales' unfortunate polo accident, which caused the cancellation of a number of his engagements. There were more non-Royal VVIP flights this year than there had been for some considerable time.

HIGHLIGHT OF THE YEAR

The highlight of the year was a visit to The Queen's Flight by Her Majesty The Queen and HRH The Duke of Edinburgh on 21st December. Her Majesty flew into Royal Air Force Benson in Andover XS790 for her last flight in this aircraft to be met by the Captain, Air Commodore The Hon T.C. (Tim) Elworthy, CBE.

Her Majesty graciously agreed to be photographed with members of the Flight, and then toured exhibits in the hangar showing how the Flight is being updated. During the visit The Queen met members of the Flight and their families.

Prior to departure in BAe 146 ZE700 for Christmas at Sandringham, the Chairman of British Aerospace, Professor Roland Smith, presented Her Majesty with the log book for the third BAe 146, ZE702, and a silver model of the BAe 146. The new BAe 146 should be in full operation early in 1991, replacing the last of the Flight's Andovers.

Earlier in the year HRH The Duke of Edinburgh had paid an informal visit to the Flight, and met Flight members in the hangar.

TOURS

HM The Queen Mother, HRH The Princess of Wales, HRH The Duchess of Kent and HRH The Duchess of York all carried out visits to Northern Ireland in aircraft of The Queen's Flight.

Amongst eleven tours carried out during the year, three were by HRH The Duke of Edinburgh, three by HRH The Princess Royal and two by TRH's The Prince and Princess of Wales. These tours ranged from Africa, USA, Russia and the Far East through to Australia, the latter being the longest tour to date undertaken by the BAe 146.

On 17th February HRH The Princess Royal left Lyneham in a BAE 146 for a tour of West Africa routing via Casablanca – Banjul – Dakar – Bakel – St. Louis – Dakar – Timbuctou – Mopti/Barbi – Bamoko – Lyons and returning to Lyneham on 27th February. One amusing experience, the Commodore (who shall remain nameless) bought some sun lotion in Dakar, not realising that it was tanning lotion he had bought in error. After rubbing it all over himself he realized his error when he found that the palms of his hands had turned a dark brown – exactly opposite to the locals who had dark backs to their hands and much lighter palms. Saluting at the bottom of the aircraft stairs was a little embarrassing to say the least – much to the amusement of the Princess!

From 17th to 30th April a proving flight was flown in BAe 146, ZE701, to Russia in preparation for a tour by HRH The Princess Royal. HRH boarded the BAe 146 at RAF Lyneham on 24th May and flew to Moscow/Shermetyevo – Omsk – Irkutsk – Ulan/Ude – Irkutsk – Omsk – Ashkhabad – Volgograd – Kiev and back to Lyneham landing on 6th June 1990. This was the first Royal visit to Russia since the Tsar was murdered.

Prior to the official Christmas stand-down, HRH The Prince of Wales flew in BAe 146 ZE701 to visit the British troops stationed in the Gulf.

A tour to Pakistan by HRH The Princess of Wales was cancelled due to a change in the political situation in that country. HRH The Prince of Wales had to cancel a tour to Brazil due to the after effects of his polo accident.

FLYING ACHIEVEMENTS

Flight Lieutenant A.H. (Tony) Guttridge, MBE, fixed wing navigator, and Sergeant S.D. (Steve) Collins, Air Steward, joined the ranks of those members who have achieved 500 Royal Flights.

Flight Lieutenant R.H. (Dick) Stanton, MVO, fixed wing navigator, joined those members who have achieved 1,000 Royal Flights.

Squadron Leader M.I.S. (Ian) Anderson, MVO, who has been on the Flight for 15 years, became the first fixed wing navigator to achieve 1,500 Royal Flights.

THE QUEEN'S FLIGHT ASSOCIATION

Air Vice-Marshal Sir John Severne succeeded Air Commodore Sir Archie Winskill as President of The Queen's Flight Association. Sir Archie agreed to become the Association's first Life Vice President.

1991

A RECORD FLYING ACHIEVEMENT – NEW BAE 146 – GOODBYE TO THE LAST ANDOVER

This was a year of record flying achievement and major changes in both personnel and equipment. On 21st June, Group Captain G.H. Rolfe, CBE, ADC, succeeded Group Captain Mike Harrington ADC, BA, FBIM, as Deputy Captain of The Queen's Flight. On 22nd November, Group Captain A.N. (Adam) Wise, LVO, MBE, ADC, succeeded Group Captain David Greenway OBE, ADC, as Station Commander Royal Air Force Benson and Deputy Captain of The Queen's Flight.

BAe 146

On 14th January the third BAe 146, ZE702, was finally accepted by The Queen's Flight, having been returned to Marshall's of Cambridge after the official hand over ceremony so that the interior fit of the aircraft could be finished to the standard of The Queen's Flight. The aircraft's first Royal task was to fly HM The Queen from RAF Marham to Southampton Airport on 21st January. The last Andover, XS 790, was handed over to The Royal Aircraft Establishment at Bedford on 31st January.

FIXED WING FLYING

The extra capacity conferred by a third BAe 146 resulted in a fairly dramatic increase in tasking, some of which was due to Royal Flights in support of the Gulf War effort. There was also a large increase in the number of Ministerial flights. The increase in flying led to an establishment bid for a fifth BAe 146 crew at the end of the year.

There were tours to South America and the Falkland Islands, Brazil, The United States of America, Papua New Guinea, Chile, Pakistan, Southern Africa, the Far East, Morocco and the Arabian Gulf. BAe 146, ZE702 became the first RAF aircraft to land at Tehran Airport for many years whilst on a Ministerial flight to Turkey and Iran. Flight Lieutenant R. P. Austin became the first co-pilot to complete 500 Royal Flights.

ROTARY WING FLYING

This was a record-breaking year for the Wessex, with tasking in the early part of the year being particularly heavy. On 17th January HM The Queen was flown from RAF Marham to Buckingham Palace; this was Her Majesty's first helicopter flight in England. The Wessex crews were again privileged to fly HM The Queen later in the year when Her Majesty visited Northern Ireland a further eight times during the year. The Wessex visited Northern Ireland a further eight times during the year, flying members of the Royal Family to many different sites in the Province. In addition, the helicopters were tasked three times to Germany and twice to France.

On 28th February Squadron Leader Derek James, a Wessex navigator, became the first member of The Queen's Flight to complete 2,000 Royal Flights. On the same flight his pilot Lieutenant Commander C.W. Pittaway became the first Royal Navy pilot to complete 500 Royal Flights.

ENGINEERING SUPPORT

Engineering Support for the flights kept the groundcrew very busy. An example of the high standards achieved was during a Royal Tour of Chile in BAE 146 ZE701 which suffered an engine problem. The need to change the engine was diagnosed on 21st September and a spare engine was delivered to Chile late on 23rd September. The engine was changed and all checks completed by 0830 hours on 24th September so that the Royal Tour could proceed uninterrupted.

Although this was not a record breaking years for all Royal flying, both types of aircraft were well used, especially the BAe 146's which carried out more Royal and Ministerial flights than in any previous year. The flying included the first circumnavigation of the world by a BAe 146 whilst carrying out a Royal Tour.

Several major changes took place during the year. In the spring Wing Commander Neil Thurston took over as Officer Commanding of the Flight from Wing Commander Nigel Beresford. A fifth BAe crew was added to enable full use of the three aircraft. Several experienced aircrew retired from the Flight after many years service.

The Flight was privileged to receive two Royal Visits during the year. The first being a formal visit by HRH Princess Alexandra and The Hon Sir Angus Ogilvy in May. The second visit was an informal one by HRH The Duke of Edinburgh in December.

FIXED WING FLYING

This year HRH The Duke of Edinburgh carried out a world tour in the BAe 146. The tour began in Australia and continued with visits to New Zealand, Japan, Alaska, Canada, United States of America, Guyana, Brazil, Barbados and the Bahamas. The tour lasted for 38 days and a total of 45,000 miles were flown, with the aircraft crossing the equator four times and the International Date Line once. This tour is described more in Chapter 10.

During the year the Flight also carried out three tours to Egypt, two tours to the Caribbean and single tours to Scandinavia, Canada, the Pacific, Argentina, India and the Balkans. The Flight also supported State Visits by HM The Queen to both France and Germany; two aircraft were used to support each of these visits. However, the major part of the fixed wing flying continued to be completed on internal United Kingdom and European flights.

ROTARY WING FLYING

This was a quieter year for the Wessex crews. Even so they recorded four Royal flights to Royal Navy ships, three flights to Northern Ireland, four flights to Scotland, and flights to the Channel Islands, the Scilly Isles and Northern France. The Wessex was also involved in many other flights in England and Wales. The Flight was privileged to fly HM King Carl Gustav XVI of Sweden during His Majesty's visit to this country.

The fitting of a Global Positioning System (GPS) to the Wessex has greatly enhanced the aircraft's navigation capability and made the finding of landing sites at night or in poor visibility a great deal easier.

In September the Helicopter Support Section was equipped with a new Rapid Intervention Fire vehicle as part of a programme to rationalise and renew helicopter support vehicles. These vehicles proved to be a great improvement over the Range Rover fire vehicles that have been used to supplement the unreliable and clumsy Bedford Helicopter Support vehicles that have now been retired.

ENGINEERING

Over the past year the Flight has maintained high standards of engineering support, despite the increased utilisation levels on both aircraft types and in particular the increase in short notice tasking brought about by the surge in Ministerial flying in the BAe 146. To meet the increased tasking the Wessex was transferred to a flexible pattern of Primary Servicing and in December approval in principle was given for the BAe 146 to increase its minor cycle from 18 months to 2 years.

Utilisation of the Wessex has increased over the past three years so that the flying hours are unable to cover all tasks. As a result of the extended use of the BAe 146 in the busy flying months, engineering work must often continue late into the night to ensure aircraft availability the following day.

1993

The beginning of the year saw Air Commodore The Hon Tim Elworthy, CBE, retire from the Royal Air Force but he retained his appointment as Captain of The Queen's Flight as a Civil Servant under the same terms of service as his predecessors. At the end of the year the Station Commander of RAF Benson, Group Captain Adam Wise, LVO, MBE, ADC, relinquished his post as both Station Commander and Deputy Captain of The Queen's Flight. In future the post of the second Deputy Captain will be filled by a retired officer.

Between February and June 1993 the Government Efficiency Unit carried out a Scrutiny of Royal and VIP flying. Its report was radical but complimentary about the Flight and its work. Its most controversial recommendation concerning the Flight was a proposal to introduce some civilians into the engineering workforce. There has been considerable and prolonged debate about much of the Scrutiny Report, both its findings and proposals. Some of the recommendations have been challenged and further investment appraisals have been undertaken and other suggestions put forward. At this stage options vary from an enlarged Queen's Flight at Benson with additional aircraft and expanded role, to the amalgamation of all Royal Air Force short range communications aircraft into a single unit at Northolt with the engineering work undertaken by a civilian contractor.

The issues are being debated at high level alongside other proposals relating to the size and shape of the services. The Flight awaits the results of these deliberations with some trepidation in the knowledge that whichever option is chosen The Queen's Flight will change radically from that we know.

FIXED WING FLYING

The BAe 146 continued to demonstrate its versatility and reliability whilst carrying out flights all over the world. The aircraft covered Africa extensively, with two tours to East Africa and tours to both South and Western Africa. This year also saw the aircraft operating in many of the former Republics of the USSR. This was often the first visit by an aircraft of The Queen's Flight to these countries which made it challenging for the crews.

The aircraft were also used extensively across the Atlantic, with flights to The United States of America, Mexico, Canada and the Caribbean. The aircraft supported the State Visit by HM The Queen to Hungary and the visit by HM The Queen to Cyprus to attend the Commonwealth Heads of Government Meeting. The aircraft were active throughout the United Kingdom and Europe and made five visits to The Republic of Ireland and 13 visits to Northern Ireland.

BAe 146 crew with HRH The Princess of Wales at Chitral, Pakistan.

Rotary Wing Flying

This was a quieter year for the Wessex, with tasking down on previous years and no overseas tasks. One aircraft underwent a major servicing and repaint and the other a minor servicing removing them from tasking for four months. Both Wessex were grounded for four weeks in the summer following a fatal accident involving a Search and Rescue Wessex Mk.2 in Wales. Fortunately most of this grounding took place during the summer stand-down and so only 7 tasks were lost. During the rest of the year 8 tasks were completed in Northern Ireland and HRH The Prince of Wales was flown on 2 tasks in Scotland, visiting the west coast on one and the Orkney and Shetland Islands on the other. The highlight of the year was when HM The Queen was flown by Wessex during a Royal Visit to Northern Ireland.

Engineering

This year saw an emphasis placed on improving the efficiency of the engineering and supply support functions. Communication facilities were significantly enhanced by the installation of a multi-terminal computer system. The provision of further portakabin accommodation for the Supply Section enabled spares and resources to be managed from a central location. The introduction of increased 1st Line Shift manning allowed periods of heavy flying/maintenance to be addressed in a more flexible and prioritised manner and the adoption of a two-year maintenance cycle for the BAe 146 brought immediate benefits. Central to the success of these ventures was a robust Quality Assurance policy which withstood the test of an External Audit with distinction.

1994

The Future of The Queen's Flight

On 23rd June 1994 The Secretary of State for Defence, The Rt. Hon. Malcolm Rifkind, MP., made the following statement to the House of Commons:

"Following the Efficiency Scrutiny undertaken last year, it has been decided that The Queen's Flight, currently based at RAF Benson, will move to RAF Northolt to join the other RAF Communications aircraft of No. 32 Squadron. Rationalisation into a single co-located unit, which will be known as No. 32 (The Royal) Squadron, will enable the RAF to continue to provide a flexible and cost-effective service to The Royal Family and the other VIP customers. The high standards associated with The Queen's Flight will be fully maintained. The new arrangements will include a new centralised tasking and monitoring organisation to ensure the best use of all the assets available."

The disbandment of The Queen's Flight and the merger with No. 32 Squadron at Northolt to form No. 32 (The Royal) Squadron is due to take place on 1st April 1995. The aircrew, the helicopter support personnel, some service policemen and a handful of the engineering manpower will transfer to Northolt but the great bulk of the Flight will be posted elsewhere. The engineering support will be in the hands of a civilian contractor who currently supports the No. 32 Squadron aircraft. The Captain and the two Deputy Captains will transfer to Northolt and become Air Equerries with responsibility for ensuring the Royal Family's needs for aircraft are met but will have no command responsibilities within the new organisation.

Fixed Wing Flying

This year the BAe 146's supported tours by HM The Queen to the Caribbean and Russia. When Wing Commander Neil Thurston flew The Queen into Moscow Airport, Her Majesty became the first British Monarch to set foot on Russian soil. On entering Russian airspace the Royal aircraft was escorted by a formation of five SU 27 Fighters until it landed at Moscow. Later in the visit The Queen was flown from Moscow to St. Petersburgh by BAe 146 before leaving Russia on HMY Britannia.

During the year members of the Royal Family flew to Ethiopia, Eritrea, Vietnam, Hong Kong, Ivory Coast, United States of America, Canada, Mauritius, Israel, India, Pakistan and South Africa. The aircraft were also busy in Europe with several flights to Croatia and Hungary in connection with the conflict in Bosnia. There were also 15 flights to Northern Ireland during the year.

BAe 146 at Chitral, Pakistan

On 29th June ZE 700, whilst on a flight from Aberdeen to Islay with The Prince of Wales at the controls, burst two tyres on landing and ran off the end of the runway at Islay. The aircraft suffered damage to the nose section but all on board escaped injury. Repair and Recovery teams from RAF St. Athan and engineers from the Flight recovered the aircraft and carried out temporary repairs. ZE 700 was eventually flown back to Benson on 18th August where, assisted by a team from British Aerospace, the Flight engineers carried out major repair work. The work was completed by 4th November but the aircraft then underwent a scheduled major servicing, which meant that it was not available for the rest of the year.

ROTARY WING FLYING

The Flight celebrated 25 years of Royal Flying in the Wessex on 27th June 1994. XV 732 carried out the first Royal Wessex task on 27th June 1969, flying TRH The Duke and Duchess of Kent from Maidstone to Coppins. On 27th June 1994 HRH The Duke of Kent was flown from Canterbury to RAF Benson in XV 732. During the 25 years the two Wessex have completed nearly 9,000 Royal and VIP Flights.

The highlight of the year in rotary wing flying was the "D" Day celebrations. Both Wessex were involved in flying members of The Royal Family to Portsmouth, then both aircraft positioned to Normandy to fly HM The Queen, HRH The Duke of Edinburgh and HRH The Princess Royal to various landing sites. HRH The Prince of Wales, HRH The Princess Margaret, HRH The Duke of York, HRH The Duke of Gloucester, HRH The Duke of Kent and several Ministers were flown by other RAF and Army Air Corps Helicopters. Despite poor weather and an extremely complicated operation order involving 50 helicopters from 4 nations, all the flights were carried out successfully. The climax to the day being when all 5 Queen's Flight Aircraft were on the ground at Caen Airport at the same time disembarking and embarking passengers. Fortunately all the passengers embarked on the correct aircraft.

ENGINEERING SUPPORT

Much of the engineering effort was directed towards the recovery and repair of ZE 700. However, the requirement to operate with only 2 BAe 146's, resulted in these aircraft being tasked more heavily than usual, which meant that long hours had to be worked to keep the two remaining aircraft on task.

Following the announcement of the disbandment and move to RAF Northolt, much of the engineering effort has been directed towards planning the transfer of equipment to RAF Northolt, whilst maintaining a full tasking capability throughout the period of the move.

1995

Although the first three months of 1995 were to be sad ones for the Flight, they were also to prove to be extremely busy for all concerned. Much of the effort was directed towards moving engineering equipment from RAF Benson to RAF Northolt, so that the aircraft could remain fully operational during the period of the move. It says much for the quality of the Flight personnel that, despite the difficulties, the standards for which the Flight has become renowned, were maintained. The aircraft were handed over to the civilian contractor in their usual immaculate condition on 1st April 1995, despite the BAE 146's carrying out four overseas tours in March.

ROYAL VISITS

The Flight was honoured to receive a visit from Her Majesty The Queen and HRH The Duke of Edinburgh on 7th February during which Her Majesty graciously agreed to be photographed with members of the Flight. Her Majesty and His Royal Highness then met members of the Flight and their families and members of The Queen's Flight Association and their families; nearly 1,000 people were in attendance in "D" Hangar. At the end of the visit The Captain presented Her Majesty with a silver picture frame embossed with The Queen's Flight Crest, which had been bought with monies contributed by Flight and Association members.

Whirlwind XR486, Wessex XV732 and BAe146 ZE700 outside The Queen's Flight hangar, February 1995.

The Flight was also honoured to receive visits from HRH The Prince of Wales, HRH The Duke of York, HRH The Prince Edward, HRH The Princess Margaret, TRH The Duke and Duchess of Kent and HRH Princess Alexandra. Her Majesty Queen Elizabeth The Queen Mother graciously invited members of the Flight to a Reception at Windsor Royal Lodge.

THE FINAL FLIGHT

On 31st March 1995 at the end of a visit to The Queen's Flight at RAF Benson by HRH The Princess Margaret, HRH was flown from RAF Benson to Windsor Royal Lodge by Squadron Leader T.E. Duggan in Wessex 732. On departure from RAF Benson the aircraft carried out a flypast so that Her Royal Highness could wave farewell to the Flight members who were assembled outside the hangar. This was the last Royal Flight to be carried out by The Queen's Flight.

MUSEUM OF ROYAL FLYING

The Queen's Flight Museum was moved to RAF Northolt and reopened by No. 32 (The Royal) Squadron as the Museum of Royal Flying. It was officially opened by HRH The Duchess of Gloucester on 22nd April 1998.

HRH The Duchess of Gloucester opens The Queen's Flight Museum at RAF Northolt.

REUNION:

"Three Knights" – Air Vice-Marshal Sir John Severne, Air Commodore Sir Archie Winskill and Air Commodore Sir Timothy Elworthy. Three Past Captains at the Association Reunion Dinner, May 2001.

8. Engineering and the Engineers

The Queen's Flight Engineers had a straightforward task. To provide three 100% serviceable fixed wing aircraft and two 100% serviceable helicopters in immaculate condition to meet about 800 Royal Flights a year, and to ensure that whenever they flew, they could not only be operated with maximum safety but also depart and arrive within five seconds of their planned time. The task was unique, and it is interesting to compare the challenge that it brought with the requirements of a typical small airline.

Although most airlines fly more hours per day on each aircraft they can, and routinely do, fly with various parts unserviceable. The aircraft are designed to allow this to be done to give the airline some flexibility to repair the inevitable unserviceabilities at the least inconvenient time. The Queen's Flight never despatched an aircraft from base with even the least important system inoperative, because they needed to ensure the maximum probability of completing each task.

Nearly all airlines fly back and forth between a limited range of airports, most of which have the airline's own maintenance facilities. The Queen's Flight aircraft were often weeks away, operating from small, remote airfields in far-flung continents.

Provided a commercial airliner is reasonably clean and tidy, it is acceptable for airline use. The Queen's Flight aircraft were constantly in the public eye and needed to be fit for a Queen inside and out, and so they accordingly were always kept in immaculate condition.

Standards were set in the early days.

Left: A view of the Vikings in the hangar showing their highly polished surfaces.

Right: Hand polishing the propeller

Most airlines consider they are doing well to despatch 97% of their aircraft within fifteen minutes of the scheduled time. The Queen's Flight achieved 99.95% despatch reliability within their five-second target. They tried to achieve 100% but when operating a complex machine such as an aircraft, this is almost impossible – they knew this best from those occasions when they almost didn't make it! As an example, an Andover had an electrical generator problem on the way into Leeds Airport whilst taking a Royal passenger to visit the city. Once the passengers had departed, the Crew Chief diagnosed a faulty voltage regulator but did not have a replacement in the small on-board spares package. A call back to base rapidly had a spare part and an electrician and tool-kit ready to go, but only about three hours to the planned departure time with the Royal passenger. Leeds was too far to get there in time by road but luckily one of the Wessex Helicopters was available. The normal flight time by Wessex is ninety minutes and, allowing for the time to change the regulator and check the system on a ground run, it would be a close call. The hangar team rapidly prepared the Wessex and it was despatched with the rescue team within fifteen minutes of the call for help. Luckily a very strong southerly wind gave the Wessex a much-needed 'push'. The job was done with about ten minutes to spare and the Royal passenger knew nothing of the drama needed to achieve the planned departure. Since then they had other problems with those voltage regulators and one was carried in every on-board spares package.

This is the sort of activity that went into the achieving of almost 100% despatch reliability. Of course, when overseas, a similar occurrence in any of the hundreds of less accessible places the Flight visited was a different matter. For that reason, each aircraft on tour carried a much wider range of spare parts and a team of four engineers to keep it in perfect order. Re-supply facilities were also arranged via commercial or military airfreight to replace any parts used. Technical support and spare parts could be on their way immediately in response to a call from the aircraft on HF radio from anywhere in the world, at any time of day or night.

Arrangements to airfreight parts were made by the small supply section, which for very good reasons was a fully integrated part of the engineering organisation. Many of the aircraft's critical parts were subject to additional quality assurance procedures during manufacture or overhaul to enhance their safety and reliability. Where a similar item, such as a Wessex main rotor gearbox, is also in the rest of the MOD inventory, ours were specifically identified and closely controlled by our supply section. Even the transportation of such equipments to and from repair at the manufacturers was done with our own vehicles and drivers. For additional safety and reliability, most components were removed and serviced more often than those on the equivalent military aircraft. The servicing work carried out within the confines of our one hangar at Benson was greater in scope than that on any other unit in the Royal Air Force.

It was unusual to have the combination of both helicopters and fixed wing aircraft on the same unit. It was also very rare to find the same group of engineers both handling aircraft on daily flying operations and carrying out complete overhauls, often lasting several months, on the same machines. The Queen's Flight engineers had the unique opportunity to exercise their skills in both these areas and also to work in our workshops stripping and repairing components such as engines, gearboxes and electrical and avionic black boxes removed from the aircraft. This broad field of employment gave immense job satisfaction and required the very best tradesmen, who had a total commitment to their work.

Each year at least five large scheduled servicings were undertaken, one on each aircraft. The shortest of these took four weeks, and careful long-range planning was needed to ensure that only one Wessex or Andover was serviced at any time. In the 1950's, aircraft utilisation was low, but since then there was a five-fold increase in tasking and there was rarely the luxury of a reserve aircraft. The Queen's Flight maintained a rigid policy of working on every returning aircraft until it is completely serviceable, regardless of the time of day or night or the effort involved.

Andover in The Queen's Flight hangar

The aircraft typically left Benson early in the morning and returned in late afternoon or early evening. Most engineering work was therefore done overnight. Even the smallest defect was always fully investigated and repaired immediately it occurred; where a small engine or hydraulic oil-leak might be technically within limits, it was fixed to prevent the risk of an aborted task at a later date. Additional checks were also carried out on many of the aircraft systems prior to every Royal flight to give the best possible assurance that the aircraft would remain serviceable throughout its flying task.

Engineers would work throughout the night to complete servicing schedules or to carry out repairs to aircraft required for the next day's tasks.

Once the aircraft were technically perfect, they were cleaned inside and out and then inspected by the duty engineer to ensure they were in immaculate condition for the next day's tasks. Two shifts of engineers worked overnight and they saw many dawns as they handed over to the day shift that despatched the aircraft away again. The Queen's Flight record shows that those policies paid off, as their Andovers and Wessex experienced less than half the rate of random equipment failures suffered by the same aircraft in normal squadron service.

The repair of unserviceable aircraft, even when operating from base at RAF Benson, could often be a problem. The Royal flying task was very seasonal; there was almost no activity around Christmas and during August when the Royal family take their holidays; by contrast, the spring and early summer months required all three Andovers and both Wessex to fly on most days. Out tasking assumed that the aircraft were 100% available, unless booked out many months in advance for scheduled maintenance.

There were many periods when two of the Andovers were away overseas on tour and the one remaining aircraft flew day after day for several weeks without a break. In those situations it was essential that replacement parts were immediately available and that the engineering support organisation could respond in a very quick time to deal with any situation that arose.

The Queen's Flight enjoyed the advantages of a largely independent engineering organisation controlled by a Squadron Leader Engineer. This ensured the maximum integration and co-operation of the 120 men of the fifteen trades under his command. The main aircraft engineering tradesmen were backed up by painters, ground equipment fitters, suppliers, motor transport fitters, drivers, carpenters and clerks, all of whom played an equally crucial role in achieving the task. Although the bulk of this team worked a 'routine' day, they were difficult to keep away from the hangar when a problem arose. As an example, An Andover needed an engine and propeller change after the aircraft arrived at RAF Lyneham at eight o'clock one Saturday morning. The duty shift at base contacted off-duty personnel, and a replacement engine; propeller, tool-kit and engineering team were loaded in our truck and on the way before 11 a.m. Luckily, that day there was a spare Andover; any spare aircraft are always kept ready to go and this aircraft undertook the task. A second team worked overnight and into Sunday, when the repaired aircraft was air-tested and recovered from Lyneham to be ready for tasking again on Monday morning.

The esprit de corps of this excellent team constantly made all the difference between success and failure and was greatly enhanced by the awareness of the value of our role. All tradesmen had the opportunity to fly on several occasions in the year on tasks carrying members of the Royal Family. Every trade was also involved in the essential task of keeping the exterior of the aircraft looking immaculate. Each aircraft had a weekly full wash and polish, undertaken by personnel of Sergeant and below. This usually took about an hour and the aircraft looked as if it had been covered in a swarm of bees with about sixty tradesmen elbow-greasing to their utmost. Nevertheless, contrary to popular belief, the polishing of aircraft constitutes only a small part of our work, and the chance for all trades to work together to produce a gleaming machine was enjoyed by most.

Each man, from the aircraft cleaners to the most highly skilled aircraft fitters, was selected at interview from the best available in the RAF. All members of The Queen's Flight were volunteers and normally served for a minimum of five years. Most of the engineers filling the important senior management posts had their tours extended and served between ten and fifteen years on The Queen's Flight; in this time they had risen from basic Junior Technician rank through Corporal, Sergeant to Chief Technician.

A few tradesmen of outstanding technical ability and personality were selected as aircraft Crew Chiefs. On both Andover and Wessex they flew with the aircraft at all times and were totally responsible for servicing the aircraft when away from base. On long overseas tours they were assisted by three other tradesmen and experienced the tremendous challenge of maintaining The Queen's Flights standards, often under the most rudimentary working conditions. Although the helicopter crewmen did not travel so extensively, they had an important additional role: because of the small size of the Wessex, they were also the stewards responsible for serving refreshments to the Royal passengers and for their comfort and safety on board. This unique combination required them to be in immaculate order, serving coffee, perhaps only minutes after being in overalls while servicing the aircraft. The breadth of operational and engineering experience of the Crew Chiefs made them excellent engineering managers. With the total dedication of all our personnel, this was a major factor in our ability to do the job.

In striving to maintain such levels of excellence, we were only keeping to the standards passed on to us by our predecessors on the Flight.

Wing Commander W. T. (Tom) Bussey, LVO, OBE, BEM, RAF (Ret'd), first joined The King's Flight in 1939 as a Corporal, and then promoted to Sergeant serving until 1942. He rejoined as the Engineering Officer in 1948 until 1950 and returned again as the Senior Engineering Officer of The Queen's Flight from November 1955 until May 1961.

In September 1939 Tom Bussey was promoted to Corporal and posted to The King's Flight at RAF Benson. The Flight then consisted of one Airspeed Envoy and one Lockheed Hudson Aircraft. Tom recalls that on his arrival at The King's Flight the personnel were: Captain: Wing Commander E. H. Fielden, The Engineers: Flight Sergeant Jenkins and Sergeant Hussey plus Mr. G. Prescott, a civil servant and Secretary to the Captain.

"My first interview on arrival at The King's Flight was with Jenkins and Prescott. After much searching into my background and service I was told that they did not expect me to stay as the Captain (who was away for two weeks collecting the Hudson) had asked for someone to look after the whole aircraft and I was not qualified. However the Envoy had to be serviced ready to leave and I could do that and see the Captain on his return. I enjoyed this task and got on well with Hussey and Jenkins who seemed impressed with my work and my tools some of which I had made myself. I saw the Captain on his return and he agreed to let me stay for the time being due to the good report he had received from Jenkins. I was to fly with him the next day when the Envoy went into storage. A further member, LAC Reed, arrived with the Hudson. The Captain, Reed and I delivered the aircraft into storage and I was told that I could remain with the Flight permanently if I successfully completed the Hudson Airframe Course. This I did and went on to do the instrument course at Sperry, Brentwood, to enable me to qualify to service the aircraft away from base. Very little flying was done during the Phoney War, but with the fall of France I became especially busy. I did a Vickers K gun course (front gun on the Hudson) and a bombsight course.

At this time the C-in-C Bomber Command's aircraft arrived, a Percival Q6 with a two man servicing team. At the same time I sat a remustering examination to Fitter IIE and was promoted to Sergeant. Just prior to the Battle of Britain I flew with Sir Charles Portal as he visited bomber crews returning from pounding the channel ports prior to the expected invasion. During the Battle of Britain I flew every flight with The Duke of Kent when he visited airfields in support of the hard-pressed pilots. We conveyed His Majesty The King to the Orkney Islands to visit the ships in Scapa Flow that had been recently attacked by aircraft.

Tom comments on the Engineering Pre-King's Flight: "Whilst I did not serve in the Prince of Wales Flight, i.e., before the advent of The King's Flight, my early experience with Jenkins and Hussey indicated a standard of aircraft maintenance far in excess of normal Service requirements at that time. In the early days of The King's Flight such high standards were implemented and maintained by careful selection of personnel, especially NCOs, and insisting on the very closest supervision by these people. This modus operandi was greatly assisted by extremely close liaison with the relevant aircraft company's nominated representatives".

The King's Flight was disbanded in March 1942 and we were all moved to Gravely in Bedfordshire to form No. 161 Squadron and subsequently moved to Tempsford. The Squadron was concerned with the clandestine operations and we were involved with the supply of equipment and personnel to the resistance organisations in Europe".

Tom was promoted to Flight Sergeant, awarded the British Empire Medal and mentioned in dispatches before leaving No.161 Squadron in 1943 for commissioning in the Technical Branch.

Wing Commander Bill Lamb, MVO, RAF (Ret'd), served two tours as Engineering Officer, the first from 1950 to 1952. He remembers:

In 1950 The King's Flight was equipped with five Viking C2 aircraft, two of which were specially equipped and used exclusively for Royal Flights (VL246 and VL247). Two aircraft were standard commercial 22-seat passenger aircraft and were used for support and training flights (VL232 and VL233). The fifth aircraft (VL248) was fitted out as a workshop, but by 1950 was 'mothballed' in storage. Externally, all the aircraft appeared alike and were maintained to the same high standard.

Parachutes were carried for all passengers and crew. Two eight-man dinghies were fitted in the upper rear of the engine nacelles. The fuel tanks were crash-proof and bullet-proof to the same pattern as the later Wellington bombers: the Viking wings and engine nacelles were in fact to the Wellington design of geodetic construction.

The flight deck provided for an aircrew of four; a pilot and flight engineer at the dual controls and navigator and signaller at a sideways-facing desk. A crew lavatory and the galley with steward's position were aft of the flight deck, as was the rearward-facing seat for the Captain of The King's Flight.

The Royal aircraft were kept in a state of basic readiness at all times as the engineering staff were given only short notice, usually less than twenty-four hours, of a Royal flight. When a Royal flight was notified, the aircraft was serviced to schedule requirements and then fully air-tested. The 'social engineering' was then carried out to ensure that the aircraft was immaculate both inside and out. The aircraft finish was bare unpainted aluminium and the whole exterior surface was hand-polished with metal polish and dusters. Not surprisingly, some skin panels had to be replaced over the years. All personnel took part in polishing, including clerks, typists and drivers, some sixty men in all; the whole task took about 200 man-hours. The undercarriage and radio aerials were chromium-plated and this saved a lot of cleaning work. There was never a problem of the chrome plating peeling off, as had been forecast by RAE.

The hangar was unheated and dimly lit by small ceiling lights. Considered opinion agreed that the winter in RAF hangars extended from 1 September to the following July. Certainly condensation was a major problem, especially when it came to polishing aeroplanes, and the only alternative to wet floors and walls was to keep the doors open and endure the blast. Aircraft servicing was carried out with the aid of torches and lead-lamps.

When preparation was completed, the aircraft was inspected by the Engineering Officer and the Flight Sergeant i/c Flight (only one Flight Lieutenant and one Flight Sergeant in 1950). This took about an hour and included checking documentation, fuel-state, appearance, correct flags, panels secure etc. There was no insurance factor applied in checking engineering work as the Captain's policy was 'one man, one job' and the full responsibility that went with it. This policy extended to one pilot being considered quite enough, second pilots were never carried, although the aircraft had dual controls.

The embarking or disembarking of the Royal Family was attended by personnel of The King's Flight as far as possible. Placing steps against an aircraft door may seem a simple enough task, but a combination of local airport workers and nervous officials was a recipe for embarrassment. The steps hitting the doorframe with a resounding thud, or being positioned a foot clear of the threshold, were experiences, which led to the Captain to direct that we do it ourselves. For aircraft positioned at London airport a 'steps party' was sent from Benson, while away from base, the flight engineer and the steward became expert in quickly assembling dismantled steps carried in the hold. One near-miss occurred on an overseas tour when the local airport manager had special, hydraulically adjustable steps flown in from Cairo. The suspicious engineer required a full dress rehearsal and as the airport manager stepped from the aircraft, the steps gently subsided amidst a fountain of hydraulic fluid.

When an aircraft returned from a flight, it was re-prepared to a basic readiness state without delay, no matter what time of day or night it was. The fuel state was brought up to two-thirds full only, to prevent fuel having to be unloaded if the maximum disposable payload was required on the next flight. All galley equipment was pre-prepared but stored in the hangar. Dust-sheets were placed on the furniture and floor and all doors locked.

During 1950 and 1951, probably due to the prolonged illness of The King, there were only ten or twelve Royal flights per month, which resulted in each Royal aircraft flying about 200 hours per year. The other two aircraft flew about 400 hours per year on training and support flights. The life of main components between Major servicing or factory overhaul was; Viking airframe and associated components, 800 hours; Bristol Hercules 634 and components, 800 hours; DH propellers and components, 800 hours; wheels and tyres 200 landings. It was realised that the level of aircraft utilisation would result in the two Royal aircraft taking four years between major servicing whilst the two support aircraft would take only two years. The situation would soon arise where the support aircraft would have a better modification state than the Royal aircraft and would have newer components fitted.

A decision was made as a matter of internal policy that all 'lifed' components on the two Royal aircraft would be removed at half-life and fitted to the two support aircraft where the remaining life would be used prior to overhaul at the normal time. Higher authority was not consulted, and it was never the intention that components supplied to The King's Flight should only be used for half the normal life. However, this policy was subsequently adopted by the Air Ministry as one of the additional safety and reliability measures to be applied to The Queen's Flight aircraft.

A personal recollection of the Engineering on The King's Flight from Mr. A. W. (Buzz) Cousins, RVM, a former Member of the King's Flight who became the Flight Sergeant i/c:

In 1946, whilst on embarkation leave to join an SDL team in Germany (charged with discovering German Luftwaffe Instrument and Auto-pilot innovations which might help the RAF), I was recalled to an Air Ministry Board and posted to The King's Flight at RAF Benson, as the first Senior NCO to arrive and be greeted by Flight Lieutenant George Pearson, our Engineering Officer.

Joining "The King's Flight" from AM SDL in 1946, Wing Commander Bill Tacon arrived with Aircrew Members and the ground crew arrived in droves. Flight Lieutenant Pearson had his hands full welding us into a team and preparing all trades for the projected Royal Tour of South Africa.

Initially all trades were accommodated in small workshops in the hanger sides, but space was at a premium and "The Ancillary trades", (Instruments, Electrical and Radio) moved into a wooden hut, placed behind the hanger. Our Vickers Viking Aircraft were all brand new and many bods attended courses at Vickers Weybridge, where the Vikings were built, resulting in good contacts being built with production, Service and drawing office staffs.

The third aircraft to arrive was VL 248 – a "Flying Workshop", fitted with Workbenches, Canvas racks of spare parts for all trades and boxes of tools. Being a "tail wheel" aircraft it soon became evident that working on benches at an angle of 15 degrees was a bit of a hazard and most of the Instrument, Electrical and Radio spares disappeared into sections, to form the basis of a good servicing stock pile – saving the delay of indenting for and drawing spares from the Station Stores.

The spares were regularly tested and were immediately available, to maintain Flight Lieutenant Pearson's principle of never closing the hanger doors with an unserviceable aircraft in the hanger – we worked until the aircraft were 100% serviceable, ready for any call. Paper-work followed in due course and replacements were drawn straight into the section stocks. Any unavailable spare was immediately the cause of an "AOG KING'S FLIGHT" order, which was often supplied direct from Vickers Weybridge, by our own transport. VL 248 was restocked with fully tested spares for its journey and we all flew to South Africa in our Vikings, via Libya, Heliopolis, Wadi Halfa, Khartoum, Entebbe, Salisbury & Pretoria, ending up at SAAF Base Brooklyn, Capetown, with four night stops on the way!

At Benson, we were visited by Service Representatives from Vickers Aircraft, Smiths Instruments, Sperry Gyroscope Company, Rotol and Dowty on a regular basis and they helped to answer any of our problems and ensured that all AOG Kings Flight requests were actioned immediately, if not normally available from RAF Stores.

Before departure to South Africa, we were all kitted out with newly designed & manufactured Tropical Khaki, tailored from beautiful soft material instead of the normal RAF issue (organised by Air Commodore Fielden) and had our photographs taken in the civilian clothing we were to fly in, for Civil Passports to be issued to transit through Libya.

Shortly after we all arrived safely at Brooklyn, a SAAF artist, Flight Sergeant Lowe, was asked to paint new crests on both sides of the noses of all 5 Vikings. He made stencils of a crest & did a marvelous job, painting in oils. My recollection is that the crest differed from the simple 'Crown and The King's Flight' scroll, was a larger round painting on the lines of a Squadron Plaque, with Heraldic motives and he worked non stop for a week.

There were two subsequent consequences to his effort – Firstly – some time after we all returned to Benson after the tour, a new pilot, being trained on circuits & bumps, landed a Viking with the Brakes ON. It skidded along the Benson E – W runway on its nose and stayed there overnight until a large crane was organised. Somebody became very worried that the local press would arrive to photograph the aircraft – crest and all – as it was in full view of the Wallingford to Oxford road. A crew of our riggers was dispatched and they cut off the crests on both sides of the aircraft with tin snips! Somebody (who?) must have those crests – they were never seen again – but they would make a marvelous addition to the museum collection! We had an uneventful return trip to Benson in April 1947.

Life was never dull on TKF, there was always something new to do, or to learn, and the Air Commodore was always a source of "Foreigners" or "Gash jobs" to keep us occupied. Sometimes they were from his home, sometimes from Buckingham Palace and we had our share in the Electrical & Instrument Sections. One memorable "job" was to clean and re-condition a 40 mm 'bofors' gun barrel, which had been converted to fire buckshot from a punt, at ducks. The barrel hadn't been cleaned for years and we made a 'pull through' from a roll of emery cloth, on the end of a broomstick. We had to splice new restraining and attachment ropes, to hold the barrel in the punt, but we never did see it in operation (reputably bagging a dozen ducks a shot). Watches, clocks, electrical equipment were interesting challenges.

One day in 1948, our Flight Sergeant. 'NCO i/c' disappeared overnight. The next morning Flight Lieutenant Lamb took me into the Air Commodore's Office and He asked "How would you like the job of NCO i/c the Flight?" That was a complete surprise and took a bit of thinking about. I replied that Yes, I would have no difficulties handling the job, (I often stood in when necessary), but it was an appointment traditionally held by a Senior Rigger or Fitter NCO, as they were trained in aircraft handling and I was worried what all the other SNCOs on the station would think of an Instrument Basher taking over as NCO i/c the most prestigious Flight in the RAF. I suggested that perhaps I take it on for a period of 3 months or so, to allow time for a suitable FS to be selected for the job – and we all agreed to that course of action and a DRO was posted on the Flight notice board.

The next morning, Flight Lieutenant Lamb walked into the office and said "I have my first job for you Chiefy, polish all the Aircraft, ready for a Royal flight." Out of the frying pan, into the fire.

I called all the section chiefs together and said "Every trade would provide hands to polish all aircraft", to immediate cries from the Radio/Radar Sergeant that they had always been excused because they had to keep their hands clean, to be able to adjust sensitive 'crystals' in their equipment! Codswallop! Instrument bashers have 'crystals' in their equipment too and they were all hermetically sealed components which could never be 'adjusted'. All hands started the cleaning operation, with 'brasso' and cleaning pads – normally a two or three day's operation.

The next morning, at 09.00 hours the Officer Commanding, Wing Commander Tacon, walked into the hanger, leading all the Aircrew wearing white overalls, and asked to be allocated an aircraft to polish! I took the crew off VL 246 and they started – but soon they spread themselves amongst the men polishing the other aircraft and that was a great fillip to team spirit from then on.

Our constant polishing efforts produced lovely shining Vikings, but eventually corrosion set in where we had rubbed away the top hardened surface of the 'Alcan' aluminium sandwich, exposing the soft aluminium core. Much re-skinning had to be carried out at Weybridge.

I started to introduce a few long awaited innovations. "Duty Crews" normally accompanied our aircraft on all flights, to handle re-fueling, cleaning, chocks, drip trays, steps and other sundry items. I asked our Fitter Sergeant Hardyman to train all other trades to do the work, so that they could also take their turn at "Duty Crew" work and he did a good job of it, saying that would help to spread the load.

In 1949, we prepared for a Royal Tour of Australia, checking and sending spares and ground equipment to RAAF Richmond Airbase, which was to be our base. One Viking was dispatched to Australia on reconnaissance, to sound out if RAAF equipment was compatible with the needs of our aircraft, (Electrical supplies, starter trolleys with the right connectors, Oil & Petrol, work shop facilities, Engine and Electrical / Radio / Instrument spares etc: and a team of all trades travelled as a duty crew. When they returned we all had a spot of leave, but on the night before we were due to take off, the tour was postponed and then cancelled, because His Majesty was very ill. We never did go to Australia.

Mr. S.A. (Jack) Frost, RVM, (Chairman of The Queen's Flight Association from May 2000), a former Flight Sergeant, Technician, Line Manager and Helicopter Crew Chief and Manager, on The Queen's Flight also remembers and writes:

"The first Engineers were two civilians, Mr. T. Jenkins and Mr. Hussey who maintained the King's personal private aircraft. Upon the formation of The King's Flight in July 1936 they were given appropriate RAF NCO status and posted on the strength of the new unit. In the early days people who serviced aircraft were known as tradesmen. Flight Mechanics, Mechanics, Fitter One or Fitter Two. Specialisation and new trade structures encompassed the word Technician and now all seem to be known under the generic heading of Engineer.

Royal Air Force Engineers entered the service as Boy Entrants, Apprentices or Direct Adult Entry. Trade training was a thorough and rigorous process followed with a competitive system of promotion based on experience, examination and performance.

To serve with either The King's or Queen's Flight a tradesman would be one who had volunteered and successfully completed a series of interviews at 'The Flight'. The final decision would then rest with the tradesman.

The King's Flight Engineers worked in a hangar that was unheated and dimly lit by small ceiling lights. There were five Viking C2 aircraft, two of which were specially equipped and used exclusively for Royal Flights. Two were standard commercial 22-seat passenger aircraft used for support and training flights. The fifth was equipped as a workshop aircraft but was not greatly used and eventually 'mothballed' into storage. A Flight Lieutenant Engineering Officer with a Flight Sergeant and sixty tradesmen set the basis of engineering excellence that was to become the hallmark of all who passed through The Flight's hangar at Benson. There was no insurance factor applied to checking engineering work in those days, the Captain's policy was 'one man, one job' and the full responsibility that went with it.

The tradesmen of The Kings Flight had a completely different working environment to that which followed. It was a harder life. Aircraft were built differently and would seem quite crude in their sensibilities to the requirements of the man doing the servicing. The service environment was perhaps not as close as it became in later years. The day of the technician was in its infancy, these men were Mechanics and Fitters in the cusp of change.

A reflection of the long lasting friendships formed from that time can be witnessed at reunions, when fifty years on after all ceases to exist they set an example of loyalty to their fellow Engineers that can but be admired.

Engineers new to The Queen's Flight became Queen's Flight Engineers with the help and guidance of their new colleagues. Accepting the exceptional servicing standards required to maintain one hundred percent serviceability, never leaving an aircraft with a problem, each and every post flight defect to be cleared as soon as possible after landing. There was no back up aircraft on The Queen's Flight; each aircraft that was scheduled for a flight was expected to carry it out. Engineers came to know the aircraft and were accustomed to them on an individual basis. An intimate knowledge of the way each machine performed would be accumulated to the extent that diagnosing a defect became almost an automatic reflex. The utilisation rates were often one hundred percent and could be maintained at this level for long periods of time. It was a secular world serving on The Queen's Flight, the understanding of each other that resulted from this produced exceptional team work and an almost unconscious combining of skills and knowledge.

The Queen's Flight would achieve ninety-nine point five per cent despatch reliability within a five second target. One hundred per cent availability with aircraft that were one hundred per cent serviceable for all scheduled tasking.

Aircraft managers and trade managers combined their planning and scheduling skills with which to deploy The Flight's resources, the results presented to the Engineering Officer at 'white coat' meetings. Long term plans for scheduled servicing, the manning and support for aircraft on overseas tours. The management of the airmen and their well being. Innovations and ideas as to how to do things better. The Engineer needed many skills.

There were fifteen different trades some of which had a work centre known as a 'Bay'. These Bays were home to the trade concerned, the hub for its specialist activities. A place where a radio became many magical components, where an engine could be delved into and gearboxes examined. The riggers had their hydraulic shop with which to care for all those valves, pistons and rams that made life easy for the chap at the aircraft controls. An instrument shop which ensured a true and accurate story was told to those who needed to know, that Navaids could tell one beacon from another and safely take the aircraft from one continent to another. Automatic piloting systems easing the pilot's way through roll, pitch, yaw, climb and descent. The electrical bay from where myriad components were serviced to provide all that AC and DC. Solenoids, shunts, bus bars, terminals, fuses, batteries, all that tied the whole thing together and provided the energy with which the rest to operate. Safety equipment had a bay for its tradesmen and a place in which to store and maintain life rafts, lifejackets, emergency beacons and all of the other survival aids. There was a trim shop that could produce an interior fit of great comfort and simplicity. The riggers who worked in the trim shop, always striving for perfection carried out much design work and greatly improved on the original. The painters and finishers applied the protection and finish to aircraft of immaculate appearance. Suppliers ensuring the on time delivery of every item of equipment for the aircraft and The Flight, from engines to royal standards and national flags, office furniture to aircrew watches. No matter where in the world an item was required they provided a door-to-door delivery service. The motor transport section where a wide variety of vehicles were maintained. Drivers on twenty-four hour call vital to the needs of all.

The Bay was a focal point, the place where problems were solved and solutions found, and the gathering place when not out on the floor. The diligence and perseverance of the Bays became the foundation of aircraft reliability.

Some tradesmen became Crew Chiefs and were assigned to flying duties. Their role to ensure the engineering integrity of the aircraft away from base and to blend in with the aircrew, monitoring the aircraft in flight and giving advice when needed. The helicopter Crew Chief had an additional duty, the safety and comfort of the passengers and attending to their needs in flight. Being a Crew Chief was a unique experience, part hangar floor and part upstairs, often not one thing or the other but probably the key link between the two worlds.

The Crew Chief would be accompanied by a selection of tradesmen for extended overseas tours. Such overseas tours became a total team effort in which people became better known to each other. All hands were turned to for the inevitable polish. The 'hands' included The Flight's policemen who ensured security both at home and away; they became renowned as the 'Mr. Fixit' for the occasions when something needed arranging.

A Senior Engineering Officer had charge of the downstairs and was fortunate in having the services of two Warrant Officers, one of whom would be responsible for Engineering Records. The Senior Non Commissioned Officers of the Flight were such that there were very few problems for the Senior Engineering Officer to contend with. The heart and soul of The Queen's Flight resided on the hangar floor; it was where everything started and where it always finished.

It would not be a proper thing to single out individuals for particular mention; such stories must be told elsewhere. As a group they were quite exceptional, people of humour ability and dedication who would always rise to whatever the occasion demanded.

The Queen's Flight, the hangar floor, home of unwritten traditions and the foundation of success for so many of its engineers, should history once again turn full circle it might yet see the like again".

SNCO Engineers and other SNCO Members of The Queen's Flight 18ᵗʰ April 1973.

Left to right: Colin Carswell, Jim Hill, Vic Brooker, John Stevens, Dave Ovenden, Dave Longland, Pete Dale, Dave Trenchard, Chris Fair, Mick Turner, Dave West, Jim Hutton, John Cresswell, Bob Norris, Pat Rowan, 'Bud' Abbott, Tony Johnson, Ron Tooke, Ray Herrington, Ray Seal, Bill Hood, Bill Race, Tony Sutherland, Gordon Goucher (Air Steward), 'Taff' Cochlan, Eric Friend (WO i/c Security) and Jim Leyborne.

STEWARDING AND AIRCRAFT INTERIORS

One of the smallest yet most important elements of The Queen's Flight was the Flight Steward's section, an enthusiastic and dedicated team of four Flight Stewards who looked to the comfort and needs of the Royal Family when travelling in the Andovers and Wessex of The Queen's Flight. Specially selected for Royal duties on the basis of the highest professional standards and personal qualities, the Stewards had previously served for at least one tour of VIP duty with either No.10 or No.32 Squadrons of the Royal Air Force, before joining for a minimum tour of five years. In professional terms their work was extremely demanding and embraced many more facets than that of their civilian counterparts or other Flight Stewards within the Service. Collectively and individually, the Flight Stewards were required to be able to perceive and anticipate the in-flight needs of the Royal Family, their households and the flight crew; it was hoped that the other aspects of their duties, the safety of the passengers during an in-flight emergency, would never have to be put into practice, but regular training ensured that the Flight Stewards would have been able to respond appropriately in the very unlikely event of such a need arising.

Much of the Flight Stewards' daily routine involved planning and preparing for Royal Flights, and even a short duration flight within the United Kingdom required careful preparation and careful attention to detail. For a short journey or a series of journeys, the knowledge gained by experience of the Royal Family's likes and dislikes allowed the Stewards to cater appropriately, without constant reference to the Royal Households. The catering requirements were ordered from a civilian 'in-flight' caterer and collected in purpose-built 'air-larder' boxes early in the morning of the flight, the food subsequently being served as required from the Andovers small galley.

For Royal Tours overseas, The Flight Stewards needed to maintain a much closer liaison with the Household staffs, to determine the in-flight catering requirements for a series of trips which could have covered a four-week period and which must be planned around the formal lunches and dinners which were to be attended by the Royal party in the host countries visited. The Flight Steward's planning would have started as soon as the provisional flight itinerary was produced, some two to three months in advance of the journey, and would take into account the time of day and duration of each flight, availability of fresh food and potable water, variety in the menus and any special requests from the Royal party.

Determining the requirements was the simplest part of the exercise; the difficulties arose in actually obtaining the necessary supplies once outside the United Kingdom and, perhaps, away from the established air-routes. Provisioning could have come from the dedicated 'in-flight' caterers at major airfields or, where facilities are known to be wanting, food and beverages may have to be flown in by scheduled airline from our caterer in London; this required careful study of airline timetables to ensure that the provisions arrived before our departure, whilst still remaining suitably fresh.

In some corners of the world, even this facility was unavailable and the Stewards could encounter primitive catering establishments which are unhygienic and do not measure up to the standards required for Royal catering. In this situation, ingredients are purchased in local shops and markets, and food was prepared from the basic raw materials to produce meals of the highest standards of hygiene and nutritional value. The importance of all this careful planning cannot be over-emphasised and whatever catering service was eventually decided upon, it was this attention to detail which ensured the very best of service wherever in the world the flight may be.

About one week before departure, the final and precise catering plan would have evolved and the detailed arrangements would be telexed to the appropriate agencies along the route. Once the flight was under way, the preparation of meals, given the limited storage and cooking facilities of the Andover galley, was a difficult task. The area was very restricted in size and was equipped with only one small grill and a hot plate, a hot cup unit and a boiler, all of which would only work when airborne. To produce a five-course meal to the very high standards required needed more than just the ingredients and ingenuity; flair and imagination were essential qualities expected of a Steward on The Queen's Flight.

Nevertheless, the Spartan galley of the Andover was a great improvement over that of the earlier Vikings, as remembered by a former member of the Flight, who provides an insight into cabin services in the 1950s:

"While the aircraft exterior was being polished, the three stewards prepared the interior and loaded the cutlery, glass and crockery into special racks. Catering supplies were prepared by the same stewards in the galley in the hangar. The stewards were in fact batmen/waiters who were paid 1s.6d. (7.5p) per day flying pay. Food was a problem, as rationing was strictly observed by the Royal Family: in 1950 bread was rationed and the meat ration was 10d (4p) worth per week. Eggs were sometimes available and the King enjoyed a four-minute egg. In an unpressurised aircraft the temperature of boiling water varies with altitude, but such was the engineering expertise available that the galley displayed a graph showing the boiling time of a 'four-minute egg' at various altitudes. Incidentally, the egg was boiled in the hot-water geyser, but it was washed first so the tea was not polluted."

The Andover galley was situated immediately behind the flight deck and thereafter the aircraft interior was sub-divided into three compartments: A, B, & C. Compartment A was forward and next to the galley. It included a large pannier which had been specially adapted and designed by the Interior Furnishing Section of The Queen's Flight to enlarge and enhance the preparation surfaces available to the Steward; also included was a table and four seats, mainly for the use of supplementary crew such as security and engineering support staff. A curtained bulkhead separated compartment A from B. In this latter section were two tables, each with four seats and two small wardrobes, one each to port and starboard side of the centre aisle. Compartment B was used mainly by members of the Royal Household such as private secretaries, personal protection officers and the flight Commodore. It was segregated by a partition and door from compartment C. This section was for the exclusive use of Royal passengers and comprised two tables, each with two chairs. To the rear of the compartment was an entrance vestibule where the Flight Steward positioned himself to greet the Royal passengers as they boarded the aircraft.

The memories of a previous member of the Flight provide another interesting insight into the Viking aircraft of the 1950's:

"Accommodation in the Royal aircraft provided for eight passengers in two saloons, each equipped with four large armchairs; two facing forward, two facing aft. The seats were remarkable in that they were steel-framed and stressed to 25g with a parachute cunningly concealed in the upholstery. The seats were also remarkably uncomfortable, a matter on which HRH The Duke of Gloucester expressed forthright views. Between each pair of seats was a white GPO telephone which connected to a small telephone exchange located at the seat provided for the Captain of The King's Flight, Sir Edward Fielden. The telephones provided only internal communications. To the rear of the saloons was a lavatory and wardrobe and at the extreme rear of the aircraft a small cabin with a divan bed.

The décor was royal blue for carpets, curtains and upholstery, with walls, ceilings and doors in cream PVC, the whole effect being one of spacious luxury, rather after the style of the Royal Daimler cars."

9. Helicopter Operations and the Helicopter Support Section

Wessex HCC Mk. 4 – XV733

To reserve a helicopter for a visit the Royal Household concerned would contact the Secretary to The Queen's Flight as far in advance of the visit as possible. This allowed the Flight to get maximum efficiency from the helicopters by attempting to 'dovetail' as many of the flights as possible on that date.

With two helicopters and three crews to share the workload, HRH The Duke of Edinburgh and HRH The Prince of Wales had personal pilots allocated to them, who invariably flew with them when the Royal Pilots flew the helicopters themselves.

Once the crew received details of a forthcoming flight they made arrangements to carry out a proving flight by contacting one, some, or all of the following: the Lord Lieutenant's office of the county involved, the county police and the organisers of the actual visit. The police were the closest contact as they were invariably involved with every visit, not only from the security aspect but, more importantly, from the Flight point of view, their identification and organisation of all helicopter landing sites that were to be used.

Having obtained as much information as possible from all the contacts, the crew would then arrange, at a mutually convenient date, well ahead of the visit, to carry out a proving flight. Not to check the route and timings but to ensure that the landing site was acceptable from the Flight's point of view. Particular regard was given to the site's size, surface, approach and departure flight-paths and, if appropriate, its acceptability for night operations. The Senior NCO in charge of the support crews flew on the proving flights.

On arrival at the site, all the interested parties would discuss the details of the arrival and departure of the helicopter, together with other details such as medical cover, security, crowd control and other arrival and departure details. Organisers were reassured that the aircraft would always endeavour to arrive exactly on time to ensure the visit started off on the right foot. "Never early, may perhaps be late but it won't be our fault. Don't panic, no news is good news, don't ring us, we'll ring you".

Obviously not all venues needed a proving flight; some sites were used regularly and so were accepted without further ado, provided the Flight and the police contacts were happy that nothing radical had changed since the last visit.

The selection and planning of a route for a helicopter flight may at first sight appear to be a simple operation of joining the departure and destination with a straight line. This would be the case when overflying terrain that is flat, unpopulated and weather free, but as ideally all Royal helicopter flying required maintaining visual contact with the ground, a number of factors influenced the selection of the route.

As the helicopter flew at a relatively low altitude, the worst possible weather conditions were assumed at the planning stage and a route selected to avoid high ground, which in the case of mountainous areas could mean a twisting track, following valleys. The overflight of densely populated areas was also avoided, to reduce the nuisance factor.

A further consideration in route selection was that a protected zone (Royal Low-Level Corridor) was promulgated, warning other users of the airspace to keep clear or cease activities that would endanger or jeopardise the Royal helicopter. Airfields and danger areas were therefore avoided, to disrupt their activities as little as possible. In the case of large civilian airfields where it would be impractical to disrupt their activities, set controlled routes were flown. Once the helicopter route had been selected, details were published in the form of NOTAMs (Notice to Airmen), ideally ten days in advance of the flight, in order to provide a protected zone around the flight.

Various other agencies had to be informed of the movement, such as en route airfields for communications, operators of large danger areas if closure was required, search and rescue organisations, and the Meteorological Office for en route weather forecasts.

The navigator for the flight, having decided on the route and producing the necessary warning signals, would prepare mapping in the form of ¼ inch to 1 mile charts and a large scale strip map of the entire route on which all hazards had been annotated, along with timing details to maintain a very strict schedule.

At the planning stage, the possibility of bad weather during the flight, which would make it impossible to maintain visual contact with the ground, would be considered. A plan would be produced to carry out the flight under Instrument Flight Rules (in cloud) with details of instrument let-downs to airfields close to the destinations – the idea being whether the Royal passenger should disembark at that airfield and complete the journey by road, or that after the let-down, the flight could be continued beneath the cloud. The weather on the day of the Royal Flight was always in the lap of the gods, probably the only factor over which The Queen's Flight had absolutely no control.

Royal helicopter flights rarely started and finished at airfields. The pick-up points were mainly in Central London or at one of the Royal residences scattered across the country, and the destinations could have been anywhere, literally *anywhere!* This meant the crew had to maintain visual contact with the ground on the last stages of the journey, so fog, very low cloud or icing conditions were factors which gave significant problems and probably forced the cancellation of the Royal Flight. If that was the case, a 'no go' decision was made as early as possible in order for the Royal Household to make alternative arrangements. Even if the weather curtailed the early part of a day's programme, the conditions were monitored and efforts made to pick up the schedule later in the day.

Notwithstanding any weather problems, the actual flight was by now very much a known quantity in that virtually all contingencies had been covered by all the intricate planning preceding it.

Virtually all, for it would have been foolish to be complacent, particularly where aviation is concerned. Never let it be said that the Flight didn't start every day with its eyes open.

The majority of the helicopter operations were in essence quite straightforward, but occasionally a more complex operation came along which required significant liaison with other agencies outside their normal sphere.

Visits by members of the Royal Family to Northern Ireland invariably made use of the helicopters. These visits normally involved flights to several different venues, all in the same day, so the speed between sites and the security en route afforded by a helicopter were invaluable advantages to all concerned. Usually the Royal passenger would arrive in Northern Ireland by using a Queen's Flight Andover and then taken on tour by the awaiting helicopter, accompanied by other units of the security forces. All the arrangements were made on a very strict 'need to know' basis, so the visits to the Province came as a great surprise to most people.

HM The Queen does not normally fly in helicopters. However, during her visits to Northern Ireland in August 1977 and to Normandy in June 1984, we had the honour of carrying Her Majesty to her venues, thereby easing the security problem considerably and making what, in both cases, would have been a major logistical exercise into a relatively simple matter.

The Queen made her first helicopter flight, in Wessex XV732, from HMS Fife, the escort to HMY Britannia, to Hillsborough Castle, returning the following day in XV733 (pictured).

A tour of the Western Isles by TRHs The Prince and Princess of Wales proved to be a major logistics exercise. Because of the nature of the terrain, difficulty of access to many of the sites involved the support of a Sea King helicopter. So one from the Search and Rescue Flight at RAF Lossiemouth was enlisted for the three-day tour. Their involvement enabled us to pre-position our support crew ahead of the Royal helicopter by a series of leapfrog manoeuvres. Additionally, the Sea King carried a Medic throughout and acted as search and rescue back up during the flights over water and mountainous terrain. Indeed, without their participation, the intense three-day schedule would have been impossible and the number of venues would certainly have had to be reduced.

Embarrassing moments are not really in the terms of reference of The Queen's Flight – at least, none which would be readily admitted. However, incidents do occur which could fall into this category. One such occasion was precipitated by the unpredictability of our arch-enemy, the weather.

"We were flying Their Royal Highnesses The Prince and Princess of Wales from West Yorkshire to Central London. Because of the distance involved, combined with the number of passengers carried, a planned en route refuel was organised at East Midlands Airport. The forecast was not wonderful, but nevertheless suitable for an instrument approach into East Midlands if the weather proved unsuitable for a visual transit.

To cut a long story short, the instrument approach option was taken in view of updated actual reports from East Midlands whilst en route, which indicated that the weather situation was deteriorating somewhat faster than had been predicted. The weather at RAF Finningley, however, remained good as a diversion – unfortunately, it would be back the way we had come.

During the instrument approach to East Midlands, the weather 'socked in' in no uncertain terms, much to everyone's surprise. A diversion to the known good weather at RAF Finningley was commenced without any further ado. It must be said that in a situation like this the crew feel a great deal of sympathy for the hierarchy of the diversion airfield, imagining the pandemonium at having to organise a Royal visit with only fifteen minutes warning – still, if you can't take a joke, etc!

After landing, the Royal party were whisked away to join a scheduled train passing through the local station on its way to London. The helicopter was refuelled to maximum capacity now that it was without passengers, and took off with enough fuel to fly through the bad weather to its base at RAF Benson. After leaving RAF Finningley, the helicopter was able to fly visually for several miles before having to climb and continue to base."

A few days later, when the same crew flew The Prince and Princess again, they were very red-faced when the lady herself enquired how it was that she saw a very bright red Wessex helicopter whizzing past the hastily commandeered 'Royal train carriage' at a great rate of knots, heading the same way as they were? – It turned out that 'Sod's Law' applies to The Queen's Flight as well as to everyone else – how were we to know it was their train? Our blushes were proved unnecessary when we saw the tongue in cheek and wry smile!

HRH The Princess of Wales made frequent use of The Queen's Flight helicopters, an ideal means of transport for fulfilling a crowded engagement calendar with speed and convenience.

Here, Her Royal Highness is seen carrying out her first visit to Northern Ireland in Wessex HCC Mk.4 – XV733

HELICOPTER SUPPORT SECTION

Quite early in its helicopter operations, the benefit of The Queen's Flight having its own crash-rescue and fire fighting facilities became obvious. There was a real need to have the basic capability at the sites which were being used throughout the country, and the extra benefit of using dedicated men who knew the Flight's operation and who could take on the responsibility of organising the landing-sites before the arrival of the helicopter was soon appreciated. They were vital to the safe, timely and polished arrivals we made with the helicopters.

The Fire Section was formed in 1954 with two Land Rovers carrying dry powder extinguisher packs; each crewed by a Corporal and a Senior Aircraftman, both firemen. In 1960 a third Land Rover and crew were added.

With the change to the Wessex Mk.4s in 1969, the Flight took delivery of three specialist vehicles. The manning was now one Sergeant, two Corporals and six airmen. One Land Rover was retained. The Fire Section soon became the Helicopter Support Section, a title that more accurately described their function, but the main reason for their existence remained fire fighting and crash-rescue, so the vehicles were, crewed entirely by RAF Firemen. The crew of a helicopter support vehicle (HSV to us) was a Corporal and two airmen.

It was of great benefit to The Queen's Flight to have its own helicopter support crews pre-positioned at landing sites.

Their experience of operations was not only of valuable assistance to the police and visit organisers, but was a great advantage to the aircrew to be in radio contact with the Flight's 'men on the spot', who had set up the landing site, providing the mandatory crash rescue vehicle (shown left) and fuel 'on tap' if required.

Those original HSVs served The Queen's Flight well for sixteen years. They were built on a Bedford chassis, with four wheel drive capability, and were petrol-engined. They carried a hundred gallons of light water (foam), which an engine-driven fire pump could deliver through two branch lines, and as much of the equipment of the professional fireman such as axes, hydraulic cutting equipment, ladder, stretcher, first-aid kit, as reasonably could be fitted into this type of vehicle. For their support operation on the landing site, they carried a large canvas 'H' marker, lengths of rubberised matting which could be pinned securely to bridge over wet ground between helicopter steps and car or hard-standing, a lighting system for night helicopter operations, radio to communicate directly with the helicopters, and up to 198 gallons of aviation fuel, in jerrycans, which could be hand-poured through the appropriate filter into the helicopter tanks. (So that's why firemen need to be fit!). These HSVs had a large cabin in which it was envisaged that heavy spares (even a complete engine-change unit for a helicopter) could be carried – they never were, but the cabin gave enough space for modified aircraft seats to be fitted to give cruise comfort for the crew. The HSVs also had a 24-volt system which could provide engine-starting power for the helicopter from a large-capacity battery installation.

The Flight still needed a smaller vehicle to solve the problem of access to sites via narrow lanes and gateways, over bridges with load-bearing limitations, or on small ferries. The Land Rover was changed for a standard Aircraft Crash Rescue Truck (TACR Mk2, a six-wheeled stretched Range Rover with a 200 gallon foam tank) and in 1977, and then in 1979, to cope with the steadily increasing task, a second TACR Mk2 and an extra crew were established.

The vintage HSVs were replaced in 1985. The new ones had all of the same facilities, but better – twice the foam facility, a diesel engine, a pumped aircraft-refuelling system, a site light on a rising stem with a tremendous light output for illumination of the scene, and even a domestic water boiling unit to replenish the helicopter's vacuum flasks.

So the establishment was now a Sergeant in charge of five vehicles and four crews. A summary of operations now follows:

As you will have gathered by now, the usage rate of the helicopters could peak, with both of them flying on tasks for many consecutive days. A look at a typical task for one helicopter on one day which might be used to carry a passenger from a country residence to an engagement in, say, the Midlands in the morning, then on to a second engagement, perhaps in East Anglia, with a return to central London in the evening, which we will assume to be after dark.

This clearly meant the use of four landing sites. We will be familiar with the starting-point and with the central London site, but the two other venues could require considerable research and a reconnaissance visit to find suitable sites.

The Sergeant in charge of the section would always have accompanied the proving flight, to discuss possible approaches and the optimum landing-point with the pilot, to check the means of access for the HSV, to make a sketch of the site, to find somewhere for the firemen to change from uniforms into fire suits, to note telephone contact numbers and generally to arm himself with all the needs to brief the crew of the HSV which he would allocate.

Closer to the date, the Sergeant organised vehicles and crews for the week in which the task fell. For this task three vehicles would suffice – one to cover the departure point in the morning, and then proceed to the London site to set up the area for a night approach, the other two for the other two sites. (You can imagine that the planning becomes more complicated when you consider the movements of the other helicopter on the same day, then co-ordinate this day with the preceding and subsequent ones.) The Corporals of the crews would be briefed by the Sergeant, and whenever possible by the aircrew. They would pick their own routes and decide on their departure time, planning always to arrive on site at least one hour before the scheduled landing time for the helicopter.

So, involved in the task are three HSVs – call them A, B and C – and four sites, 1, 2, 3 and 4. Crew A would drive to Site 1. Arriving there before the helicopter left base, having driven through areas of fog, but finding that Site 1 was clear; the Corporal would telephone the information back to base where it was gratefully received by the pilot as confirmation of the met man's best guess.

Crew B meanwhile arrived at Site 2 (the helicopter was still en route to Site 1), where they were provided with a room in which to change, and even a welcome cup of tea, before proceeding to the adjoining sports field which happened to be an ideal landing-site. The ground was firm and dry – no need for any matting, just peg out an 'H' so that everybody knew where the helicopter would touch down (including the pilot).

While they were doing this, the local police Inspector would tell the Corporal that a hundred or so youngsters would be turning up soon from the nearby school, and where would he suggest they stand? Then a few dozen people would gather along one side, and he'd have to ask them to move as the helicopter would be approaching right over that area; the ambulance had arrived and parked by the HSV; the Managing Director wanted to know where to put the cars; the Corporal tries to explain that despite where the helicopter door was on a proving flight, the wind was now blowing from the opposite direction so the door would be on *this* side, but in any case there would be plenty of time to move forward. And 'Would you like to stay well back over there, sir, until the rotor stops?' He's seen it all before – wet grass-cuttings, dust, hats and skirts all on the move, displaced by six tonnes of helicopter downdraught. At least there were no arguments about red carpets today. This one was easy; he still remembers being swamped by 3000 people in a public park the first time they carried a certain young Princess.

With the spectators safely organised in a good viewing position and the HSV strategically parked, the crew await the radio call from the helicopter, fending off the inevitable question of 'Will it/he/she/they be on time?' with the usual 'Yes, unless we hear otherwise' or 'No news is good news'.

The Lord Lieutenant for the county would arrive to meet and greet HRH, then, with about fifteen miles to run, the helicopter would duly call: 'Rover Zero Four, this is Kittyhawk Five. We'll be on time.' The HSV driver acknowledged, passed the suggested landing direction to the pilot, adding any relevant reminders such as 'low wires on the approach', and would alert the Corporal who would be on the field to marshal the helicopter down and direct/invite the meeters and greeters towards the helicopter as it shut down. Just as the rotor stopped, the door would be opened (on time to the second, of course) from within by the Crew Chief, who lowered the steps for HRH to descend. One more Royal flight completed.

The necessity of having pre-positioned support crews for The Queen's Flight helicopters is underlined by the many remote places to which they were flown, far from any kind of aviation support facilities.

When HRH had departed the scene and the immediate interest in the aircraft had died down, the firemen provided chocks for the aircraft and helped the Crew Chief fit intake and exhaust covers. A top-up of fuel was needed at this stage of the day, so the HSV was carefully positioned, electrically earthed and bonded to the helicopter, the fuel hose run out and, when the Crew Chief had checked a fuel sample to ensure no water content, the firemen dispensed the required amount – all carefully metered and logged, of course.

Meanwhile Crew C was on the way to Site 3, having left base in the late morning. They would be squeezed into the somewhat cramped interior of a Range Rover, a much smaller vehicle than the Bedford HSV, but still a heavy machine with its 200-gallon water tank and a load of equipment, including spare aircraft batteries. Even so, it was capable of moving along quite briskly under the power of a big V8 petrol engine, but you are aware of the body-roll when cornering with a ton of water aboard. Access to their site was via a low archway, which a Bedford could not negotiate; the landing-site was a fairly small area quite close to a building, which HRH was visiting, but with clear approaches for the helicopter over open countryside apart from the odd tree. The helicopter would land beside the path here and HRH could walk straight into the building.

It would be nearly dusk when the helicopter departed from here towards London. Crew C would then drive further north to make a pre-arranged night stop, putting them within reach of their next task near Sheffield the next day.

In London, Crew A arrived in mid-afternoon after their 120 mile drive, parked the HSV in the usual secure area, had plenty of time for a meal and were at Site 4 in daylight, setting up the familiar night landing-aid. This was a geometric pattern of battery-operated lights which delineated an approach-path direction and safe angle clear of obstructions which the helicopter would be able to recognise and follow, even on a dirty wet night with a failed landing-lamp. In the absence of any other message, the Corporal would switch on the lights thirty minutes before the helicopter was due – he knows it could be early on the return flight as timing is not important on the home run. The HSV was also equipped with an eye-catching strobe light which could be used to assist the helicopter crew with their initial identification of the site.

The expected call eventually comes: 'Rover Zero Five, Kittyhawk Five with you in five minutes.'

'Roger, Kittyhawk Five. Approach one nine zero degrees. Glidepath at ten degrees.'

The helicopter would land – usual shutdown routine – a chauffer would drive the car almost to the cabin door – HRH descended from the cabin as the last few thousand engine rpm whined down – smiled thanks towards the cockpit and exchanged gentle banter about the time-keeping or the weather – He would get into the car to the Palace before his evening engagement (how do they keep up the pace?).

By now, the fog was beginning to threaten again, so more fuel would be taken on to increase the diversion options for the helicopter, plugging into the HSV's battery power now for the helicopter's lights and for the re-start. All this took no more than fifteen minutes, and the helicopter departed for the last hop back to base. One of the firemen from Crew A was given a lift back in the helicopter, leaving the Corporal and one man to return with the HSV – not much more than an hour's run in reasonable traffic that evening.

Of course, they're all out again tomorrow. The aircraft would be serviced overnight; and the vehicles would be immaculate in their dark blue finish when they departed again. The wives were remarkably understanding, and with luck, half of the firemen would get both Saturday and Sunday off that weekend. Two crews would have to depart on Sunday to be in Scotland on Tuesday – but it could all change before then.

"That was a simple day. We used nine sites one day last month (and only one of them twice), and seven the next day. It all went like clockwork, as it usually does, but you can guess what a flurry of activity is generated when one vehicle suffers even a minor breakdown. Then the initiative is with the Corporal whose vehicle it is, but we get the same response from our MT section as the engineers give to an aircraft with a snag, and if it can possibly be fixed in time, it is".

As well as all points between Land's End and John o'Groats, we've taken Royal passengers in our helicopters (and therefore needed firemen on site with their equipment) to the top of Snowdon, to the Western Isles (even St. Kilda, which is off the top left-hand corner of most people's maps of the UK), to the Shetlands, the Orkneys, the Channel Isles and the Scillies. We sometimes need a little help from other friendly services to get them there with their kit, but there they are, with portable fire-extinguishers and a radio (hand-held now); 'Kittyhawk Seven from Rover One…'

Note: Wessex XV 732 has been granted to the Royal Air Force Museum at Hendon whilst XV733 was sold, at public auction in London on 25th October 2001, to the Helicopter Museum at Weston-super-Mare.

The History of The Queen's Flight Fire Service

The Fire Section of The Queen's Flight was responsible for covering all helicopter movements of the Flight whether they had Royal or VVIP passengers operating away from a normal airfield environment.

The section was established in 1954 with two Corporals and two Senior Aircraftman Firemen. Equipped with two short wheel based Land Rovers both carrying 100lb 'KER' dry powder packs.

In 1957 both vehicles were exchanged for long wheel based Land Rovers and the dry powder was increased to 200lb per vehicle. An extra crew and vehicle were established in 1960 to help meet the extra commitments.

In 1968, with the re-equipment of The Queen's Flight with the Wessex HCC Mk.4 helicopters, a requirement existed for the reorganisation of the Fire Section. In that same year three specially designed helicopter support vehicles (HSVs) were built by Marshalls of Cambridge. The vehicles carried 100 gallons of premixed foam and up to 198 gallons of aviation fuel, Avtur F34. This fuel was carried in 4.5-gallon jerry cans and poured into the Wessex by hand by the fire crews. Equipment on the vehicle included hydraulic rescue gear, hand tools, fire extinguishers, first aid equipment and an air powered chisel. The section manning was increased to make it one Sergeant, two Corporals and six Senior Aircraftmen.

In 1971 an SAC was disestablished to make way for another Corporal, but five years later returned to give the section three, three man crews with a Sergeant in charge of the section.

Things stayed as they were until 1979 when the section took delivery of two Truck Airfield Crash Rescue Mk. II vehicles (TACR II's) an extra crew was also brought in but the TACR's could only be deployed to sites where the aircraft didn't require a refuel.

A Truck Airfield Crash Rescue Mk. II. The original colour was blue.

After seventeen years and 468,000 miles the three HSV's were replaced in 1985. The new vehicles were designed and manufactured by Edgehills Hook. They now carried 900 litres of premixed foam and 545 litres of Avtur, this time complete with its own integral fuel pump. It also carried a power saw, hydraulic rescue equipment, air bags, hand tools, extinguishers and first aid equipment. The vehicles had a halogen stem light that was powered by the vehicles own generator. It also had the capability to supply the Wessex with power for engine starts or any other aircraft power requirements.

A Helicopter Support Vehicle in service from 1985.

Due to the amount of work the section was now involved in it was decided to increase the section manning by two SAC's, so by the end of 1989 the section consisted of fifteen men, one Sergeant, four Corporals and ten Senior Aircraftmen.

1989 was one of the busiest years the section was to be involved in. In that year they covered 631 aircraft landing sites throughout Great Britain and North West Europe, covering a total of 98,000 miles and delivering 60,000 litres of Avtur to the two Wessex helicopters.

THE JOB

When a crew were tasked they were required to arrive at a set location one hour before the helicopter was due to land. They were to set up the landing zone and lay markers for the helicopter's arrival by day or night. For night operations the crew were to arrive during daylight hours and set up the BARDIC night landing system, using an angle approach indicator and a standard NATO 'T'. This equipment is more commonly used by Army units operating in the field.

The fire crew's were responsible for liasing with the local police with security foremost in mind but also for the safety of the reception party and the local public who turned out in their hundreds.

Only when the fire crew were sure that everything was ready would the pilot be informed. He would usually call the crew about ten miles from the site via the VHF radio and would request details about the site. The crew would pass back the suggested approach heading, landing heading, ground wind speed and direction plus any other information that may be of use to the pilot.

A member of the fire crew would then be required to marshal the helicopter and when shut down ensure the safe departure of the passengers. When the helicopter was fully shut down and the passengers safely away the fire crew were then responsible for the safety of the aircraft. Also assisting the helicopter Crew Chief with his turn round duties before the helicopter departed. If the helicopter was to remain on the site for a prolonged period of time the batteries would be disconnected and the helicopter secured. If the helicopter required fuel the fire crew were responsible for the safe delivery of it.

Depending on how many tasks the fire crew had been detailed for that week there may have been a requirement to move to another location in any part of the country as soon as they had finished that day's task. If the helicopter requires fuel again at the next site whoever was in charge of the crew would have to organise the collection of the fuel and also arrange where the crew would stay overnight to ensure that they would arrive on site for the following day's tasks. Avtur has been collected from RAF stations around the country and at most civil airports, even at Search and Rescue fuel dumps in the North of Scotland when the need arose. The busiest time of the year for the section was during the summer months, particularly June and July when a crew could be out all seven days of the week.

With the amount of tasks the section were covering in 1990 and the discovery that the TACR II's were over their legal axle limits and so the need for extra vehicles to carry their equipment it was decided to change the whole vehicle fleet, because of the problems encountered with the HSV's carrying both foam and Avtur it was decided that they would be kept apart. It was decided that the following vehicles would be required:

a.   A rapid intervention fire vehicle.

b.   A support vehicle.

c.   A refuelling vehicle.

After many meetings and trial vehicles coming and going, the support vehicle chosen was the Land Rover Discovery TDI. They were production models with equipment added that the section had requested. This included cellnet telephones, a ground to air VHF radio, Whelen two tones and public address system fitted by Woodway Engineering to certain specifications and an emergency lighting bar roof mounted. The lighting bar included white and green lights which were used for night landings when the pilot needed site identification. He would normally call the fire crew about ten minutes before landing to ask for strobe lights. In good weather conditions the vehicle was visible from ten miles away.

The vehicle also carried support equipment that included aircraft batteries, 'H' landing markers, crowd control barriers and if required the BARDIC night landing system plus any personal equipment required by the crew.

Rather than have a third vehicle as a base for the refuelling equipment it was decided to incorporate a trailer. These trailers, based on a four-wheel chassis capable of carrying 1270 litres of Avtur, were produced by Mainways and NEI Thompsons of Birmingham. Due to regulations regarding fuel and accompanying equipment the fuel was delivered by using a hand pump.

The Land Rover Discovery in shown in front of Wessex XV732. The fuel trailer on the right was introduced in 1991.

The last vehicle, a rapid intervention fire vehicle, after much deliberation Scania was chosen to supply the vehicle chassis and running gear. In addition Carmichaels of Worcester were contracted to supply the vehicles fire fighting capabilities, the new vehicle being capable of carrying 1800 litres of foam. The foam delivery system is fully automatic with the use of new technologies. The vehicle was equipped with Clan Lucas cutting gear, incorporating a combi tool and pedal cutter. In addition the vehicle held first aid equipment and three compressed air breathing apparatus with two spare cylinders, used in conjunction with the air bag lifting equipment. The vehicles communication capabilities were the same as the Discoveries, as was the lighting bar fitted to the roof.

The Land Rover Discovery and fuel trailers were delivered in the summer of 1991 and the first Scania in April 1992 after weeks of trials that included several days at the Fire Service Training Headquarters at RAF Manston.

10. Tours Overseas

The unique qualities of The Queen's Flight inspire a special esprit de corps amongst its ex-members. To foster this, The Queen's Flight Association was formed in 1982. One of its members, Wing Commander W. T. (Tom) Bussey, LVO, OBE, BEM, RAF (Ret'd), served no less than three tours with the Flight. – the first as a Corporal from 1939 to 1941, the second as an Engineering Officer from 1948 to 1950 and thirdly as a Squadron Leader and the Senior Engineering Officer from 1955 to 1961. As a flight mechanic, he was closely involved with Royal flying in the early days of the 1939-45 war.

Tom writes: "The Hudson aircraft, N7263 underwent several modifications on receipt in August 1939 to suit its role. Most of the modifications were done at Farnborough. Radio sets were duplicated in an effort to ensure absolute communication. An IFF set was fitted and three Vickers K guns were added to its armament, one in the nose-cone and one on either side of the rear fuselage at window positions. Had the threatened invasion of the country materialised, bomb racks were available, and it was anticipated that the aircraft could have been used for this purpose if needed. Fuselage fuel-tanks were manufactured and fitted by Cunliffe-Owen Aircraft Company of Southampton to give the aeroplane long-range capacity. All the extra equipment was stored at Benson.

After the fall of France the normal complement of the aircraft was: pilot, Wing Commander Fielden; Jenkins, engineer, in the right-hand cockpit seat; Figg, wireless operator; Reed, dorsal turret gunner; Bussey, front gunner; Morley, acting steward and side-gunner; Jenkins would move to the other side-gunner position in the event of enemy aircraft in the vicinity.

Our passengers were mainly HRH The Duke of Kent, who was on the staff of the Inspector General of the Royal Air Force at that time, and TRH The Duke and Duchess of Gloucester. On one occasion we carried the King of Norway and another passenger, I believe, was a Belgian princess. (Because of the close security condition that prevailed we were never told in advance who our passengers would be.)

On 9 August 1941, we had HM King George VI on board from Inverness to Hatston in the Orkney Isles. On this occasion we were escorted by a Hurricane squadron of Czech pilots who, being so proud of being given the honour of escorting the King, orbited the aircraft rather too closely in vics of three, to the consternation of the Captain. During the flight, German aircraft had attacked shipping along the Orkney coast and this had alerted the Royal Navy in Scapa Flow. Having dropped our passenger, our flight-path took us near to Scapa as we departed the island, and a trigger-happy naval gunner took a shot at us, much to the Captain's annoyance.

On another journey from Scotland, we had passed Barrow-in-Furness in bad weather and low cloud on our way to Rhyl. As we dropped out of cloud to search for our pinpoint, we found ourselves right over a convoy heading for Liverpool. Again we had a very hostile reception, but we were lucky. As the Captain commented, "Thank God the Navy cannot shoot!"

We experienced two enemy air raids on Benson airfield during the Battle of Britain. On one of these a stick of bombs straddled the airfield, the last one exploding near the hangar and spraying it with debris. One dropped within feet of the hangar but did not explode. Several air-raid warnings were given and during these the Captain always sat at the entrance to the shelter with a Thompson machine-gun at the ready.

During the invasion threat we made adaptors to enable the three Vickers K guns normally carried on the aircraft to be used for the defence of the hangar.

Earlier, during the phoney war, Jenkins and I were returning to the aircraft at Paris airport in heavy rain. The French guard was standing under the mainplane out of the weather. As we alighted from the vehicle he attempted to shoulder arms and, in doing so, managed to push his bayonet through the mainplane. After this incident, on Royal tours overseas we always insisted that bayonets were not carried by local troops guarding our aircraft.

A similar incident was to occur at Jesselton, North Borneo, on 1-2 March 1959 during Prince Philip's world tour. After convincing, with great difficulty, the local guard commander that bayonets must not be fixed whilst his troops were in the aircraft vicinity, Squadron Leader Ken Hannah and I returned at dusk to check, to find the guard without bayonets but peacefully cooking their evening meal on an open fire almost under our aircraft wing-tip. Having put that right, we were awakened at two o'clock next morning with the news that one of the guards had accidentally loosed off a round from his rifle which had penetrated the leading edge of the mainplane and scored the top of the cockpit as it passed. We effected the necessary repair and Prince Philip was able to carry on his tour early next morning as scheduled."

Royal flying during the 1939-45 War was still supervised by the Captain of The King's Flight, Edward Fielden, who retained this appointment even though the Flight itself was disbanded. Air Commodore J.L. Mitchell, LVO, DFC, AFC, AE, RAF (Ret'd) – not to be confused with his namesake of the same rank who later became Captain of The Queen's Flight – was involved in wartime Royal flying, including HM King George VI's dramatic and hazardous visit to North Africa in June 1943:

"I was posted to No. 12 OCU at Benson in early May 1940 for operational training on Fairey Battles, at that time supporting No. 98 Squadron at Rheims. I was then an Acting Pilot Officer Observer, one of the first to be commissioned into the RAFVR. On reporting to my flight I was despatched, inevitably as bog-rat, to fetch the Oxometer. My journey round the station to find this mythical piece of equipment took me past a hangar in which half the floor-space was screened off from the Battles. I found it contained a Lockheed Hudson (N7263) and a Percival Q6 (P5634). These aircraft were the residue of The King's Flight, conveniently located near London, Windsor and the home of the Air Equerry and Captain of the Flight. This Hudson was fitted with its Atlantic ferry tanks, and turreted. Coincidentally, as it turned out for me, the crew of this aircraft was found from No. 24 Squadron at Hendon, the VIP transport squadron of the RAF.

In May 1943, three years later, I was posted to No. 24 Squadron for duty with the York flight, then at Northolt. A personal aircraft for Mr. Churchill had been delivered to the squadron: this was *Ascalon*, the second prototype, LV633, luxuriously equipped (for the time) with a private cabin and toilet, a dining saloon-cum-conference room seating eight, and eight further sleeper-style bunks forward of the galley. For the first time on long-range flights, the PM was to have an all-RAF crew. It was captained by Wing Commander H.B. Collins, the OC of 24 – an ex-Imperial Airways Captain of some considerable experience. I was the navigator.

After completion of its clearance trials at Boscombe Down, the York had made its maiden flight in May 1943 – a rendezvous at Gibraltar with the Boeing Clipper flying-boat bringing Mr. Churchill's party from the TRIDENT Conference in Washington. After visiting Algiers and Tunis and inspecting the Mareth Line from the air, we returned to Northolt on 5 June. Mr. Churchill commented to the Captain at the time, 'You will be wanted shortly for a very important passenger.' Who could be more important than the PM himself? A few days later, the presence of Group Captain 'Mouse' Fielden inspecting *Ascalon* brought back my Benson memories.

On the evening of 11 June the arrival of the Guardsmen batmen with luggage in Palace cars dispelled any doubts in our minds about the identity of 'General Lyon'. At briefing, the AOC-in-C of Transport Command (Ginger Bowhill) addressed a few words to us about the historic occasion.

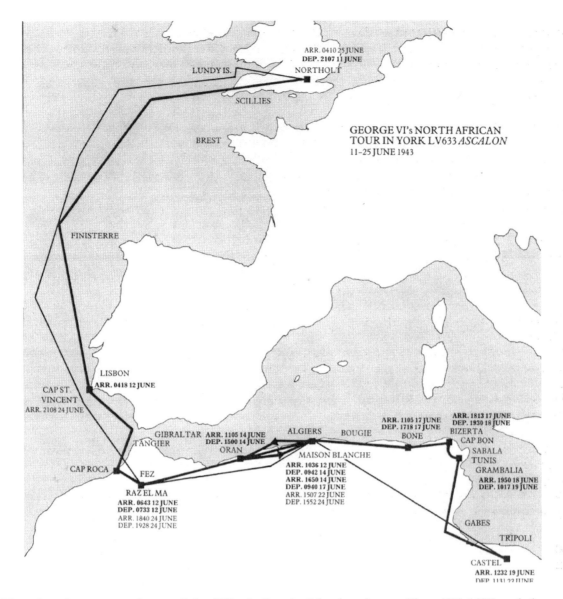

The map contains the following labels:

GEORGE VI's NORTH AFRICAN
TOUR IN YORK LV633 *ASCALON*
11-25 JUNE 1943

NORTHOLT
ARR. 0410 25 JUNE
DEP. 2107 11 JUNE

LUNDY IS.

SCILLIES

BREST

FINISTERRE

LISBON
ARR. 0418 12 JUNE

CAP ST.
VINCENT
ARR. 2108 24 JUNE

GIBRALTAR ARR. 1105 14 JUNE
DEP. 1500 14 JUNE
TANGIER
ORAN

CAP ROCA

FEZ

RAZ EL MA
ARR. 0643 12 JUNE
DEP. 0733 12 JUNE
ARR. 1840 24 JUNE
DEP. 1928 24 JUNE

ALGIERS   BOUGIE   BONE

MAISON BLANCHE
ARR. 1036 12 JUNE
DEP. 0942 14 JUNE
ARR. 1650 14 JUNE
DEP. 0940 17 JUNE
ARR. 1507 22 JUNE
DEP. 1552 24 JUNE

ARR. 1105 17 JUNE
DEP. 1718 17 JUNE

ARR. 1813 17 JUNE
DEP. 1930 18 JUNE
BIZERTA
CAP BON
SABALA
TUNIS
GRAMBALIA
ARR. 1950 18 JUNE
DEP. 1017 19 JUNE

GABES

TRIPOLI

CASTEL
ARR. 1232 19 JUNE
DEP. 1131 22 JUNE

The aircraft was routed out of the UK via Lundy Island and a position 49N 10W and thence southwards, a roundabout route to keep beyond the likely range of Ju 88 night-fighters operating from the Brest Peninsula. The flight went smoothly but the landing forecast for Gibraltar was fog and, along with all the other aircraft destined for the Rock, a diversion was ordered to the RAF staging post at Ras el Ma (Fez). For security reasons we had been allocated a call-sign within the block of ferry aircraft that night from the UK to North Africa – the Royal flight call-sign to be used only in dire emergency. Thus Ras el Ma had no reason to differentiate between us and the other aircraft. By chance, the direct secure link between Gibraltar and Ras El Ma was temporarily out of action. Guarded RT messages got no reception and so we took our turn in the circuit and found ourselves parked alongside an Albermarle whose crew and passengers' appearances caused some Royal comment. Their embarrassment was in no way matched by the unfortunate Station Commander's, who was woken with the news of the Royal arrival, having had a somewhat hectic Mess party the night before. We continued on to Algiers (Maison Elanche) an hour later, after refuelling and revictualling passengers, crew and aircraft.

After two days at General Eisenhower's Supreme Headquarters in Algiers, HM flew to Oran to review the US Fifth Army under General Mark Clark, on the La Senia airfield; this was but an hour and a half's flight in each direction.

While HM and his party were on the saluting-base watching the march-past, a stray US Colonel approached the York – with the inevitable camera. The crew, who were at ease in the shade of the wing, were asked, 'Say, fellows, who's the big shot?' On being told that it was HM The King, the Colonel thought for a bit and then exclaimed, 'Gee, I guess that makes you all dooks and oils.' We humbly explained that such honours and dignities had not yet been conferred upon us and he went on his way somewhat disappointed. He might have been pleased to know that on the morning we returned to the UK, we were summoned to the Palace where HM made all the flight-deck crew MVOs (4th Class), now LVO.

On 17th June, HM's tour of British Army units took him to Bone and Tunis, and two days later on to Tripoli, where he embarked in the cruiser HMS *Aurora* to visit the garrison in Malta. On his return to Tripoli he reviewed representative units of the Eighth Army before flying back to Algiers.

The homeward journey started on 24 June and we again staged at Ras El Ma to avoid any risk of fog at Gibraltar – this time with adequate warning. A wide Atlantic track was flown, similar to outbound, with Royal Navy ships on station at the major turning points, listening on the guard frequency for any mishap. The flight was uneventful but for a much stronger tail-wind component than had been forecast. By five hours out it was clear that we were very much ahead of schedule. Speed was reduced, but the Air Equerry came forward to enquire the reason for the change in engine settings. After explanations, he ordered the Captain to resume normal cruising speed: HM had no wish to be in the air longer than was necessary, as there was always a risk of interception as we neared UK, even over London. We landed at Northolt nearly an hour early but fortunately our adjusted ETAs were being passed by ferry Control at Gloucester to the AOC-in-C, so that he and the Chief of the Air Staff were on hand. Mr. Churchill, arriving a little later, found the Royal party already taking coffee in the Officer's Mess.

Just a year later, the PM let it be known that he was lending His Majesty 'his' aircraft again, forgetting perhaps that all RAF aircraft belong to the Crown. This time Rabat Sale was chosen instead of Gibraltar as the intermediate staging-post. It was an all-RAF airfield with good met facilities and good approaches. Most important from a security point of view, it had the great advantage that it was not overlooked by the Duty Spy at La Linea.

Our crew was the same and we were joined, of course, by the Air Equerry, Group Captain Fielden, temporarily spared from commanding RAF Tempsford. We left Northolt at 2310 on 22 July, slightly late closing doors as a doodlebug (V1) flew right over the airfield, fortunately without stopping. The Royal Party, which included HM Queen Elizabeth and the Princess Elizabeth, were inspecting the interior of the aircraft and there was not an air-raid shelter within a hundred yards!

Weather was good for the eight-hour flight; a PAMPAS recce had been made by Mosquito in the afternoon as far as Finisterre to check on cloud-tops, so for once met had been confident in their forecast. Two hours later, the flight was continued to Pomigliano (Naples), the RAF staging-post for the Headquarters at Caserta. This was a rather bumpy trip over lunchtime, across a typical Mediterranean cold front situation. The York was to remain at Pomigliano, being too large for forward airfields and too demanding on fuel to operate further north, while HM continued to the forward areas in General 'Jumbo' Wilson's Dakota (FZ631) named *Freedom* and flown by Squadron Leader Penfold. Ten days later the York was standing ready for departure to the UK via Rabat, but was delayed on take-off by an unusual Naval manoeuvre: HM was being hosted by C-in-C Med., whose driver got lost on the rather tortuous route through the back streets of Naples, selected for security reasons to keep away from the main boulevards. Land navigation had proved too much, and some naval expletives were said to have been used.

Homeward, the weather on the Atlantic leg did produce a few bumps in the tops of the cloud. Before turning in, HM came forward to appraise the flight-deck. That he knew his star recognition was evident from the interest he took in our navigation methods and progress. As we landed at Northolt on time, yet another doodlebug made its appearance.

It is interesting to compare our wartime operations with present-day practices. The aircraft was new to the service at that time, but based on the wings, tail empennage and undercarriage of the well-proven Lancaster. As to the engines, Rolls-Royce had not only their name at stake but also a strong commercial interest in the performance of the aircraft in hot weather. Thus we had a permanent Rolls representative at Northolt and direct access to Derby at all times.

Planning was the same as for the PM's flights and we were fortunate that in our relationship with No. 10 we dealt through the SASO of Transport Command, Air Vice-Marshal H.G. Brackley, formerly of Imperial Airways and widely experienced over the Atlantic and Empire routes. As the intermediary between the requirements of the Palace and No. 10 (via the Chief of the Air Staff) and the Captain of the aircraft, his knowledge and judgement saved us from a lot of petty interference by well-meaning but often ignorant staff officers at various levels anxious to be in on the act.

Minimum need-to-know was the rule but with the added handicap that but for established RAF bases, we could not be sure of what facilities we should find on arrival; there could be little way of pre-flight reconnaissance. With HM's flights, at least we were sure of the itinerary, but this was not always true of the PM's, for whom we had to make adequate provision for victualling as well as for the more mundane matters of navigation and fuel: there were little problems like keeping the bed-linen aired in Russia and the refrigerator running in Tunis!"

When The King's Flight re-formed early in 1946, its first Officer Commanding was New Zealander Wing Commander Bill Tacon, DSO, DFC, AFC (now Air Commodore E. W. Tacon, CBE, DSO, LVO, DFC, AFC); He recalls some of the problems he faced in re-establishing the unit:

"When I arrived at RAF Benson on 12 June 1946, I found that the news of the impending arrival of four aircraft, twenty officers and one hundred and twenty airmen was unwelcome news to the Station Commander, particularly as it was unknown under whose command we would be operating. We were allocated the hangar which was then in use for the second-line servicing of the PRU Mosquitos, and this was the filthiest hangar on the station. Flight Lieutenant George Pearson, the Engineering Officer, arrived at around this time and it wasn't long before we had sorted out the various offices, crew-rooms, storage space etc – but we were then faced with the awful problem of getting the hangar and offices clean. The hangar floor was covered in oil and grease and the offices were far from satisfactory. George (pictured) and I discussed the problem and I suggested that the quickest way would be to use petrol on the floors. Provided we took a few precautions, it should work. I really admired the way George went about the job; he opened both ends of the hangar, stationed men on all approaches to the hangar to keep away unwanted intruders, had a line of airmen across the width of the floor with bass brooms, then brought up the petrol bowser which poured petrol over the floor as the men scrubbed with the brooms.

As they reached the other end of the hangar, more men came in with high-pressure fire hoses and washed away the sludge. Some hours later, George and I heaved a great sigh of relief that not only had nothing gone wrong but we also had a clean hangar, and after a few days with paint brushes, the place was really transformed.

Some weeks later, there was a complaint from the local water conservancy council in Wallingford about oil and petrol in the river flowing through the town. We admitted to an oil-spill, apologised and assured them it was not likely to happen again. That was the Flight off to a clean start."

Bill Tacon had just eight months to prepare the Flight and its new Vickers Vikings for the Royal Tour of South Africa in 1947:

"The first time The King flew in South Africa was on 8 March 1947 from Bloemfontein to Bulfontein and return, along with Princess Margaret. On the return flight he sat in the co-pilot's seat and, I suppose to make conversation, said to me, "I believe this is a very safe aircraft and can fly very well on one engine" to which I replied, "If, sir, you look out to your right, you'll see that the starboard engine is feathered and we are flying on one engine". I don't know how impressed he was – but I know 'Mouse' Fielden wasn't, and I received a right royal blast from him about endangering the life of the Monarch.

During the Royal Tour we had to return to the UK urgently on Palace business; my crew and I left Cape Town on 25 April 1947 and arrived in Benson 32 hours 30 minutes later on 26 April. What all the hurry was about I don't recall, but it certainly proved that The King's aeroplane, VL246, was a reliable machine and that it was possible to fly 65 hours 50 minutes in four days."

On 30 March 1948, my crew and I, with 'Mouse' Fielden in the co-pilot's seat, set off for Australasia and New Zealand on a proving flight for the planned Royal Tour (later to be cancelled because of His Majesty's ill-health). The autopilot failed after we left Malta and the whole trip was flown manually. We arrived in Auckland, New Zealand, on 6 April, having flown 50 hours and 50 minutes in seven days. After visiting fifteen airfields in New Zealand and discussing tour arrangements, we left for Canberra. In Australia we visited some forty-four airfields before setting off for the UK from Perth, Western Australia on 6 May. Arriving back at Benson on 13 May, we had flown some 311 hours 25 minutes in six weeks – and no autopilot except for the first seven hours.

With Bill Tacon on the tour of South Africa was Flight Lieutenant Brian Trubshaw, who went on to achieve great distinction as Chief Test Pilot and Divisional Director at Filton for British Aerospace. He it was who flew the British-assembled Concorde and he recalls:

"I joined The King's Flight in the middle of 1946, I remember being interviewed in the Air Ministry by Air Commodore (as he was then) Fielden, who selected eight pilots. The four senior ones were made the captains of the four Viking aircraft which were going to be the equipment for the Royal Tour of South Africa scheduled for 1947. I, being one of the junior ones, was therefore a co-pilot and assigned to the No.4 aeroplane, which was fitted out as a workshop.

The early days we spent training vigorously on the Viking, which was not a particularly nice aeroplane from some points of view, although it did pretty noble service in the Flight over the years. We did run into some engine-surging troubles on one of the first proving flights during a take-off from Nairobi. That was quite an exercise; because the aeroplane really paddled down the runway from side to side as each engine surged in turn. That problem was eventually fixed, but only just in time for the tour of South Africa to take place.

Also during this initial build-up period, we did a bit of flying around the UK in the Dominie (RL951) and in fact I was in the Dominie on the night of 11 November 1946 when it ran out of fuel over Oxford and we came down in a field near Mount Farm. The accident smashed the aeroplane to pieces, but none of the individuals on board had even one scratch. I was actually sitting in the back of the aeroplane when I found the navigator sitting at my feet and said to him, 'What the hell are you doing down there?' whereupon he said 'We're about to crash!' So I came out of my slumbers and began to take a little bit of interest, and I also realised that it was kind of quiet outside because neither of the engines was running.

We got back into the Mess after the accident and there was the Benson 'gen' man called Pudsey, a Mosquito pilot, sitting at the bar, which was in the hall in those days. Pudsey said to me, 'I don't like the sound of this. Meet me at the back of the Mess in fifteen minutes.'

Still being a little bit shaken, I went to see what Pudsey was up to and found he was loading petrol cans, ropes, axes and all sorts of stuff into his car. 'What are you going to do?' I asked. He replied, 'We're going to burn it'

We set off on this venture in Pudsey's car, but by the time we got to the wreckage, there were a couple of rather nasty Alsatians walking around it with their Corporal handlers, so we just retired to the George in Dorchester and finished the evening there.

Then the Tour came off, and off we went to South Africa. The No.4 aeroplane brought up the rear and when we got to Tabora (it took the workshop, as it was called, some time – you couldn't put much fuel in it, because it was carrying all those spare parts), we found the No.1 aeroplane, that was with 'Mouse' Fielden and Bill Tacon, waiting for us and in need of a new gill motor, necessary for the air-cooling of the engine, I immediately went into the great book of words to see which rack this would be located in and was somewhat horrified to find that we didn't have a gill motor on board. Those who knew 'Mouse' Fielden will well appreciate that he was far from pleased.

The tour itself was uneventful. We spent most of the time based in Cape Town, but we moved both to Pretoria and to Rhodesia as it was then, when the Royal party moved to those areas. After a most enjoyable tour and our return to England, the Flight was cut into two, but I was one of the lucky ones who were kept on.

We immediately started on another venture as part of selling air transportation to the Royal family: it was decided that the mail would be delivered to Balmoral by helicopter. The two junior people, of whom I was one as there were now only four pilots left in the Flight, were taught how to fly helicopters for this particular purpose. This was an amazing experience because we used the old Hoverfly Mk. I, which was made by Sikorsky. Its cruising speed and maximum speed was sixty miles an hour, so it took us some thirteen hours to fly these two things up to Aberdeen from Benson.

We started the mail run by driving over to Balmoral on the first day to have a look at the cricket ground that was going to be our landing strip; in fact we were honoured to have lunch with the Royal Family and then were sent back to Aberdeen to fetch the helicopters. We brought them over and all the younger members of the Royal Family jumped in and out of them all afternoon, having a good look at them. I remember a very embarrassing experience when the late Prince William of Gloucester, on getting out of my helicopter, put his hand on the hot exhaust – he let out a bellow which could be heard all around the high ground north of Balmoral and I should think the echo could have travelled even further. The burn was not too bad, I am glad to say, and with a little tenderness from his mother all was quickly restored.

Flt.Lt. A. J. Lee & Flt.Lt. E. B.Trubshaw

We then started the mail runs proper and on the first morning were met by the Court Postmaster – who used to get extremely upset if he was only called 'the Postmaster'. He took us both to the senior servants' hall for breakfast, where we had a very hearty occasion. When we got back to Aberdeen, though, I had a call from Sir Harold Campbell, who was the Equerry in Waiting at the time, to say that The Queen was very upset that we had been taken to the senior servants' hall; of course we must have breakfast, but in future it would be in the dining room. The other pilot, Alan Lee, and I were a little bit nervous about this and were rather shy in asking for the toast to be passed. But it was a most amusing time – we went to the Ghillies' Ball and found ourselves doing all sorts of dances unfamiliar to us. Finally in that summer of 1947, we had a dinner party at Balmoral given for the two of us and that was really a very memorable occasion.

In the summer of 1948 we started up again on the mail run to Balmoral, but this time we did it quite differently in that we were working up to the Royal Tour of Australia and New Zealand scheduled for the autumn of 1948, so we were not actually based at Aberdeen in quite the same manner as we had been in 1947. With the cancellation of the Royal Tour, those of us who had been on the Flight since its re-formation in 1946 were obviously time-expired on our duty period, and were posted elsewhere. I still managed to keep in touch with the Flight, though, because 'Mouse' Fielden in fact got me my job as a Test Pilot with Vickers Armstrong. Without his guidance I would certainly never have gone into the aircraft industry, so I owe him a particular debt as far as my future life has worked out. When I went to Vickers, we still used to have the Vikings back from the Flight for their major servicings and it was my privilege to do the test flying on them and then deliver them back to Benson, so contact was maintained for a great many years."

Africa seems to have been an eventful area for the Flight, and reference has already been made in an earlier chapter to the first arrest of an aircraft of The Queen's Flight when Wing Commander Attlee's Heron (XM296) was detained at Goa, in Mali in 1961. Now Air Vice-Marshal D.L. Attlee, CBE, LVO, RAF (Ret'd) recounts the incident in his own words.

"I suppose my suspicions that all was not as it should have been were first aroused when the controller failed to answer the initial call for landing instructions, for we were expected and well within range. The crew and I had been very well entertained the previous evening by the French Commandant of the Beau Geste-type Algerian oasis of El Golea. We had taken off at sunrise for In Salah, another, smaller watering and refuelling place in the middle of the Algerian desert. Now, at midday on Sunday 9 July 1961, we were at 9,000 feet approaching Goa, a town on the banks of the Niger and some 200 miles east of Timbuktu.

Goa was not a planned refuelling stop on the route to Accra. It had been substituted for Tessalit only thirty-six hours before leaving England at the insistence of the Air Attaché in Paris. He had assured us that Tessalit had just been abandoned by the French and there was no fuel available. Both Tessalit and Goa are in the Republic of Mali, a former French African colonial territory, and there should have been little difficulty over changing airfields within the same country. So I was surprised, when we eventually made radio contact, to be asked if we had authority to land. I knew we had, but without a piece of paper it was going to be difficult to prove. And we certainly had not got the authority to land anywhere else, even if we had the fuel to get there.

I was certain that we had a small problem on our hands when we taxied in. I had never before been marshalled to a parking-place by a number of natives inexpertly waving Tommy-guns and rifles. I was also a little perturbed to see a small crowd of Europeans apparently behind a barbed-wire fence.

What appeared to be a company of fully-armed Mali police surrounded the aircraft, and, when we got out, they inevitably asked for the authority to land? A lengthy explanation then took place, which became more and more one-sided since it was conducted entirely in French, a language in which none of us was proficient. It became evident that the aircraft was not to be moved or refuelled, but it was quite impossible to discover a way round the impasse. The situation was not made much easier by the arrival from behind the wire of a number of French army and air force officers, none of who could speak a word of English. One explained that even French aircraft had to have written authority for every landing, which was apparently only obtainable from Bamako, the capital of Mali and about 600 miles to the west. And it was Sunday.

The first hopeful sign was the arrival of a Police Lieutenant. Up to now the police had been 'controlled' by an enormous and very dim Sergeant. Now he and his men fell silent, while the Lieutenant had the story told to him in our halting French. He was prepared to be sympathetic and thought the incident could be forgotten, but some of his men took him to one side and changed his mind for him. However, he did allow the aircraft to be taxied to the refuelling point, although one of the crew had to remain with him as a 'hostage'. At the same time, barrels were being placed along the taxiway and runway to prevent an unauthorised departure.

While the refuelling was being carried out with the assistance of French air force personnel, another member of the crew, whose French was the least basic, was driven into the town of Goa, some five miles away, to see the Governor of the Province. During more lengthy explanations, still in French, the Governor showed that he knew quite well what the aircraft was doing, where it was going and why. But it appeared he had not the authority to release it, and he would have to cable his government in Bamako for instructions. Furthermore, he forbade the crew to send a message to the British Ambassador in Bamako. And it was Sunday.

Back at the airfield, the French Commandant had arrived and at last I thought we should get some sense out of someone. But it transpired that the French had practically no influence with the Mali officials; not only were they unwelcome guests, but they were leaving in three weeks for good. The wire had been put up not so much to keep the French in, as the Malis out. The Commandant was prepared to, and did, put every facility under his control at our disposal, but he was extraordinarily reluctant even to talk to the local provincial Governor. He did eventually phone, but his arguments made no impression at all. He also agreed to send a signal to Bamako over the French forces network, but I am sure that this would not have been done if I had mentioned that the Governor had banned all cables to the capital.

The aircraft now had to be locked up in a hangar pending further instructions. This meant starting the engines, which also supplied power to the HF radio. The opportunity was too good to miss. With luck, we should be able to talk to Accra direct, but the distance to the hangar was only about fifty yards, which did not allow much time. By some inefficient taxying the distance was slightly increased but, although Accra could hear us, they could not understand the message. However, the French operator at Niamey did and, efficient as ever, undertook to relay the message. Subsequently, we learnt that the punch was lost, as we had used the word 'arrested'. When this was relayed by a Frenchman, it came out as 'stopped'. In Ghana, they knew we were 'stopping' at Goa and took no notice. And anyway, it was Sunday.

After parking the aircraft, the crew were ordered into an ancient French bus and taken to the hotel in Goa. This was, I think, called the 'Splendide'. Outwardly, it might once have lived up to its name, with Automobile Association Afrique and International Tourist signs still hanging outside, though why anyone should want to spend a night in Goa, I cannot imagine. Inside, the hotel was anything but 'splendide'. It had been shut for three months, there was nothing to eat or drink and it was indescribably filthy. We quickly decided that this was no place for a night-stop and demanded to be returned to the French officer's mess. The wrangling and argument with and between Mali officials over this one simple point lasted for four hours.

During the discussion, we were approached by a Mali who was slightly better dressed than his compatriots – he even wore a tie – and who introduced himself as Georges Segou. His suggestion that we might like a beer was the most constructive remark any Mali had yet made. Leaving the debating Malis, Georges led us for about a hundred yards along the banks of the Niger, where a flock of naked children were splashing in the muddy and sluggish water, to an adobe house which also did duty as the local bistro. The beer was a well-known French brand. It came out of a fridge which worked, and cost the equivalent of ten shillings a bottle. Since we were guests, we thought it would be impolite to offer to buy a round too early.

Over the first glass, we discovered that Georges' French was even worse than ours and his English, of which he claimed some knowledge, bore no resemblance to any language yet heard. In fact, his invitation to drinks was about the only intelligible phrase he knew and it was obviously well rehearsed. It was, therefore, not before the second beer that we realised that Georges must be some sort of 'commissar', and that he was trying to obtain a 'confession' from us. Through some elementary French, a few words of English and some complicated signs, he indicated that we should trust and confide in him. He said he was anti-communist, anti-French, pro-British and pro-

Russian. He was not certain about America. We interrupted this line of conversation, before it passed the bounds of credibility, by suggesting another beer. Georges promptly ordered whisky and continued by asking whether we could fly him to France, or anywhere as long as it was out of Mali and not into Ghana.

Georges was becoming something of a bore, and a most tenacious one. He followed us back to the hotel, where the same Malis, aided by some other disinterested parties, were still arguing the next move. Fortified by the beer, our French became more fluent though less accurate, we singled out the most influential looking Mali and again demanded a car to take us back to the airfield. Strangely, and in spite of Georges' protestations, it arrived within an hour; accompanied as far as the gates by Georges, we returned to an excellent dinner and comfortable beds in clean rooms. Shortly after midnight, the French duty officer told us that we were free to go, and at seven the next morning we took off for Accra.

I returned to Goa some five months later in a similar aircraft. The French had gone but the same Malis were there, all smiles and co-operation. Of Georges there was no sign. We refuelled in twenty minutes and were off. All was in order. And it was not Sunday."

Squadron Leader Graham Laurie (Kitty 4) describes the preparation and flights carried out for an Overseas Tour carried out by HRH The Princess Anne, with official engagements for the Foreign and Commonwealth Office and also included visits to projects for the Save the Children Fund, of which HRH is the President, to Africa during November and December 1985.

'Mbeya Tower, this is Kittyhawk Four. Field in sight, landing at 0756 for doors open on the hour, will call downwind right-hand for runway 13'. The end of the first 'Royal' sector is almost upon us, the culmination of six months' work involving The Queen's Flight, HRH The Princess Anne's Household, British Embassies and High Commissions, the Save the Children Fund and the various host Governments, to name but a few. The provision of air transport for overseas Royal Tours is an important role for The Queen's Flight. This particular tour, carried out by Princess Anne in November-December 1985 was to Tanzania, Mozambique, Zambia and Sudan. It comprised a large number of official engagements on behalf of the Foreign and Commonwealth Office but also included visits to projects run by the Save the Children Fund of which Her Royal Highness is President. In many cases the Andover landed at airfields and strips not normally served by even internal airline services.

We are often asked why our Andovers go these vast distances to fly members of the Royal Family and why local pilots who know the area are not used. All Royal Flying revolves around safety, engineering, security and quality of catering as well as the basic flying operations. For many it is hard to understand how a crew fresh from UK can be more suitable than the local crews. We have normally seen the airfield before during a proving flight (in this case made in October 1985), or on a previous tour. A crew used to operating with each other and used to the Royal flying environment will have no hesitation in diverting if conditions dictate. Certainly there will be no 'pressing on beyond reasonable grounds', whereas an operator who knows the area backwards may continue; the annual accident summaries continue to have far too many reports bearing this out!

The planning of this tour began with a dialogue of signals between the British Embassies and High Commissions with the office of HRH The Princess Anne, with suggested programmes to be followed in the various host countries. The Queen's Flight is often asked the nearest suitable airfield or strip to a particular place. We check maps, Aerad and Jeppersen Flight Guides and we also check with No.1 AIDU (RAF Northolt) who stores the Air Information Publications (AIP/Air Pilots) of most countries in the world and with the British Embassy or High Commission concerned. In many cases we never hear of that particular place again. Slowly, however, a draft programme evolves.

In this case our own proving flight (in Andover XS793) was to be combined with the recce to be done by the Royal Household. Whilst the Private Secretary and Personal Protection Officer visited the various sites to be visited by HRH, the crew checked with the airfields, fire cover, air traffic facilities, refuelling installations, in-flight catering kitchens and airport security. At the planning stage of this tour, it was clear that at many of the destinations fire cover and air traffic facilities would have to be found from outside. We were also getting some conflicting reports on the state of various strips in the Sudan. The rainy season had only just finished and the situation was changing daily. Some of the strips would have to be visited by light aircraft before taking the Andover in, even on the prover. We also had the added complication that at the end of the proving flight, the aircraft was required at Nairobi to complete a Royal task with HRH Prince Philip, so we could not afford any damage on a strip on our proving flight.

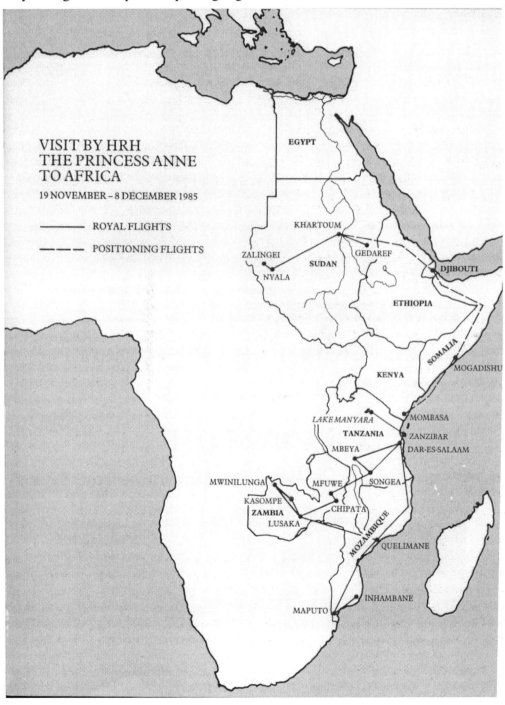

103

Back at Benson, the plan for the proving flight and the draft programme for the Royal tour were studied by the crew. The performance manuals were used to work out our take-off performances – somewhat limited on 1000-metre strips in temperatures expected to be ISA +20. In some instances fuel would need to be positioned especially for us. Were the logistics to do this feasible? We re-checked our planning to ensure the positioning of the fuel really was essential for the task to be completed. Unfortunately, on this tour, it most certainly was! We also had to guarantee supplies of water methanol, which is used in the Rolls Royce Dart engine to restore power in both hot and high-altitude conditions. Again the schedule was checked to see if this also needed to be positioned. We had already heard that Mozambique had none in the country and supplies could not be guaranteed even if specifically ordered.

The Save the Children Fund operated a Cessna 210 (G-BFLC) in Sudan and this was to prove invaluable during the proving flight. We were able to visit two of the most limiting strips in this light aircraft prior to committing the Andover. As it transpired, all the strips in the Sudan, although far from ideal, were suitable for the limited operation we required.

In Tanzania it was another story; the strip at Lake Manyara near the Ngorongoro Crater was marginal in length, so again it was visited by light aircraft first. Although the approaches were satisfactory, the first third of the runway had too many loose stones to be safe. However, the captain and navigator were assured that labour would be provided for a working party to do whatever we considered necessary. We therefore agreed that with the work completed, we would land the Andover at Lake Manyara on the Royal tour. Fire cover would drive the 3½ hours from Kilimanjaro International Airport. We also arranged for an expatriate pilot to fly his light aircraft in to act as Air Traffic Control and to confirm that the work requested had been carried out.

At Songea, also in Tanzania, we learnt that the refuelling would be from 45-gallon drums as there was no bowser. This in itself does not present a problem, except that a short stopover was planned and it could take between two and three hours to hand-pump the fuel into our tanks. Luckily, in this case the programme was amended to give us an overnight stop.

Mozambique presented us with few problems, as we were operating from tarmac runways throughout. So we thought! on arrival at Quelimane we had considerable difficulty getting fuel supplied. Eventually we had to get authority from the Regional Governor, and we were made only too aware that the war in the north of Mozambique was still a reality. We were the first aircraft of The Queen's Flight to visit Mozambique, but in spite of this initial setback, the overall impression was one of friendliness and a keenness to help.

Our final point of call on the proving flight was to Zambia, where two of the five destinations had been visited eighteen months previously with HRH The Prince of Wales. More over-wing refuelling from drums at Mfuwe, but again it transpired the Royal party required a night-stop. The aircraft was then duly handed over to a new crew in Nairobi for their visit with HRH Prince Philip to Madagascar, whilst we flew back to the UK by RAF VC-10 for just thirteen days prior to picking up XS789 for the Royal Tour.

The aircraft of The Queen's Flight are on the Military Register, which means we have to apply for diplomatic clearance to overfly or land in every country on our route. The workload of the signals alone for the navigator is considerable. The route, point of entry and exit from each country, together with the time, has to be quoted. Some of the clearances only come through a matter of forty-eight hours before they are required. Our Operations staff collates the replies and the clearance numbers, which have to be quoted on the flight plans. Luckily, this time most came through speedily, and when we left the UK, only Mozambique and Sudan were outstanding; as they were both receiving the Royal visitor, we did not anticipate any problems.

So it was 12 November when we departed Benson. The crew consisted of captain, co-pilot, navigator, crew-chief, steward and policeman (our basic crew) plus three engineers to give us adequate trade cover to keep the aircraft running for a month and over a hundred hours flying. The

Royal programme was confirmed; fuel in position, catering orders confirmed, and the availability of bottled water checked as in many places the local water was suspect. Certainly it was essential for the crew to take great care, in order to stay fit for the four-week trip. The co-pilot had collected the 'imprest', in this case considerable sums in Sterling and US dollars, to pay our bills around the route. The Queen's Flight or not, cash in hand and an American Express card say far more than 'Our Embassy will pay'! Throughout the trip, much of the co-pilot's time away from the aircraft will be spent settling hotel bills, aircraft handling bills and the like.

We soon reached Dar-es-Salaam in Tanzania, where we were to meet up with the Royal party. On our arrival the first check is 'Are there any changes to my published programme?' This must be followed by a check of the host country's own programme and any anomalies discussed. Luckily this tour was remarkably clear from such problems.

Our real job had begun: to get HRH from place to place safely, comfortably (not always easy in the heat of midday in Africa) and on time. The navigator has declared his 'doors time' some months previously; now the team has to make it. We rely on the Royal party running to time and in this we are lucky that they do their job in such a professional manner that they are normally at the aircraft very close to the appointed time. It is easy to lose time in the Andover but very difficult to make it up. We try to find out early on in the exercise which runway will be in use at our destination, as this will often vary taxy times, so our planned touch-down time needs to be adjusted. We can fine tune at the last minute but must avoid an obviously slow taxy and even worse, the opposite! Once on the ground it is simply a matter of taxying to the agreed spot and shutting down on time, so that the door can be opened to the second! This always assumes that we are parking where it was agreed on the proving flight and that the red carpet is rolled to the back door. This is hard to get through to many people, as all first class airline passengers alight at the front. Again, this tour proved successful in this respect.

While the Royal passenger is away from the aircraft, the crew clean the inside and outside of the aircraft before anything else is considered. The overall cleanliness of the aircraft is always commented upon. But cleaning 'a little and often' is essential for it to stay that way. The worst surface to operate from is the 'murram', a red natural surface found in many parts of Africa; the dust gets everywhere. We often chat to the inevitable crowds who have gathered to watch five or six Englishmen polish an aircraft in the heat of the noonday sun!

We also visit the fire-crew. At one destination, the local airport fire officer proudly showed us his Land Rover and fire trailer, which, he announced, had been made in England in 1839. The plate he pointed out on the side did indeed say 1839 – manufacturers since 1839. We could not spoil his image of British reliability. We had a report of the fire engine at an airfield not far away that had appeared in the original draft programme. The fire engine there is pushed out at the start of flying and pushed back at the end of the day. The pushing is necessary as the engine was taken out for repair some months previously! This would be bad enough but worse – it does not contain any water. The reason is simple enough from the locals' viewpoint: it is too heavy to push when full!

The tour is a gruelling one, and HRH The Princess Anne works a full day from the start on 18 November until 9 December, when the tour finishes in Khartoum. Our input works well, the aircraft remains serviceable, and the only slight 'hiccup; is an enforced overshoot at Gedaref in Sudan; a vehicle bringing a young girl to present a bouquet to HRH drove past a guard and onto the strip as the Andover was on approach. We landed successfully at the second attempt. The explanation was simple – the guard was a Private, the driver a Captain. At least Lieutenant-Colonel Peter Gibbs (Private Secretary to HRH The Princess Anne) could understand that one.

So it was 8 December when the twin flags flew for the last time on the Andover (HRH's personal standard on the left, the host nation on the right) as we completed our involvement in this tour, except, that is, to fly home a number of gifts presented to HRH by the four countries concerned.

Behind every successful tour is a dedicated team. Not just the engineers down the route, but the Operations staff and engineers at base, and the MT drivers ready to rush spares to Heathrow should we need them. In this case we were lucky, since the aircraft stayed one hundred per cent serviceable within our existing route spares. The General Office staff prepares all the visa applications; the signals staff at RAF Benson send out our diplomatic clearance requests; the staff at our Embassies and High Commissions see to all our needs and liaise with the respective foreign governments. And when we return, the Accounts staff has to check all the bills we have paid, over ninety per cent of which are in US dollars as most countries insist on visitors settling accounts in hard currency. Hundreds of people outside, as well as the entire strength of The Queen's Flight, work together to produce the end result – a tour fit for a Princess.

The second detention of a Queen's Flight aircraft was on a Route Proving Flight being carried out by Kitty 4 in an Andover CC Mk.2 (XS 789) and involved a check on an airfield some 100 miles east of Harare in Zimbabwe. The Captain of the aircraft, Squadron Leader Graham Laurie, (Kitty 4 1981-1995 then No. 32 The Royal Squadron until 2000) relates the story of 'Aberdeen 2':

"In 1982 HRH The Princess Anne was to complete a 20-day tour of African and Middle Eastern countries, in her capacity as Patron of Save the Children Fund (SCF).

The Andover XS 789 left RAF Benson on Sunday 10th October, positioning to Johannesburg. En-route, however we needed to do some late notice proving in Zimbabwe. Normally tour programmes were settled weeks before departure, but the nature of SCF work, necessitates a more flexible response. The trips to Victoria Falls and Lake Kariba (Binga) were confirmed but we would need to prove a strip called 'Aberdeen 2', situated in the Inyanga National Park. The Air Attaché explained that there was still some 'political' doubt about a royal visit to this area (the home of the 5th Brigade), however our proving flight had been approved by the Ministry of Defence and the requested fire cover had been put into the strip.

Monday 18th October dawned bright and sunny. We departed Harare for Aberdeen having spoken with a DC-3 pilot from the Zimbabwe Air Force about the strip. The surface was 'natural surface' but he explained that there were many loose stones on the early part of the runway, which also had a marked slope after about a quarter of its length.

The flight over to Aberdeen was pleasant enough, as we approached the area Brian Sowerby came forward from the delights of his 'Doppler' with the trusted topographical map. We could see the army camp clearly and when nearly in the overhead position we picked out the strip or at least a strip. On the map there was more than one Aberdeen! A careful check of approximate length, runway direction confirmed we had 'Aberdeen 2'. We could see the fire engine a few hundred yards from the strip on the edge of the army camp. We made a low pass to check for hazards in the undershoot, the runway and overshoot; we could also clearly see the slope. Turning downwind we positioned for landing. Air Traffic was not being provided for the recce but we had been told they would cover any subsequent Royal Flight.

The approach and landing were fine; yes the strip was a little rough! I could hear the crew chief wince as we reduced speed, fairly rapidly to minimise any damage. There was no obvious parking area so we moved just off the strip close to the fence next to the army camp and closed down.

Out we jumped into the searing heat and dust (much of our own making). Mike Darling, the co-pilot had spotted a guard up near the threshold, so set off to have a good look at the surface and 'have a fag'. Whilst he was away a vehicle approached and a Major dressed in combat kit emerged. I greeted him in a friendly manner but all he appeared to want to say was 'you have no permission to be here'. We then started the pantomime of 'oh yes we have', 'oh no you haven't'. That did not work, so we resorted to shouting louder! Still no joy and all suddenly became clear, when he drew out his pistol and said 'if you try to get away I will shoot out your tyres'. I could tell from those around me that they believed him as well!

After a while Mike Darling returned from his stroll, unaware of the fracas. More guards arrived and the Major said he would speak to his Officer Commanding. We continued to busy ourselves with cleaning duties which did not appear to upset them. During that time we also decided to use some of our meagre battery supply to try and make contact with Harare. We decided to listen out on Harare Approach on VHF; we could hear a number of aircraft but not the Air Traffic Controller. Eventually we made contact with an Air Zimbabwe 707 and the Captain relayed our message to Harare Approach for onward relay to the British High Commission. We arranged to listen out in 30 minutes for any reply.

Outside things had relaxed, but it was equally clear we were going nowhere. There were further comings and goings with more guards, plus the odd person just driving by for a look! As the half hour approached the group outside made a diversion, whilst we switched on the batteries to hear a Swissair DC 10 calling us. A message from the British Air Attaché – 'Keep your chins up, we are doing everything possible for you; please call again at 1400'. Wing Commander or not if I could have reached him I would no longer be a Squadron Leader!!

We called back in the three hours that had lapsed to hear a Zimbabwe Air Force Islander that had been sent up as 'aerial relay' telling us that the problem was about to be resolved and the MOD was just trying to get a message to the Commander of the 5th Brigade in our area. You've guessed it, in about 30 minutes the Major came back and said he had personally been working for 3 hours on our behalf, he had persuaded his Officer Commanding to let us go 'as an action of goodwill'. I enquired about the fire crew for our take off? 'Oh they are for you are they', the Major said, 'they were very difficult to understand'. I am not surprised if he waved his pistol about in front of the young Zimbabwe Air Force firemen.

The return trip was uneventful; as we landed an ex-patriot voice in the tower said 'welcome back'. We proceeded to the Zimbabwe Air Force ramp to be met by guess who, the Air Attaché, who was keen to point out just how hard he had worked on our behalf. I explained that by far the most important thing was to get a message back to Buckingham Palace, over what had happened and that Aberdeen 2 was not suitable for a royal visit!

The Station Commander who was keen to get a report on proceedings joined us; we left the ground crew cleaning the aircraft and 'dressing' the odd bit of stone damage and proceeded to Station Headquarters. When we reached his office the Station Commander asked me to write a brief report. He pulled open his desk, looked over his shoulder and handed me some paper saying 'sorry but this is all I've got'. He was smiling and as I looked at the headed paper, I could see why, it read 'Air Force of Southern Rhodesia, Salisbury'!

Whilst writing the report we were told that the Air Force had wanted to get out the DC 3 'Gunship' and fly to Aberdeen to 'sort them out'; somehow I feel the softly, softly approach was better. I was just finishing writing up proceedings when into the room came the said Zimbabwean Officer. Pleasantries were exchanged and the Station Commander said to the young Supply Officer that we were all going to the Officers' Mess bar, and how we had asked to meet as many Zimbabwe Officers as we could during our short stay (as you do!). On the way we collected the ground crew and with plenty of 'top cover' they joined us for a beer or two. After a brief discussion we explained to the Station Commander that there was this room in Meikles Hotel that could do with a bit of livening up any time after 7.00pm. We also mentioned that we would love to meet the crew of the Islander and any of the others involved in the proceedings.

The party was a huge success, all the tribulations were soon forgotten and the ex-patriot members of the Zimbabwe Air Force had a ball! The following morning we departed for Swaziland and more proving before heading for Johannesburg and the first Royal sector. Before this could take place there was another small matter of a party with the local RAFA. At the end of the evening somebody came in with the Sunday papers; there we were in the headlines on the front page, with the story of our escapades in Zimbabwe. Dougie Barr (TQF Adjutant) had also rung through to let us know he had spoken to our families as 'The Sun' had got hold of the story as well.

Our first Royal sector was back to Matsapa, Swaziland and immediately following the arrival ceremony, whilst putting the aircraft to bed, the British Press corps surrounded us, wanting their two penn'th! The following day the reports were filed in UK and pictures of Mike Darling, myself plus the interviews we never gave! In fact as I was supposedly giving this 'exclusive' interview in my hotel, I was still at the airfield, but this time, being hosted by the Royal Swazi Flying Club! The tour went very well; it was hard work and play with 56 sectors of which 25 were Royal in 14 countries. Finally I am happy to report that the Zimbabwean part of the Royal Tour went off without an arrest, nor a visit to Aberdeen 2!"

Squadron Leader Ian Anderson, Kitty 3 Navigator, a member of The Queen's Flight from 1975 until 1992, recounts this Global Tour ('A Great Swan Song' is his description) in the BAe 146 aircraft in 1992, picking up HRH The Duke of Edinburgh in Australia after a Royal Visit to that country:

In the spring of 1991 during a flight within the United Kingdom, HRH The Duke of Edinburgh said that he would like to take the Bae146 round the world. I was used to this sort of ad hoc planning so I produced the Sunday Times map of the world from my navigation bag and in the 30 minutes that the flight lasted we worked out a possible route. The main problem would be crossing the Pacific Ocean, as the BAe 146 did not have the range to fly from Honolulu to San Francisco. The planned route would be East-about so the only feasible way would be to go via Japan and the Aleutian Isles into Alaska.

The flight was due to take place the following spring so I pointed out to HRH that I would be retiring in September 1991 so someone else would be the navigator. He didn't think that was a good idea and could I not stay on for the tour. I needed no arm-twisting and the Royal Air Force agreed to keep me on for a further 6 months.

After several meetings at Buckingham Palace and innumerable phone calls from the Private Secretary the precise route began to take shape. It was to involve an "empty" transit to Australia to pick HRH up in Adelaide after a visit to Australia with Her Majesty The Queen was over. The tour would involve visits by HRH to New Zealand, Japan, Canada, California, Guyana, Brazil, Barbados, and the Bahamas.

So in February 1992 we set out. The crew consisted of myself and Geoff Williams, Malcolm Brecht, Don Gordon, Brian Beach, Dickie Bird, Mick Hind, Neil McGlynn and Tom Kerr. The first day was a pretty standard route for Queen's Flight aircraft heading east involving refuelling stops at Rome and Cairo before an overnight stop at Bahrain. The next day brought on the first "little" problem. We had been keen to avoid refuelling at Bombay as bitter experience told us that we could not expect to get away with a 30 minute stop there. We had therefore, with a lot of hassle, managed to get diplomatic and military clearance from the Indian authorities to refuel at Goa. Unfortunately, nobody had told Air Traffic at Goa that we had such permission and no amount of argument would persuade them to let us land. So we had to divert back to (you've guessed it) Bombay! When you know how much red-tape you are up against for a stop at Bombay when it is has all been planned and cleared in advance you can appreciate that we were dreading the stop there. However we were able to contact The Queen's Flight Operations and have them advise Bombay that we were coming and so with the help of a British Airways manager we got out in just over an hour – a very pleasant surprise.

After Bombay we proceeded to Colombo where we had our second night-stop. A couple of gin and tonics in the crew bar helped us get over the trauma of that day. Next day we refuelled at Changi (Singapore) and Surabaya (Indonesia) and on to the night-stop in Northern Australia at Darwin. The following day was an easy one leg (3hrs 30mins) to Adelaide (South Australia) where we had a couple of rest days for aircraft preparation before starting the Royal flying.

The first country to be visited by HRH was New Zealand arriving at Wellington after refuelling at Melbourne. After three days at Wellington, during which time I took the opportunity to fly to visit my sister who lives in Christchurch, we moved to Auckland for two nights.

The next country where HRH had a visit planned was Japan. To get there from Auckland involved refuelling at Brisbane (Australia) and Port Moresby (Papua New Guinea) and an overnight at Andersen (right spelling!) US Air Force Base on the island of Guam. From there we flew direct to an island called Ishigaki, which is just about the southernmost part of Japan. I have no idea what HRH was there for but it was something to do with WWF. We were there just for one night before flying to Osaka for another one night visit. The next day we did a forty-minute flight to Atsugi for another WWF meeting and then we went to Kushiro in the North of Japan. We had travelled from the semi-tropical Ishigaki to a very cold and snowy Kushiro. Our second day there was March 6th which was Geoff Williams' birthday so we had a party arranged by the Air Attaché from Tokyo which started in the crew bar and after dinner in the hotel finished in a Karaoke bar. On the morning of March 7th we left Kushiro and flew to Shemya US Air Force Base in the Aleutians to refuel. This is just about the bleakest, coldest and windiest place you can imagine and we were surprised to find the USAF welcoming party all in shirt-sleeve order. It is their idea of a gimmick! Then it was on to Anchorage where, as we had crossed the International Date Line, it was March 6th all over again – so we had another birthday party!

From Anchorage we flew to Vancouver where we had a very welcome three days off. Then followed a series of one-night visits at Medicine Hat, Monterey, Nassau and Georgetown (Guyana). These legs involved refuelling stops at Calgary, San Francisco, Dallas and Barbados.

The next country on the itinerary was Brazil where the first nightstop was at Manaus, which is on the Amazon. The crew visited an interesting hotel, which was built in the tops of trees with rope ladders and walkways. There were lots of monkeys around and a tank containing an electric eel, which could light a lamp. After Manaus it was on to Sao Paulo for one night where, because of warnings about how dangerous it was on the streets, we all stayed in the hotel. Our final visit in Brazil was the capital, Brasilia. This is such a boring city that all the locals push off to Rio de Janeiro at every opportunity. However, the crew were very kindly invited to a party at the Defence Attaché's house, which was a lot of fun.

That was the last official visit of the tour but as Prince Philip wanted to have a few days of R & R at Eleuthera we flew there from Brasilia via Belem and a night stop in Barbados. While he was at Eleuthera the crew had to put up with five days off in Nassau. Then it was homeward bound via Bermuda with a final twist. The last night stop should have been at Gander but the weather there was not good so we diverted to Halifax (Nova Scotia). This was a very good move as the crew and passengers were accommodated in the Sheraton hotel and, as it was my last night stop ever with the Flight, it was my pleasure to be the guest at a party given by the crew and Prince Philip, which included dinner followed by some entertainment in the crew bar. On the final day it was off to Gander, Keflavik, Heathrow and Benson. The trip took 104 flying hours and we covered 45,306 miles. It was truly a great swan song.

PERSONALITIES

11. The First Captain & Others 1936–1961

This chapter and the chapters that follow show just a quick pen-picture of some of the personalities who served under each successive Captain of The King's Flight and The Queen's Flight. Each chapter will be headed by the Captain and then the other Members alphabetically. Members who served under more than one captain are fitted in to help balance the length of the chapter. A description of the role of the Captain and that of the Officer Commanding is given in this chapter.

CAPTAIN OF THE QUEEN'S FLIGHT

The title 'Captain of The Queen's Flight' can be traced back to the London Gazette of 20 July 1936 which stated, inter alia: 'The King has been graciously pleased to make the following appointment to His Majesty's Household, to date from the 21st July 1936: Flight Lieutenant Edward Hedley Fielden, AFC, Captain of The King's Flight.'

'Mouse' Fielden, as he was known to all his friends, was the only pilot of the one and only aircraft of The King's Flight, and therefore 'Captain' accurately described his role. Later with twenty-two officers and one hundred and sixty airmen of many trades, together with three civilians, in The Queen's Flight, the Captain no longer flew the aircraft, but he was in overall command of The Queen's Flight with the responsibility for all aspects of its operations.

When The King's Flight was re-formed after the war, the Flight carried out about 130 Royal Flights a year, but since the introduction of helicopters in the mid-1950's there was a steady increase until the Flight was flying over five times that number of flights annually with the same number of aircraft. Many of those flights were overseas and required a considerable degree of planning and research; the Captain therefore had two Deputies, both serving Group Captains, to assist him in that task.

In addition to being responsible for everything that happened on the Flight, the Captain was required to advise HM The Queen and members of the Royal Family on all aspects of aviation; ranging from planning the air travel arrangements for a major State Visit overseas by The Queen, involving up to fifty passengers and eight tons of baggage, to arranging a parachute jump or a flight in a glider for one of the young Princes. The work was thus very varied and demanded a broad practical knowledge of all aspects of flying.

Special engineering rules were laid down by all three services for the preparation of military aircraft for flights by members of the Royal Family. These rules were designed not only to add that little bit of extra safety to the exercise, but also to ensure, as far as possible, that the aircraft would be one hundred per cent serviceable on the day. It was not feasible, therefore, for a member of the Royal Family to fly at very short notice in a military aircraft because it would not have been possible to carry out the necessary checks and prepare that aircraft in the limited time available. Of course, aircraft of The Queen's Flight were maintained at all times to those exacting standards and very short-notice Royal flights in their aircraft were occasionally carried out.

When The Queen flew overseas for a State Visit, the aircraft of The Queen's Flight were not big enough to take the load, so an aircraft was usually chartered from British Airways for the task. If flying to Australia, Canada or New Zealand, Her Majesty would probably be offered an aircraft from their Air Force or national airline; indeed, pilots and crews from those Commonwealth countries have rendered notable service in flying members of the Royal Family many thousands of miles safely and comfortably. However, the Captain of The Queen's Flight would have been closely involved with the planning for all such flights and would still accompany The Queen, even though the aircraft did not belong to The Queen's Flight.

In other countries it was a well-established procedure that The Queen would only fly in aircraft of The Queen's Flight (except in the USA, the President has on occasions invited her to make use of Air Force One). If, then, Her Majesty flew overseas in an aircraft of British Airways and wished subsequently to fly to an airfield that was too small for that aircraft to use, The Queen's Flight would pre-position its own BAE 146 or Andover for that particular exercise. Both aircraft had exceptionally good short-field performances and were well used to flying into remote airfields all over the world.

The Captain was an Extra Equerry to Her Majesty The Queen and was the only member of the Flight who was a member of the Royal Household. As such he was in constant touch with the Private Secretaries of those members of the Royal Family who flew with the Flight. He was responsible to the Chief of the Air Staff for the safe and efficient operation of The Queen's Flight and he was therefore in close contact with the Ministry of Defence, HQ Strike Command and HQ No.1 Group to ensure that the Flight was able to meet its tasks as effectively as possible.

OFFICER COMMANDING

The Captain of The Queen's Flight was in ultimate command, and with the assistance of two Deputy Captain's, he made all the detailed travel arrangements with the various Royal Households. The Officer Commanding had the responsibility to ensure that the aircraft were available to meet the tasks and that the Flight was correctly administered. The analogy given to explain the division of responsibilities was that the Captain could be likened to the travel agent who dealt directly with a customer and made the reservations, whereas the Officer Commanding was responsible for running the airline which then took the customer on his or her journey.

In the case of The Queen's Flight (in the Andover days), the airline consisted of three Andover fixed-wing aircraft and two Wessex helicopters and around 185 men of all ranks. To fly the Andovers there were four crews, the OC being captain of one, and there were three crews for the Wessex. As both HRH The Duke of Edinburgh and HRH The Prince of Wales flew the Andover and the Wessex whenever possible, one of the crews on each aircraft type were designated as the personal crew to each Prince and, as far as was possible, would always fly with them to provide an element of continuity.

To support the flying task, the Flight had its own dedicated engineering, administrative, operations, security and helicopter support staffs, relying on RAF Benson, the home station, only for accounting, medical and accommodation services. In a way, The Queen's Flight was a 'mini' RAF station within a station, and the OC's duties ranged far and wide, from dealing with the selection of officers to join the Flight, to welfare and discipline problems (few), to discussing aircraft servicing programmes with the Senior Engineering Officer. The OC also served as one of the Andover pilots and usually flew as the Captain of the aircraft carrying either HM The Queen or HM The Queen Mother.

With the sheer variety of responsibilities, coupled with varied and interesting flying the post of Officer Commanding was immensely satisfying, but all who have held the post agreed that the greatest satisfaction came from seeing the standards which were achieved by all the men and women who supported the flying task, and who were in fact The Queen's Flight.

Air Vice-Marshal Sir Edward Fielden GCVO, CB, DFC, AFC (deceased)

Captain of The King's Flight and The Queen's Flight. 21st July 1936 to 31st December 1961
Senior Equerry to The Queen, 1962-69; Extra Equerry to The Queen, 1970-76
Captain of The King's Flight, 1936-52; Captain of The Queen's Flight, 1952-62

Born 4th December 1903. Educated at Malvern and the Royal Air Force College. Joined the Royal Air Force Reserve 1929; Appointed Pilot to The Prince of Wales, 1929; Extra Equerry 1932; Equerry to King George VI, 1937; Extra Equerry to The King, 1946; Extra Equerry to The Queen, 1952. Died 8th November 1976.

Sir Edward ("Mouse") Fielden worked both for the Royal Air Force, which he joined in 1924 with a short service commission, and for the Royal Family. He became the private pilot to The Prince of Wales in 1929 and subsequently held an unbroken connection with the Royal Family for over 40 years.

When The Prince of Wales became King Edward VIII in 1936, he formed The King's Flight; Mouse Fielden was the only pilot of the one and only aircraft (a Rapide) and was appointed "Captain of The King's Flight" with the rank of Wing Commander in the Reserve. In 1952, on the accession of Queen Elizabeth II, the Flight became The Queen's Flight and in 1962, on relinquishing command he was created Senior Air Equerry to HM The Queen, which post he held until 1970. He was then appointed Extra Equerry until he died in 1976 at the age of 72.

When The King's Flight was disbanded in 1942, it formed the nucleus of No. 161 Squadron with Fielden as the Squadron Commander. This squadron was engaged in highly secretive work in connection with the French resistance movement, Fielden acting as pilot on many hazardous missions. For these operations the French awarded him the Legion d'Honneur and the Croix de Guerre avec deux Palmes.

Although the Flight was not reformed until 1946, he retained the appointment of Captain of The King's Flight throughout the war, because he was still responsible for any flying carried out by The King.

Mouse Fielden was a perfectionist in all his activities, and many of his exacting philosophies were continued until the disbandment of The Queen's Flight.

He cherished highly the honour that he had been decorated by four British Monarchs: George V (AFC 1929), Edward VIII (MVO 1936), George VI (DFC 1943, CVO 1943 and CB 1946) and Elizabeth II (KCVO 1952 and GCVO 1968).

Wing Commander T.H. (Archie) Archbell, DFC, RAF (deceased)

GD/Pilot: The King's Flight. 1944-1945

Born in Durban, South Africa in 1914. Archie was educated at Michaelhouse. He joined the Royal Air Force in 1938 and trained at Hamble and South Cerney. Posted to No. 216 (BT) Squadron in Cairo Heliopolis flying Valencias and Bristol Bombays.

In 1939 he was appointed OC the newly formed 173 Squadron with a variety of aircraft including: Loadstars, Proctor, Avro Anson, Argus, Audax Magister, Lysander, Lockheed, Beaufighter, Blenheim, Hurricane, Moth Major, Percival Golf, Scion Senior, Boston (VIP), Oxford, JU51, Savois-Machetti, SM79. Passengers flown included King George of Greece; Lord Trenchard and Generals Alexander; Montgomery; and Wavell.

In 1944 Archie was posted to Blakehill Farm as Wing Commander Operations for briefing and dispatching on D-Day. Flew Dakotas tugging Gliders and dropped paratroopers of 6th Division; conveyed casualties back from Normandy. Later in 1944 was posted to Hendon as OC No.24

Squadron then standing in for The King's Flight. Archie flew Their Majesties The King and Queen from the Channel Islands to Northolt; this was the first flight of a Queen of England.

On the stage Jersey to Guernsey he had an escort of 36 Spitfires whilst on the return trip from Guernsey to Northolt the Dakota was escorted by 36 Mustangs with Naval Vessels patrolling the seas below.

Another flight to Londonderry had TM The King and Queen and Princess Elizabeth as passengers. Archie well remembers flying Sir Charles Hambro to Germany and returning with 20 ex Prisoners-of-War from Hindelsheim who were in a shocking state of health.

In 1945 Archie took three weeks leave to go back to Durban and marry Betty, a girlfriend from before he joined the RAF. Betty remembers travelling to England on the Carnarvon Castle, like a troopship but comfortable and living at the Bedford Arms (£4.00 a week with three meals a day) in Oakley, then a village but now a housing estate.

In 1945 he was posted to No. 47 Group, near Bedford as Wing Commander Flying before moving on in 1946 to the RAF Staff College at Bracknell. Archie retired from the RAF in 1947 for personal reasons and returned to South Africa where he flew commercially until his left arm was severely injured in an accident (on the ground). He joined Unilever and spent twelve years in Salisbury, Rhodesia and Nyasaland before being transferred back to Durban and retirement in 1977. Both Archie and Betty enjoyed playing golf and travelling overseas for many years until Archie had a fall which restricted his movements. Sadly, Archie died on 12th March 2003.

Warrant Officer Victor Bennett, MBE
L Tech ST, The King's Flight, March 1949 – September 1950
L Tech ST, The Queen's Flight, January 1955 – 1965

Victor Bennett was born on 30th May 1929 and after receiving education at the Stanley Technical School in South Northwood, London, joined the Royal Air Force as an Aircraft Apprentice Instrument Maker on 13th February 1945.

He joined The King's Flight as a Corporal at the end of his improver year in March 1949 and stayed until September 1950 when he was posted to No. 82 Squadron at Takoradi, Gold Coast (Ghana) operating Lancaster's and Dakotas, carrying out map surveying.

After detachments to Lungi, Sierra Leone and Kano, Northern Nigeria, the Squadron moved to Eastleigh, Kenya with further detachments to Tabora, Tanganyika (Tanzania) and Livingstone, Northern Rhodesia (Zambia) until October 1952 when the Squadron returned to the UK to re-equip with Canberra aircraft.

Vic then jumped at an opportunity to re-join The Queen's Flight in January 1955 where he stayed for the next ten and a half years (which he admits were the most enjoyable of his career).

Vic, pictured (right) circa 1959, in the back of HRH Prince Philip's personal Heron, was Sergeant i/c the Instrument Section and was involved in three Royal Tours: Kenya and Uganda in 1959, India, Pakistan and Nepal in 1961, and Mexico and the Caribbean in 1964. During his time with the Flight he progressed through Chief Technician to Flight Sergeant.

He was then posted to Trade Standards where he spent three years producing and marking promotion exams. With promotion to Warrant Officer in September 1968, Vic was involved in getting Phantom Simulators into Coningsby where he stayed until 1980 when he moved to Cottesmore and a change of scenery to Tornado Simulators.

Vic remembers his time at Halton well. Having learnt to play the bagpipes in the Boys' Brigade he was greeted with open arms into the Apprentice Band which resulted in many outings including the Victory Parade, performances in the Royal Albert Hall, the Royal Tournament, Lord Mayor's Shows and Wembley Stadium. He was the leading piper for his last year at Halton. On one occasion he thought he was going to end up in police cells when, whilst piping a bunch of well oiled ex-apprentices along Victoria Street at about 10.00 p.m. during an apprentice reunion, they were surrounded by a number of policemen. Luckily, they only told them that it was all right up until 11.30 p.m. as long as they kept moving, so got a police escort instead!

As for The Queen's Flight Vic remembers well the "tasks" that were handed down from the top. Some of the tasks became legendary and members will no doubt remember such tasks as the five bar gate; the bucket; the tractors and the triangular collar stiffeners. There was a flourishing cricket team, which played against local village teams, and aviation companies such as Sperry Gyro and the tug-of-war team which twice won the Transport Command championships. He remembers there were some very good sportsmen on the Flight and that they usually did very well on station sports day.

Left to right: Norman Hooper, Ron Tooke, Vic Bennett (drinking), Alec Graham, Bill Williams and Wing Commander Hyland-Smith. Vic cannot remember what the trophy was for!

In 1959 Vic and his wife, Margaret, decided to move out of married quarters and buy a house locally, starting a trend on the Flight. Everyone thought they were crazy but were soon followed by Ron Tooke and Tony Johnson.

They moved into a house in 1961 at the cost of £2,705, which is now on the market at around £192,000. In those days an extra three shillings a day was payable if you found your own accommodation, which was essential to help with the mortgage.

Vic retired from the Royal Air Force on 30th May 1984 as **the** Senior Warrant Officer. During this time of almost forty years he was awarded the MBE, Meritorious Service Medal, War Service Medal, Long Service and Good Conduct Medal and Bar, plus an AOC-in-C's Commendation.

After retiring from the service, Vic worked on the Community Programme for a few years but his main interest has been as a case worker for SSAFA/Forces Help. At the age of 50 he took up singing and joined the Cranwell Singers and together with his wife, has performed in all the 11 most popular Gilbert and Sullivan operettas plus numerous other productions which has given a lot of pleasure to the people of Sleaford and District, besides raising quite a lot of cash for local charities. Otherwise life now remains very quiet!

Flight Sergeant Alfred Ernest BRYAN, BEM
The King's Flight, Electrical Fitter Air, February 1949–October 1949

Alf was born in May 1929 and educated at Barrow-in-Furness Grammar School. He became an Aircraft Apprentice at Halton in February 1945 followed by an Improver year at St. Athan before joining The King's Flight in February 1949. After TKF Alf served mostly with Bomber/Strike Command and Technical Training Schools with 5 years as a Systems Fitter (the RAF eventually called them Mis Fit) on THOR.

His final appointment was in the MOD Engineering Branch. In May 1969, Alf joined Works and Bricks under its various titles serving at the Royal Mint, RAF St. Athan, Driving Vehicle and Licensing Centre and as District Works Officer at Brawdy and Gutersloh before retiring in September 1998.

Wing Commander W. T. (Tom) Bussey, LVO, OBE, BEM, RAF (Ret'd)
Corporal, later Sergeant, The King's Flight. September 1939 – March 1942
Senior Engineering Officer, The King's Flight. 1st June 1948 – 1st June 1950
Senior Engineering Officer, The Queen's Flight. 21st November 1955–8th May 1961

William Thomas Bussey was born on 30th December 1913 and educated at a local school in middle of fen, two and a half miles from his home. Left School at 14 years of age. Tom joined the Royal Air Force in May 1935 as an Aircraftsman General Duties Group 5. Remustered to Fitters Mate Group 4. Later remustered again to Flight Mechanic Engine Group 2.

His first posting was to Cambridge University Air Squadron in May 1937 as a qualified LAC.

In September 1939 he was promoted to Corporal and posted to The King's Flight at RAF Benson. The Flight then consisted of one Airspeed Envoy and one Lockheed Hudson Aircraft. Tom recalls that on his arrival at The King's Flight the personnel were: Captain: Wing Commander E. H. Fielden, The Engineers; Flight Sergeant Jenkins and Sergeant Hussey plus Mr. G. Prescott, a civil servant and Secretary to the Captain.

"My first interview on arrival at The King's Flight was with Jenkins and Prescott. After much searching into my background and service I was told that they did not expect me to stay as the Captain (who was away for two weeks collecting the Hudson) had asked for someone to look after the whole aircraft and I was not qualified. However the Envoy had to be serviced ready to leave and I could do that and see the Captain on his return. I enjoyed this task and got on well with Hussey and Jenkins who seemed impressed with my work and my tools some of which I had made myself. I saw the Captain on his return and he agreed to let me stay for the time being due to the good report he had received from Jenkins. I was to fly with him the next day when the Envoy went into storage. A further member, LAC Reed, arrived with the Hudson. The Captain, Reed and I delivered the aircraft into storage and I was told that I could remain with the Flight permanently if I successfully completed the Hudson Airframe Course. This I did and went on to do the instrument course at Sperry, Brentwood, to enable me to qualify to service the aircraft away from base. Very little flying was done during the Phoney War, but with the fall of France I became especially busy. I did a Vickers K gun course (front gun on the Hudson) and a bombsight course.

At this time the C-in-C Bomber Command's aircraft arrived, a Percival Q6 with a two man servicing team. At the same time I sat a remustering examination to Fitter IIE and was promoted to

Sergeant. Just prior to the Battle of Britain I flew with Sir Charles Portal as he visited bomber crews returning from pounding the channel ports prior to the expected invasion. During the Battle of Britain I flew every flight with The Duke of Kent when he visited airfields in support of the hard-pressed pilots. We conveyed His Majesty The King to the Orkney Islands to visit the ships in Scapa Flow that had been recently attacked by aircraft.

Tom comments on the Engineering Pre-King's Flight: "Whilst I did not serve in the Prince of Wales Flight, i.e., before the advent of The King's Flight, my early experience with Jenkins and Hussey indicated a standard of aircraft maintenance far in excess of normal Service requirements at that time. In the early days of The King's Flight such high standards were implemented and maintained by careful selection of personnel, especially NCOs, and insisting on the very closest supervision by these people. This modus operandi was greatly assisted by extremely close liaison with the relevant aircraft company's nominated representatives".

Tom lists amongst his memorable moments having His Majesty King George VI on board the Hudson in 1941.

"The King's Flight was disbanded in March 1942 and we were all moved to Gravely in Bedfordshire to form 161 Squadron and subsequently moved to Tempsford. The Squadron was concerned with the clandestine operations and we were involved with the supply of equipment and personnel to the resistance organisations in Europe".

Tom was promoted to Flight Sergeant, awarded the British Empire Medal and mentioned in dispatches before leaving No.161 Squadron in 1943 for commissioning in the Technical Branch.

As a Pilot Officer, Tom was posted to India becoming the Officer Commanding 56 Staging Post at Santa Cruz. Promoted to Flying Officer and subsequently Flight Lieutenant on posting to Poona. Finally he was posted to Mauipar for one year before returning to England in September 1946. A tour at No. 49 Maintenance Unit, Lasham in 1946/47 was followed by No. 30 Maintenance Unit Sealand during 1948 before moving to Benson to join The King's Flight as their Engineering Officer for the period 1948-51. Appointed to be a Member of the Royal Victorian Order (MVO).

After leaving The King's Flight in 1951, Tom attended a Service Engineering Specialist Course at Henlow in 1952, before being posted overseas again to Air Headquarters, Habbaniya, Iraq as Eng.2. in 1953. Promoted to Squadron Leader. On returning to the United Kingdom in 1955, Tom was once again posted to Benson and The Queen's Flight as the Senior Engineering Officer; 1955-61. Promoted to be a Lieutenant in the Royal Victorian Order (LVO).

Among his memorable moments on The Queen's Flight, Tom remembers accompanying Her Majesty Queen Elizabeth II and Prince Philip on their visit to Kaduna (Durbar), Nigeria in 1956; accompanying His Royal Highness Prince Philip on his visit to Borneo Sarawak in 1959; and accompanying Her Majesty Queen Elizabeth II and Prince Philip on their visit to Nepal in 1961.

Posted to HQ Flying Training Command for two months before being promoted to Wing Commander and off to Malta as OC Engineering Wing RAF Luqa; 1961-65. Appointed to be an Officer of the Most Excellent Order of the British Empire. (OBE). Returning to the UK in 1965 to Command No.3 Apprentice Wing at RAF Halton until 1967 and then OC Engineering Wing at RAF Binbrook before retiring from the Royal Air Force in 1967.

Tom joined the National Coal Board smokeless fuel development team as Head of Services, Promoted Assistant Chief Engineer in 1970. Retired 1978. President of the Coventry Branch of the Royal Air Force Association in 1980/82, Tom is now active in the Chippenham Branch of RAFA.

Flight Sergeant A. W. (Buzz) Cousins, RVM, C Eng, MRAeS, AIMM
Instrument Fitter, The King's Flight. 1946-1951

"As a boy I won a scholarship to "Devonport High School", Plymouth. My father enrolled me in 'The Royal Naval Barracks Boy's Brigade, HMS Drake', but after moving to live in South Wales, I escaped from the Navy in 1938 by passing the examination to join the RAF as an Aircraft Apprentice Instrument Maker, at RAF Cranwell; No.1 E & W School. My hobbies were Horology, Philately and Photography.

War started in 1939 but there was no reduction in our 3 years apprenticeships and I joined the RAF proper in July 1941, as an AC1. Ten of my course was given flying instructions on a Vickers Valencia twin-engined Bi-plane transport aircraft, to ready us for "Auto Pilot specialisation". There were 5 operational sets of Smiths Mark 1a Auto-pilot set up in the cabin, in addition to the normal aircraft set – and all could be engaged at once – Mechanically – so 5 Instructors were carried to watch apprentices little fingers during training!

After a stint at No. 9 B. & G.S. Penrose, working on Whitleys, Blenheims, Harts, Fairey Battles, Bombays, Harrows and Henleys, (the Mark 1a Auto pilots in all but the Harts and Henleys were particularly interesting), I was posted overseas after a lot of air raids, during which the Luftwaffe put the camp hot & cold water systems out of action, and I put the camps Electrical supply out of action, (all sections constructed wooden "Tanks & Armoured cars" – to look as though we were well defended – unfortunately our Tank's long "Gun Barrel" shorted out the power and everybody had to be billeted in Pwllheli, until the camp was fit to occupy again!

As a Corporal, I found myself i/c the Instrument section of 3 Tiger Moth Squadrons, at SAAF Potchefstroom, in the Transvaal, South Africa, having been off-loaded in Capetown with 19 other NCO's, from the "Rieno Del Pacifico", a troopship on it's way to Singapore and we helped to expand the E.A.F.T.S. Luck was with me. During the next 3 years we worked on Tiger Moths, Airspeed Oxfords, Harvards, Miles Ministers with Mercury engines, training Pilots and Navigators. I did a stint at No 1 Air Depot, Voortrekershookta as a Sergeant, i/c Repair & Overhaul of Gyro Instruments, including the Sperry A3A Auto Pilot units, from the SAAF, and re-developed a great interest in Automatic Pilots. Returning to England in 1944, to Transport Command at RAF Great Dunmow in Essex, we worked on Halifax's, Stirlings, Wellingtons (Mark 4 & Mk. 8 Auto-pilots), Dakotas (Sperry A3A Auto-Pilots) and Horsa Gliders.

Victory in Europe Day (V.E. Day) was a memorable one for me – the day I earned my "nick name" BUZZ". It was my luck to draw duty as "Orderly Sergeant" that day – The camp was overrun with Army Glider Pilots, Americans, Poles and Czechoslovaks and every mess had bands and big parties. The Pilot Officer Orderly Officer and I entered the Airman's mess at 23.00 hours, to close it down. As we entered, the band stopped playing and the dancers all turned to look at us in dead silence. The O.O. turned to me, saluted and said, "Carry on Sergeant" in a loud voice and walked out! Surveying the scene I decided that there was only one thing to do and without saying a word I took off my hat, ceremonial belt and revolver and hung them on a coat rack. The band started playing again and the mob went wild. A WAAF sitting at a table just inside the entrance came over to me and said "What's your name Sarg" and then quipped 'What's buzzin cousin' and the next morning everybody in the camp was calling me "Buzz".

In 1946, whilst on embarkation leave to join an SDL team in Germany, (charged with discovering German Luftwaffe Instrument and Auto-pilot innovations which might help the RAF), I was recalled to an Air Ministry Board and posted to The King's Flight at RAF Benson. I was the first Senior NCO to arrive and be greeted by the Engineering Officer, Flight Lieutenant George Pearson. Wing Commander Bill Tacon arrived with Aircrew Members and the groundcrew arrived in droves. Flight Lieutenant Pearson had his hands full welding us into a team and preparing all trades for the projected Royal Tour of South Africa. (Details of the preparations and how Buzz became the SNCO i/c the Flight can be seen in Chapter 8, Engineering and the Engineers).

Before departure to South Africa, we were all kitted out with newly designed & manufactured Tropical Khaki, tailored from beautiful soft material instead of the normal RAF issue (organised by Air Commodore Fielden) and had our photographs taken in the civilian clothing we were to fly in, for Civil Passports were to be issued to transit through Libya. That passport caused me a lot of problems later on, travelling in the Middle East as a "Smiths Rep".

Years later, As a "Smiths Rep" I had "AFRICA" as my area of responsibility for 3 years – any Airline or Air Force in Africa with an Instrument, Auto Pilot, Pilot or Ground staff training problem – I was Mr. Fixit. The SAAF took delivery of a Squadron of Shackleton Mk.3. aircraft from Avros and I flew with them to Brooklyn Air Base, spending 2 months there. One day I visited the Sergeant's Mess and asked for FlightSergeant Lowe, the painter of the crests on the Vikings, but he had left the SAAF. I discovered that after TKF returned to England he had requested and been honoured by the granting of the Title "By Appointment to His Majesty King George VI", the first time that a serving SNCO had received such an honour – and he was now working as a Commercial Artist in civil life.

Her Royal Highness Princess Elizabeth's 21st Birthday was celebrated in Cape Town by a Gala Ball on April 21st, 1947. The Ball was held in the Town Hall and attended by most of the Aircrew. A few ground staff were co-opted for local duties – helping guests alight from their cars etc: and filling in wherever asked. When we had time off, getting out of camp was sometimes a bit of a problem – Local people were lined up with their cars at the gates, asking us to visit their homes for the weekend, or go on sightseeing trips around the Cape. They all wanted to entertain us – and the crew of HMS Vanguard had the same problem when leaving Capetown docks! We made many friendships with those most hospitable South Africans. I wasn't surprised at their actions – the same thing happened continuously during the war, outside every RAF and SAAF Air base and many RAF Airmen married South African wives, as a result.

One weekend three buses arrived in Brooklyn camp after the Wing Commander accepted an invitation for the whole Flight to visit a winery, at Stellenbosch, in the hills about 50 miles east of Capetown. It was a most interesting day, visiting the vineyards, sampling the wines, joining a string of natives, singing and dancing naked as they did the conga, round and around in great vats, stomping grapes into juice, sampling the wines, eating lunch, African fruits, sampling wines, tea and then returning to Brooklyn with buses full of crates of wine to sample! What a marvelous day out, with Sunday to recover! South African White wines are nearly as good as Australian! We had an uneventful return trip to Benson in April 1947.

A memorable occasion in 1948 was a visit to the flight by the 'Punch' Magazine cartoonist Mr. Pat Rooney. He was preparing drawings of many of our members, which eventually resulted in a full "centrefold" in an issue of 'Punch'. He presented many of his original drawings to members and I treasure my original.

Life was never dull on The King's Flight, there was always something new to do, or to learn, and the Air Commodore was always a source of "Foreigners" or "Gash jobs" to keep us occupied. Sometimes they were from his home, sometimes from Buckingham Palace and we had our share in the Electrical & Instrument sections. One memorable "job" was to clean and recondition a 40mm 'Bofors' gun barrel, which had been converted to fire buckshot from a punt, at ducks. The barrel hadn't been cleaned for years and we made a 'pull through' from a roll of emery cloth on the end of a broomstick. We had to splice new restraining and attachment ropes, to hold the barrel in the punt, but we never did see it in operation (reputably bagging a dozen ducks a shot). Watches, clocks, electrical equipment were interesting challenges.

On another occasion, Mr. Prescott brought me over a pewter teapot, "from Buckingham Palace", leaking where the spout joined the polished and engraved teapot body. Tommy Shore & I looked at it, decided to seal the joint inside the pot, with solder, to maintain it's outside appearance. My small soldering irons were obviously not man enough to transfer enough heat, so Tommy heated up his much larger Iron with a gas jet and I started to 'tin' the inside of the pot, ready to apply more 40-60 solder. Unfortunately we didn't realise that the melting point of Pewter was lower than the melting point of solder and the complete spout fell off! Cap in hand, I took the pieces into the Air Commodore's office. He turned to Mr Prescott and said "Take him to the Tower". You can't win them all! After that my "Crown" came through, substantive at that!

All good things come to an end and after 5 years, the end of my second 'tour' on The Queen's Flight, (as it was now re-named), was approaching. Then another even bigger surprise – Flight Lieutenant Lamb took me into the Air Commodore's office one morning – I was to be posted and he asked "Where in the RAF would you like to be posted"! I didn't have a clue! Eventually the Engineering Officer said "How about if I take Buzz on a tour of various Establishments, to see if their work is of interest to him, and if they will have him? We drew up a list of St. Athans, (Instrument training base); R.A.E; C.S.D.E. Radar Establishment, Air Ministry, with RAE Farnborough as my No.1 wish.

We went there first. A marvellous posting for anyone. The Scientist i/c the Instrument Laboratories was particularly interested in my Automatic Pilot experiences and General Instrument knowledge, but pointed out to us that only Commissioned Officers could be posted to the RAE. Stumbling block. But Flight Lieutenant Lamb thought of an answer and we visited CSDE at RAF Wittering. Wing Commander Otter was the OC and he grilled both of us for an hour, and then explained the work of CSDE. He suggested I be posted to his control, then after some indoctrination in CSDE requirement I would be sent on detachment to Farnborough, as he needed someone to join a team of Flight Sergeants led by a Flight Lieutenant to carry out investigations on Auto Pilot and Sperry Compass system problems. After TQF it is possibly the most interesting Establishment in the RAF, with the most interesting and demanding workload.

Life after The Queen's Flight: I spent a most interesting 5 months working at RAE Farnborough, after a fortnight at RAF Wittering, learning how to compose & write official reports before being posted on attachment to RAE. Early in January 1952, I was told that the RAF Adjutant, in the RAE Admin building, wanted to see me in his office, next to the RAF Orderly Room. As I walked into the Orderly Room, a strange performance was being acted out – The Orderly Room Corporal was standing over an LAC, who was kneeling in front of him, on the polished floor. The Corporal was touching the LAC on each shoulder, with a long wooden ruler – with not a word being said. He then used the ruler to point to the Adjutant's door and I went in; to be congratulated by the Adjutant on being awarded the Royal Victorian Medal (Silver) and he handed me a letter signed by Air Marshall Sir Aubrey Ellwood, KCB, DSC, announcing the award. (The letter had been forwarded from CSDE Winthorpe and took a little while to reach me).

My first investigation involved RAF Mosquitoes, employed on Air Sampling flights at very high altitude. The Mossies were stripped of everything possible, to fly as high as possible, but were experiencing navigation problems on their return to the UK. We had lots of Sperry Gyroscopic compass equipment, returned to RAE on 1022's for investigation, our team noticed that control box 'Yaxley' switches were broken, overriding their stops, (used to select the compass function, in the box). We visited Units & discovered that Pilots & Navigators were wearing two sets of 24 volt heated underwear & gloves, to combat the cold at 45,000 feet. This changed their manual dexterity – they just couldn't feel the switch stops & turned the knob too far – switching off Detector monitoring of the Gyro system – with disastrous results. There was no room to fit a beefier 'Paynton' or similar switch, so I invented a simple solution and made some 'cup washers' on a lathe, to fit under existing screws and stop the selector knob plate being turned any further. Sperry's put out an urgent Mod and their M.D. invited me to have lunch in the Director's canteen at Brentwood. I was offered a job "if ever I left the Air Force", as a Sperry Rep.

Back at CSDE, joining No.1.Team, I wrote the sections covering Instruments in the manuals for Jet Provost & Neptune aircraft & learnt all about time & motion study. I also helped with the 7 minute refuel & re-arm turn round study for the Hunter fighter. Meeting Frank King, Aviation Service Manager for Smith's Aircraft Instruments one day, he offered a job as a "Service Engineer" and helped get me out of the RAF before my "Queen's Year" had expired, at the end of my 12 year + engagement.

Smiths allocated 'Areas of responsibility' to their Engineers and Representatives, for 2 or 3 years, to work with Air Forces and Civil airlines in their 'area'. Set up servicing or overhaul facilities or investigate and fix problems. My history with Smiths was:

1952-54: England & Ireland, including monthly visits to The Queen's Flight, as a Service Eng, then as a service Rep; 1954-56: Anywhere in the Middle East, Istanbul to Calcutta (always jabbed up to move in 24 hours.); 1956-59: Anywhere in Africa, North and South. As a Service Representative. 1959-63: Europe, including 3 years as an "Honorary Hauptman" in the Deutche Luftwaffe. As Serv. Rep; 1963-67: Chief Inspector & Workshop supervisor of Smith's Industries LAP Depot, as a Senior Service Rep; 1967-69: Aviation Service Manager, Smiths Industries Australia Pty. Ltd. 1969-72: Servicing Co-ordinator, NIC Instrument Company, Essendon Airport, Melbourne; 1972-74: General Manager, Martin Electronics, Essendon Airport; 1972-2001 Proprietor, Kitson Electronics, (My own Instrument manufacturing company).

As you may see, I've travelled the world as a civilian, and it is surprising how many times this has revolved around experiences in the RAF & TKF in particular; Viking aircraft of several British airlines, and of Iraqi Airlines and Central African Airlines for instance and specialising in Autopilot work on SEP 1, Mark 9, SEP 2, Mark 10, SEP 5 (on RAF Belfast and BEA Trident aircraft) & SEP 6 system in Fokker F28. This travel presented marvelous opportunities to practice my hobbies of Stamp Collecting and Fishing.

I visited and flew with Air Lingus, BEA, BOAC, Middle East Airlines, Turkish Air, Iraqi Airlines, Misrair, Air India, Indian Air Force, German Air Force, South African Airways and SAAF, Central African Airways, to name a few, Including the RAF Valiant Squadron in a SAC competition in the USA.

One problem I had in Beirut was caused by my English Passport, issued in the RAF originally for the Royal Tour of South Africa and still in use, now over one inch thick. Arriving there from India, my passport was taken away & my bags were emptied and inspected three times, before an Immigration officer arrived and demanded "Where is your Uniform?" He said, "Your passport describes you as a Regular Airman in the RAF. We think you have come to Beirut to train rebel pilots and we are looking for your uniform"! Luckily the General Manager of Middle East Airlines was there and waited an hour – he certified that he had asked Smiths to send me to Beirut, to install and certify Smiths SEP 1. Autopilot Overhaul equipment, for Vickers Viscount 700 aircraft use – and I was freed. I soon had a new passport issued on return to England two months later!

Back in England for a while, promoted "Chief Service Representative", Smiths put me in charge of their new Technical Services workshops at London Airport. With ARB and MOD appointment as Chief Inspector, I also combined those duties with Workshop Supervisor, so controlled Service and Inspection – the first time that had been authorized, and all twenty of my Technicians became Inspectors as well as Service men. I ran a 24-hour Exchange service for Instruments and Autopilots for RAF Belfast aircraft and Airlines in England and anywhere in the world, guaranteeing a 24-hour turn-round time, even to China. (but it usually took 14 days to get the u/s item back from China, instead of the normal "over the counter" exchange system we ran).

Then one day, the General Manager of Smiths Australia offered me the job of Aviation Service Manager in Melbourne, and we became "Twenty Pound Poms". I had to recruit 20 service technicians to take with me, 19 migrated eventually, with their families. That job lasted less than two years before the company folded and I found local jobs for all except one technician, who returned to England with his family.

I transferred to N.I.C. Instrument Company, at Essendon Airport, as they took on Smith's Service needs, as "Servicing Co-ordinator", arranging Instrument service for the RAAF, RAN, TAA, Qantas, Ansett and G.A. aircraft, working closely with RAAF & RAN Representative Engineering Officers.

In 1969, the RAAF Resident Engineer Officer introduced my family to the pursuit of 'gold prospecting' and we joined a Prospecting Club, camping in the Victorian 'Golden Triangle' with our caravans whilst 'prospecting'. It's a most interesting & rewarding hobby the whole family enjoys, camping in the 'bush' for 5 to 10 days at a time and in 1969 I invented a prospecting metal detector, to avoid the back breaking 'Panning" method of seeking Gold.

Completing the manufacture & setting up of SEP 2. Autopilot service & overhaul equipment for the RAAF and TAA at NIC, I took on the appointment of General Manager of "Martin Electronics", also at Essendon Airport. The company had designed and put an EPIRB into production we had factories at Essendon & Bankstown, Sydney.

Whilst still at NIC, in 1972, and continuing my metal detector efforts, I invented and patented a "Letter Bomb Detector" & started my own instrument manufacturing company, Kitson Electronics (using my wife Marjorie's maiden name). One week later an order for 7 units arrived from the PMG and we were in business. After one of the first batch of 10 "Postal Protection Units" saved the life of Australia's Prime Minister (his security officer made the diagnosis), production went ahead and there are now six models, from simple hand operated, to conveyor systems, in operation worldwide (including three I donated to Her Majesty through (now Sir) David Smith at Government House in Canberra, who had already become a friend, and they were in the control of another Australian (also now Sir) William Heseltine, the Queen's Private Secretary at Buckingham Palace.

My 'aviation' interests continued. I had joined the Royal Aeronautical Society in England, became an Associate Fellow in 1974 and was Chairman of the Victorian Branch for four years in the 1980s. As an inventor, I joined the Inventors Association of Australia in 1972 and later was Victorian and Federal president for seven years, so you can appreciate that life in Australia is interesting and rewarding, in all fields of endeavour."

Group Captain J.E. (John) Grindon, CVO, DSO, AFC, RAF (Ret'd) (deceased)
Officer Commanding, The Queen's Flight. 1st March 1953 – 9th September 1956

 Born 30th September 1917 in Newquay, Cornwall just 26 days before his father was killed at Ypres; John was educated at Dulwich College and as a Flight Cadet at the Royal Air Force College, Cranwell, 1935-37. Joined 98 Squadron at Hucknall, Nottinghamshire equipped with Hawker Hind single-engined light bombers. In June 1939 he was posted to No. 150 Squadron, a Fairey Battle light bomber squadron that, shortly after the declaration of war, was despatched to France to support the British Expeditionary Force as part of the Advanced Striking Force.

Posted back home for a navigation course during the so-called "phoney war" in the winter of 1939-40 he missed Hitler's *blitzkrieg* drive to the channel coast. After two postings as an instructor in Canada and a spell on the navigation staff at Bomber Command John returned to operational flying as a flight commander with No.106 Squadron.

After five weeks and 13 operational sorties he was appointed the Officer Commanding of No. 630 Squadron equipped with Lancaster bombers. Shortly before the end of the war he took command of No. 617 Squadron, the Dambusters Squadron.

John served as Chief Instructor, Long Range Transport Force, 1946-49 and in training appointments before becoming the Officer Commanding of The Queen's Flight from March 1953 to September

1956. A tour as a V-Bomber Captain (Vickers Valiants) and Station Commander of RAF Honington followed in 1956-57.

Group Captain Grindon retired at his own request in 1959 and took up a career as a Director/General Manager in printing/publishing from 1961 to 1971 and with the Metropolitan Police, New Scotland Yard from 1976 to 1981. It was during the latter period that John discovered horse racing and after his second retirement he frequented racecourses several times a week until ill health prevented him doing so. Sadly he died on 11th November 2001.

Decorations: CVO 1957; DSO 1945; AFC 1948.

Chief Technician David Kennedy (Ken) Hicks, RVM
Airframe Fitter, The King's Flight and The Queen's Flight, 1951-1959

Ken (Taff) Hicks was born on 5th February 1922 and joined the Royal Air Force as a Halton Aircraft Apprentice (No: 574954 – 38th Entry) on 15th September 1938. On completion of his Apprentice Training in July 1940, Ken was posted, aged 18, to No.222 Natal Fighter Squadron at Kirton in Lindsey. The Squadron, equipped with Spitfires, soon moved to Hornchurch, and as an AC2 Fitter II Airframe, found himself thrown in at the deep end, just in time for the Battle of Britain.

Ken remembers: "Chiefy asked me "Can you draw?" I nodded, "Good, on every new Spitfire delivered to this Squadron I want you to paint the letters 'ZD' on the side of the fuselage, and then I'll tell you which letter to paint on the right of the roundel." I was kept busy, with three aircraft in the first week, two of them with the letter 'E'. On seeing other Spitfires with cannon and bullet holes being repaired, it dawned on me that the new aircraft were replacements for the Spitfires that had been shot down. With all the scrambles, bombing and night work I hardly had a thought what went on in the air.

I was keen to learn all I could about the Spitfire. I was detailed to work with an experienced fitter an LAC I GC, who referred to me as 'sprog'. My first job with him was a complete tail section change on a Spitfire, which had been shot to pieces with cannon shells. So with two spanners and a lead lamp I had to crawl inside the tapering fuselage to the rear end and undo 52 5/16ths nuts and bolts. It was August, it was hot, and in that confined space with no air, I began to wonder what I'd let myself in for. But, with the new unit bolted on and all the controls re-connected, I experienced a sense of achievement as I helped push the aircraft out of the hangar for ground runs and air test.

The next aircraft for us was a Spitfire of 603 Squadron that had a shell hole in the centre of the fuselage roundel, in through the red and out of the other side in the white 'inner ring'. That was a metal repair-riveting job. For small bullet holes, with no internal damage, the holes were filed smooth and a fabric patch doped on, anything to get it flying again. With three Spitfire Squadrons at Hornchurch, we were often called upon to work on other Squadron aircraft to spread the workload, which was the natural thing to do.

A bullet through the tail wheel tyre was a piece of cake to fix. Just four split pins and castellated nuts to undo, and split the hub, then slide on the new inner tube and tyre, assemble the hub, inflate and re-fit. Priority was given to an aircraft that could be finished that night, so we often burned the midnight oil to get the job done. On completion of the work we opened the hangar doors, pushed the aircraft out in the pitch black of the night and ran the engines until the exhaust stubs glowed. Enemy aircraft could be heard overhead, bombs were dropping in the distance leaving a red glow in the sky. Searchlights were converging to lock on, and shrapnel pieces from our own Ack-Ack guns were pita-patting all around us.

The Spitfire guns were freezing up at altitude, because there were gaps in the heater ducts from the rad to the guns. To put this right was one hell of a job, through a small round inspection hole under the wing, just sufficient to get one hand in at a time. The gaps in the round duct had to be sealed by fitting Basle Leather secured by two jubilee clips. All the aircraft had to be done, so I had to work nights on that job, talk about being a contortionist! I was in the hangar one day, when an instrument basher checking his air pressure gauge, pressed the firing button. They had pushed the wrong aircraft into the hangar – this one was armed! So there was me, crouched down behind my toolbox with armour piercing and tracer bullets whizzing around the hangar. I thought to myself " I could get unlucky in this game".

Was it dangerous on front line airfields? Well at 18 years of age I had no fear, everything was happening, it was exciting! RAF Hornchurch was buzzing with "Gen" most of it "duff", but the bombs were genuine, they made you stop and think that these guys are not playing; this is serious stuff.

One day I looked up and saw rows of brown earth jumping up in the air on the other side of the airfield, they were coming towards me, I could actually see the bombs leaving the Dorniers at about 6,000 ft., dozens of them. I did 100 yards in 10 seconds to the air raid shelter. Our airfield was bombed on August 24th, August 26th, twice on August 31st and twice on September 2nd. Not only did they bomb us by day but by night as well.

I was sitting in a lovely hot bath in the barrack block when a bomb landed right outside, what a predicament, it was pitch black and I was covered with slivers of window glass and red brick dust, and not much else – I thought "Get out of that one". A new cookhouse had been bombed, and I had been bombed out of my billet. A few nights later I was in a Sutton hospital ward when a land mine took the roof off over my head.

Six of us then had to sleep in a lean-to against the hangar – very convenient for our work. One morning we woke to find, right outside the lean-to, a green parachute and attached to it a big black land mine with a clock going tick-tock, tick-tock. Later I helped roll the disarmed land mine up two planks onto a lorry, which then took it to Canvey Island Flats, where it was blown up.

How well did we get to know the Pilots? Maintenance Personnel working in the hangar very seldom saw the Pilots. Occasionally one would come over and taxi a serviced aircraft back to the dispersal flights. Once at the entrance to the Station, I saw a Sergeant Pilot with a loosely bundled parachute under his arm having just thumbed a lift back to Camp after having had to bail out. I thought "Good on you mate". I'd buy him a drink any day, and on my money that would have been a big item, as I was only getting three pounds and ten shillings a week.

On two occasions I was fortunate to strap Douglas Bader into his cockpit, this was at Coltishall, where his aircraft was parked just outside his hangar office. Although he was OC of the other Squadron, Chiefy used to grab me to see him off. As for his flying – we all thought he was a nutter, without warning, he used to fully open the throttle and blow you off the wing of the aircraft. Still he was GOD.

One day I remember, when the airfield was being bombed and we were in the air raid shelter I heard an aircraft taxying, looking out I saw a Hurricane with the Pilot beckoning me with his arm. I ran out and jumped on the wing. He was a Polish Pilot and he was lost, he said, "Where am I?" The map he had on his knee was of the East Coast, so I turned it over and pointed to Hornchurch. He then gave me the thumbs up, checked his fuel gauge and promptly took off again.

As far as our social life was concerned, I remember having quite a few days off. On these occasions the favourite was to catch the tube to the Smoke and do the West End. There was always one of us who knew the ropes, and provided we were back at work the next morning everything was OK. The Red Caps were always a bit of a menace so we gave them a wide berth. One of our Squadron ACH GD's had a car and he often used to run us places, the snag was that Chiefy knew about this, so he used to say "Harvey – I want to borrow your car tomorrow night, make sure it's full of petrol won't you?" Petrol coupons did not run to much so aviation fuel was used to give the old car a bit of a boost.

I didn't have any leave during the Battle of Britain; it never entered my head to have any. Some of the blokes used to have compassionate leave but we felt sorry for them, as it was usually a sad tale that they told. The food in the cookhouse was nothing to write home about, but it was wholesome and adequate. The food rationing was strict for us, and we did not mind that the aircrew used to get extra flying rations.

One always felt that you were part of your Squadron and were proud to be part of that Squadron but the blundering Air Ministry Records Office used to post us individually willy-nilly at the drop of a hat. The consequence was, just when you had a good servicing team running smoothly you were split up and posted away, invariably overseas, never to see each other again".

In 1941 Ken was posted to Rhodesia with the Rhodesian Air Training Group, serving at 28 EFTS Mount Hampden (March 41), then RNAS Wingfield, Capetown (Oct 43), and PDC Capetown until 1944. Returning to the UK and Wales to 78 MU Binea, St. Athan and 45 MU Llandow (1944-45) before another overseas tour in Egypt and the Middle East serving at PDC Middle East (Jan 46) and 133 SP at RAF Almaza (1946) before going on to 231 Wing at Kabrit and 107 MU at Kasfereet in 1947.

In 1948 and 1949 Ken was at No. 2 School of Technical Training at Cosford before posting to Abingdon for Operation Plain Fare, the Berlin Airlift, and service at RAF Gatow working on York, Dakota and Hastings aircraft.

After eight months at Bassingbourn, Ken joined The King's Flight as a Corporal/Technician on 29th November 1950, promoted to Sergeant and then Chief Technician in 1954 whilst serving and finally left The Queen's Flight on 11th May 1959. He was awarded The Royal Victorian Medal (Silver).

One of Ken's biggest achievements whilst serving was in the sport of sailing having been selected to represent Transport Command; the Royal Air Force; Inter-Services; and Inter-Services versus University. Ken gives a big thanks to The Queen's Flight for allowing him the time off to take part in this activity.

After leaving The Queen's Flight, Ken was posted to Germany with No. 79 Squadron equipped with Swifts as part of the 2nd Tactical Air Force, stationed at RAF Gutersloh (1959); RAF Jever-Sylt, (1959-61) and back to Gutersloh in 1961 before joining 71 MU at Bicester at the end of 1961, Little Rissington, Hullavington in 1963, with short stays at St. Mawgan, Upavon, Bassingbourne and Chivenor before returning to RAF Benson in November 1963.

Retiring from the RAF on 1st June 1968 Ken went to work for the Martin Baker Ejection Seat Company until 1972 when he joined Austin Rover Unipart Company at Cowley before his final retirement thirteen years later in 1985. Now well into his final retirement Ken spends many hours looking after welfare cases for the British Legion and is a strong supporter of the Royal Air Forces Association at their Oxford Branch.

Pilot Officer T. Jenkins, MVO, RAF (Ret'd)
(Originally Mr, later Flight Sergeant, later commissioned)

Mr. T. Jenkins (left) joined 'Mouse' Fielden in 1927 in the early days of Royal Flying as the engineer. Jenkins or 'Jenks' as he was known, remained with Fielden on The King's Flight (Flight Sergeant) and in No. 161 Squadron at Tempsford. (Pilot Officer) (right)

Air Commodore Sir (Arthur) Dennis Mitchell, KBE, CVO, DFC*, AFC (deceased)
Deputy Captain, The Queen's Flight, 6th November 1956 – 7th October 1959

Born 26th May 1918, Sir Dennis was educated at the Nautical College, Pangbourne and the Royal Air Force College at Cranwell. Joining the RAF in 1936, he served in India, Burma, UK and North-West Europe during the war years from 1938-1945.

He attended the Army Staff College, Camberley and later the Flying College at RAF Manby.

From 1948 to 1949 he was serving at RAF Delegn in Belgium, then with the US Air Force, from 1951 to 1953, and with the Headquarters Allied Air Forces Central Europe, NATO, at Fontainebleau from 1953 to 1956, until he was appointed the Deputy Captain of The Queen's Flight in 1956.

Leaving The Queen's Flight in 1959 he was appointed OC RAF Cottesmore in Bomber Command from 1959 to 1962, before returning to be the Captain of The Queen's Flight from 1962 to 1964. He was appointed ADC to The Queen, in 1958-62 and has held the appointment as an Extra Equerry to The Queen since 1962.

After leaving the Royal Air Force, Sir Dennis founded Brussels Airways; Aero Distributors SA; Founder and Managing Director, Aero Systems SA since 1972; General Agent, Spantax SA. Sadly Sir Dennis died in Brussels on Christmas Day 2001.

Decorations: KBE 1977; CVO 1961; DFC 1944, Bar 1945; AFC 1943; Awarded French Croix de Guerre, 1945.

Dennis A. Sealey
Instrument Repairer I, The King's Flight, June 1946–March 1949

Born on 2nd March 1922, Dennis went to school in Walthamstow, London before joining the Royal Air Force as a Boy Entrant trainee instrument fitter at RAF Cranwell in February 1939. Dennis says that his career continued without distinction or much promotion (he says three years in the Sudan didn't help) until he joined The King's Flight in June 1946.

He well remembers being on the Royal Tour of South Africa in 1947 when HRH Princess Elizabeth was celebrating her twenty-first birthday and on that day was given about twenty minutes to get on his "best blue" and join the Captain, the OC Wg. Cdr Bill Tacon and Warrant Officer Morrison before being driven to Government House where they were received by Sir Michael Adeane, the King's Private Secretary.

The party were each introduced to the Princess, glasses of sherry raised and a toast, proposed by the Captain, followed by the presentation of a diamond set brooch in the shape of RAF Wings, which appeared to greatly please the Princess. Thirty-nine years later, at the reception at St. James's Palace to celebrate fifty years of Royal Flying, he knew HM The Queen would most probably be wearing the wings brooch and so with a bit of pushing and the help of the Captain, Sir John Severne, he was able to have another chat with Her Majesty. A couple of moments that he cherishes and which he thinks are unique. Dennis only served ten years in the RAF before retiring to enter into business in his own account as a Watch and Clock Repairer and Jeweller.

Group Captain Roy Charles Edwin Scott, CBE, MVO, AFC*(deceased)
Officer Commanding, The King's Flight. 1st January 1950 – 31st July 1952
Officer Commanding, The Queen's Flight. 1st August 1952 – 28th February 1953

Born 11th January 1918 and educated at Wellington College, New Zealand; and Victoria University, he joined the Royal New Zealand Air Force in 1939 (Reserve 1938); and served in the Royal Air Force from 1940 until 1968.

He flew with No's 207 and 103 Squadrons in Bomber Command from 1940 to 1941 until moving to Flying Training Command in 1942 and to Transport Command in 1943. He attended the Royal Air Force Staff College.

As a Wing Commander he was appointed OC Transport Command Examining Unit 1946-49, and in 1950 was appointed OC The King's Flight, until 1952, when he became the OC The Queen's Flight after the death of the King, until 1953.

Group Captain Scott served as the Air Attaché, Berne from 1953 until 1956. He became the Deputy Director of Air Transport Operations, at the Ministry of Defence in 1961 before becoming the Deputy Air Commander, Borneo, from 1964 until 1965.

Retiring from the Royal Air Force in 1968, he worked in the Department of the Environment until 1971, when he was appointed Principal of the College of Air Training at Hamble, where he worked until 1981. He died on 2nd July 1982.

Frederick William Silvester, RVM
A Fitt E, The King's Flight 1948–1953; A Fitt E, The Queen's Flight, 1956–1966

Fred Silvester was born on 13th July 1921 and went to the Polytechnic Secondary School in Regent Street, London. He joined the Royal Air Force as a twenty-year old in July 1941 and after training as an Aircraft Fitter Electrical saw service at 13 OUT, RAF Harwell; 51 Base, RAF Swinderby; Emergency Landing Unit, RAF Woodbridge; RNAS Lee-on-Solent; RNAS Eglinton; and Transport Command Development Unit, RAF Brize Norton.

Fred was posted to The King's Flight at RAF Benson in August 1948 until October 1953 and posted back again to The Queen's Flight in December 1956 to March 1966. Most of his time at Benson was spent as SNCO i/c Electrical Section. He was awarded the Royal Victorian Medal (Silver) for his contribution to Royal Flying.

He retired from the Royal Air Force in February 1974 from RAF Brize Norton holding the rank of Warrant Officer.

Air Chief Marshal Sir (Thomas) Neville Stack, KCB, CVO, CBE, AFC (deceased)
Deputy Captain. 15th July 1959 – 25th November 1962

Born 19 Oct 1919, educated at St. Edmund's College, Ware and Royal Air Force College Cranwell. Sir Neville Served on flying boats during the war, 1939-45 (mentioned in despatches); and stayed with Coastal Command from 1945-52;

A change to Transport Support flying in Far East and UK from 1954-59 followed, before his appointment as Deputy Captain of The Queen's Flight from July 1959 to November 1962.

After leaving The Queen's Flight he returned to Transport Support in the Far East during 1963-64, before returning to the UK as Commandant at the RAF College, Cranwell from 1967-70 and returning overseas again as UK Permanent Military Deputy CENTO, Ankara from 1970-72.

Knighted in 1972, Sir Neville became AOC-in-C, RAF Training Command from 1973-75, and appointed to be the Air Secretary, from 1976-78. He was appointed Air ADC to The Queen 1976-78. Gentleman Usher to The Queen 1978-89 and Extra Gentleman Usher since 1989.

On retirement from the Royal Air Force, Sir Neville became Director-General of Asbestos International Association from 1978-89; became a Member Council CRC 1978 (Member Executive Committee 1978-88); President of Old Cranwellian Association; Governor of Wellington College 1978-90; A Freeman of the City of London and a Liveryman of the Guild of Air Pilots and Air Navigators. FRMetS; FBIM 1978-88.

Decorations: KCB 1972 (CB 1969); CVO 1963; CBE 1965; AFC 1957;

Air Commodore E. W. (Bill) Tacon, CBE, DSO, LVO, DFC*, AFC*, RAF (Ret'd)
Officer Commanding, The King's Flight. 1ˢᵗ May 1946 – 31ˢᵗ December 1949

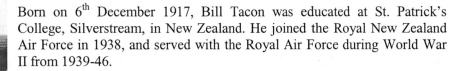

Born on 6ᵗʰ December 1917, Bill Tacon was educated at St. Patrick's College, Silverstream, in New Zealand. He joined the Royal New Zealand Air Force in 1938, and served with the Royal Air Force during World War II from 1939-46.

Serving with Coastal Command flying Beaufighters he was shot down over Den Helder in 1944 and was held Prisoner of War for nine months.

Bill transferred to the RAF in 1946 and was appointed Officer Commanding, The King's Flight at RAF Benson from 1946 to 1949. One incident that Bill relates with relish, and for which he received a reprimand, was with The King sitting in the right hand seat on a Viking flight, when he commented that he believed these planes could fly on one engine. Bill said, "Look out the left hand window sir". When he did so he saw that Bill had feathered that engine. The powers that be were not amused.

Overseas tours as OC Flying Wing, Fayid, Egypt (Canal Zone) from 1951 to 1953 and as Station Commander, RAF Nicosia, Cyprus, from 1955 to 1958.

Appointed Lecturer at the School of Land/Air Warfare, at Old Sarum, from 1960/61, he was appointed Commander Royal Air Force, Persian Gulf, from 1961 to 1963. Returning to the UK he was appointed Commandant, Central Fighter Establishment, 1963-65, and Air Commodore, Tactics, HQ Fighter Command Bentley Priory, from 1965 to 1968. His final tour was as AOC Military Air Traffic Operations from 1968 to 1971.

Now retired and living in Auckland, New Zealand where, sadly, it has been reported in February 2001 that he has suffered a series of strokes and is now in hospital care. His sight is very poor and he is unable to write or walk though he is mobile through use of an electric chair.

Decorations: CBE 1958; DSO 1944; MVO (4ᵗʰ Class now LVO), 1950; DFC 1940 (Bar 1944); AFC 1942 (Bar 1953).

Captain (Ernest) Brian Trubshaw, CBE, MVO, FRAeS (deceased)
Flight Lieutenant Pilot, The King's Flight, 1946–1948

Brian Trubshaw was born on 29ᵗʰ January 1924 and educated at Winchester College.

He joined the Royal Air Force in 1942, completing his flying training in the USA flying a Stearman biplane.

He served with Bomber Command in 1944 flying Stirlings and Lancasters until in 1945 he was posted to Transport Command until 1946.

Being rated 'exceptional' as a pilot he joined The King's Flight in 1946 until 1948 when he became a student at the Empire Flying School in 1949 and then instructed at the Royal Air Force College at Cranwell from 1949-50 before leaving the service in 1950.

Brian had a most distinguished career in Civil Aviation and will be most remembered for being the first Briton to fly the Concorde. He was given permission to leave the RAF in 1950 to become an experimental test pilot for Vickers Armstrong where he remained for thirty years becoming chief test pilot in 1960 and Director of Test Flights in 1966 until 1980. Brian worked on the development of the Valiant V-Bomber, the Vanguard, the VC10 and the BAC 111. In 1980 he became Divisional Director and General Manager (Filton), Civil Aircraft Division BAe plc until he ended his career in 1986. He became a part-time member of the board of the Civil Aviation Authority from 1986 until 1993 and worked as an aviation consultant.

In 1962 the British and French Governments signed an agreement to develop a supersonic transport aircraft and Brian was selected as the BAC test pilot. He piloted Concorde on its first British Flight from Bristol Filton to RAF Fairford in Gloucestershire on 9th April 1969. He continued with the programme after the test flight and, on January 21st 1976, flew the British version to Bahrain on its first commercial passenger flight.

Brian Trubshaw was appointed MVO in 1948, an OBE in 1964 with subsequent promotion to a CBE in 1970. He received many aviation awards and honorary appointments including Warden, Guild of Air Pilots 1958-61; Fellow, Society experimental Test Pilots, USA; Hon DTech Loughborough 1986; Derry and Richards Memorial Medal in 1961 for his work on the Valiant jet bomber and again in 1964 for saving Britain's prototype VC-10 from disaster on an early test flight; Richard Hansford Burroughs Memorial Trophy (USA), 1964; R.P. Alston Memorial medal 1964; Segrave Trophy 1970; Air League Founders' Medal in 1971 for his outstanding work on the development of Concorde; Iven C. Kinchloe Award, USA, 1971; Harmon Aviation Trophy, 1971; Bluebird Trophy, 1973; and the French Aeronautical Medal, 1976. He died in his sleep at his home in Tetbury, Gloucestershire on 24th March 2001.

Air Marshal Sir Richard Wakeford, KCB, LVO, OBE, AFC
Officer Commanding, The Queen's Flight. 1st July 1959 – 1st January 1961

Photograph shows Wing Commander R. G. Wakeford, OBE, AFC, taking delivery of the second Westland Whirlwind HCC8, XN127, on 5th November 1959. Flight Lieutenant John M'Kenzie-Hall and Flight Lieutenant Ralph Lee behind

Born 20th April 1922. Richard was educated at Montpelier School, Paignton and Kelly College, Tavistock.

Joining the Royal Air Force in 1941 and after training flying Catalina flying boats in Coastal Command from 1942 to 1945, operating out of India, Scotland, and Northern Ireland.

A change of role saw him flying Liberator and York transport aircraft on overseas routes from 1945 to 1947 when he attended a course at the Central Flying School and graduated to become a flying instructor at the Royal Air Force College at Cranwell before moving on to the Central Flying School Examining Wing 1947 to 1952. Ground appointments from 1952 to 1958 included two years on the staff of the Director of Emergency Operations in Malaya.

Sir Richard was appointed Officer Commanding, The Queen's Flight from July 1959 to January 1961. A tour on the Directing Staff, RAF Staff College followed until 1964 and subsequently appointments as Officer Commanding RAF Scampton; SASO, HQ 3 Group Bomber Command; Assistant Commandant (Cadets) RAF College, Cranwell.

He attended the Imperial Defence College in 1969 before being appointed Commander Northern Maritime Air Region, and Air Officer Scotland and Northern Ireland, 1970 to 72 and Director of Service Intelligence, Ministry of Defence, from 1972 to 1973. A posting overseas as ANZUK Force Commander in Singapore from 1974 to 1975, was followed by an appointment as Deputy Chief of Defence Staff (Intell) from 1975 to 1978.

Sir Richard has also held the following appointments: HM Commissioner, Queen Victoria School, Dunblane; Vice-Chairman (Air) Lowland T&AVR; Trustee, McRoberts Trusts (Chairman 1982-); Director: Thistle Foundation; Cromar Nominees; CStJ 1986. Secretary, RAF Benevolent Fund, Scotland since 1978.

Air Commodore James Wallace, DSO, LVO, DFC, AFC (deceased)
Deputy Captain. 25th April 1960 – 5th August 1962

Born 28th July 1918. Educated at Mountjoy School and Kilkenny College, Ireland. Joined the Royal Air Force in 1938.

He served in the Middle East, 1939-41; with the Desert Air Force 1941-43; psa 1942; In Italy 1943-44 and North-East Europe, 1944-48; Appointed Officer Commanding No. 41 Squadron, Fighter Command, 1949-51, before joining Fighter Command Duxford Wing, 1951-53: jssc 1953; British Joint Staff, Washington, DC, 1954-56; NATO (France), 1956-58; Fighter Command, 1958-60:

Appointed Deputy Captain of The Queen's Flight 25th April 1960 to 5th August 1962 before becoming Director of Public Relations (RAF) MOD, 1964-67; and retiring from the Royal Air Force in 1967. Civilian appointments held include, Spitfire Productions Ltd, 1967-70: Director, Promotor (Europe) Ltd, 1970-73; Area Warden, Wiltshire National Trust 1974-75; Walsh Security Service, London Hilton, 1976-77. Air Commodore Wallace died 17th September 1980.

Decorations: DSO 1944; LVO 1962; DFC 1942; AFC 1953; Legion d'Honneur, Croix de Guerre (French), 1945.

12. The Second Captain & Others 1962–1964

Air Commodore Sir (Arthur) Dennis Mitchell, KBE, CVO, DFC*, AFC (deceased)
Captain, The Queen's Flight. 21st March 1962 – 1st August 1964

Born 26th May 1918 at Staplehurst in Kent, educated at Bloxham School, Banbury and the Nautical College, Pangbourne before becoming a Cadet at the RAF College, Cranwell. The Army Staff College, Camberley and RAF Flying College, Manby.

Joined the Royal Air Force in 1936, served from 1938 to 1945 in India, Burma, UK and NW Europe. He was awarded a DFC and Bar in 1944 for his courageous leadership of squadrons under his command in the north-west Europe Campaign.

He became an exceptional and highly experienced pilot. In the late 1930's he had honed his flying skills over the unforgiving mountainous terrain of the North-West Frontier of India. Flying a No.20 Squadron biplane Hawker Audaw he provided cover for trucks supplying the forts guarding the Kyber Pass. This involved several hours on patrol followed by overnighting at a fort with a lively evening guaranteed.

Returning from one such mission, his Audax was brought down by a tribesman's shot which hit the plane's radiator. Fortunately, he was rescued by a passing armoured car, and thus spared from presenting the tribesmen with the "goolie chit" which was carried by pilots patrolling dissident tribal areas and promised a handsome reward in gold for returning them with their private parts intact.

After two years of frontier fighting, Dennis became an instructor until December 1941 when he was posted to No. 146 Squadron, an operational squadron still equipped with the obsolete Audax. With the fall of Singapore early in 1942 and the invasion by the Japanese of Burma the RAF were in desperate need of modern aircraft, so some 100 Curtiss Mohawk American fighters were landed at Karachi. After being assembled at No. 301 Maintenance Unit, he air tested them before they were delivered to operational squadrons. He was awarded the AFC in 1943.

On his return to the UK at the end of 1943, the Air Ministry intended to send him on an extended flying training course instead of an operational unit. He attracted the attention of Air Vice-Marshal Basil Embry, the AOC of No. 2 Group, of the 2nd Tactical Air Force and so was given a posting in February 1944 to No. 226 Douglas Mitchell Squadron and took command in June.

As OC he led perilous cross-channel daylight attacks on enemy communications targets and airfields in preparation for the invasion of Normandy. In 1944 he was awarded the DFC early in the north-west Europe campaign and received a Bar after its conclusion. In the final weeks of 1944 Air Vice-Marshal Embry called him to use his experience at No. 2 Group Headquarters and also in a special posting to the Group's No. 139 Wing, which included No's 98, 180 and 320 Mitchell squadrons.

A subsequent citation paid tribute to Dennis Mitchell's "inspiring leadership, untiring efforts, courage and high standards of operational efficiency in squadrons under his command". Referring to a period of intensive bombing operations prior to the final assault on the German Army, the citation praised his "constant supervision of the organisation on the ground and leadership of attack on the more difficult targets that materially contributed to the effectiveness of a long series of operations"

During the post-war 1940's he served at No. 2 Group Headquarters, British Air Forces of Occupation, No.84 Group and the Air Ministry, before learning to fly the Gloster Meteor, the RAF's first jet fighter.

Following a brief spell as OC of No. 26, a Hawker Tempest Squadron in Germany, he was posted to Brussels in 1948 as a member of an RAF delegation responsible for determining the need of the future Belgian Air Force. In this period he met and married Comtesse Mireill Cornet de Ways Ruart.

His next posting was to the US Tactical Air Command Headquarters, 1951 – 1953, where he volunteered for a tour with the United States Air Force in the Korean theatre which included difficult and dangerous flying. To reassure his wife, he told her he was on a four-month flying course and arranged for a friend based there to send a weekly postcard describing the joys of golf and swimming! His next posting was to the training, plans and inspectorate division of Allied Forces Central Europe at Fontainebleau in France during 1953 – 1956.

Appointed Deputy Captain of The Queen's Flight at RAF Benson in 1956 until 1959, at a busy time when the two-engine Vickers Viking were being retired in favour of the four-engine de Havilland Herons and two helicopters were being added. It was also a busy period for Royal Tours which included HM The Queen Mother's visit to Australia in 1958 and, later that year HRH The Princess Margaret's tour of Canada, the West Indies, British Guiana and British Honduras. In 1958 he flew on tours to South America and Nigeria. He was appointed ADC to The Queen in 1958.

In 1959 he was appointed Officer Commanding RAF Cottesmore, Bomber Command until 1962.

Returning to The Queen's Flight as Captain in 1962, he was appointed Extra Equerry to The Queen. His arrival coincided with the replacement of the Herons by two-engine turboprop Hawker Siddeley Andovers. It is said that the Treasury resisted purchase of the Andovers but when the Captain bluntly informed officials that in the absence of Andovers it would be better to hand the entire Royal operation to BOAC, funding became quickly available.

After leaving The Queen's Flight and retiring from the RAF in 1964, Air Commodore Dennis Mitchell founded Brussels Airways, an air taxi operation, and went on to develop Aero Distributors in Belgium. He was the Founder and Managing Director, Aero Systems there in 1972 and became the representative on the continent of leading British and American aviation companies.

Decorations: KBE 1977; CVO 1981; DFC 1944 Bar 1945; AFC 1943. Awarded French Croix de Guerre, 1945. Sir Dennis died in Brussels on Christmas Day 2001 aged 83.

Air Vice-Marshal D.L. (Donald) Attlee, CB, LVO, DL
Officer Commanding, The Queen's Flight, 2nd January 1961–21st July 1963

Born 2nd September 1922. Educated at Haileybury. Completed Pilot training in Canada, 1942-44; and remained a Flying instructor from 1944-48.

Appointed to Staff Duties at Training Command, 1949-52; before joining No. 12 Squadron, 1952-54; Posted to Air Ministry, Air Staff, 1954-55; and RAF Staff College in 1956; back to flying with No. 59 Squadron, 1957-59.

Appointed Officer Commanding of The Queen's Flight, 2nd January 1961 until 21st July 1963: before moving to HQ RAF Germany, 1964-67; and returning to be the Officer Commanding of

RAF Brize Norton, 1968-69; Attended Imperial Defence College in 1970; before moving to MOD Policy Staff, 1971-72; Director of RAF Recruiting, 1973-74; Air Commodore Intelligence, 1974-75; AOA Training Command, 1975-77 before retiring in 1977.

Became a fruit farmer 1977-2000. Chairman, Mid-Devon Business Club, 1985-87; Member Board of Mid-Devon Enterprise Agency, 1983-93; Member Mid Devon District Council 1982 until May 2003 (Vice-Chairman 1987-89, Chairman 1989-91); Deputy Lieutenant Devon 1991.

Decorations: CB 1978; LVO 1964.

Warrant Officer J. James Baker, RVM, BEM (deceased)
Royal Air Force Police, The Queen's Flight, Easter 1962–July 1972

Jim Baker was born on 25th July 1917 and went to the small village school at Crux Easton in Hampshire. Prior to his enlisting in the RAF he was employed as Under Gamekeeper on Lord Carnarvon's Estate at Highclere, Berkshire from 1931 to 1938 when all the young employees were laid off because of the 1939-45 war looming on the horizon. Jim was then employed as Under Gardener to the Nicholson Gin Owner from 1938 to 1940.

27th March 1940 saw Jim Baker enlisting in the Royal Air Force at RAF Cardington (that place sounds familiar – editor) and off to square-bashing at Morecambe. His first posting was to RAF Brize Norton hoping to muster to Mechanical but finished up on a RAF Police Course for six weeks at RAF Uxbridge. On the Passing-Out Parade of No. 191 Course, Jim was selected as the smartest 'Irk' on parade, then with five others of different trades paraded outside Station Headquarters to be presented to HM King George VI. It was a very hot day so all six 'Irks' was allocated an airman each to prevent their buttons from tarnishing and to remove dust from their shoes. Standing to attention for 45 minutes in the glowing sun before The King arrived, Jim was asked "How long have you been here?" and was about to reply when the OC replied "Six weeks your Majesty", the latter replied "Standing here in this heat", dead silence from the OC.

On posting after the course Jim was to join the elite RAF Mobile Police that comprised one Sergeant and six acting Corporals. The job was mostly of a disciplinary nature being moved from one location to another wherever there was an influx of servicemen.

Posted to Iceland in 1942 and employed as RAF Dock Police at Reykjavik docks. Escorted on motor cycle all heavy equipment, cranes, earth moving equipment to move and excavate lava rocks etc. for the new airfield which is now Keflavik. Awarded BEM for Bravery whilst in Iceland.

Returning to the UK early in 1945 and stationed at Princes Gate Court, South Kensington he fell foul of a 70-year-old Officer Commanding and was posted back to Iceland on the day Germany surrendered. On the way, by train, to Gourick, people everywhere were going crazy with excitement due to the war being over. Boarding a Yankee bottomed boat called the 'Florence Nightingale' the tannoy blurted out "Now hear this – This is a dry ship en-route to Iceland, there are no alcohol drinks or spirits, only coke".

"Re-posted back to UK in October 1945 and stationed in Reading with my previous OC from Iceland. The Reading Unit closed down and moved to RAF Halton in 1946. Posted to RAF Horsham St. Faith (now Norwich Airport) in February 1947, at this time I was 'signing on' at six monthly intervals because so many were leaving the Service and for one year I was moving from

Horsham to Halton until the situation caused by the releases stabilised, but I eventually led a normal life with a secure posting to Horsham in 1948. It was there that a Wing Commander friend inveigled me into signing to age 55, this I did and never regretted it, a wonderful life.

Boxing Day 1951 I was posted to RAF Lunenburg, Germany, as SNCO of the Field Punishment Detention Unit followed, in 1952 by a posting to RAF Gatow, a wonderful posting and plenty of excitement with our not so liked neighbours. The highlight was the responsibility I had for the Security of the Foreign Secretary, Mr. Anthony Eden and his entourage when they attended the Four Power Conference held in Berlin with Molotov, Dulles and the French Foreign Secretary, at the end of which we were given a first class party and Mr Eden thanked us personally for our services.

Posted to RAF Bishop Briggs in August 1954, and staying on camp one weekend, I decided to have a gate check of persons leaving for the weekend; two arrested who had in their possession one dozen fisherman type black macs and a pile of new sheets with pillow slips and other stores. On Monday morning all hell was let loose, how dare I arrest two airmen, what with the Equipment Officer and the Adjutant not speaking and me in the middle – later that morning the airmen appeared before the OC on charges of Improper Possession, the corridors blocked with half the Station personnel to await the outcome; the charges were dismissed. Later the OC asked for me and asked if he had been too lenient in dismissing the charges as the airmen said they were taking the macs for their friends who were going to attend the football match in case it rained and the sheets were being taken home to be washed!

However, as Mr. Churchill said, "This is their finest hour", it was certainly mine as I was moved to RAF Watton in October 1954 as a result of being 'too keen and upsetting the smooth running of the Station'. Whilst at Watton I was promoted to Warrant Officer and served as Provost Security and Liaison Officer for Suffolk at RAF Felixstowe in 1955.

In 1957 I was posted to RAF Halton as Sheriff, a wonderful posting. In 1958 I was posted to Cyprus, interviewed and recommended to be District Warrant Officer at HQ Cyprus and RAF El Adem. 1958-59 dodging bombs and bullets from the so-called EOKA terrorists and always ready for action with a loaded .38 or sten under the pillow for silent hours!

Tour expired in 1961 and after leave a move to RAF Sydenham, Belfast. Later that year my former OC from Cyprus paid a visit to Belfast and during a conversation informed me that he had put my name forward as a prospective Security Warrant Officer with five others for the post of Security Officer at The Queen's Flight. Obviously my face must have fitted as I was accepted for the post and moved to TQF Benson at Easter 1962 where I remained until the age of 55 in 1972, and enjoyed every moment, a very responsible job that I regretted leaving, but all good things come to an end. Whilst at TQF I was awarded the Royal Victorian Medal.

Loyalty to The Queen's Flight was so over powering that I had to move from Wallingford as I could not see myself static on the ground when that silver streak was taking off and landing and me not with it, so I moved to the Norfolk area, but kept in touch.

On leaving the Service and residing in Norfolk I applied for many jobs of varying positions, for a time when asked my previous appointment, the mention of TQF was accepted as some kind of disease as none had heard of it. However I tried my hand as pallbearer for the local undertaker, then painting and decorating, both worthless tasks. After an interview I was accepted by Securicor as their Security Salesman. Although this was an ideal post, the three-day week arrived, the last in was the first out and that was me. My luck did change however in 1973 when I secured a position with the Civil Engineering Construction Industry as Entertainment and Welfare Officer at RAF Bircham Newton purchased by the former in 1966, and they are now called CITB and CECOL. I remained there until the age of 65 in 1982.

From then on I did not live a life of luxury or become lazy but worked for a couple of Solicitors and three Doctors in garden design, but by 1996 I found it was all in the mind what I could do and also found my body was telling me different. I now lead a quieter life and doing as I am told.

In 1978 I was Secretary to the Heacham and North West Norfolk Wildfowlers Association, a full time job that now is even greater with so many laws etc. I retired from this in 1994 because it took up so much time and hassle and I found that my brain wasn't functioning as it used to!" Jim died on 19th October 2001 at his home in Framlingham Earl, Norwich.

Decorations: RVM, BEM with two C-in-C Commendations being received.

Squadron Leader John E. M'Kenzie-Hall, MVO, FFB, AMRAeS, FBIM
Helicopter Pilot, The Queen's Flight, 1957-1964

John M'Kenzie-Hall was born in Tasmania, Australia on 7th June 1923, and was educated at Trinity College, Melbourne, Geelong Grammar School, Melbourne, Australia and Bordersley Green Technical College in Birmingham, England.

John saw wartime service with the RAF (1940-43) as a pilot with Fighter Command and flying instruction duties with the RAF and the United States Army Air Corps (the latter following his attending the inaugural course at the Central Flying School, Randolph Field, Texas).

From 1943-44 as a Flight Lieutenant he became the Assistant Chief Flying & Gunnery Instructor at a Civilian Flying School in the USA (No.1 BFTS – Joint American and British).1944-45 saw John in the Royal Navy and the Fleet Air Arm as a Night Fighter Pilot with 891 Squadron and flying with, but not posted to, the Admiralty Flight at Heston as a VIP Pilot with the rank of Lieutenant Commander (Acting).

At the end of the war, from 1945-48, John went to Tanganyika as the Produce Manager, Bovill Matheson and Company, returning to the UK and rejoining the Royal Air Force in 1948 with the intention of flying on the Berlin Air Lift but arrived too late and was posted to the Central Flying School at RAF Little Rissington to renew his Instructor's Category and then on to the Royal Flying College at RAF Manby. General duties as Basic and Advanced Flying Instructor and a Flying Training Command's Instrument Rating Examiner followed until 1952.

After Helicopter conversion he was posted to Malaya in 1952 as a member of the first helicopter casualty evacuation squadron, No.194 Squadron, then to No.155 Squadron, in the post of Operational Training Officer and Operational Pilot. John commanded the Far East Jungle Rescue Team (Malaya and Borneo). He was also an Instrument Rating Examiner for the Far East Air Force. John was a fixed wing Captain and the Chief Flying Instructor at the Kuala Lumpur Flying Club.

Returning to the UK in 1955 he was a Flying Instructor and Operational Training Officer to the Joint Experimental Helicopter Unit of the Army until 1957.

Joining The Queen's Flight in 1957, John was responsible to the Captain, Sir Edward Fielden, for the operation of the short-range helicopter aircraft. He was appointed Personal Pilot and instructor to HRH the Duke of Edinburgh. As the project officer with Westland Aircraft Company he had responsibilities for the specification, manufacture and supply of the helicopter aircraft to The Queen's Flight. As the Helicopter Flight Commander he was also responsible for the selection of helicopter landing sites in restricted areas and the operation of the fire service crews and transport. John left the Flight and retired from the Royal Air Force due to an injury in 1964.

From 1964 until 1972, John was appointed Deputy Director of the National Federation of Housing Societies with responsibilities for the promotion, servicing and administration of a £25m. housing fund, together with the promotion, development and servicing of 2000 member organisations comprising charitable trusts, housing associations and societies. 1972-73 he was appointed Deputy Chairman, GEP Consulting Group Limited. As an Associate Partner, Geoffrey Edwards Partnership and Associate Partner, International Airports Consultants he was involved with the production of housing developments for BEA, BOAC and the Broadcasting industry and project management and client liaison in the field of airport development and the attendant operational infrastructure. From 1973-78 as Group Director, Omnium Housing Association Limited, his duties involved responsibilities and accountability for large sums of public monies, management and development policy for public housing projects, and national representation within the field of housing and housing legislation involving negotiations with local government, central government and both Houses of Parliament.

John is the author of 'Low cost Homes to Rent or Buy', written in 1971 which is a definitive textbook on the function, formation and operation of housing societies and associations and he frequently contributes to professional and public journals on housing with occasional contracts with BBC Sound and Television on general housing matters.

John is also the author of 'Hoverhawk', the story of helicopter flying on The Queen's Flight.

Decorations: MVO

Wing Commander E. W (Bill). Lamb MVO, MBIM, RAF (Ret'd)
Flight Lieutenant, Engineering Officer, The King's Flight, 14th August 1950 – 6th February 1952
Squadron Leader, S.Eng.O., The Queen's Flight, 6th February 1952 – 22nd April 1953

Bill Lamb was born on 18th January 1923 and educated at Cockburn High School, Leeds and then at No.1 School of Technical Training, RAF Halton after joining the Royal Air Force as an Aircraft Apprentice on 5th September 1938. He was commissioned from the rank of Corporal Fitter II (Eng) on 28th April 1944.

Towards the end of the war, from 1945-46, Bill served in Burma at No.132 RSU as Crash Inspector and Field Repair Officer for the South Burma area.

"No. 357 (SD) Squadron, equipped with Lysanders, was trying to maintain agents operating in Japanese Territory. The monsoon season was in full blast and the weather precluded parachute drops of either men or supplies. The SOE agents were in the Karen Hills and the Lysanders were the only way of getting men in or out. The ceiling was generally about "100 ft with rain squalls". Casualties were high – five out of twelve aircraft in six weeks and no replacements. When one crashed on a 400 yards jungle strip, the 357 Squadron Flight Commander thought it might be possible to get it out – as they definitely needed the aircraft.

It was my job and I thought it might make an interesting story for some of the 'old hands' of Tempsford – many of whom served on The King's Flight: two Deputy Captains I believe were pilots in that rather hazardous business. I had three one-way flights in the black Lysander – and very interesting it was too! The Operations had to be in daylight".

Bill sent in a couple of photographs but they are too old and discoloured to reproduce but they show Flying Officer E.W. Lamb with a Sergeant Weaver with a No.357 (SD) Squadron Lysander V9885 at Lipyekhi Strip in the Karen Hills in July/August 1945 together with Karen Locals and Ghurkha Paratroops of Force 136 (SOE).

After Burma, Bill served in Singapore from 1946-47 with No. 648/81 Squadron as Squadron Engineer Officer, doing Photographic Survey of Far East Area (Burma, Java, Malaysia, Indo-China and Siam).

Back to the UK and in 1948-50 was a Project Officer for the Canberra, Shackleton and Hunter aircraft at the Central Servicing Development Establishment at RAF Wattisham before being posted to The King's Flight as the Engineering Officer on 14th August 1950 and to The Queen's Flight on 6th February 1952 staying until 22nd April 1953.

Wing Commander Bill Lamb on his last flight in the Royal Air Force

Departing The Queen's Flight and off to RAF Henlow for the Senior Specialist Engineer Course in 1953 before going overseas to RAF El Adem in Libya as the Senior Engineer Officer. Then further east to Egypt and No. 103 MU at RAF Abyad and then north to Cyprus with the MU to RAF Akrotiri in 1955-56. Returning to the UK saw duty on the Special Duty List, being seconded from the Department of the Assistant Chief of Air Staff (Intelligence) from 1956-59 and on to HQ Flying Training Command in 1960.

On 21st January 1961 saw a return posting to The Queen's Flight as Senior Engineering Officer at RAF Benson until 16th March 1963 when with promotion to Wing Commander saw a posting as Station Commander to RAF Safi in Malta. 1966-68 saw a tour at MOD as Engineer Policy I before a move to RAF Swanton Morley as CSDE Engineer Secretariat from 1968-72. Moving to Wales and Management Services at RAF St. Athan from 1972-74 was followed by a tour as Station Commander at RAF Cardington from 1974-76 where Bill made his last flight in the RAF in an experimental airship GBAWL piloted by Santos Dumont in March 1976.

Decorations: MVO.

Group Captain Eric E. Lake, MVO, CEng, MRAeS, MBIM, RAF (Ret'd)
Flight Engineer, The Queen's Flight, 1952-1954
Senior Engineering Officer. 28th January 1963 – 10th September 1966

Born in York in 1923, Eric Lake enlisted in the RAF in December 1941. Trained initially as an Engine Fitter and subsequently as a Flight Engineer served with No. 206 Squadron, Coastal Command, flying Liberators based at St. Eval in Cornwall and Leuchars in Scotland.

1945-48 saw a change of role to Transport Command, firstly with No. 206 Squadron flying Liberators, converted for trooping, and subsequently with No. 51 Squadron flying Avro Yorks and an appointment as Flight Engineer Leader on that Squadron in 1947.

1948-51 saw a flying tour at the Experimental Flying Department, RAE Farnborough followed by a ground tour in 1951-52 as a Flight Commander in the Initial Training Wing at RAF Cranwell.

"In 1952, my first tour of duty with The Queen's Flight was as a Flight Engineer on Vikings. (The Vikings did not carry a second pilot; the right hand seat was occupied by experienced flight engineers who were also responsible for ground servicing away from base). I flew mainly with Squadron Leader R.G. (Ron) Churcher (pilot), Flight Lieutenant M.D. (Maurice) Rafferty (navigator), and Flight Lieutenant W.D. (Bill) Rees (air signaller). (The late Bill Rees will be remembered by many as he served on the Flight for a long time, later becoming Adjutant). I left on transfer to the Engineer Branch in 1954."

1954-57 was spent at the RAF Technical College, RAF Henlow, followed by a tour in the Far East Air Force in 1957-60 as OC Aircraft Servicing Flight at RAF Tengah.

A Staff appointment at HQ Fighter Command in 1960 lasted only a few months before being posted on promotion to Squadron Leader as Eng. Plans at HQ Flying Training Command from 1960-63.

"A return to The Queen's Flight, this time as Senior Engineering Officer in 1963. A hectic but satisfying tour, with first the introduction of new turbine-engined helicopters, and then the introduction into service of the Andover. Initially the Andover was operated alongside the Herons. The Andover presented several problems in the early days. All were overcome by the ground servicing team, with a mixture of skill, ingenuity and dedication upon which, The Queen's Flight has always been able to rely. I was privileged to lead a top flight servicing team, headed by Warrant Officer Ron Tooke (to whom nothing was impossible) with indispensable support of the unflappable Warrant Officer Bob Norris, who operated as my technical adjutant. I left in 1966 on promotion to Wing Commander".

OC Engineering Wing at Wildenrath in Germany followed until 69, when Staff Appointments took over, firstly 1969-72 at the Ministry of Defence; 1972-74 at HQ Strike Command, leaving on promotion to Group Captain and then 1974-78 as Senior Training Officer, No.1 School of Technical Training, RAF Halton. (1975 Appointed ADC to HM The Queen).

"Following retirement from the RAF in 1978 I joined the Engineering Industry Training Board and after my second retirement I worked for several years as a self-employed consultant.

Among my memorable moments I remember introducing the Crew Chief concept with the introduction of the Andover. This did not meet with the universal approval of higher authority and a request for help with cross training was refused. (At the time there was a formal training course for Bomber Command Aircraft Servicing Chiefs in being which could have been useful). Consequently training was accomplished in-house. Later I was asked on whose authority Queen's Flight SNCOs were being permitted to undertake work outside their basic trade boundaries. Swallowing hard I replied that it was on my own authority; nothing more was heard so I concluded that someone was clearing his own yardarm. If justification of the crew chiefs' value was needed, it came early.

During Royal Visit to one of the African States we suffered one of our very rare engine failures. Fortunately, it occurred when the aircraft was scheduled to be on the ground for 48 hours. The Flight sprang into action and a Benson-based Argosy was loaded with a replacement Dart engine and a team to replace the defective engine. It took off within hours of receiving the signal. On arrival they found that the crew chief had already removed the defective engine, which was sitting safely on a cushion of old tyres, and all ready to install the replacement engine. This was quickly accomplished and the aircraft air tested. The Royal Tour continued on schedule. The crew chief concerned was Sergeant Fred Bloor (basic trade; electrical fitter).

A minor problem with the introduction of the Andover concerned the cabin warning signs (No Smoking-Fasten Seatbelts). Prince Philip pointed out that the sign was unreadable in bright daylight. There followed a lengthy period of trial and error with different combinations of illuminators, screens, filters, etc. Flight Sergeant Silvester and his electricians were driven almost to distraction before a sign, which met with Royal approval was eventually produced. This episode resulted in one of the Flight's traditional "Christmas Presents". A faithful reproduction of the cabin sign was made. It was portable and fitted with an internal battery. When activated, however, bells rang, lights flashed, warning flags appeared and the sign illuminated to read very clearly "Fags Out" and "Belt-up". Air Vice-Marshal Fielden took it to the Palace to show Prince Philip who, we learned, roared with laughter and insisted on keeping it as a personal souvenir.

One of our helicopters was carrying HRH The Duke of Edinburgh to visit the Royal Naval College at Dartmouth, when the instruments indicated an engine problem. Sensibly the pilot immediately carried out a precautionary landing in a convenient field. At the time I was spending a few days leave in Devon. I was just sitting down to lunch when I received a telephone call from the OC to tell me that the helicopter had force-landed and to give me a map reference. Coincidentally, the location was only a short distance from my hotel and I went there immediately. By the time I arrived at the site, the Royal party had been whisked away by a Royal Navy helicopter and I later heard that, a few minutes earlier, the sky had been "black with aircraft". As I walked across the field towards the helicopter, Ron Kerr, the pilot, looked all around him for another helicopter, stared at me in disbelief, and said, "Where the hell did you come from?" He could not believe that even The Queen's Flight could produce an Engineer Officer at the scene so quickly. Inspection revealed that his decision to land had been the right one and I spent the remainder of my leave in the field as we replaced the defective engine".

Frederick William Silvester, RVM
A Fitt E, The King's Flight 1948–1953
A Fitt E, The Queen's Flight, 1956–1966

Fred Silvester was born on 13th July 1921 and went to the Polytechnic Secondary School in Regent Street, London. He joined the Royal Air Force as a twenty-year old in July 1941 and after training as an Aircraft Fitter Electrical saw service at 13 OUT, RAF Harwell; 51 Base, RAF Swinderby; Emergency Landing Unit, RAF Woodbridge; RNAS Lee-on-Solent; RNAS Eglinton; and Transport Command Development Unit, RAF Brize Norton.

Fred was posted to The King's Flight at RAF Benson in August 1948 until October 1953 and posted back again to The Queen's Flight in December 1956 to March 1966. Most of his time at Benson was spent as SNCO i/c Electrical Section. He was awarded the Royal Victorian Medal (Silver) for his contribution to Royal Flying. Fred retired from the Royal Air Force in February 1974 from RAF Brize Norton holding the rank of Warrant Officer.

Warrant Officer Ronald Frederick Tooke, MBE, RVM, BEM
A Fitt P, Warrant Officer i/c Engineering, The Queen's Flight, 1957–1976

Born in 1921, Ron Tooke was taken as an infant by his parents to India when his father, serving in the RAF, was posted to RAF Lahore where they lived in the winter moving to the Murray Hills for the summer. Later they moved to Simla, 8,000 feet high in the Himalayas and moving down to New Delhi for the winter. Ron went to school at the Lawrence Royal Military School at Sanawar and St. Edwards High School in Simla.

When he was sixteen, in 1937, he came to England and completed a two-year Engineering Apprentice course.

In May 1939 Ron joined the Royal Air Force and trained as a flight mechanic at RAF St. Athan before being posted to No.17 Hurricane

Fighter Squadron in January 1940 during the Battle of Britain, operating from Kenley, Debden and Martlesham Heath.

During the fall of France, he was one of six ground crew detached to Le Mans Race Course in France with some Hurricane aircraft. They flew over in a Dragon Rapide with the seats taken out and they sat on their kitbags. The Hurricanes operated out of Le Mans for a few days but then did not return. They were close to a road and after five days, the refugees streamed past, followed by two soldiers who told them the Germans were only three miles away. They had a lorry so they all climbed aboard and after much hiding and sleeping in the woods arrived at St. Malo, which they found deserted except for an old trawler that a fisherman was trying to start. After threatening him they were able to start the trawler and put to sea.

It was dark and the sea very rough so everyone was seasick when the engine failed. In the early hours of the next morning the trawler was found and towed into a port. They dragged themselves ashore onto the cobblestones and slept. Awaking to brilliant sunshine they were told they were on the island of Jersey. There was a threat of a German invasion in Jersey at any time and there was only one small boat left, and after being given food, they were 'squeezed' onboard and sent on their way to England.

By this time Dunkirk was over and they returned to No.17 Squadron at RAF Martlesham Heath where Ron stayed until the end of the Battle of Britain. He was then sent to RAF Halton to complete a six-week Fitter 2E Course and returned to Martlesham Heath.

In November 1941, he was posted to No.89 Squadron, a Beaufighter Night Fighter Squadron, which went by troopship to the Middle East by way of South Africa. The Squadron operated from RAF Abu Suer. The camp had previously been bombed out and they lived in holes in the sand, one of each trade in each dug-out, sleeping on the sand with no beds or mattresses. He was there from December 1941 until early 1943, when one of each trade was detached to Calcutta, flying by Empire Flying Boat from Cairo via Basra and Gwalior to the Hougly River in Calcutta.

The Army RTO Officer telephoned the OC of the Transit Camp, but he didn't know anything about them, however he agreed to come over to see them. He was more than an hour away so they waited where they had been dropped. After an hour a staff car pulled up and out stepped the OC, **he was Ron's father**, he had last seen him when he arrived in England in 1937 and he had no idea that he was there!

Next morning two of the Squadron Beaufighters arrived at Dum Dum airport and the groundcrew prepared them for operations. The first night, Flight Sergeant Paing shot down three Japanese aircraft in four minutes. The next night Flying Officer Cromby shot down two more. The following day the unit moved further into Burma where they were joined by a Squadron of Beaufighters from the UK. The small detachment was disbanded and Ron was posted to the Air Headquarters Communications Flight in New Delhi.

Lord Wavell was the Viceroy and Ron found himself the crew chief on his aircraft, a Dakota. Admiral Lord Louis Mountbatten, the last Viceroy, replaced Lord Wavell. He received a York aircraft to replace the Dakota and Ron was transferred as crew chief onto the York. Sir Claude Auchinlech was the Commander-in-Chief Punjab and he attended the Victory Parade in London and Ron accompanied him as the crew chief on his aircraft. Returning to New Delhi he was posted to RAF Palam, New Delhi.

In 1943, in New Delhi, he met someone who was teaching in the Convent. They had known each other as children during their school days in Simla. They were married on July 22nd 1944 and had their honeymoon in Simla where they had both spent a lot of their childhood.

When the partition of India came in 1947 they left India by troopship, the SS Otranto, with their son and baby daughter. On arriving in UK in July 1947 Ron was posted to RAF Abingdon, on second line servicing of York aircraft. Their second son, David was born at Abingdon in 1948.

In the winter of 1948/49, he was detached to Wunsdorf in Germany for five months on the Berlin Airlift and on return was posted to the Rectification Flight at RAF Lyneham working on Hastings aircraft from 1949 until 1954. During this time he remembers going to Moscow via Templehof airfield in the Berlin Zone where a Russian Pilot and Navigator joined the crew to fly to Moscow. There were Doctors and Nurses on the aircraft and after spending the night in a Russian hotel they prepared for the return with four prisoners of war, stretcher cases, returning via Templehof to drop off the Russian crewmembers and then on to RAF Abingdon so that the patients could go to the nearest hospital in Oxford.

From 20th October to 5th December 1952, Ron was the Engine support groundcrew for two Hastings aircraft supporting two Canberra aircraft of No.12 Squadron, RAF Binbrook on a 24,000 miles Goodwill Tour led by Air Vice Marshal Sir Dermot Boyle, with air displays at Rio de Janeiro, Brazil; Montevideo, Uruguay; Buenos Aires, Argentina; Santiago, Chile; Lima, Peru; Bogotá, Columbia; Caracas, Venezuela; Mexico City, Mexico; Havana, Cuba; Kingston, Jamaica; Cuidad Trujillo, Dominican Republic and Port of Spain in Trinidad.

In June 1954 Ron was awarded the British Empire Medal and in December of that year was posted to RAF Benson as the Flight Sergeant on the Ferry Unit. This unit ferried aircraft all over the world. In 1957 he was selected for interview, along with 13 others, to replace Warrant Officer Booker (who was going to OCTU for a commission in the Engineering Branch) on The Queen's Flight. Interviewed by Sir Edward Fielden and the very next day posted to The Queen's Flight!

Warrant Officer Ron Tooke served under four Captains' of The Queen's Flight, Sir Edward Fielden, Sir Dennis Mitchell, John Blount and Sir Archie Winskill. His contribution is included under the second Captain purely in an attempt to equalise the number of pages in each chapter of the 'Personalities'.

In the New Year's Honours List on 1st January 1976, Warrant Officer Ron Tooke was appointed to be a Member of the Most Excellent Order of the British Empire (MBE) and the story of the time he spent with The Queen's Flight may be summarised in the following extract from the Citation on which that award was made.

"During his unique tour of duty Warrant Officer Tooke has been responsible for the servicing of a wide variety of Royal aircraft and has loyally served a succession of Monarchs, Captains of the Flight, Officer Commandings and Engineering Officers. The results he has achieved are truly outstanding. His sustained efforts throughout the period of his 18 years have been largely responsible for the establishment within the Flight of the highest possible standards of engineering and discipline; this in turn has achieved unsurpassed aircraft serviceability and availability. Warrant Officer Tooke's outstanding qualities are his personal commitment, no matter what obstacles are presented, to serve the Royal Family through the medium of The Queen's Flight. He is utterly loyal and will willingly subordinate his personal life to achieve the aims of the Flight. Although dedicated and forceful Warrant Officer Tooke takes a sincere and compassionate interest in the lives of The Queen's Flight airmen and their families. Without exception, he has personally visited every airman who has been ill or bereaved, either in hospital or at home, throughout his 18 years tour.

During extended Royal Tours overseas Warrant Officer Tooke has overcome daunting engineering problems, coercing the resources and authority of whatever agencies are available to ensure success".

13. The Third Captain & Others 1964–1967

Air Commodore J. H. L.(John) Blount, DFC (deceased)
Captain, The Queen's Flight. 2nd August 1964 – 7th December 1967

John Blount was born in London on 24th November 1919 and educated at Harrow School before entering the Royal Air Force College at Cranwell in January 1938. Flying Training was carried out in the Avro Tutor, Hart and Oxford aircraft.

Graduating in October 1939 John was posted to the School of Army Cooperation War Course at Old Sarum flying Lysander aircraft. Moving to the photographic Reconnaissance Unit at Heston from November 1939 until November 1940 saw a move to the Harvard, Spitfire and Blenheim aircraft.

His logbook records on 1st April 1940 he flew from Heston to Shawbury to collect a Spitfire in a Hudson N7301 flown by a Wing Commander Fielden (Could it have been 'Mouse' Fielden?) His Spitfire Photographic Reconnaissance Operations are logged as starting in June 1940 and his longest sortie was four hours and thirty minutes when he flew from Heston and landed at RAF Turnhouse, Edinburgh on 26th August 1940, a long time to be airborne in a Spitfire, and one can only wonder where he had been. Several of his flights were logged as 'height tests'; one is also left to wonder how high these sorties went.

Moving to No. 3 Photographic Reconnaissance Unit at RAF Oakington in November 1940 he flew several types of aircraft; Spitfire, Tiger Moth, Hornet Moth, Magister, Cygnet and Owlet but continued his operational flights in the Spitfire. One sortie flown in December 1940 is logged as being flown at 30,000 feet to photograph condensation trails. Further research has revealed that some of his operational sorties included photographic reconnaissance flights over Cologne, Brussels, Nannheim, Hamm, Osnabruch, Bremen, Bremerhaven, Ruhr, Hamburg, Hanover, Rotterdam, Frankfurt, Amsterdam, Arnhem, Magdeburg, Brest and Emden.

Pictured (left) in his Spitfire days, John was posted missing in April 1941 whilst flying in Spitfire X4712 when he was shot down by an ME109 over the island of Texel (Holland). He survived and was held a prisoner-of-war in Stalag Luft III.

October 1945 saw John at No. 21 (P) Advanced Flying Unit at RAF Wheaton Aston flying various types of aircraft; Oxford, Tiger Moth, Magister, Dominie and Liberator with a detachment to No. 1517 Beam Approach Flight at RAF Chipping Warden in November 1945 flying the Airspeed Oxford and the Link Trainer. Having successfully completed the A.F.U. Course in January 1946 he was posted to No. 21 O.T.U. at RAF Moreton-in-Marsh and a conversion to Wellington aircraft but still managing to get himself a couple of flights in a Hurricane, PG426, during the course.

By now a Squadron Leader, John was sent to fly Lancaster aircraft at No. 1653 H.C.U. at RAF North Luffenham from August to October 1946 when he was appointed Officer Commanding of No. 214 Squadron at RAF Upwood until April 1947 when he was posted to No.15 Squadron at RAF Wyton flying Lincolns' until January 1950. He flew Lincoln LS/C in the Battle of Britain Flypast over London on 15th September 1948 and a few days later on the 18^{th,} the Battle of Britain Flypast over aerodromes in the South of England. In November 1949 he flew Lincoln LS/D, RF532, to Shallufa in the Middle East to take part in 'Operation Sunray'.

In January 1950 John was posted to the Officer's Advanced Training School at RAF Bircham Newton as a Wing Commander until June 1951 when he was moved to No. 75 School of Recruit Training at RAF Bridgnorth. In August 1952 he became a student at the Royal Air Force Flying College at Manby where he converted to Meteor Mk. 4 and 7, Vampires and the heavier Valetta and Lincoln aircraft successfully, graduating in May 1953.

A move to Germany and No. 34 Wing at RAF Gutersloh followed flying Meteor Mk. 9 and 10 aircraft. He was also checked out on the Meteor Mk.7 and on 13th September 1954 his logbook reveals he flew a local sortie with his cousin Lieutenant Blount as his passenger.

Returning to the United Kingdom in December 1954 he presented himself to the RAF Staff College Course at RAF Bracknell in January 1955 until December 1955 but still managing to fly a Meteor Mk.7, Balliol, Anson and a Chipmunk during that year!

A tour at the Cabinet Office from December 1955 to November 1957 also didn't stop John from flying. Types flown during this period included Balliol, Anson Mk.19, Meteors Mk 7 and 8, and Vampire.

Appointed to be the Station Commander at RAF Syerston as a Group Captain (No. 2 Flying Training School) in November 1957 until January 1960 with Provost, Jet Provost, Meteor Mk. 7 and 8 and Vampire T11 aircraft saw John getting plenty of flying.

Diplomatic Duties followed with his appointment to be the Air Adviser to the British High Commissioner in New Zealand from April 1960 until September 1962 when he returned to the UK to be appointed to be the Deputy Director Air Plans 2 at the Ministry of Defence.

He was appointed to be the Captain of The Queen's Flight from 2nd August 1964 arriving just in time to see the re-equipment with the Andover aircraft. Amongst the overseas tours he flew with the Flight were HRH The Princess Margaret and Lord Snowden to the British Trade Week in Copenhagen in September 1964; HRH The Duke of Edinburgh to Mexico and the Caribbean in October/November 1964; The State Visits of HM The Queen and HRH The Duke of Edinburgh to Ethiopia and the Sudan in February 1965; The visits by HM The Queen and HRH The Duke of Edinburgh to Berlin in May 1965, and to Barbados in February 1966 (this one flying in a VC10 aircraft); and the Tour of Australia and New Zealand by HM Queen Elizabeth The Queen Mother in March to May 1966.

Tragically, Air Commodore John Blount was killed, at the age of 48, in the crash of The Queen's Flight Whirlwind Helicopter XR487 whilst flying from RAF Benson to the Westland factory at Yeovil to discuss the VVIP Wessex helicopter. John was a second-generation airman and the second also to die in an air crash. His father, Air Vice-Marshal Charles Blount, was killed on 23rd October 1940, at the age of 46, whilst taking off from RAF Hendon to visit his command, No. 21 Army Cooperation Group.

Group Captain J.L. (John) Gilbert, CVO, DFC
Deputy Captain, The Queen's Flight, 17th January 1966 – 30th January 1968

Born 19th December 1921. Educated at Bradfield College, Berkshire from 1935-1940. Joined the RAF in April 1941.

As a Squadron Leader, John saw service as Air Staff, HQ MEAF, Cyprus during 1955-57; Attended RAF Staff College Bracknell in 1958; and a short tour in the Air Secretary's Department at the Ministry of Defence in 1959 before being promoted Wing Commander and in 1960 appointed as the Officer Commanding of No. 48 Squadron (Hastings aircraft) 1960-62 (held "A" Category as a pilot 1961-62).

After attending the Joint Services Staff College in 1963 John was posted to the Joint Services Warfare Staff at the Ministry of Defence from 1964-65 and on promotion to Group Captain, was appointed Deputy Captain of The Queen's Flight from January 1966 to the end of January 68 when he retired from the Royal Air Force.

On his retirement John became the Operations Manager (Aprons), British Airports Authority, London Heathrow Airport from 1968 until 1984.

Group Captain Alexander Roualeyn (Sandy) Gordon-Cumming, CMG, CVO
Deputy Captain, The Queen's Flight, 28th December 1966 – 17th October 1969

Born 10th September 1924 and Educated at Eton College, Sandy Gordon-Cumming joined the Royal Air Force in 1943.

Graduating in 1944 he served as a flying instructor in South Africa and at Tern Hill and Cranwell; Sandy also served as a Pilot with No.72 (Vampire) Squadron, at RAF North Weald; and No.73 (Vampire) Squadron in Malta.

He was appointed Officer Commanding of No.29 Squadron (Javelins) at RAF Leuchars.

Staff Appointments included Inspector of Mountain Rescue, Chiefs of Staff Secretariat, Transport Command, and Imperial Defence College.

He was appointed Deputy Captain of The Queen's Flight from December 1966 to October 1969.

Retiring from the Royal Air Force in 1969 with the rank of Group Captain he became a Civil Servant with the Board of Trade as a Principal Officer, dealing with EFTA and EEC trade negotiations; In 1973 to the Department of Trade and Industry; transferring to the Air Division dealing with the launch of the BAe 146 at the Department of Trade and Industry.

Seconded to HM Diplomatic Service from 1974-78, serving in the Foreign Office as Counsellor (Aviation and Shipping) in Washington, USA, dealing primarily with the grant of landing rights for Concorde aircraft.

He retired in 1984 as Director, Invest in Britain Bureau, Department of Industry, (1979-84).

Decorations: Appointed CMG in 1978. Appointed CVO 1969.

Terence (Terry) J. Holmes, RVM, BEM, MISM
Fireman, The Queen's Flight, 1965-68 and 1973-78

Terry Holmes was born on 12th July 1937. He joined the Royal Air Force, reporting to RAF Cardington in August 1955. After basic training at RAF Padgate and trade training at RAF Sutton-on-Hull and RAF Weeton his first posting to RAF Shawbury lasted from 1956-1962.

Overseas in January 1962 to RAF Changi, Singapore with detachments to Malaya, Labuan Island and RAF Gan before returning to the UK and RAF Honington in 1964.

In 1965 Terry was selected for The Queen's Flight and Helicopter Support Duties (Fireman) and stayed for three years before being posted, on promotion, to RAF College Cranwell.

In 1970 he was posted to RAF Salalah (Oman) for a one-year tour before returning to RAF Cranwell and in 1973 was selected for a second tour on The Queen's Flight in charge of the Helicopter Support Section.

1978, again on promotion, was posted to RAF North Coates but in 1979 was selected for secondment to the Sultan of Brunei Armed Forces and served for five years in Brunei as the Fire Advisor to the Sultan's Armed Forces. Returning to the UK for a four-year tour to RAF Brize Norton in 1984, Terry was once again posted overseas in 1988 to RAF Wildenrath. In 1989 he was posted to RAF Kinloss with a detachment to the Falkland Islands as The Force Fire Officer, returning to Kinloss and a posting back to Wildenrath where he served as the Station Fire Officer until Wildenrath closed and he retired from the Royal Air Force in 1992.

Terry started a second career as a Building Manager with Jones Lang Wootton and after 18 months became an Area Building Manager with the same company, followed by further promotion to Area Facilities Manager. Jones Lang Wooton are now known as Jones Lang LaSalle, Chartered Surveyors and International Real Estate Advisers and Terry is still in their employ as a Regional Facilities Manager looking after a portfolio of properties in East Anglia.

Terry has two memorable moments from his career, firstly his visit to Buckingham Palace where HM The Queen invested him with the Royal Victorian Medal and his visit to the Dorchester Hotel, London where HM The Sultan of Brunei invested him with the PJK for Meritorious Service to the Brunei Armed Forces.

Decorations: RVM (Silver); BEM;

Medals: General Service Medal with the Dhofar clasp; The Queen's Silver Jubilee Medal; Meritorious Service Medal; Long Service and Good Conduct Medal with clasp; Pingat Jasa Kebaktian (Brunei) Sultan's Personal Medal and General Services Medal (Brunei Armed Forces).

Sergeant William (Bill) R. Hood
A Tech A, The Queen's Flight, 1964-1968 & 1972-1977

Billy Hood joined the Royal Air Force in November 1958 and went to RAF Bridgnorth for his initial training and on to RAF Weeton for technical training. His first tour was with No. 41 Squadron at RAF Wattisham before going to Germany, firstly to RAF Gutersloh and then to Berlin and 'Checkpoint Charlie'. Billy did a one year unaccompanied tour to RAF Gan, his comments "God's island in the sun! Only one woman on the island (a WVS lady). What did I do to deserve that"?

From the hot to the cold, and to RAF Marham where he helped in the scrapping of the Valiant fleet because of multiple cracks in the main spars of the mainplanes.

Following a "good show" at Marham, in 1964 he was selected for a posting to The Queen's Flight where he served for five years before taking his family with him to Singapore, firstly to RAF Seletar and then to RAF Changi.

Bill tells the story of how he met his wife in Trafalgar Square, she tripped over his holdall, and believe it or not, her surname was also Hood! His youngest daughter, Hazel, was born in Changi hospital and, another remarkable co-incidence, she is now married to Richard Sowerby, the nephew of Brian Sowerby (K4Nav), the Association's current Secretary.

Whilst in Singapore Bill was seconded for six month's to the Air Attaché Saigon to help maintain his aeroplane (Devon 968 callsign MONPD).

In February 1971, Bill and his family were welcomed back to the UK on the first day of decimal currency and in the middle of a postal strike! Posted to the flying training school equipped with Gnats at RAF Valley for 9 months, he remembers a bleak windy place where the trees had the 'Anglesey lean' and having as his Officer i/c, Squadron Leader Rigg, the brother of the actress Diana Rigg.

A further tour of six years on The Queen's Flight followed where he travelled all over the world on proving and Royal Flights. As part of the support crew he was often given the task of handing out the 'pills and plasters' when required so was given the nickname 'Doctor Billy'.

In 1977 Bill was posted to C.I.O. Brighton for two years on recruiting duties before moving to RAF Halton where he was in charge of training aids which encompassed the hospital, the dental training centres and the apprentices and flight line mechanics. He retired from Halton as a Flight Sergeant and is now living in Eastbourne in Sussex.

Brian Anthony Johnson, BEM
A Fitt P, The Queen's Flight, 1954 – 1973

Brian Johnson served on The Queen's Flight from 1954 until 1973. He served under four Captains and is included in this particular chapter because of the time served by the fourth Captain allows more personalities to be included in the fourth chapter.

Brian was born on 29th September 1933 and was educated at Manchester Grammar School. He joined the Royal Air Force on 20th June 1949 and after apprenticeship and engineering training served on No. 41 Fighter Squadron from January 1951 to February 1954.

Selected to join The Queen's Flight in 1954, Brian, for nineteen years, served as engineer/fitter servicing Viking, Heron, Whirlwind and Andover aircraft.

He served as a Crew Chief on Andover aircraft from March 1965 to September 1971 and as the Propulsion Trade Manager from September 1971 until August 1973.

On retiring from the Royal Air Force in September 1973, Brian served with Pento Motorhomes as Sales manager until June 1979 when he joined Auto Sleepers until he retired in September 1998. He lives with his family in Brightwell-cum-Sotwell.

Colin Lumby
MTD, The Queen's Flight, November 1962 – September 1973

A Yorkshireman, Colin Lumby was born on 5th April 1935 and went to the Primrose Hill Secondary Modern School in Pudsey, near Leeds. Joining the Royal Air Force on a 3-year engagement on 5th September 1952 he went to St. Athan for trade training as an Engine Mechanic Liquid Cooled after completing his recruit training at RAF Cardington.

March 1953 saw Colin on board the Troopship Dorsetshire en-route, for 33 days, to Singapore joining the Far East Flying Boat Wing on the Sunderland Major and Minor Servicing Team from April 1953 to March 1955 then to RAF Kuala Lumpur on the Auster Mk 6/7/9 Servicing Team with No. 656 AOP Squadron. Returning to the UK in August 1955, again by sea, 31 days on the RMV Capt Dobson before the end of his three-year term of service.

Work as a civilian for four years obviously didn't suit him so, in September 1959, he rejoined the RAF and trained as an MTD at RAF Weeton. After three years at CSDE RAF Swanton Morley in Norfolk, Colin volunteered for, and was posted to The Queen's Flight in November 1962 where amongst his most memorable moments he remembers the winter of 1962/63 when RAF Benson was snowbound and he was part of the team helping operate the Heron aircraft out of London Heathrow from a BOAC hangar for a number of weeks; travelling from Aberdeen to Portsmouth on HM Yacht Britannia; being the personal driver to Air Vice-Marshal Sir Edward Fielden from 1966 until he retired as Senior Air Equerry in 1970; attending a Reception and Dance at Buckingham Palace in December 1970; 19th April 1971, the 25th Anniversary of The Queen's Flight and the visit by HM The Queen followed by the dance in the hangar; 1971-1973 personal driver to the Captain of The Queen's Flight, Air Commodore Sir Archie Winskill; 1st June 1973 and the award of the AOC's Commendation, being promoted Sergeant, before departing to the MT Squadron at RAF Lyneham in September 1973.

Colin left Lyneham in December 1975 for RAF Masirah where his tour was cut short due to his developing migraine and eye problems so in April 1976 he went to RAF Wattisham before volunteering for a post at the RAF MT Driving School at St. Athan where he served from July 1977 until his retirement from the RAF in February 1979 on completing his 22 years service.

As a civilian again, Colin was appointed Agent for British Road Services Tyre fitting and repair facilities including mobile roadside repairs until February 1980. He then went to Gleeson's Plant as Transport Co-ordinator for heavy plant movement by HGV, operating throughout the UK liasing with County Council weight restrictions and Police escorts until the Branch closed in November 1980. Joining an Independent Builders Merchants as Buyer/Supervisor/Manager during the next 15 years before resigning in September 1996 to start his own company in Office/Home building maintenance and final retirement in March 2000.

On 26th June 1986 Colin and his wife attended a reception to celebrate the 50th Anniversary of The King's Flight at St. James's Palace accompanied by their son David who was serving on The Queen's Flight as a fireman with the Helicopter Support Unit. Colin is very proud that his son served on The Queen's Flight from 1984 to 1986.

Warrant Officer Robert (Bob) Norris, RVM, BEM
Aircraft Fitter, The Queen's Flight 1958 – 1973

Bob Norris was born on 5th August 1918 and went to Stamshaw Grammar School in Portsmouth and a Junior Technical School before joining the Royal Air Force as a Halton Apprentice in 1934.

Bob is a 'character' and the way he has presented his service career, from Apprentice in 1934, pre-war and through the war years, to joining The Queen's Flight as a Flight Sergeant in 1958, in his own way, is shown without any alterations.

Joining The Queen's Flight in 1958, Bob served under four Captains' of The Queen's Flight, Mouse Fielden, Sir Dennis Mitchell, John Blount and Sir Archie Winskill, until he retired in 1973. His unique contribution to these 'Personalities' chapters is included in Chapter Three purely to provide some uniformity in the number of pages in each chapter and is presented to you in his own way in three parts:

PART 1 – 1918 TO 1945

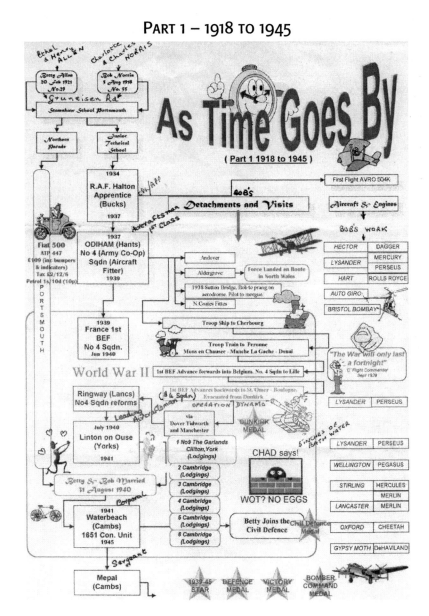

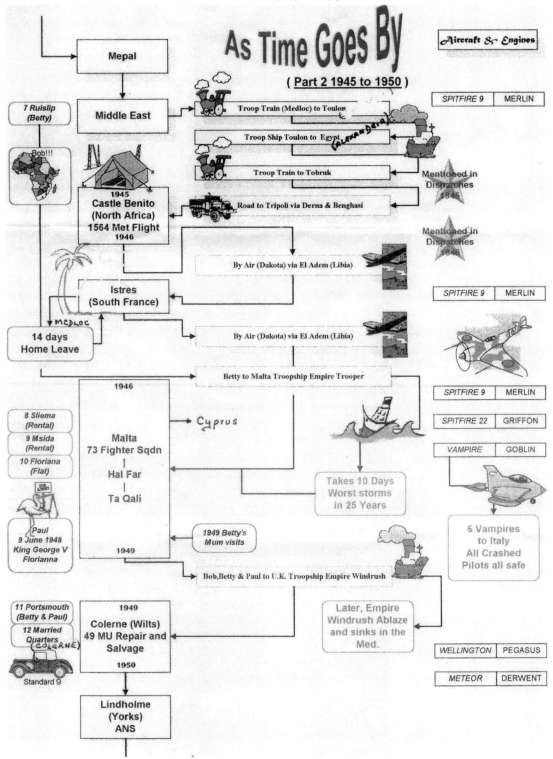

As Time Goes By

(Part 2 1945 to 1950)

Aircraft & Engines

Mepal

7 Ruislip (Betty)

Middle East

Bob!!!

1945
Castle Benito
(North Africa)
1564 Met Flight
1946

Troop Train (Medloc) to Toulon

Troop Ship Toulon to Egypt (Alexandria)

Troop Train to Tobruk

Mentioned in Dispatches 1945

Road to Tripoli via Derna & Benghasi

Mentioned in Dispatches 1946

By Air (Dakota) via El Adem (Libia)

SPITFIRE 9	MERLIN

Istres (South France)

MEDLOC

14 days Home Leave

By Air (Dakota) via El Adem (Libia)

Betty to Malta Troopship Empire Trooper

SPITFIRE 9	MERLIN

SPITFIRE 9	MERLIN

8 Sliema (Rental)

9 Msida (Rental)

10 Floriana (Flat)

1946

Malta
73 Fighter Sqdn
|
Hal Far
|
Ta Qali

Cyprus

Takes 10 Days
Worst storms
in 25 Years

SPITFIRE 9	MERLIN
SPITFIRE 22	GRIFFON
VAMPIRE	GOBLIN

Paul
9 June 1948
King George V
Florianna

1949 Betty's
Mum visits

1949

6 Vampires
to Italy
All Crashed
Pilots all safe

Bob,Betty & Paul to U.K. Troopship Empire Windrush

11 Portsmouth (Betty & Paul)

12 Married Quarters (COLERNE)

Standard 9

1949
Colerne (Wilts)
49 MU Repair and Salvage
1950

Later, Empire
Windrush Ablaze
and sinks in the
Med.

WELLINGTON	PEGASUS
METEOR	DERWENT

Lindholme
(Yorks)
ANS

As Time Goes By

Flight Sergeant

(Part 3 1950 to 1958)

Aircraft & Engines

WELLINGTON	PEGASUS
VARSITY	HERCULES
PROVOST	ALVIS
PROVOST	GNOME

13 Married Quarters

Ford Squire

Geoff
29 July 1952
Chippenham
Cottage Hospital

1950

**Hullavington
(Wilts)
ANS - FTS**

1956

AOC COMMENDATION 1952

LONG SERVICE 1955

AOC COMMENDATION 1956

By Superconstelation Via LAP - Shannon - Gander - New York - San Francisco - Hawaii

1956

**Christmas Island
Pacific Ocean
H-Bomb Tests**

Code name "Grapple" 1957

BANG

BRITISH EMPIRE MEDAL 1956

AUSTER	CLOCKWORK

FRIGATE BIRDS DON'T LIKE BEING DISTURBED

By Hastings Via Hawaii - San Francisco - Edmonton - Montreal - Goose Bay - Lyneham

14 Skellingthorpe (Rental)

15 Married Quarters
(RAF SWINDERBY)

Hillman Minx

1957

**Swinderby
(Lincs)
ANS**

1958

WELLINGTON	PEGASUS

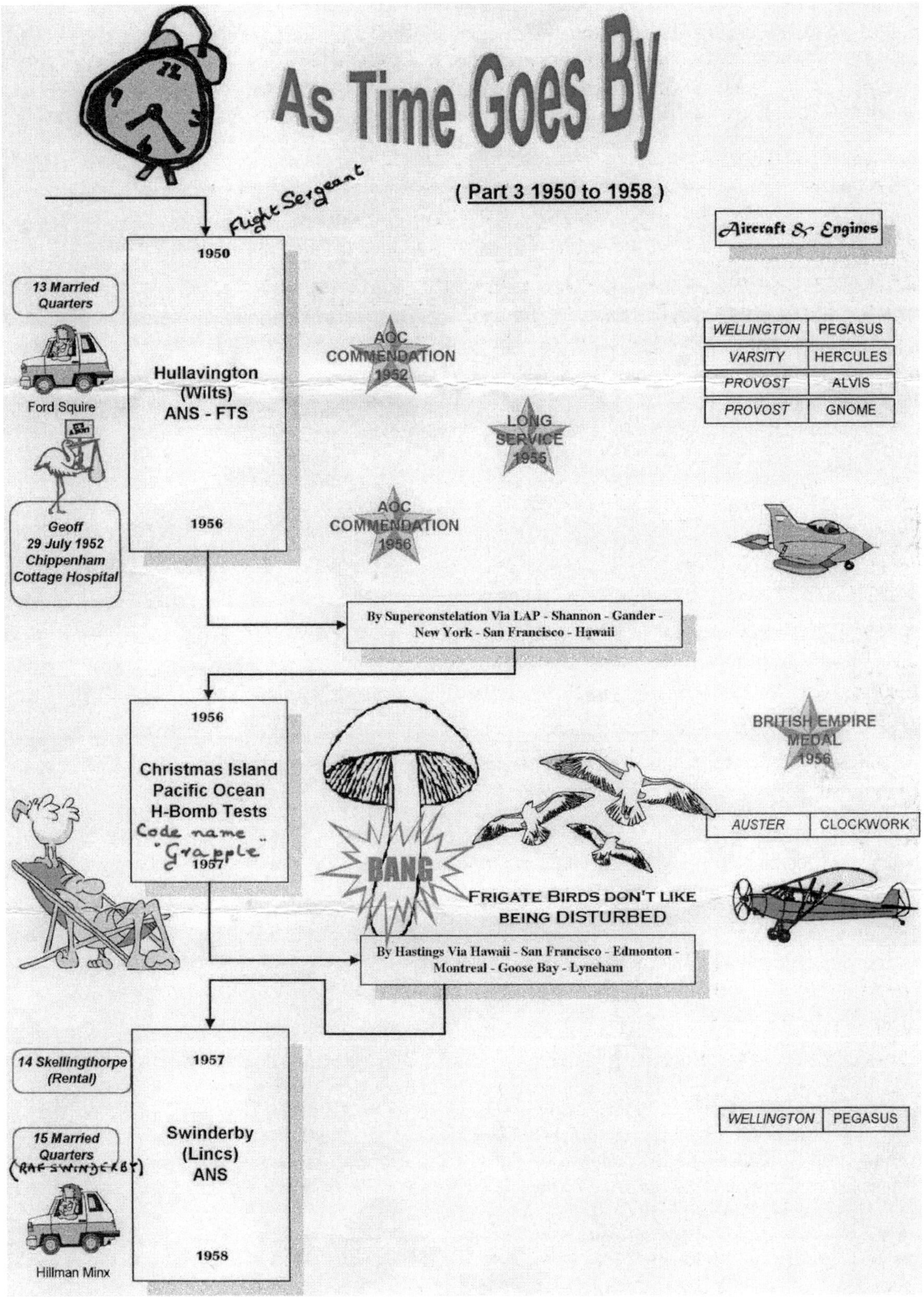

Group Captain Anthony W. Ringer, CBE, LVO, AFC*, RAF (Ret'd)
Officer Commanding The Queen's Flight 22 July 1963 – 4th February 1968

Tony Ringer was born on 22nd August 1921 and attended the King Edward VII Grammar School at Market Harborough before joining the Royal Air Force in September 1940. Pilot training was carried out at No. 11 EFTS Perth, No. 8 SFTS Montrose and No. 20 OUT at Lossiemouth.

January 1942 saw Tony at No. 44 Ferry Group at Harwell and on his way as one of eighteen Wellington Mk. 1Cs to Egypt via Portreath, Gibraltar and Malta before joining the aircrew-holding unit at Shallufa.

During March/April 1942 he joined No. 40 Squadron at Fayid then ME Echelon to India via Habbaniya, Shaibah, Sharjah, Karachi. Asansol and Pandaveswar with No. 215 Squadron flying operational sorties, supply dropping, and day and night bombing before moving south to St.Thomas's Mount, Madras for coastal patrols.

In October 1942 moved the Squadron to Rawalpindi (Chacklala) for paratroop training for the Ghurkhas and in 1943 to Jessore in Bengal to continue day and night operations over Burma and the Bay of Bengal until repatriated by sea in November arriving at Falmouth in November 1943.

After conversion to the later Mks of Wellington, Tony served as QFI at No. 12 OUT at Chipping Warden, at No.14 OUT at Market Harborough and No. 26 OUT at Wing. After completing a staff course at the Bomber Command Instructors School in April 1946 he remained on the staff of BCIS flying Wellingtons and Lancasters at Finningley and, in July 1947, at the Bomber Command Instrument Rating and Examiners Flight at RAF Scampton.

Leaving Scampton he joined No. 50 Squadron flying Lincolns and in January 1948 moved to Headquarters, No. 1 Group at Bawtry as PA to the AOC, first Air Vice Marshal Guest then Air Vice Marshal Mills. Tony was also the OC of the Communications Flight at Lindholme.

In January 1950 he joined the Central Flying School Examining Wing at Brize Norton and later at Little Rissington. He held a CFS A1 category.

Moving on to the Royal Air Force Flying College at Manby in July 1952 he completed No. 4 Course and remained on the staff as Deputy Syndicate Leader until the 4th May 1955 when he was appointed Bomber Command Liaison Officer at Handley Page, Radlett.

Appointed to be OC 'A' Squadron (Victors) at No. 232 OCU at Gaydon in May 1957 before taking up the appointment as Wing Commander, OC No.3 Group Standardisation Unit, Valiants and Victors in July 1959. In September 1961 he was appointed to be Wing Commander Training at No.3 Group HQ at Mildenhall.

His appointment to be Officer Commanding, The Queen's Flight at RAF Benson followed in 1963, after which, in March 1968, he attended the Senior Officers War Course at the Royal Naval College at Greenwich.

A tour with NATO In October 1968 in the Policy Branch, Allied Forces Central Europe at Brunssum was followed by his appointment in February 1971 to be the Officer Commanding and RAF Henlow and Commandant OCTU.

His final tour of duty was as the Air Adviser to HE the British High Commissioner, British High Commission in Canberra, Australia from March 1973 until his retirement from the Royal Air Force in August 1976. His total flying hours was 6000 in 46 different aircraft types.

Decorations: CBE, LVO and AFC and Bar.

Squadron Leader H. G. (Fred) Sealey, MVO
Fixed Wing Navigator, The Queen's Flight, 1962-76

Horace George (Just call me Fred) Sealey was born on 9th February 1926. Fred joined the Royal Air Force as an Aircraft Apprentice at RAF Cranwell in February 1942 and trained as a Wireless Operator Mechanic.

He began his flying duties as a Wireless Operator/Air Gunner with Coastal Command flying Sunderland and Catalina flying boats.

Fred later trained to be a Navigator and again in Coastal Command flew in Shackleton aircraft before being posted to Bomber Command where he flew in Canberra aircraft. In 1962 he was posted to The Queen's Flight where he flew as the Navigator in Kitty Three crew as Personal Navigator to HRH The Duke of Edinburgh until he retired in April 1976.

A memorable occasion for Fred occurred at London Heathrow Airport. The Kitty Three crew had positioned the Andover ninety minutes before their Royal Flight with HRH Prince Philip at the north side VIP lounge with plenty of time to file the flight plan, check the weather and be ready for HRH to arrive.

The crew exit on the Andover is at the front of the aircraft and is reached by a high ladder that stands at an angle of about twenty degrees to the vertical. It would be sensible when using this exit to face inwards to the ladder and use both hands. However, he did not but came down face forwards with a brief case in his hand. He came down far faster than he expected, having caught his heel in the top rung and landed on the ground nose first! On coming round a few moments later, Fred remembers hearing a voice suggesting his nose may be broken. A fair amount of blood was spilt on the tarmac and his best uniform. He was obviously in no condition to continue with the task and he was whipped off to casualty where he was patched up and very well looked after.

The Queen's Flight reacted in its usual efficient style and got hold of the nearest available navigator who was Squadron Leader Phil Fearn. As it was still early in the morning he had not yet left his home in Henley and was able to arrive in time to replace Fred on that flight.

The OC's wife, Anne Ringer, telephoned his wife Cynthia, to say she was not to worry but Fred had fallen out of the aeroplane but that he was all right. Fred recovered quite soon but had to endure two black eyes for a while including attendance at a Royal Garden Party.

Retiring to the North of England in April 1976, Fred became the County Emergency Planning Officer for Northumberland and since his second retirement now spends many hours carrying out voluntary work for SSAFA/Forces Help and the WRVS.

J. R. (John) Welch, RVM, BEM
A. Tech A, The Queen's Flight, 1963 to 1972 and 1974 to 1977

Born 17th April 1943 in Mere, Wiltshire, John was educated at the Gillingham (Dorset) Grammar School from 1955 to 1959. A real country boy, who spent most of his free time rough shooting and helping out on local farms, he was never away from home, even for a holiday, until he joined the Royal Air Force.

Coming from a family with a service background, his father served on the Somme at 17 years old, and was invalided out with mustard gas poisoning, three of his uncles served in the Royal Air Force during the Second World War (one with DFC and OBE – one (Reginald) was lost in action whilst flying a Typhoon, John took his name later in life as a mark of respect), and one uncle in the Army, it was no surprise when he followed their lead and joined the Royal Air Force as a Halton Apprentice in January 1960, the 94th Entry, as an Airframe Fitter.

In 1963 John was posted to The Queen's Flight as a Corporal Airframe Fitter and rose to Chief Technician before he left in 1972. John was awarded the Royal Victorian Medal (Silver) on leaving the Flight in 1972.

From 1972 until 1974 John was sent to Cyprus to work on helicopters with No.84 Squadron with the United Nations at RAF Nicosia, Cyprus as the Airframe Trade Manager. At RAF Nicosia in 1973 John and pilot (Barry Hobkirk) escaped with only minor injuries from a Westland Whirlwind Mk 10 (XL 110) that suffered an azimuth star failure that resulted in the loss of one complete main rotor blade and total destruction of the aircraft. How did they escape? FAST! Reason for failure, Westland's forgot to add the grease track to the main spherical bearing, the rest is history and John has a balance problem to contend with because of injuries sustained.

RAF Nicosia 1974 – Coup followed by Turkish invasion, quite an eventful few months. Learnt how to keep his head down; his family was evacuated under fire (ground and air) and eldest daughter (only 9) received a citation for bravery from the Girl Guides Association – protected sister (7) by lying on top of her whilst under fire. Many, many sandbag tales not enough time or paper; would not have missed it for the World! Interesting point, between his father-in-law (33 years RAF) and John they caught all 3 Cyprus problems.

At end of Cyprus tour, by longhand letter from Ron Tooke via his OC, he was told he was to return to The Queen's Flight as Trade Manager and to please tell Pete Baughan (at Akrotiri) that he was to return to be i/c First Line. Neither of them was asked, it was assumed that they would return. In 1974 John returned to The Queen's Flight as Airframe Trade Manager until 1977.

John tells a few memorable and a few funny and memorable incidents during his second tour when he flew as support crew on quite a few overseas trips with Kitty 3:

"Whilst grounded at Bangkok for a week (that was boring!), I was charged with looking after a jar containing king leaches that had been gifted to Prince Philip for use on his Polo ponies injuries. The water had to be changed every day but no chlorine (very difficult); needless to say I failed, the stench was unbearable but not as bad as having to tell HRH!

With 23 passengers and HRH to feed on a 1½ hour internal flight (Gdansk to Warsaw) we had ordered set seafood meals; no such luck, whole lobsters etc. to prepare in a hurry but unfortunately no sharp knife except the Captains penknife! We coped but only just, fortunately Prince Philip enjoyed our predicament and the lobster.

Requested by Prince Philip's Valet for a pot of HRH's special tea; not a problem I thought as I gave it to Prince Philip. Unfortunately, those of a certain class don't seem to like the tea bags left hanging down the side of the silver pot! Not many brownie points that day.

On behalf of my team I received the Silver Jubilee Medal during second tour and on posting, on promotion to Flight Sergeant, I received a signed framed photograph of the Queen and Prince Phillip".

During his second tour John enjoyed attending, with Margery, such functions as a day at the Palace and a Christmas Ball at Windsor Castle with the famous Joe Loss and since leaving the RAF has enjoyed many Victorian Order Services at Windsor, a British Empire Service at St Paul's Cathedral and of course, again with Margery, the Garden Party at the Palace.

In 1977 at RAF Shawbury as a Flight Sergeant, John set up the Wessex Helicopter Aircrew Twin-Engined Continuation Training Flight for which he received the BEM on behalf of his team. He states it was a very interesting tour; with 5 Wessex Mk 5's (Navy) and had to operate using their offshore servicing system on a land based RAF station with RNAS Yeovilton as his HQ. He had 2 (very helpful but very thirsty) Chief Petty Officers to assist him. As a further interest his AOC's inspecting officer (Jock Rae) for his GSE and the Station Commander, Group Captain Wilson, were both ex-The Queen's Flight.

John returned to Oxfordshire in 1979 on posting to RAF Abingdon as the Repair Liaison Officer on the Repair and Salvage Squadron until his retirement from the Royal Air Force in 1983

Decorations: Royal Victorian Medal (Silver), British Empire Medal, United Nations (Cyprus) Campaign Medal, Silver Jubilee Medal, LSGC Medal

On leaving the Service John attended a Technical Author Course and worked until 1987 for the Pergamon Press firstly from 1983-85 as a Technical Author responsible for compiling operating and maintenance manuals for British Gas onshore terminal and offshore platforms, and from 1985-86 as a Technical Author responsible for compiling operating/training manuals and training modules for Marathon Oil Brae 'B' oil production platform.

In 1986-87 as a Senior Technical Author responsible for compiling component maintenance manuals to military specifications of AVA8B Harrier and Phantom aircraft, and until June 1987 as a Senior Technical Author responsible for compiling training packages, comprising lecture notes and visual aids, for CONOCO Southern Basin Gas Development.

A move to the Martin-Baker Aircraft Company Limited in 1987 saw John as a Technical Author responsible for compiling and amending publications to AVP70 on aircraft emergency escape systems for the British Armed Services. Liaison visits to Service units and civilian contractors. In 1990 John became a Senior Technical Author using DL Pager DTP system and SGML, responsible for compiling publications to MIL-M-819A (AS) on aircraft emergency escape systems and associated ground support equipment with liaison visits to United States Navy Service units.

In 1996 John moved to AWE Aldermaston until 2001 as Project Technical Author/Sub-Contract Liaison Officer and after an Aldus PageMaker DTP Introductory Course, using Microsoft Word 97; responsible for converting to '97' from out-of-date software as necessary, while compiling and amending approximately 900 Operating and Maintenance Manuals for the Main Process and its associated mechanical, electrical and instrumentation Utility Systems.

Courses attended during this period included a Management Partnership Course; Direct Security Vetting appropriate to a Nuclear Environment; Windows 98 and Word 97 experience to advanced level and Safety Courses appropriate to a Nuclear Environment. John was also responsible for compiling and amending Operating Instructions for the remote Control Room, and as Sub-Contract Liaison Officer; responsible for estimating, controlling and checking work sub-contracted to two Agencies.

At RAF Halton John had started shooting smallarms as a competitive sport and carried this on until 1997, having successes both in the service and afterwards. He was, for many years a member of the RAF Pistol and Sub-machine gun teams. John shot both the smallbore and fullbore rifle for Oxfordshire and was the County fullbore champion for many years. In 1973 John finished on a high, coming 43rd in the Queens Hundred in the Imperial Meeting at Bisley out of 1200 competitors from around the World. He continues to rough shoot and help out on 2 local estates during the shooting season (back to being a country boy).

During the IRA bombings in the UK and shortly after the Bournemouth incidents, whilst roost shooting pigeons on the Orchards at Harwell on a Sunday evening, he encountered (at dusk in the wood he was in) a suspicious looking and acting lone stranger! He had a chat and escorted him off the site. The following Thursday evening he settled down to read the 'daily' and to his horror there was an identikit wanted drawing of guess whom? Yes his friend, unfortunately his nickname was Mr. 'Gaunt' and was wanted as an IRA suspect for the Bournemouth bombings. Quick visit to Didcot Plod Station; panic and recorded interview which was sent immediately to Bournemouth CID! As a follow up he thought he had better tell the owner so next day he met him outside of his office and stared to tell his tale. He stopped John in mid-sentence and whisked him inside as he said 'don't let the girls hear'. Apparently the previous Saturday a 'blown' safe with more explosive inside had been found amongst the fruit trees. Recently he was told that his encounter had been reported in a 'Daily' but he did not see it. What made him go cold following his encounter was that he would not have been alone, so where was his mate?

14. The Fourth Captain & Others 1968–1982

Air Commodore Sir Archie Winskill, KCVO, CBE, DFC*, AE
Captain of The Queen's Flight: 15th February 1968 – 27th January 1982
Extra Equerry to HM The Queen

Born 24th January 1917. Educated at Penrith and Carlisle Grammar Schools. Originally had an ambition to make a career in the Merchant Navy but with the slump in 1933 the entire fleet of The Northern Shipping Company, to which he had been articled, was laid up and he was taken on by the LNE Railway Company to be trained for higher echelons. A five shilling (25p) flight with Alan Cobham's circus in a field near Carlisle in 1932 plus a friendship with a World War I pilot turned his thoughts to other fields and he joined the newly created Royal Air Force Volunteer Reserve as a weekend pilot in 1937.

Called up before WW2 he completed three operational tours flying Spitfires. The Battle of Britain; Sweeps over Occupied Europe; and North Africa (Operation Torch 1942-43); Awarded the DFC in 1941 and a Bar to the DFC in 1943. Credited with five aircraft destroyed and three probables.

Twice he evaded capture having been shot down over enemy territory. Firstly in 1941, flying one of 36 Spitfires from 41 Squadron escorting Blenheim bombers on a raid from Tangmere to the St.Omer railyards when his plane was hit in the ailerons and elevators and spun out of control. "I

jumped out quite low and landed without injury in the cornfield, staying within eyeshot of the aircraft. Once the Germans realised there was no one onboard, they searched the whole area for a couple of days, but the idiots never thought to look in the corn and spread a wider net.

The locals obviously saw my parachute and that first night an 18 year old French farm boy, Felix Caron, walked around the field and sought me out. He had a bowl of soup with him and said "Are you hungry?" He was very brave and visited me twice until the hubbub died down. Then I went into the village and lived and worked with them until I could move on, I was extraordinarily lucky". The villagers helped him to evade capture by dressing him as a French peasant, (see picture), then contacting underground organisations which smuggled him across France and over the Pyrenees, arriving back in Britain three months later, where he was awarded the Distinguished Flying Cross.

(Note: The two met again in 1998, Sir Archie being 81 and Felix 75 by this time and together they visited the field where Sir Archie's aircraft crashed).

No longer allowed to fly over Europe because of his knowledge of escape routes, he was posted to Scotland and then to North Africa with No. 232 Squadron. There, in January 1943 he was brought down by ground fire whilst attacking a sensitive target, landing his Spitfire successfully on the sea. Later over Tunisia in 1943 when he parachuted out after being struck by ground fire, and returned to his squadron, crossing the front line with the help of friendly Arabs.

He ended the war as a Wing Commander and was the Chief Flying Instructor of The Central Gunnery School; Graduated from Army Staff College; and was awarded a Permanent Commission in the RAF. After a tour of duty in the Air Ministry, 1945-47; he reverted to the rank of Squadron Leader and was given command of No. 17 Squadron in Japan, and had the task of leading a fly past over Tokyo of 72 Commonwealth aircraft, on the 20th November 1947 in honour of the marriage of HRH The Princess Elizabeth to Prince Philip.

A tour of duty in Malta, 1948-49, was followed by secondment to the Belgian Air Force as Air Advisor to the Belgian Government and formed their first Meteor Jet Wing, 1950-52; Staff duties at HQ Fighter Command, 1953-54, followed, and then graduation from the Joint Services Staff College; Station Commander, RAF Turnhouse, 1955-56, which included Wing Commander Flying of the Scottish Auxiliary Vampire Jet Wing, Edinburgh/Glasgow/Aberdeen; Posted to RAF Germany as Group Captain Operations, 1957-59; Graduating from the RAF Flying College where he flew the Canberra bomber and the Hunter fighter jet. He then commanded RAF Duxford, 1960-61, established with one day and one night fighter squadrons equipped with the Javelin and Hunter aircraft.

After a tour of duty in the Ministry of Defence, 1962-64, he was seconded to the Foreign Office as Air Attaché, British Embassy, Paris, 1964-67. There he was involved in Anglo French aviation projects, (including Concorde, Martel Missile, Jaguar aircraft and helicopters). His next appointment was Director of Public Relations, Ministry of Defence (RAF) i.e. Spokesman for the RAF dealing with the media. It was in November 1967 that a helicopter of The Queen's Flight crashed and killed the Air Commodore and two Squadron Leaders and one Flight Lieutenant. A truly poignant disaster with its effect on the morale of such a specialised unit dedicated to the air travel of members of the Royal Family. Sir Archie was selected by the Air Board to replace the Air Commodore and restore morale of the Unit.

Liveryman GAPAN 1978-; Freeman of City of London 1978.

Decorations: KCVO 1980 (CVO 1973); CBE 1960; DFC 1941 Bar 1943: AE 1944.

Flight Sergeant Roger J. Church, RVM
Eng Tech Av, The Queen's Flight, 1971-74, 77-83

Roger was born on 1st March 1943 and educated at the West Greenwich Central School in London. He joined the Royal Air Force in August 1961 and had a variety of postings before joining The Queen's Flight's Avionic Bay.

A summary of his service shows that he served at RAF Scampton servicing ECM Vulcan B2's for one year; RAF Geilenkirchen in Germany with No. 11 Squadron, Javelin Mk 9 for three years; RAF Wittering 100 & 39 Squadrons, Victor Mk.2; Headquarters Strike Command as Technical Advisor to Crystal Bank; RAF Little Rissington with Jet Provost's Mk.3, Mk.4, Mk.5, Chipmunks and Varsity's; The Queen's Flight at RAF Benson; RAF Little Rissington again, this time servicing PTRs Red Arrows and Red Pelicans; RAF Cosford, servicing all the various types of aircraft used for training; Second tour on The Queen's Flight; before moving to RAF Wyton on Electronic Warfare; and RAF Sealand as QA Manager for ATE test programs.

Roger retired from the Royal Air Force in May 1988 and has worked as the New Equipment Manager for Plandale 1988-91; Sales Support Manager for IMTEC from 1991-1998; and at RAF Sealand as the Cryptographic Maintenance Engineer.

Decorations: RVM (Silver). LSGM.

Warrant Officer Peter M. Dale, RVM
Eng Tech Av, The Queen's Flight, 1967-1978

Peter (Dizzy) Dale was born on 12th August 1941 and educated at Yately Manor, Nr. Canterbury and Clarks College Guildford.

Joining the Royal Air Force as a boy of 15 on 11th February 1957, Peter served until September 1996 when he retired as the Warrant Officer i/c Trade Training Avionics at RAF Cosford.

"Dizzy" joined The Queen's Flight as a shift Corporal and left as a Chief Technician, Trade Manager for the Avionics Bay. Whilst serving with the Flight he was a member of the "Golden Eagle" team in support of the Prince of Wales learning to fly and undertook many overseas flights with the Andover as engineering support.

His career in the Royal Air Force is listed as:

RAF Cosford, Wolverhampton	1957-1958	RAF Oakington, Cambridge	1958-1961
RAF Yatesbury, Calne, Wiltshire	1961-1962	RAF Oakington, Cambridge	1962-1964
RAF North Front, Gibraltar	1964-1966	RAF Benson, Wallingford	1966-1967
The Queen's Flight, RAF Benson.	1967-1978	RAF Cosford, Wolverhampton	1978-1982
RAF Wyton, 51 Sqdn, Huntingdon	1982-1985	RAF Sealand, 3 Sqdn, Chester	1985-1987
RAF Cosford, Wolverhampton	1987-1996		

On retirement Peter took up a post as an Instructional Officer, Grade D Civil Service, teaching Electronics at RAF Cosford.

Decorations: RVM (silver), MSM, SJM, LSGM with bar.

Air Commodore Michael C. Darby, MVO, BSc(Eng), RAF (Ret'd)
Senior Engineering Officer, The Queen's Flight, 26th October1970 – 15th March 1973

Michael was born on 1st August 1937 and educated at Brockenhurst and Bristol University.

Joining the Royal Air Force in 1955, he retired in 1990 before going on to teach maths and physics at the Royal Grammar School, High Wycombe.

His career history in the Royal Air Force shows that his first tour as the Junior Engineering Officer with No. 85 Squadron at RAF West Raynham was followed by a tour as Engineering Officer at the Day Fighter Combat School at RAF Binbrook.

After training he was posted as the Search and Rescue Helicopter Pilot at RAF El Adem in Libya before returning to the UK as a Trials Officer at the Aeroplane and Armament Experimental Establishment at Boscombe Down, followed in 1970 by a three-year tour as the Senior Engineering Officer at The Queen's Flight.

After attending a Staff College Course, Michael was posted as the Engineering Inspector of Flight Safety before going to Cyprus as Officer Commanding, Engineering Wing at RAF Akrotiri. A tour as a Deputy Director at the Ministry of Defence followed before being appointed Station Commander at RAF Swanton Morley.

A Course at the Royal College of Defence Studies was followed by another tour in the Ministry of Defence as a Procurement Director before becoming Air Commodore Engineering and Training at Headquarters RAF Support Command.

Married with four grown up children Michael is now happily retired with his wife in Somerset.

Group Captain D.L. (Eddie) Edmonds, CVO, AFC*
Deputy Captain, The Queen's Flight, 16th March 1973 – 31st March 1978

Joining the Royal Air Force in 1942, Eddie Edmonds went to Southern Rhodesia under the Empire Training Scheme for his basic flying training. He stayed on and was trained to be a flying instructor and posted to the Flying Instructors School to instruct future instructors.

Eddie returned to the UK in Aug 1945 as a Flight Lieutenant and was posted to No.61 Eastern Reserve Group until his release from the Service in 1947. Eddie returned to Southern Rhodesia and joined the Southern Rhodesia Civil Service in 1947.

Re-joining the RAF in 1949 he carried out a Flying Refresher Course and Jet Conversion on Meteor aircraft before being posted to No.74 (F) Squadron in1950. He became the Training Officer for No.610 County of Chester Auxiliary Squadron at RAF Hooton Park in 1952.

Selected for an Exchange Posting with the Royal Canadian Air Force in 1954 he was posted to RCAF Gimli in Manitoba, Flying Training T33 aircraft, and was appointed Deputy Chief Flying Instructor. Back to the UK in 1956 he became a Flight Commander on No.1 (F) Squadron at RAF Tangmere flying Hunter Mk.5 aircraft.

He was detached to Cyprus for the Suez Emergency and was promoted to Squadron Leader in January 1957. The same year he moved to No.12 Group as Flight Safety Officer. In 1958 Eddie was posted to RAF Alhorn in Germany to reform No. 26 Squadron with Hunter Mk6s, moving the Squadron to RAF Gutersloh until Dec 1960 when the Squadron was again disbanded.

A ground tour at No.13 Group Headquarters as Operations (Day) in 1961 followed before being promoted to Wing Commander and a move to command a Boy Entrant Wing at RAF Hereford in 1962. He attended the Air Warfare Course at RAF Manby in 1964 before moving to RAF Little Rissington as the Chief Instructor at the Central Flying School, Little Rissington from 1964 to 1966. He was involved with the formation of the Red Arrows and he reformed and led a four aircraft Red Pelicans formation and aerobatic team in 1965.

A short tour at Flying Training Command Headquarters followed in 1967 before being promoted to Group Captain and being selected as Air Adviser to the British High Commissioner, in Australia in the same year. He returned to the UK to be appointed Station Commander, Varsity Flying Training School at RAF Oakington from 1971 to 1973.

He was appointed Deputy Captain of The Queen's Flight in 1973 until his retirement in 1978. In 1981 he was appointed Custodian, at Berkeley Castle in Gloucestershire, where he stayed until his final retirement in 1990.

Decorations: Awarded AFC 1957; Bar to AFC 1967; Appointed CVO 1978.

Sydney Arthur (Jack) Frost RVM
A Fitt P, The Queen's Flight, 1967-71 & 1973-74

Son of a serving Royal Marine, Sydney Arthur (Jack) Frost was born in 1934 at Gillingham in Kent. Spending his early years as a spectator of aerial warfare Jack attended State Primary and Secondary Modern Schools before entering the Royal Naval Dockyard at Chatham as a 'messenger boy'. In September 1950 he joined No. 2 School of Technical Training at RAF Cosford, 11th Entry Boy Entrants, as an Engine Mechanic.

On completion of his training in the spring of 1952, Jack was posted to RAF Manby, a boy/airman. Involved in the 'great floods' rescuing residents of Chapel St Leonard's and sandbagging the seawall at Mablethorpe.

Qualified to Fitter then promotion to Corporal. Early in 1954 he went off to the Far East Air Force at RAF Seletar West Camp, where he joined the Field Repair and Salvage Flight and Jungle Salvage Team, recovering or repairing broken aeroplanes in Malaya, India, Burma and Laos. Survived a Court-martial, sea snake bite and some parachuting, albeit with a broken leg.

1957-59: Back in UK and off to RAF Colerne, building Hastings and Valetta power plants, living in a hut with ten bods and ten motorcycles, great fun but not a very inspiring occupation!

1959-62: Off to the Southern Hemisphere and No.1 Air Trials Unit Royal Australian Air Force at Woomera. Normal aircraft maintenance with duties as a 'flying spanner' on fixed and rotary wing aircraft. Wandered the desert in search of Aboriginal Antiquities contributing 'finds' to the South Australian Museum. In collaboration with an RAF rigger operated the Woomera lemonade factory. Travelled extensively in the outback experiencing the true Australia; sheep stations to mission stations, opal mines to gold mines. Walked from Woomera to Port Augusta in 19 hours, shot 'roos' for their skins, trudged Tasmania up and around Cradle Mountain. The Pom who went bush!.

1962-64: RAF Hullavington promoted to Sergeant – Quality Control – Command Power Plant Bay. NCO i/c a flight at Sir Winston Churchill's funeral.

1964-67: Far East Air Force, No. 103 Squadron Whirlwind Helicopters RAF Seletar. Promotion to Chief Technician. Contributed to deployment capabilities and field operations. Sponsored by Group Captain Hutton the Station Commander (brother to Flight Sergeant Hutton TQF) and the Air Vice-Marshal RAF Engineering, made application to join The Queen's Flight. Returned to UK pending interview and selection for service on The Queen's Flight.

1967-71: The Queen's Flight. Technician, Helicopter Crew Chief/Helicopter Manager. Introduction of the Wessex helicopter. Produced a paper with recommendations for the review of helicopter servicing.

1971-73: No. 33 Squadron, Puma Helicopters. NCO i/c Line Shift promoted Flight Sergeant and appointed NCO i/c Squadron Engineering Flight.

1973-74: The Queen's Flight Line Manager. Then retirement from the Royal Air Force.

1974–76: Aircraft fitter at CSE Aviation, Kidlington, Oxford, Ministry of Defence Police Officer and British Aircraft Corporation.

1977-82: BAC Saudi Arabia, Dhahran and Tabuk. Spent time exploring the deserts and mountains, Tabuk to the Red Sea. Discovered Stone Age rock carvings and archaeology from ancient times.

Traced journeys of St John Philby, the one time British advisor to King Fiesal. Returned overland to UK.

1982-83: not working by choice/ part time Security Guard.

1983-85: enlisted in The Sultan of Oman's Air Force, appointed Staff Officer Engineering (Mods), Oman Ministry of Defence.

1986-91: Manager Spares and Repairs at Schenck UK, a large-scale international multi-disciplined engineering company. Redundant 1991, enjoyed retirement since that date. Member of The Royal Air Force Boy Entrants Association, Chairman of The Queen's Flight Association. 2000 – 2003. Awards: 1970 QCVSA, 1972 RVM.

Corporal J.E.F. (Joe) Gibbons
Supply, The Queen's Flight, 1966-1976

Joe was born on 12th June 1925 and went to the South Oxford School until he was 14 years old. When he was 16 years old (1941) he joined the ARP as a messenger and when he was 17 he went on war work in an Oxford factory making spares for Spitfire and Hurricane aircraft. He had to register for Armed Forces in 1943 when he was 18 years old and joined the Local Defence Volunteers (LDV), later to become the Home Guard. He was not called up, presumably because he was on war work, but he volunteered and was accepted for the Royal Air Force on 11th September 1944

Posted to Arbroath in Scotland for his 'square-bashing' then on to RAF Kirkham, Nr. Blackpool for equipment/assistant training in November 1944. Two months later saw Joe at No.233 MU at RAF Market Stainton in Lincolnshire, a bomb dump, all the bombs being stacked along the country roads and at times, everybody had to help unload the bombs. On one occasion a lorry load turned up and for some reason, no unloading slings were available, so it was decided to manhandle the bombs by rolling them along the bed of the lorry and dropping them off at the end onto the grass verge. After the unloading and stacking it was pointed out by someone that the red label on each bomb read, 'Do not drag or drop'. 2000 Italian Prisoners of War were sent to the camp then they disappeared and 2000 German Prisoners (SS Troops) were dispersed around the camp.

Joe moved to RAF Barnham in Norfolk in March 1947 where they were clearing mustard gas and in November of that year left the RAF with his demob group and went back to the factory in Oxford who was, at that time, then producing car spare parts.

In June 1958 he moved to work at the Pressed Steel (Oxford) factory, hanging doors on the Sunbeam Rapier Line, but the car recession came in 1959 and under the union rule of last in, first out, was out of work. In January 1961 Joe rejoined the RAF in the supply trade and after RAF Cardington went to RAF Kirton-in-Lindsey on the supply course. No square bashing! After the supply course a posting to RAF Duren in Germany (another bomb dump) where he first met John Barber who had been posted from The Queen's Flight on promotion. Tour-expired and in November 1963 posted to RAF Benson in the Electronic Supply Group and after two years was detached to RAF Hereford on a supply course and was promoted Corporal shortly after arriving back at Benson and in April 1966 was posted to RAF North Luffenham but didn't go because, at the same time, a vacancy arose on The Queen's Flight for a Corporal Supplier and Joe was selected. Here he again met up with John Barber who was the SNCO i/c the Supply Section.

Joe left the RAF at the end of his tour on the Flight in January 1976 and worked for ML Aviation at White Waltham Aerodrome maintaining records of Ministry of Defence equipment that the company had loaned in support of defence contracts and retired in June 1990 aged 65. Still living in Benson village Joe and his wife remain life members of the Married Families Club at RAF Benson and had no hesitation in joining the The Queen's Flight Association on its formation and volunteered to serve on the Committee serving for eighteen years responsible for the sale of the TQF/TQFA souvenirs. Such is his desire to be involved with the Association, even though no longer a member of the Committee, Joe retained until recently responsibility for the sale of ties and blazer badges. He is ever enthusiastic for the Reunion Dinners, having only missed one since 1982, and despite having ten operations and two replacement knees; Joe maintains he will be there whilst he is able to draw breath.

Wing Commander S. (Stan) Hitchen, LVO, AFC, MRAeS, RAF (Ret'd)
Officer Commanding, The Queen's Flight, 21st November 1975 – 6th December 1979

Born 8th May 1936 and educated at North Manchester Grammar School; and Brockenhurst County Grammar School. Stan joined the Royal Air Force in 1954.

After training and graduating as a pilot in Canada, he flew with No.5 (Venom) Squadron in 1957, at RAF Akrotiri in Cyprus. After conversion to the Transport Role he was back in Cyprus from 1958-59 with No.70 (Hastings) Squadron, this time at RAF Nicosia.

Back to the UK, another transport OCU and conversion to the Beverley , and a posting to No.53 Squadron at RAF Abingdon, 1960-62; No.34 (Beverley) Squadron, Seletar and Borneo in the Far East, 1962-64 (Awarded QCVSA);

Home again and to the Central Flying School at Little Rissington in 1965 for training as a flying instructor.

A tour as a Flight Commander Varsity Instructor, at RAF Manby, 1965-66; was followed by another overseas tour as Officer Commanding, No.84 (Beverley) Squadron, at RAF Khormaksar, Aden, 1966-67.

Returning to the UK Stan was appointed Officer Commanding, Standards Squadron at No.5 FTS Oakington, from 1967-70, attended RAF Staff College, Bracknell, 1970, followed by a tour at the Ministry of Defence in Operations Requirements, 1971-74.

A student at the Air Warfare College, Cranwell, 1974, before being appointed Officer Commanding of No.46 (Andover) Squadron, at RAF Thorney Island, 1975; and Officer Commanding, The Queen's Flight, Benson, 1975-79.

Retiring from the Royal Air Force in April 1980, Stan took up a career in Civil Aviation; Orion Airways, Training Captain, Airbus/Boeing 737, 1980-88; Britannia Airways, Training Captain, Boeing 737, 1989-94; GB Airways, Boeing 737, 1994-96; Air Foyle, Chief Training Captain, Boeing 737, 1996-97; Pilot Training Consultant All Marks Boeing 737, 1998-date.

Decorations: LVO 1979; AFC 1967; QCVSA 1964.

Group Captain D. St. J. (Derek) Homer, LVO, RAF (Ret'd)
Deputy Captain, The Queen's Flight, 7th May 1978 – 9th January 1981

Born 8th March 1936. Educated at Wrekin College and RAF College Cranwell. Joined the Royal Air Force in September 1954 and after graduating from the College joined No.65 (Fighter) Squadron in 1957. Three years later attended Central Flying School course and became a flying instructor.

Tours as a flying instructor at No.6 FTS and Edinburgh University Air Squadron followed, before he returned to No.6 FTS as Chief Instructor.

Derek gave some basic flying training to Members of the Royal Family on the Chipmunk at The Queen's Flight during 1962. He was appointed to be a Lieutenant of The Royal Victorian Order (LVO) in 1962.

Other notable appointments during his career include PSO to Commander-in-Chief Far East Air Force, 1970-72; Military Attaché to the Governor of Gibraltar, 1975-78, where he remembers Government House being known as the Convent because it had in the past been a Monastery and the Spanish word for Monastery is Conventa. It was haunted. Seemingly there was a Monk in the Monastery (Convent) who formed an amorous relationship with a Nun across the Square in a Convent. Clearly they were unable to take their relationship further, so they decided to leap off the cliffs at the southern end of Gibraltar together. She leapt, he didn't; and for 400 years or so she has been in the "Convent" looking for her lover. He never saw her, but many people did. Particularly two very young girls (aged 2 and 3), the granddaughters of a former Governor's wife and they could not possibly have known the supernatural from earthly beings.

Appointed Deputy Captain, The Queen's Flight in 1978-81; a tour of duty at the Ministry of Defence, 1982-87, before Retirement from the Royal Air Force in March 1987 to take up an appointment with the National Benevolent Institution where he still resides as Secretary. Derek finds his work at the NBI very rewarding and he finds it particularly gratifying that in the later years of his life he has been able to contribute a little to the well being of others in Society. They provide financial support for 400 or so elderly people and their families, and have homes in Westgate, Old Windsor and Tetbury, Gloucestershire. He invites you to visit them on the website on www.nbicharity.com

Group Captain E.T.I. King, LVO, RAF (Ret'd)
Officer Commanding, The Queen's Flight, 7th December 1979 – 17 December 1982

Born on 26th May 1944, educated at Strathmiglo Primary School, Strathmiglo; New Park Preparatory School, St Andrews; Dollar Academy, Dollar and the University of Glasgow. Eric joined the Royal Air Force as a Direct Entrant in 1963 and carried out his Initial Training at RAF South Cerney. Basic Training followed in 1964-65 at No. 6 FTS at Acklington winning the (Leadership Trophy & Eustace Brooke Lorraine Trophy, for best all-round student).

Advanced Training was carried out at No. 5 FTS at RAF Oakington in 1965. QFI Training at Little Rissington in 1965/66 was followed by a tour of Instructing at No.3 FTS at RAF Leeming from 1966-68 (appointed A2 Instructor in 1967).

Joined the Transport world in 1968/69 at the Andover OCU at RAF Abingdon and No. 46 Squadron at Abingdon and later at Thorney Island – 1969/73 – HS748MF, Andover Co-Pilot, Captain and Training Officer (Commendation for Valuable Service in the Air). In 1973 converted to C-130 Hercules at No. 242 OCU at Thorney Island before becoming Flight Commander Training on No. 36 Squadron at Lyneham, 1973/75.

A tour at the MOD Directorate of Flight Safety (RAF), London, 1975/77 – Desk Officer Publicity, was followed by attending the RAF Staff College, Bracknell as a student in 1977 before departing to the MOD Directorate of Personnel Management (RAF), Barnwood – 1977/79.

Back to flying duties and No 241 OCU, Brize Norton in 1979 for HS748 Andover Conversion and a tour as Officer Commanding, The Queen's Flight, Benson from 1979/83 (Member, later Lieutenant of the Royal Victorian Order).

Off to be a student again at the College of Air Warfare, Cranwell in 1983 before being posted to HQ Strike Command, High Wycombe – 1984/85 – as Wing Commander/Group Captain Contingency Plans and a later move to the MOD Directorate of Public Relations (RAF), Bracknell in 1986 as Group Captain head of the RAF Presentation Team.

Retiring on 1st April 1987, Eric has been actively engaged since in the Scottish Knitwear and Hosiery Manufacturing industry with Cumnock Knitwear Holdings Limited, Director (1988 / 1993); John Ford & Company Limited, Managing Director (1989 / date); John Ford Holding Limited, Chief Executive (1993 / Date) Holding Company, post Management Buy-out; North East Fife Enterprise Trust, Director (1990 / 1993) 'One-stop' provider on Business Advice and Training; Dollar Academy, Governor (1994 / Date) Independent, Co-educational Boarding School (Primary & Secondary) – 1,100 Pupils; Cresthigh Limited, Director, (1996 / Date) Property Development; Scottish Knitwear Association, Secretary – (1999 / Date) Knitwear Trade Association.

Professional Qualifications: Public Transport (Airline) Pilot's Licence (1982); Master of Business Administration (University of Glasgow) [Distinction] – (1990). Decorations: LVO (1983) QCVSA 1972. Eric is married with two children.

Air Commodore (later Professor) Richard A. Miller, OBE, FRAeS
Deputy Captain, The Queen's Flight, 6th December 1976 – 30th November 1978

Born 12th July 1936. Richard was educated at Northampton Grammar School; College of Art, Nottingham; Open University (DipEd, BA.Hons); Polytechnic of East London (MA, MSc).

Joining the Royal Air Force in 1956, and graduating in 1957 he was employed on normal pilot flying duties until 1970. He attended the RAF Advanced Staff Lovex in 1970 before a tour of duty at the Ministry of Defence during 1971-72, before being appointed the Officer Commanding No.36 Squadron at RAF Lyneham, 1973-75; In 1976 Richard was appointed Station Commander RAF Benson and Deputy Captain, The Queen's Flight until 1978; being appointed ADC to The Queen during this period.

He was awarded the RAF Diamond Jubilee Fellowship at the University of Southern California and Fitzwilliam College, Cambridge 1979. Returning to the Royal Air Force and an appointment as Director, Department of Air Warfare, RAF College in 1980 and as Director, Air Staff briefing, MOD, 1981-82, and Director, Public Relations (RAF) MOD, 1982-84. Retired as Air Commodore.

Since leaving the Royal Air Force Richard has held appointments with Executive Air Weapons, BAe Inc, USA 1985-86; Director, Defence Procurement Management Group, 1986-88; Dean, Continuing Education, 1987-89; Director, School of Defence Management, 1988-95 RMCS; Director of Strategic Management, School of Defence Management, RCMS, Cranfield University, 1995-97; Visiting Professor, Cranfield University 1997-99; Bath University 1999-date; Chairman, DGB Sterling Ltd. since 1998.

FIMgt; Freedom, City of London 1982; QCVSA 1965, 1970. Appointed OBE 1976.

Mr George Oakes, MVO
Secretary to the Captain, The Queen's Flight, 1966-76

George Oakes was born at Congleton, Cheshire on June 15th 1915 and was educated at St. Peter's Church School in Congleton.

From May 1940 until February 1946 George served in the Army with the Royal Artillery.

A career in the Civil Service followed with George "never in the RAF but always with the RAF". Nine years at the Headquarters at Buntingsdale Hall followed, in 1955, by a transfer to the Headquarters of the Middle East Air Force in Cyprus

From 1962 to 1966 George was a Civilian Administrative Officer at RAF Stafford before his posting as Secretary to the Captain of The Queen's Flight in 1966. In 1974 George was appointed to be a Member of the Royal Victorian Order.

He retired from the Civil Service in 1980 and took up the voluntary post of Sergeant at Mace to the Mayor of Wallingford until 1985 when he retired and returned to live in Market Drayton where he was a member of various local organisations following his hobbies of Caravanning, Motoring and Gardening.

George was a popular member of The Queen's Flight and Members will be sorry to hear that George suffered a stroke in the year 2000. "Lady" Vi reports, "He is doing quite well but is very slow".

Group Captain D.W. (David) Parsons, LVO, RAF (Ret'd)
Officer Commanding, The Queen's Flight, 1st November 1972 – 20th November 1975

Dave Parsons was born on 27th November 1935 and educated at Whitgift Middle School, Croydon (now renamed Trinity). He joined the Royal Air Force as a National Serviceman in September 1954 and was selected for Pilot Training, graduating in July 1956.

A tour as 2nd Pilot on Comet Mk.2 aircraft with No.216 Squadron at RAF Lyneham in 1957/58 was followed in 1959 by a posting to RAF Colerne with No. 24 Group Communications Squadron flying Anson's. (As he remarks – what a comedown!).

An OCU course and a tour with No. 36 Squadron as a Hastings Captain also at RAF Colerne from 1960/63 was followed by an Exchange Tour with the United States Air Force, 62nd Squadron, Sewart Air Force Base at Nashville, Tennessee as C130 B/E Captain. On 3rd March 1964 he was flying at 20,000 ft. when the forward cargo door blew out seriously damaging the aircraft wing, fuselage, engines and tailplane. He carried out an emergency landing at Knoxville and was awarded the American DFC.

Back to the UK in 1965 and off to the Central Flying School at Little Rissington to become a QFI. Promoted Squadron Leader in January 1966 and a posting to the Handling Squadron at A&EE Boscombe Down dealing with the C130 Pilots Notes/Checklists and translating USAF documents into RAF format. 1967/68 appointed Officer Commanding, 'A' Squadron at No. 242 OCU at RAF Thorney Island converting crews to the C130.

A tour at HQ Air Support Command at RAF Upavon, 1969/70 on Tactical Transport Policy and promotion to Wing Commander on 1st January 1970 saw a move to RAF Abingdon as Officer Commanding, Air Support Command Examining Unit (ASCEU), with the responsibility for the maintenance of standards and the categorisation of aircrew of all the transport force in the RAF at home and overseas.

David was appointed Officer Commanding, The Queen's Flight at RAF Benson; highlights of which he says were "getting the best transport job and the South Pacific Tour during 1974, taking Lord Mountbatten around the Far East to visit areas of his wartime command". He found it very hard to return to the RAF after such a tour!

In 1975 he was posted as Wing Commander Tasking at HQ No.38 Group at RAF Upavon until 1977 when he attended the Air Warfare Course at RAF Cranwell and promoted Group Captain in January 1978. A tour at the Ministry of Defence in Whitehall followed as Deputy Director Ops (AT) RAF before he retired on 5th April 1980 at his own request to pursue a career in Civil Aviation.

David's civilian flying career started with Shell Aircraft, London Heathrow (1980/83) flying BAe 125-700 taking Director/Senior Managers around Europe and the Middle East. In 1983 he moved to the Sultan of Oman's Royal Flight, Seeb Airport in Muscat as Deputy Commander where he flew the Gulfstream and VC10 aircraft. In July 1987, he flew the Sultan's VC10 to Brooklands Museum, the last civil flight by a VC10 and the first time one had landed at Brooklands where it remains today as part of the Museum's display.

Bristol Airport and a Captain MD83 with Paramount Airways (1987/89), a holiday charter company which closed down in 1989 was followed by Trans European Airways at Birmingham as a B737 Captain (1989/91), again a holiday charter company which closed down late 1991.

1992-2000, Dave was employed by Airtours International Airways at Manchester, once again a holiday charter company, starting as MD83 Captain, Fleet Manager 1992/93, Chief Pilot 1993/97 and Director Flight Operations 1997/2000, before retiring on 27th November 2000. He now lives in Cheshire.

Air Vice-Marshal Sir Richard Peirse, KCVO, CB
Deputy Captain, The Queen's Flight, 13th October 1969 – 1st February 1972

Born 16 March 1931. Educated at Bradfield College and RAF College Cranwell 1952. After graduation Richard flew with No.266 Squadron (Vampires and Venoms) 2nd TAF, Germany from 1952 to 1954 and served as ADC to AOC HQ 2 Group from 1954 to 1956.

Completing a course at the Central Flying School in 1956, he became a Flying Instructor at RAF Cranwell (Vampires) until 1959. A tour as Squadron Leader TF 2, No. 23 Group (Vampire/Meteor Training) followed until 1962 when he attended the Staff College at Andover for one year.

Posted to Malta in 1963, firstly as Flight Commander No.39 Squadron (PR9 Canberra) at RAF Luqa, then in 1964 as OC Ops Wing at Luqa until 1965, when he returned to the UK and the Air Secretary's Department (PA2), 1965-68.

Richard attended the Joint Services Staff College at Latimer in 1968, and was appointed Officer Commanding No.51 Squadron (Comet/Canberra) at RAF Wyton, from 1968 to 1969, and afterwards was appointed Deputy Captain of The Queen's Flight where he remained until 1972.

On leaving the Flight, he attended RCDS 1972, and was appointed Station Commander of RAF Waddington (Vulcans), from 1973-75, and moved to the Ministry of Defence with successive appointments as Deputy Director Operational Requirements 5, New aircraft systems, 1975 to 1977; Director of Personnel (Air), 1977 to 1980; Director of Operational Requirements, New aircraft 1980-81.

He was appointed Air Officer Commanding and Commandant RAF College Cranwell from 1982 to 1985 and the Defence Services Secretary from 1985 until his retirement in 1988.

Decorations: Appointed CB in 1984. KCVO 1988.

Appointed Gentleman Usher of the Scarlet Rod in the Most Honourable Order of the Bath in 1990

Note: Sir Richard is the son of the late Air Chief Marshal Sir Richard Peirse, KCB, DSO, AFC who has his own place in the history of Royal Flying, having flown Prince Albert on his first flight on the 4th March 1918 at the RN Air Station Sleaford (Cranwell) where Prince Albert was serving as a Naval Officer.

Group Captain B.A. (Basil) Primavasi, CVO
Deputy Captain, The Queen's Flight, 11 Mar 68 – 13 August 1971

Born 24th May 1921. Educated at Ewell Castle School, Ewell, Surrey. Applied for a Short Service Commission in the RAF in Mid-1939 and in June of that year attended the DH School of Flying at White Waltham for a 50 hour Tiger Moth course (Civil Service Grade). In August went to RAF Depot at Uxbridge for Commissioning and Discipline Course, Commissioned on 19th August 1939.

Attended No.12 Flying Training School at Grantham in September 1939 and on graduation posted to RAF Jurby as a Staff Pilot in January 1940. In early 1941 posted to Central Flying School, graduated as a category 'B' instructor, later regraded A1. From 1941-43 postings to various Stations followed carrying out Flying Instructor Duties, OC Station Flight and Flight Commander.

In April 1943 Basil was posted to No.96 Night Fighter Squadron, Beaufighter, Mosquito at Honily, Drem, West Malling, Ford and Odiham. (1 FW190 and 3 V1's destroyed) until August 1945 when appointed OC Mosquito Conversion Flight at 54 OTU Charter Hall. January 1947 saw a posting to the Empire Flying School Course, at RAF Hullavington, staying on after graduation as a Flying Instructor and Tutor.

An overseas tour in February 1948 saw Basil as Squadron Leader Training at HQ 205 Group, Fayid, Egypt. Returning to the UK and a RAF Staff College course at Bracknell in January 1952. A posting to the Air Ministry ACAS (OR) as OR2 (Helicopters) in January 1953 was followed by a short Helicopter Course at the Westland Aircraft Company, Yeovil in 1954.

He was appointed to be the Officer Commanding No.275 (Search and Rescue) Squadron, equipped with Sycamore Helicopters in 1955 before he returned to the Ministry of Defence, firstly in the Air Secretary's Department as P(Pol)1 in 1957 and in June 1958 as the PSO to the Inspector General.

Basil returned to flying duties in July 1960 and after completing No.16 Course at the Flying College, RAF Manby, he successfully completed the Vulcan OCU course at RAF Waddington. In May 1961 he was given Temporary Command of No. 617 Squadron, at RAF Scampton, before being appointed to reform No.50 Squadron as Officer Commanding in July 1961.

A ground tour followed in 1963 at HQ 2ATAF Rheindahlen, Germany as ACOD (Plans), before his appointment as Station Commander of RAF Cranwell in March 1965. He was appointed to be a Deputy Captain of The Queen's Flight in 1968 where he remained until 1971 and a return to the Ministry of Defence as Deputy Director of Ops Plans.

Basil was appointed Air Attaché for Tehran and Kabul in 1973 before his retirement from the Royal Air Force in 1976. Decorations: Appointed CVO 1972.

Warrant Officer Bryan Keith Rawnsley, MVO
A Tech A, The Queen's Flight, 1973 –1983

Born in Blackpool on 6th May 1930, Brian was educated at the Creighton School in Carlisle, Cumbria. He joined the Royal Air Force as a Boy Entrant on 26th May 1947 in the First Entry to be formed after the war. Throughout his service career Bryan was generally employed as an Airframe Mechanic then Fitter on a variety of aircraft that included Lancasters and Lincolns.

In 1951 during the trouble in the Canal Zone in Egypt he worked as a Team Leader rebuilding Vampires and on his return to the UK in 1954 continued to work on Vampires and Meteors.

In 1959 following an eight month course in all the allied trades to support his own, Bryan became an Aircraft Servicing Chief, a role which lasted for 7 years until his promotion to Flight Sergeant. He well remembers two flights, one the taking of Sir Winston Churchill's funeral films to Canada for their television, probably the last manned flight of this kind as the first satellite was due to come into use. The other was over 17 hours in a Vulcan Bomber non-stop on a proving flight for three aircraft to fly to Australia. Sadly his aircraft ended as a reserve!

As a junior manager he had many demanding roles, which included Shift Boss of over 70 Engineers on No. 617 Squadron at RAF Scampton working alternative days/nights for four years. Posted to Malta in 1970 on No. 13 Squadron and then on to ASF RAF Luqa and finally appointed controller for the removal of the Royal Air Force from the Island, although, in the end, we didn't actually leave. Bryan was awarded a C-in-C's Commendation for his efforts in that task.

Joining The Queen's Flight on 1st April 1973 as the Engineering Adjutant, he was appointed Warrant Officer Servicing in 1976, a post he held for nine years. Bryan was a member of the Steering Committee to introduce The Queen's Flight Association and served as Secretary/Treasurer of the Association for fourteen years.

Bryan retired from the Royal Air Force in October 1983 and joined South Oxfordshire District Council as Training Services Manager involved with the young and old unemployed until his final retirement in March 1993.

Appointed to be a Member of the Royal Victorian Order (MVO) in the New Year's Honours List 1983, Bryan was told by the Captain of The Queen's Flight that he, at that time, was the only Non-Commissioned Officer in the Royal Air Force to hold that award and that the Army and Navy also had just the one holder.

Squadron Leader W. B. (Brian) Sowerby, LVO, RAF (Ret'd)
Navigator, The Queen's Flight, 3rd January 1972 to 11th November 1985

A Yorkshireman, born in Barnsley, on 1st March 1933 and educated at Barnsley and District Holgate Grammar School, Brian left school at 15 to work as a Junior Clerk in the local Town Clerk's Office. As a keen member of the Air Training Corps he well remembers the Town Clerk telling him to "keep your feet on the ground laddie". Joining the Royal Air Force as a Direct Entry Navigator in January 1951 he completed his Initial Training at No.2 ITS, RAF Jurby in the Isle of Man, and No.2 Air Navigation School at RAF Thorney Island before being appointed to a King's Commission, sadly His Majesty died, so it became a Queen's Commission, a change of buttons on the uniform, and a passing out parade in February 1952 wearing a black armband.

Waiting for a Transport OCU Course, Brian was posted as supernumerary to RAF Topcliffe where he flew in the Hastings aircraft of both No.24 Squadron and No.47 Squadrons. One overseas trip with No. 47 Squadron was carried out under the guidance of a certain Flight Lieutenant Reg Mitchie, later of The Queen's Flight.

After completing No.242 (Medium Range Transport) OCU at RAF Dishforth he was posted overseas to No.114 Squadron at RAF Fayid in Egypt.

With 5 Squadrons of 8 Valetta aircraft each, plus the Long Range, York and Hastings, aircraft passing through made it a busy airfield. A fact, which became all too plain when Brian, in June 1953, had to take his turn at being an Operations Officer. The OC Flying Wing was Wing Commander Bill Tacon (ex OC The King's Flight), and others connected with Royal flying there were Ken Jenkins (ex Navigator The King's Flight), Vic Keay (The Queen's Flight), Mike Rayson (a future OC TQF) and Mike Hawes (future Navigator on TQF). After six months back to flying full time, this time with No.216 Squadron until tour-ex in July 1955.

A Long Range Transport conversion to Hastings aircraft, followed by a posting to No.511 Squadron at RAF Lyneham in Wiltshire in March 1956; flying the long-range routes and eventually becoming 'global' qualified. In September 1958 the squadron moved to RAF Colerne and renumbered No.36 Squadron. In December 1958, posted as Navigation Leader at the Transport Flight, A&AEE at Boscombe Down, mainly flying the Hastings, Valetta, Bristol Freighter aircraft to the overseas trials bases at Castel Benito, Tripoli, or Khartoum, for hot weather trials or to Edmonton and Fort Churchill in Canada for the cold weather. Or flying around the UK aircraft manufacturers with the 'boffins' and aircrew in the Anson or Devon aircraft, he also found the time to put on weight (three cooked meals a day or was it the Wiltshire Beer?).

March 1962 and his first posting to RAF Benson. The Argosy OCU and to No.115 Squadron for a three week build-up before the Squadron moved en-mass to RAF Khormaksar in Aden to fly routes around Africa and the Middle East. Appointed a local Navigator Examiner. Tour-ex at the end of March 1964, Brian received a posting notice to attend the Staff Navigation Course but on reporting to the Air Ministry on his return to London was told that this was cancelled and he was to be posted to the Transport Command Examining Unit (TCEU) (later TCES (Staff)) at RAF Benson as an Argosy Navigator Examiner, where he remained until October 1966 when he was sent to No.242 OCU at RAF Thorney Island to be part of a team preparing the OCU for the forthcoming arrival of sixty-six Hercules (C-130) aircraft. Delivery was expected before sufficient crews had been trained so the pressure was on! The OCU Pilots and Engineers had been sent to the USA for a full conversion, the Navigator's were sent for one week. Brian was lucky or unlucky, depending on your point of view; he arrived on a Sunday for the course to start on the Monday. Thursday of that week was Thanksgiving Day so his conversion course lasted three days and the aircraft he was due to bring back to the UK was not ready so it was back to the OCU writing the flying programme and précis notes. The urgency for the crews to be trained resulted in the OCU Staff being split into two Squadrons 'A' and 'B'. Brian was appointed Navigation Leader for 'A' Squadron under the command of Squadron Leader David Parsons (another future OC The Queen's Flight). In May 1968 he was appointed Wing Navigation Leader for the OCU with responsibility for the training, categorisation of the staff navigators and for the standards for the training of the student navigators. Awarded an AOC-in-C's Commendation for his efforts. OC Flying Wing at that time was Wing Commander Desmond Divers (another future OC The Queen's Flight!).

After four very hectic years at Thorney Island it was back to RAF Benson and the Air Support Command Examining Unit (ASCEU) as a Hercules Navigator Examiner. This unit moved from RAF Benson to RAF Abingdon in November 1970 where Wing Commander David Parsons followed him as OC ASCEU, and on 3rd January 1972, Brian was delighted to be invited to join The Queen's Flight back at Benson.

Initially crewed with Flight Lieutenant Derek Lovett (K4), he became K1 Navigator in November 1973 when Wing Commander Parsons once again, followed him to be his Officer Commanding. One year later he reverted back to K4 to resolve a case of personality clash and stayed with Derek Lovett until the arrival of David Rowe as K2 and thus the training crew until December 1981 when Graham Laurie (K4) arrived.

Brian will be remembered by most of the hangar floor personnel for his calling fire practices during his period as the unit Fire Officer. Emptying the hangar of aircraft, equipment and personnel became quite a slick performance and he still has the fireman's outfit presented to him at one of the annual dinners!

8th July 1972 gave him an early introduction into the flexibility required of a crew of The Queen's Flight. Kitty 4 and his crew were flying HRH Princess Alexandra to Blackpool and on the return flight were to 'drop in' at Wittering so that HRH could attend the reception after the wedding of TRH's Prince and Princess Richard. Twenty minutes before the time of take-off from Wittering to London, the weather broke and at the last minute the helicopters could not carry out their Royal Flights. Kitty 4 crew found themselves with HM Queen Elizabeth The Queen Mother, HRH The Prince of Wales, HRH The Princess Margaret, HRH Princess Alexandra and the Bride and Groom as passengers to London Heathrow with a quick turn round and a flight to RAF Leeming with TRH's Prince and Princess Richard on the first stage of their honeymoon. The thirty-five minute flight from Wittering to London spent arranging transport pick-ups for all the passengers soon passed. It is said the Captain's driver refused to believe it until HM The Queen Mother was sat in the back seat of his car!

Other highlights of his time with the Flight include February 1973 (flying with Kitty 4, Derek Lovett), and his first overseas Royal Tour to Ethiopia with HRH The Princess Anne. The tour went very well, but how those flies stick to one's face at Lalibella! The wisdom of carrying out proving flights was justified on this tour because we found, on the prover the previous November, that one of the landing strips was 35 miles away from the position given by the briefing.

February and March 1974 (Kitty 1, David Parsons) and the Tour of the British Solomon Islands, Papua New Guinea and Indonesia by HM The Queen, HRH The Duke of Edinburgh where they were joined by HRH The Princess Anne and Captain Mark Phillips on their honeymoon and Admiral of the Fleet, The Earl Mountbatten of Burma. The locals in PNG referred to Prince Philip as 'man belong Queen' whilst Earl Mountbatten was referred to as 'man belong all'. HM The Queen had to return to London from PNG for the UK elections so the Kitty One Crew were left to carry Earl Mountbatten from Papua New Guinea to Darwin, Bali, Singapore, Kuala Lumpur, Singapore/Tengah, and back to Darwin via Bali to rejoin HM Yacht Britannia and the Royal Party.

An excellent tour within a tour, with a wonderful personal memento of a signed letter and photograph being given to each member of the crew by Earl Mountbatten.

It was not often that the fixed wing crews made a night-stop at Wick after taking HM Queen Elizabeth The Queen Mother, north on her annual holiday to the Castle of Mey. 6th August 1974 is a date that Brian will remember for a long time. The crew were night stopping because they were to carry HM the following day to Kirkwall and back before returning to base. An invitation to take tea with Her Majesty at the Castle of Mey became a magical event.

In February 1975 Brian was lucky to be able to take the place of Alan Venier (because of his ill-health) flying with Jack Challinor (Kitty 2) on the Royal Tour of Mexico with HM The Queen and HRH The Duke of Edinburgh. The crew returned in the Royal Civil VC10 to London on 1st March, Brian's birthday, and with the usual 'standards' a cake had been arranged by the Crew Steward. Brian had to cut and serve it to the whole of the Royal Household onboard.

November 1975 and being 'detailed' as Officer i/c to build a golf course on the airfield for Sir Archie Winskill. Many members of the Association will remember those early days when the golfers from the Flight spent many hours making the wish of Sir Archie, to have a golf course where the airmen could learn to play the game of golf at little cost, come true. Once the Station Commander had given permission for the course to be built it was only a few months before the first competition was held. The golf course is still going strong with over 200 members and the golf club still acknowledges its existence was due to The Queen's Flight. Brian helped 'administer' the club for its first 21 years and now still helps out by organising the bar and cutting grass as a member of the Greens Team.

Another memorable tour in February 1977, Silver Jubilee Year, with Kitty 2 (David Rowe), and the Royal Tour to Fiji, New Zealand, Australia and Papua New Guinea by HM The Queen and HRH The Duke of Edinburgh. At the end of 1977, Brian was appointed to be a Member of the Royal Victorian Order (MVO).

If you wish to see the antiquities in Egypt it is recommended that you go with a Royal Personage. In November 1978, Kitty 2 and Crew flew HRH Princess Alexandra on a tour of the Arab Republic of Egypt and the crew were privileged to be able to join the Royal Party for the tours in Luxor. Fascinating, and to think he had wasted so much time not visiting the sights whilst passing through Luxor so many times during his early overseas tour in Egypt in 1953-1955.

Be prepared is a good motto, but on the July 1979 Royal Tour to the Independence Celebrations of the Gilbert Islands with HRH The Princess Anne, David Rowe and Brian were not prepared for the last minute news that they, as the most senior British Officers present, were to pull down the Union Jack at midnight. It was even suggested that they march out to the flagpole! A compromise was reached; the local police sergeant would march out with the new flag whilst the Officers of The Queen's Flight would stand smartly by the flagpole and lower the flag when indicated to do so! Good co-ordination of effort saw the job completed smartly (according to friends in Australia who saw the telecast). The extra people on the island for the celebrations, however, were too much for the local water supply, David and Brian had been billeted with the local Senior Air Traffic Controller and his family, and the only water available was that collected in the roof rain-water tank, so complete showers were out of the question. The after-shave came in handy!

Many tours, throughout the years, were carried out with HRH The Duke of Kent, as President of the War Graves Commission to visit War Graves and Memorials in parts of the world as far apart as Burma, Italy and France. Each and every one of them left a lasting impression.

Royal funerals overseas are something that occur at frequent intervals and the Kitty 4 crew, flying with Graham Laurie, saw Brian in Swaziland with Prince Michael of Kent representing HM The Queen in September 1982 and again later that month, the same crew flying to the South of France for the funeral of Her Serene Highness Princess Grace of Monaco with HRH The Princess of Wales, Queen Anne Marie of the Hellenes and the Grand Duchess of Luxembourg as the passengers.

On October 18th 1982, the Kitty 4 Crew became the second crew in the history of The Queen's Flight to be detained whilst carrying out their duties. On a proving flight to Aberdeen Two, a landing strip just over a hundred miles east of Harare in Zimbabwe, despite being told before the flight that everything had been cleared, just after landing the crew were detained by the Zimbabwe Army (North Korean trained!) for about four and a half hours. The full story has been covered elsewhere but the next day when the crew had moved on to Johannesburg, Brian had been entertaining a pilot friend of his, from the Argosy days at Benson and Khormaksar, and his wife to dinner and whilst seeing them off from the hotel after dinner collected the local papers which had the headline story. Back at home Margaret hadn't see the UK newspaper and knew nothing of the event until telephoned by the Adjutant and told "Don't worry, they are all right". She immediately thought there had been a crash.

Brian's route knowledge of Africa was again useful (with Kitty 4) during October and November 1982 when HRH The Princess Anne made a "Save the Children Fund" Tour of Swaziland, Zimbabwe, Zambia, Kenya, Mozambique and Yemen, and again in March 1984 when HRH The Prince of Wales toured Tanzania, Zambia, Zimbabwe and Botswana.

A very big one-off event took place during another "Save the Children Fund" Tour by HRH The Princess Anne, this time to Pakistan when the crew were delighted to be invited to be driven up the Kyber Pass as part of the Royal Party. The Pass, famous for the regimental badges painted on the hillsides and its historical past, was lined by very heavily armed tribesmen, and was not normally open to travellers.

5th October 1985 saw the passing of 5,000 hours on type whilst on a Royal Flight from Lyneham to Venice with HRH Prince William of Wales and HRH Prince Henry of Wales as passengers. Another landmark was passed on 02 July 1985 when flying from Kinloss to Edinburgh with HRH The Princess Anne on his 1,000[th] Royal Flight.

Posted to No.32 Squadron, RAF Northolt on 11th November 1985 after totalling some 6,185 days stationed at RAF Benson during his career, Brian finally retired from the Royal Air Force on 28th November 1986, spending his last day of service being 'entertained' at a happy hour in the Officer's Mess at the Royal New Zealand Air Force Base, Whenuapie in New Zealand whilst on terminal leave taking his wife Margaret around the world to show her some of the places he had visited during his travels with The Queen's Flight and the Royal Air Force. His log books show that he flew 12,519 hours and 35 minutes in 27 different types of aircraft and flew 1020 Royal Flights and he is proud of having held so many staff appointments without having completed a staff navigator's course and having held an 'A' category navigator rating for well over 20 years.

Following his retirement, Brian commuted to London daily for six years to work as a Senior Official in the Royal Household at St. James's Palace in the post of Assistant Secretary of the Central Chancery of the Orders of Knighthood, with responsibilities, amongst others, for co-ordinating the names of recipients of awards from all Government Departments, Prime Minister's Office, the three Services and all participating overseas countries and publishing them in the London Gazette, mainly on HM The Queen's Official Birthday List and the New Year's Honours List, maintaining records of all awards and arranging for the recipients to receive their insignia at an Investiture at Buckingham Palace or elsewhere. He was always very delighted to greet members of The Queen's Flight at their Investitures and to escort them through to the Ballroom to receive their insignia.

Brian retired on his 60th Birthday in 1993 and now divides his time between the golf course and his duties as Chairman and Group Tour Organiser for the Oxfordshire Branch of TQFA, and since May 2000, the duties of Secretary/Treasurer of The Queen's Flight Association including the writing of the Kittyhawk Newsletter and information for the TQFA website.

Air Vice-Marshal Don Spottiswood, CB, CVO, AFC, MA
Deputy Captain, The Queen's Flight, 7th July 1974 – 5th December 1976

Born on the 27th May 1934 and educated at West Hartlepool Grammar School and Boston University, USA (MA), Don joined the Royal Air Force in 1951, completing his training and granted his commission in 1952. General pilot duties followed until he joined No. 617 Squadron in 1962 for two years before becoming a student at the Royal Naval Staff College in 1965. A tour in the Middle East followed on his appointment to be the PSO to the Commander-in-Chief from 1966-1967.

Back to flying and an appointment as OC No. 53 Squadron, flying the Beverley from 1968 to 1970 was again followed by another period as a student, this time at the Joint Services Staff College in 1970. On graduating Don was appointed Station Commander of RAF Thorney Island from 1972 until 1975 when he was appointed Deputy Captain of The Queen's Flight, and later became the first holder of the dual appointment, with two hats, additionally as Station Commander RAF Benson in 1975 until he left in 1976.

1978 saw Don at the Royal College of Defence Studies, followed by his appointment as Secretary to IMS, HQ NATO from 1980-1983 and this tour was followed by his appointment to be the Director General of Training (RAF) from 1983-1985 and as Air Officer Training, RAF Support Command from 1985 until he retired from the Royal Air Force in 1989.

His appointments since leaving the service include Managing Director of Airwork Ltd, Bournemouth International Airport, 1989-97; Military Adviser to Airwork Ltd since 1997; Vice President, Support Services Division, Short's, 1994-97; Chairman, British Gliding Association 1989-97.

Decorations: CB, CVO, AFC.

15. The Fifth Captain & Others 1982–1989

Air Vice-Marshal Sir John (de Mitt) Severne, KCVO, OBE, AFC, DL
Captain, The Queen's Flight, 27th January 1982 – 13th January 1989

Born 15th August 1925. Educated at Marlborough. Joined the Royal Air Force in 1944.

After flying training on Tiger Moths and Harvards, his first tour was with No.264 (Mosquito) Night Fighter Squadron: followed by Central Flying School Instructors Course; RAF Cranwell and CFS instructing on Prentices, Harvards and Meteors, 1948-53;

Flight Commander No.98 Squadron, Germany, 1954-55; Squadron Commander No. 26 Squadron, Germany 1956-57;

Air Ministry, 1958; Equerry to HRH The Duke of Edinburgh, 1958-61; psa 1962; Chief Instructor No.226 Operational Conversion Unit (Lightning), 1963-65; jssc 1965;

Joint Headquarters, Middle East Command, Aden and Air Adviser to the South Arabian Government, 1966-67; Directing Staff, Joint Services Staff College, 1968; Group Captain Organisation, HQ Strike Command, 1968-70; Station Commander, RAF Kinloss, 1971-72; ADC to The Queen, 1972-73; RCDS 1973; Commandant, Central Flying School, RAF, 1974-76; Air Commodore Flying Training, HQ RAF Support Command, 1976-78; Air Commander, Southern Maritime Air Region, Central Sub-Area Eastern Atlantic Command, and Plymouth Sub-Area Channel Command, 1978-80;

Retired from the Royal Air Force 1980; Appointed Captain of The Queen's Flight, 1982-89; Extra Equerry to The Queen since 1984.

Honorary Air Commodore No.3 (County of Devon) Maritime HQ Unit, RAuxAF, 1990-95; President South West Area Royal Air Force Association; President, The Queen's Flight Association 1990-2000; CFS Association 1993-98; Taunton and District Branch ESU 1996-; Won King's Cup Air Race, British Air Racing Champion 1960; President RAF Equitation Association 1976-79 (Chairman 1973); Chairman Combined Services Equitation Association 1977-79 (Chairman 1976); Deputy Lieutenant, Somerset 1991.

"It all began when I was taken up for my first flight in a Gypsy Moth in 1935. I was 10 at the time and from that day on I knew exactly what I wanted to do with my life – fly aeroplanes. I couldn't wait until I was old enough to join the Royal Air Force, which I did in 1944. I then spent a hectic three months as a dispatch rider dodging doodle bugs whilst waiting for my flying training to begin. I received my wings just after the war ended in 1945 and I was bitterly disappointed to miss the "excitement" (as I saw it at the time with all the irresponsibility of youth!).

I trained on Tiger Moths and Harvards and then had the good fortune to join No. 264 Mosquito Night Fighter Squadron. At the end of the two-year tour I realised I had enjoyed my flying training and my first operational squadron so much that I wanted to put something back into flying. I thought the best way of doing this would be to become a test pilot or a flying instructor, but I quickly realised I did not have the brains to be a test pilot and I therefore volunteered for the Central Flying School (CFS) course to become a Qualified Flying Instructor (QFI).

At that time all CFS students on the course had to fly, not only the training aircraft, but also the Spitfire, Lancaster, Vampire and Mosquito. To add three of the classic wartime aircraft and my first

179

jet to my log book was like heaven indeed! The solo on the Lancaster was a proper solo – none of this co-pilot nonsense!

I am proud of the fact that I have had a flying appointment in every rank from Flight Lieutenant and have had the opportunity to fly a wide variety of aircraft. During my 43 years with the RAF I flew 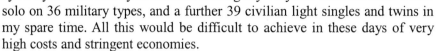 solo on 36 military types, and a further 39 civilian light singles and twins in my spare time. All this would be difficult to achieve in these days of very high costs and stringent economies.

After five years instructing at Cranwell and CFS on Prentices, Harvards and Meteors, I had two tours in Germany, the first as a flight commander on No. 98 Squadron flying Venoms and the second as squadron commander of No. 26 Squadron on Hunters. This was followed by a short spell at the Ministry of Defence when I was posted, of all places, to Buckingham Palace as Equerry to HRH The Duke of Edinburgh in 1958. This was a wonderful experience which involved a great deal of travel including going round the world in the Royal Yacht. During that time I indulged my love of light aircraft flying by joining the Tiger Club at Redhill where I was able to enter aerobatic competitions and do some air racing. I had many happy hours flying the Turbulent – an ultra light aircraft weighing 320 lbs and powered by a Volkswagen engine and in 1960 I managed to win the King's Cup Air Race in a Turbulent entered by The Duke of Edinburgh. After the race I persuaded Prince Philip (without much difficulty) to fly this aircraft and he thus became the only member of the Royal Family ever to fly a single seater. The chairman of the Tiger Club presented Prince Philip with a model of that Turbulent which can now be seen at the Museum of Royal Flying at RAF Northolt. Incidentally, if you have not yet visited the Museum, please try to do so, it is even better than its forerunner at Benson.

My next flying appointment was to be the Chief Instructor of the Lightning OCU at Coltishall. The Lightning was a wonderful aeroplane to fly and operate (from releasing the brakes at take-off to reaching 40,000 ft in two minutes can't be bad!). I then had a complete change of direction when I was posted to Kinloss as station commander in 1971. The Nimrod had just arrived and when I pointed out to the C-in-C that I had no experience of big aeroplanes and had never been in the maritime business he said, "That's exactly why you are going there, and if you fly those things like Shackletons I'll skin you alive!"

On promotion to Air Commodore in 1974 I was posted to the Central Flying School (then at Little Rissington) as Commandant. This was a fascinating appointment being responsible, not only for the pure flying standards throughout the RAF, but also for the Red Arrows. This involved the selection of the pilots, their training and their display supervision. Naturally I had to fly in the back seats to see if they did the job properly! My final appointment, before retiring from the RAF was as Air Commander of the Southern Maritime Air Region at Mount Batten. My responsibility was the tasking of RAF maritime operations in the North Atlantic and the Search and Rescue operations in the southern half of the UK. The Survival School was also at Mount Batten and I was able to escape from the office (which overlooked Plymouth Sound and was reputed to have the best view of any office in the RAF!) to fly the SAR Whirlwinds winching students from the Sound after they had been dumped into the water by friendly survival staff.

I retired for the first time in 1980 and after eighteen months unsuccessfully job hunting in Somerset I was recalled to be Captain of The Queen's Flight. When I was Prince Philip's Equerry I knew 'Mouse' Fielden well and I always thought his job must be the best in the Service – and it was! The job was much more than being responsible for the Flight, which in any case was run by the Officer Commanding, because the Captain was also responsible for all aspects of aviation advice to The Queen and other members of the Royal Family. In this respect one of the highlights for me was organising the charters of British Airways Tristars to take HM on state visits overseas, particularly the one to China in 1986 – the first time a British Monarch had ever been to that country. The tour was also supported by our first BAe 146 ZE700, which was of great interest to the Chinese because, at that time, were considering buying the aircraft. It was also our first overseas tour with the BAe 146 so there was no way it was going to go unserviceable!

During my time, with a lot of help from other people, particularly Bob Taylor, we set up The Queen's Flight Museum. I did this because I knew there was much interesting history to be preserved; I felt that once the last of us who knew 'Mouse' Fielden had left the scene, much would be lost unless we did something about it. I am therefore delighted that No. 32 (The Royal) Squadron is continuing to record and preserve the history of Royal Flying.

By far the most rewarding aspect of my seven years with The Queen's Flight was the privilege of working with such a dedicated and enthusiastic team of professionals, both up and down stairs."

Warrant Officer M. D. (Mick) Burnett, RVM
Eng Tech AE, The Queen's Flight, 1980–1990

Mick Burnett was born on 12th June 1945 and was educated at the Mile End House School in Portsmouth, He became an Electrical Apprentice (97th Entry) at RAF Halton on 10th January 1961.

1963 to 1970 saw Mick at RAF Wittering on No.139 (Jamaica) Squadron, Victor B" aircraft carrying the Blue Steel Missile.

Over to Germany in 1970 for two years to RAF Wildenrath Electrical Bay and No. 20 Squadron Harriers before returning to RAF Cottesmore for three years from 1972 with No.115 Squadron and Argosy aircraft flight checking of ILS installations.

Back to basics in 1975 with a three-year tour at RAF Halton as a Technical Instructor before, in 1978-79 moving to RAF Binbrook on the Lightening Training Flight. This was followed by a short tour at RAF Coltishall with No. 54 Squadron Jaguars (1979-80).

Moving to The Queen's Flight at RAF Benson in 1980 saw a ten year tour starting in the Electrical Bay and technical support down the routes followed by First Line Shift Boss and then Flight Sergeant First Line.

One of Mike's most 'memorable moments' was the hangar floor. As Flight Sergeant First Line, it was his responsibility to ensure the hangar floor was always a sparkling clean showpiece that greeted anyone who visited the Flight. Corporal Alan Mace and his band of GD tradesmen spent many hours cleaning and polishing to maintain it in a pristine condition. When the BAe 146 aircraft were introduced into service with The Queen's Flight, the floor, pristine as it was, couldn't stand up to the increased weight of this aircraft. The floor was subsiding and forming ruts where the undercarriage wheels travelled along the 'yellow' lines. Various ploys were tried to stop the subsidence, which included defuelling the aircraft before bringing it into the hangar.

When everything failed to stop the floor sinking, a decision was made to lay down onto the floor, interlocking aluminium panels known as portable aircraft landing strip. The Army came in with all the equipment and in three days, the strips of aluminium were laid down each side of the centreline. It was very 'green' and looked very 'tactical', quite alien to what The Queen's Flight were used to. Gone was the shiny floor and with it the moral of those who worked on it.

After a very short time it was generally agreed that the floor looked horrible, was horrible to walk and work on and was a safety hazard. It was noticeable that moral was low. Everybody 'upstairs' and 'downstairs' were unanimous, "The floor was a monstrosity". Pressure was put on the Captain to get rid of it, but to no avail, until one day when one of the Andovers, which was notorious for underwing panel fuel leaks, deposited a vast quantity of Avtur onto the floor. Of course the fuel leaked through and settled underneath the aluminium floor, which couldn't be mopped up causing a fire hazard. The decision was made – "Get rid of the floor!"

What took the Army three days to install was removed in one working day by all members of The Queen's Flight, working with great gusto. Work started at 0800 and finished at 1730 with all the panels neatly stacked and banded, thanks to Gillian Archer. By 1800 we were sitting in The Queen's

Strengthening The Queen's Flight hangar floor for the BAe 146. May 1988

Flight Social Club downing a well-deserved pint or two! The next morning the floor was back to its former glory and so were the smiles of those who worked on it. The floor was eventually dug up and reinforced, but that is another story!

On leaving the Flight in 1990 Mike was posted to No. 56 (F) Squadron, Phantoms as Squadron Warrant Officer until in 1992 moving to RAF Halton as Officer Commanding Training Resources before in 1995-96 taking a tour in the Falkland Islands as Officer Commanding Aircraft Support Flight. Returning to the UK in 1996 he went to RAF Cosford as Training Supervisor Electrical Training Flight before he became redundant and left the Royal Air Force on the 20th December 1996.

In 1997 Mike became the Contract Manager for Castrol Lubricants, setting up a lubrication programme and supervising a team of lubricant engineers at Didcot 'B' Power Station operating 4 gas turbine and 2 steam turbine generators. He retired in May 2000 and has gone to live in Suffolk where he has built a house to spend his days in leisure!

Air Commodore R.B.(Dickie) Duckett, CVO, AFC
Deputy Captain, The Queen's Flight, 14th January 1983 – 22nd February 1985

After initial training at RAF College Cranwell, 1960/63; flew fighter aircraft Hunter and Lightning for several years 1963/67;

Member of Red Arrows Aerobatic Team 1968/71;

Instructor at Lightning OCU Coltishall 1972/75;

Team Leader the Red Arrows 1975/76;

RAF Staff College 1977;

OC No.1 Squadron (Harriers) 1978/81;

Station Commander RAF Benson and Deputy Captain of The Queen's Flight, 1983-85; Royal College of Defence Studies, 1986; Senior Staff Appointments at MOD and HQ RAF Germany, 1986/93; AOC Scotland and Northern Ireland, 1993/96; Retired from the RAF in 1996.

During his period as Deputy Captain of The Queen's Flight from 1983-85, he was also the Station Commander at RAF Benson. Nevertheless, he was able to undertake several overseas tours with Members of the Royal Family, one of the most memorable being a tour with HRH The Princess Royal to visit refugee camps in Pakistan. This included an exciting drive up the Khyber Pass with heavily-armed, but thankfully friendly, local tribesmen manning vantage points along the route.

Chief Technician John R. J. Eaton
Eng Tech P, The Queen's Flight, 1971–1980 & 1984–1987

John Eaton was born on 4th June 1937 and educated in Cheltenham. On being called up for National Service, John signed on for three years in the REME as a vehicle fitter. Posted to LAD 3rd Carboneers Tank Regiment in Osnabruck, Germany and later as Artificer to headquarters R.A. 4th Infantry Division, Herford.

On leaving the Army John worked as a Specialist Printer from 1958 to 1968 when he joined the Royal Air Force. His first posting was to No. 115 Squadron at Cottesmore, Argosy and Varsity aircraft then with No. 360 Squadron with Canberra still at Cottesmore. A posting to The Queen's Flight followed in 1971 where he stayed until 1980 leaving to go as Engineer/Loadmaster on the C-in-C's Andover at HQAFNORTH in Oslo until 1983.

A second tour at The Queen's Flight followed before he moved in 1986 to RAF Abingdon as Hangar Controller on the Hawk Major Servicing Unit. John left the Royal Air Force in 1990.

From 1991 until 2000 John spent his time with VSO tours in Tanzania, Namibia and Zambia, all involved with re-building or manufacture of rural hospitals.

John remembers one particular trip whilst Crew Chief on the Andover. A Kitty 3 Royal Flight with Prince Philip to Luxembourg with TRH's The Duke and Duchess of Gloucester. At Luxembourg, John asked the caterers for a tray of fresh eggs for the next morning departure. Prince Philip asked for the morning departure to be delayed and a message to the Gloucester's Hotel failed to reach them. They arrived early, hungry for breakfast on board. Eggs arrive; Prince Philip arrives, already breakfasted. Eggs all found to be hard-boiled, the Gloucester's decline to eat them and abandon breakfast.

A sad story from his days with the VSO in Zambia. In the Western Province of Zambia, a flare up in Angola resulted in refugees pouring over the border. This was during the 'rains' and some had walked for hundreds of kilometres to safety, all were wet and starving, all were anaemic, all had worms, most had diarrhoea and Malaria. Many of the young were too weak to stand and unable to support their heads. Until the large international agencies got their act together the mothers and children came to us. We were swamped. We measured the length and weight of each child, age is a useless parameter and a 15 year old can look 8 years old. We scrounged mattresses from anywhere and fed them four or five nutritious meals a day. We gave our own blood as often as possible; an adult donor can donate enough for small four children. Many we had to feed through tubes either because they were too weak or too young to feed themselves. We didn't save all but most survived.

Squadron Leader David W. Gale, MVO, RAF (Ret'd)
Pilot, The Queen's Flight, June 1985 – December 1990

Born on 27th December 1946 and educated at Shrewsbury School, Shropshire, David joined the Royal Air Force on 24th February 1966. After Initial and Flying Training he was posted to the transport world carrying out his conversion to the Hercules (C-130) at No.242 OCU before joining No. 24 Squadron at RAF Lyneham as a co-pilot in November 1969. Just over a year later in December 1970 David was off to the sun as a co-pilot on No. 70 Squadron (Hercules) at RAF Akrotiri in Cyprus. Returning to the United Kingdom in August 1972 David successfully completed his conversion to the left-hand seat as a Captain and in January 1973 joined No. 36 Squadron (C130) at Lyneham before transferring to No. 47 Squadron (C130) (Special Forces) at Lyneham.

In June 1980 David was given an Exchange posting to the United States where he converted to the C141B Starlifter at 41st MAS, Charleston AFB, South Carolina. Amongst the special duties he was given on this tour included Flight Examiner, In-Flight Refuelling and Special Operations Instructor before returning home in March 1983.

Appointed to be the Flight Commander on the BAe 146 Evaluation Flight at No. 241 OCU at RAF Brize Norton in April 1983 gave David special knowledge and led to his appointment as the BAe 146 Training Captain (Kitty 8) on The Queen's Flight in June 1985. In December 1990 David left TQF and retired from the Royal Air Force that same month.

Since leaving he has become an Airline Pilot with Comair Airlines, (Delta Connection), based and living in Florida in the United States where he and his wife give freely of their time as volunteers for organisations involved with wildlife conservation and environmental protection in Florida.

David and Keith Millar, another TQFA member, have "started" a Branch of the Association in Florida, see the TQFA website, and I feel sure that they would be delighted to see any members at their "meetings". MVO 1990. QCVSA 1980.

Alan Gibson, RVM

A Eng Tech, The Queen's Flight, 14th February 1971 – June1979 and March 1982 – July 1990

Alan was born on 11th November 1948 and was educated at Elmore Green Secondary Modern School at Bloxwich, Walsall in Staffordshire. Joining the Royal Air Force on 6th August 1967 was posted, after his engineering training, to No. 214 Squadron on Victor Mk.1A Tankers at RAF Marham.

His first tour of duty with The Queen's Flight started on Decimalisation Day, 14th February 1971 and included, a period as a Crew Chief on the Wessex helicopter from 1977 to 1979. At the end of his tour Alan was posted to the Wessex Servicing Flight in Hong Kong before returning to the UK and a tour with No.33 Squadron at RAF Odiham.

Returning to The Queen's Flight in March 1982, Alan stayed until July 1990 during which, from 1986 to 1988, he operated as a Crew Chief on the BAe 146.

Before leaving the RAF in April 1995, he completed a tour with A Flight No. 22 Squadron at Chivenor in the Search and Rescue role. Alan still retains his connections with Royal Flying, currently operating as a BAe146 Crew Chief with Serco Aerospace at No. 32 (The Royal) Squadron at RAF Northolt.

Group Captain P.G. Pinney, CVO, RAF (Ret'd)

Deputy Captain, The Queen's Flight, 31st October 1987 – 17th November 1989

Born in August 1939 and educated at Christ's College, New Zealand and RAF College Cranwell, 1958-60, where he graduated with The Queen's Medal and other awards.

Joined No. 3 Squadron at RAF Geilenkirchen in 1961 flying B(I)8 Canberras in the low level strike/attack role in Europe, Middle East and Africa. Appointed as ADC to AOC-in-C Bomber Command in 1963.

Trained as a flying instructor in 1965 before serving as an instructor at the RAF College Cranwell and the Central Flying School at RAF Little Rissington. He then joined CFS Examining Wing flying Chipmunks and Jet Provosts and won the coveted A1 QFI category. Whilst a QFI, he flew in The Poachers and Red Pelican Aerobatic teams at Cranwell and CFS respectively.

In July 1968, he was promoted to Squadron Leader and appointed as the Personal QFI to HRH The Prince of Wales, thereby beginning the first of his two tours with The Queen's Flight at RAF Benson.

From The Prince of Wales' first instructional flight at RAF Tangmere on 30 July 1968, Squadron Leader Pinney took his small TQF Chipmunk team around the country to enable HRH to fly throughout his time as an undergraduate at Trinity College, Cambridge (flying from RAF Oakington) and the University of Wales in Aberystwyth (flying from RAE Aberporth).

During this time, HRH also found time to continue his flying lessons on the Royal Chipmunk (WP903) at RAF Benson, Marham and West Raynham, White Waltham, Valley and at Bassingbourn where he flew his first solo on 14 January 1969.

The Prince of Wales flew his last Chipmunk sortie at RAF Tangmere on 2 August 1969 when he passed his Final Handling Test (flown to University Air Squadron regulations) and his Private Pilot's Licence (flown to full Civilian standards), both with very good results. In a short ceremony later that day, HRH was presented with his Preliminary Flying Badge by the AOC-in-C Training Command, Air Marshal Sir Leslie Mavor. The Royal Chipmunk left TQF for the last time on 9 October 1969 when Squadron Leader Pinney delivered it to RAF Shawbury.

Towards the end of his 92 Royal Flights on the Chipmunk, Squadron Leader Pinney converted onto the Basset and delivered the fully instrumented twin-piston Royal aircraft (XS770) to the Flight on 27 June 1969. The Basset aircraft was acquired to allow HRH The Prince of Wales to develop his flying skills further and gain his instrument rating. It also enabled HRH to pilot himself to Royal engagements in the British Isles and Central Europe. As such, the now slightly larger Basset team included a navigator, Flight Lieutenant Tom Sneddon, who accompanied HRH on the Royal solos; the Basset team operated from even more bases than before including Turnhouse, Kemble and Aberdeen as well as flying many Royal trips from Heathrow, Paris, Germany, etc. The Prince of Wales flew his first Basset sortie from RAF West Raynham to Aberdeen on 1 October 1969, his first solo on type at RAF Oakington on 6 February 1970 and passed his Instrument Flight Grading at RAF Benson on 15 December 1970.

HRH The Duke of Edinburgh also flew the Basset and HRH The Prince William had many sorties of continuation and instrument flying training. In all Squadron Leader Pinney flew 166 Royal flights on this tour and also authorised and supervised HRH from the ground on his solo Royal flights flown during the Chipmunk and Basset phase. In January 1971 he was posted to the RAF Staff College and in June 1971 was awarded the MVO 4th class (later to become LVO). After completing the 1971 RAF Staff College course, he served in the Air Secretary's Department in MOD before completing the National Defence College course at Latimer in 1974-75. From 1976-79 he returned to the overland strike/attack role as OC 208 Squadron, flying Buccaneers and Hunters based at RAF Honington. During this time he took the Squadron on the RAF's first two fast jet low level training deployments to CFB Goose Bay in Labrador, the RAF's first two Red Flag exercises at Nellis AFB in Nevada and its first Maple Flag exercise at CFB Cold Lake in Alberta.

Sadly, all good things come to an end; in 1979 he was posted to Air Plans in MOD and then, from 1982-84, he became the RAF Exchange Officer on the Directing Staff of the Canadian Forces Command and Staff College in Toronto. On his return to the UK, he was appointed as the Service Adviser in the Cabinet Office and then, on promotion to Group Captain, returned to RAF Benson from 1987-89 as Station Commander, Deputy Captain of The Queen's Flight and Aide-de-Camp to HM The Queen. In an action packed tour, he saw RAF Benson host the Ceremonial Presentation by HM The Queen of her Colours to the Royal Auxiliary Air Force, host a major deployment and exercise by four American Squadrons and, more personally, spend over 1030 hours in the air during his 24 months tour in command. Needless to say, many of these hours were flown with The Queen's Flight where he flew on a further 384 Royal flights as well as many other sorties with Ministers and VIPs; these flights and tours took him to all continents except for South America and Antarctica.

He was promoted to CVO in the 1990 New Year Honours list shortly after his return to Central Staffs in MOD where he served for four years. During this last tour, he even managed to acquire TQF aircraft to fly with the Secretary of State to conferences in North America and Europe. Group Captain Pinney retired from the Royal Air Force in 1994 and was appointed to the Lord Chancellor's Panel where he works to this day. In his spare time, he is Treasurer of the Alpine Ski Club which is the oldest ski mountaineering club in the world; he was its President from 1988-90. He also serves as an elected Local Councillor, Church Treasurer and as a Trustee to two local Charities. What spare time he has left, tends to be spent fishing in either Hampshire or in the remoter parts of Scotland and New Zealand. He is married with three grown up daughters.

Warrant Officer Peter Stokes, RVM
Air Loadmaster, The Queen's Flight, 1970–1978 and 1983–1989

Peter Stokes was born in King's Lynn on 18th April 1940 and was educated at the King Edward VII Grammar School. Joining the Royal Air Force in 1958 he volunteered for Marine Craft duties as a Coxswain serving tours at Mount Batten and in Cyprus.

Attended the Aircrew Selection Unit at RAF Biggin Hill in 1962 he was selected for Air Quartermaster duties. After training a posting to No.114 Squadron flying the Argosy aircraft at Benson from 1963 to 1966.

A further tour overseas with No.115 Squadron at RAF Changi in Singapore followed from 1966 to 1967, before he was posted direct to Cyprus to No.70 Squadron at RAF Akrotiri to become the Air Loadmaster in the Air Officer Commanding in Chief's Crew flying the VIP Argosy.

Peter was one of the team who designed the interior and monitored the rebuild of Argosy 444 at RAF Saafi in Malta and flew with the AOC up to Air Marshal Sir Denis Smallwood until in 1970 he was selected and chosen to serve with The Queen's Flight.

On his first tour as the Senior Steward from 1970 to 1978 he highlights the award of The Queen's Warrant in 1972 and the 1977 Silver Jubilee tour with Her Majesty The Queen and HRH The Duke of Edinburgh with the Kitty 4 Crew to Fiji, New Zealand, Australia and Papua New Guinea. He was awarded the Royal Victorian Medal (Silver) in The Queen's Birthday Honours List in June 1978.

Leaving the Flight in March 1978 he joined No. 38 Group examining Unit as a Loadmaster Examiner but in September 1983 was again selected to re-join The Queen's Flight as part of a design team to bring the BAe146 to the Flight standards. His highlights of this tour include the 1986 tour of China with HM The Queen and HRH The Duke of Edinburgh, completing his 500th Royal Flight in 1987 and the 1989 Tour of Central America with HRH The Duke of Edinburgh.

Peter retired from the RAF in 1989 and was employed at RAF Benson as Estates Management Officer and in October 2000 was promoted to Executive Officer and moving to the RAF Infrastructure Organisation at Benson in June 2001. Peter is very proud that his son Nicholas followed him into the RAF and who is now a Flight Lieutenant Nimrod Captain.

Wing Commander Michael Leonard (Mike) Schofield, LVO, RAF (Ret'd)
Officer Commanding, The Queen's Flight, 12th October 1984–25th November 1988

Born 6th March 1945 and educated at The County Grammar School, Hyde, Cheshire, Mike joined the Royal Air Force, on 1st April 1964. Following Initial Training at RAF South Cerney and Pilot Training (Jet Provost) at No.7 Flying Training School at RAF Church Fenton during 1964-65 he completed his Pilot Training (Varsity) with No.5 Flying Training School at RAF Oakington in 1965-66,

Mike made his first entry into the world of transport flying with No.242 OCU (Hastings) at RAF Thorney Island, in 1966 followed by a tour as a Co-Pilot with No.24 (Hastings) Squadron at RAF Colerne, in Wiltshire.

A tour as a Captain with Royal Air Force Germany Communications Squadron, subsequently No.60 (Pembroke) Squadron, RAF Wildenrath from 1967-71, before a return to the flying training world, attending Central Flying School (No.259 Flying Instructors Course), RAF Little Rissington in 1971-72; and No.3 FTS (Flying Instructor Jet Provost) RAF Leeming, 1972-73; before returning to the Central Flying School (Staff Instructor Jet Provost) RAF Little Rissington, 1973-76.

Appointed OC Manchester and Salford Universities Air Squadron, RAF Woodvale and OC RAF Woodvale from 1976-79; Mike returned to transport flying as a Hercules (C130) Captain and Flight Commander, No.70 (Hercules) Squadron, at RAF Lyneham, 1979-82, before attending RAF Staff College Bracknell, 1982; and a tour as Desk Officer, Air Secretary's Department, RAF Barnwood, 1982-84, where he obviously managed to 'arrange' his return to transport flying and as a Captain, Andover Conversion, RAF Benson, 1984; and an appointment as Officer Commanding, The Queen's Flight, RAF Benson, from 1984-88. Mike retired from the Royal Air Force on 6th March 1989 to take up a career in Civil Aviation.

Mike flew with British Airways from March 1989 to December 1998, as First Officer and Senior First Officer, 747-100/200 and 400. He was the Assistant Flight Technical Manager for the 747-400 Fleet and latterly Captain Dash 8 and General Manager Flight Operations for Brymon Airways, a British Airways wholly owned subsidiary.

Mike Schofield retired from British Airways on 31st December 1998 and in January 1999 commenced working for the Civil Aviation Authority, as a Flight Operations Inspector, based at Weston-super-Mare Regional Office. Appointed LVO 1988.

Sergeant John Raymond Taylor, RVM, BEM, MIFireE
Fireman, The Queens Flight, 1969–1970, 1971–1977 and 1979–1983

Ray Taylor was born on 18th November 1943 and was educated at the Lincoln Road Boys School, Peterborough and the Peterborough Technical College. Joining the Royal Air Force in February 1965 and after training as a Fireman served at RAF Manby and Strubby, overseas at RAF Salalah and at RAF North Luffenham before joining The Queen's Flight.

His first posting to the Flight was as a SAC in October 1969 leaving in October 1970 to RAF Finningley on promotion to Corporal. Ray returned to the Flight as a Corporal Fireman in March 1971 and remained until again leaving on promotion, as a Sergeant, to RAF Hereford in October 1977.

He returned again as SNCO i/c Helicopter Support in September 1979 but once again was posted on promotion to Flight Sergeant to RAF Brize Norton in September 1983.

Ray retired from the RAF at the end of January 1987 and appointed as an Operational Fire Brigade Station Officer at the Atomic Energy Research Establishment at Harwell before progressing to become the Site Fire Safety Officer. He resigned in September 1998 to establish his own Fire Safety Consultancy that remains his ongoing business.

Squadron Leader Geoffrey H. Williams, LVO, RAF (Ret'd)
Fixed Wing Pilot, The Queen's Flight, 1973 – 1995

Geoffrey Hector Garratt Williams was born on 6th March 1939 and educated at Crafnant Lodge Preparatory School, St. George's College, Weybridge, Regent Street Polytechnic and Guys Hospital Dental School.

Joining the Royal Air Force in October 1959 and completing his flying training Geoff was posted as an Argosy co-pilot on No.105 Squadron at RAF Benson during the Squadron build-up before leaving en-masse to RAF Khormaksar in Aden.

After this overseas tour Geoff was off to the Central Flying School at RAF Little Rissington to become a flying instructor and to pass on his knowledge as a qualified flying instructor flying Jet Provost Mks 3 & 4 at RAF Syerston. Back to transport flying and No. 242 OCU at RAF Thorney Island to become a Hercules Captain and to RAF Lyneham as a Captain with No. 36 Squadron before returning to the OCU at Thorney Island as a QFI.

Back again to RAF Lyneham, this time as the OC Hercules Examining Unit before being selected for duty as an Andover Captain with The Queen's Flight, joining as the Personal Pilot to HRH The Duke of Edinburgh in 1973 with the personal callsign of Kitty 3. Geoff converted to the BAe146 and flew until he retired from The Queen's Flight and the Royal Air Force in June 1995. He was appointed to be a Lieutenant in the Royal Victorian Order.

Geoff recalls his happiest memories on The Queen's Flight are all central around working with such a wonderful group of people. Everybody was supportive and all relied on each other. These memories have never left him and he says they never will. One particular memory he recalls was flying HM The Queen from London Heathrow to Aberdeen and on the return journey the steward found a box full of greengages beside the seat where Lord Porchester had been seated. When he got back to Benson he telephoned Balmoral and spoke to Frank Holland, the baggage master, who told him to dispose of the said greengages! On arrival in the office next morning he passed the fruit around the office and then the hangar floor. Whilst having a drink with Sir Archie Winskill at lunchtime, he received a call from Lord Porchester who told him that HM wished him to send the box to Balmoral via British Airways. Geoff told Sir Archie who was most helpful. He told him that he was in the "s---" and to "sort it out". He rushed back to the Flight and sent people off to Wallingford, Oxford and Henley. As luck would have it a supply was found in Henley. These were purchased and he sent this new supply up to Balmoral. Geoff never heard any more of the matter (except for the Flight's usual "Christmas Present ") and he didn't even have a greengage himself!

He recalls some of his overseas tours with Prince Philip: The opening of the Opera House in Sydney in 1973 followed by the Commonwealth Games in Christchurch, New Zealand; A tour of the Banana Republics; A Gulf Tour plus Afghanistan, playing tennis in Kabul where the altitude defeated him when the balls flew far too fast; A Tour to China, a visit to Wallong to see the Panda's (he hated the State Banquets); Three flights from RAF Goose Bay in Labrador direct to the United Kingdom in the dear old Andover.

His first and last Tour with the BAe146 completely around the world. He had never before had two birthdays in one year. One in Kushiro and the next day flying to Anchorage where it was his birthday yet again!

Geoffrey retired to Cornwall where he became a committee member of the St. Mawes Sailing Club and eventually the Chairman in 1998. He now resides in Mawnan Smith, Falmouth.

Group Captain A.M. (Marcus) Wills, CVO, OBE
Deputy Captain, The Queen's Flight, 23rd February 1985–30th October 1987
Deputy Captain, The Queen's Flight, 1st February 1994–31st March 1995

Born September 1943. Educated at Sherborne and RAF College Cranwell.

Joined No.111 Squadron (Treble One – The Black Arrows) to fly Lightning's in 1966.

After a tour as ADC to the AOC-in-C Air Support Command, made a complete role change from fighters to transport for several tours on VC10s at RAF Brize Norton, joining as a co-pilot and then, on promotion to Squadron Leader, became a flight commander and a training captain.

Tours at the RAF Staff College Bracknell, both as a student and a member of the Directing Staff followed before returning to No. 10 Squadron as the Officer Commanding. During this final tour on VC10s he achieved the coveted "A" (exceptional) flying category, qualifying him to fly HM The Queen. During his tours on the VC10, he flew 5 British Prime Ministers, from Heath to Thatcher (the fifth was Sir Alec Douglas-Home, then Foreign Secretary!) as well as several long-range Royal Flights – including HRH The Prince of Wales to Salisbury for the Rhodesian Independence celebrations in 1980.

In 1984, after a tour as Personal Staff Officer to the Chief of Air Staff, he took command of RAF Benson and became Deputy Captain of The Queen's Flight, where he remained until posting to HQ NATO Brussels in 1987.

There then followed "something completely different", including the Army Higher Command and Staff Course, detachment to US Forces Europe in Stuttgart to work on Kurdish Humanitarian problems following the Gulf War, and finally posting back to the Ministry of Defence to work on the development of UK policy as a member of United Nations.

Marcus Wills returned to The Queen's Flight as a Deputy Captain in 1994. (See Ch 16).

16. The Sixth Captain & Others 1989–1995

Air Commodore The Hon Sir Timothy Elworthy, KCVO, CBE
Captain of The Queen's Flight, 14th January 1989–31st March 1995
Senior Air Equerry to The Queen 1995-2001
Director of Royal Travel 1997-2001
Extra Equerry to The Queen since 1991

Born 27th January 1938 of New Zealand parentage, he was brought up in South Canterbury. Returned to UK in 1945 and completed his education at Radley and the Royal Air Force College, Cranwell.

His career in the Royal Air Force included tours on fighter squadrons and as a flying instructor. He was appointed Squadron Commander of No. 29 (Fighter) Squadron in 1975. Having attended the RAF Staff College and the National Defence College and staff appointments including PSO to Air Officer Commanding-in-Chief, Strike Command in 1979, he Commanded RAF Leuchars, 1983 (Group Captain) and RAF Stanley in the Falkland Islands.

After attending the Royal College of Defence Studies, 1986, he became Director, Operational Requirements (Air) at the Ministry of Defence, 1988 (Air Commodore);

In 1989 he became the sixth Captain of The Queen's Flight until disbandment of the unit in 1995. He was appointed Her Majesty's Senior Air Equerry in 1995 and Director of Royal Travel at Buckingham Palace from 1997 until 2001. He has been an extra Equerry to The Queen since 1991. Sir Timothy was knighted on the 30th March 2001 when Her Majesty graciously appointed him to be a Knight Commander in the Royal Victorian Order.

He became a Liveryman in the Guild of Air Pilots and Air Navigators in 1995; QCVSA, 1968.

Decorations: KCVO, CBE.

Group Captain Peter B. Akehurst, LVO, RAF (Ret'd)
Senior Engineering Officer: (Promoted Wing Commander 1st January 1990)
5th February 1987 – 8th July 1991

Born in Salisbury, Southern Rhodesia on 31st January 1951, Peter Akehurst was educated at Ratcliffe College, Leicester and Loughborough University, 1969-73, where he gained a Degree in Aeronautical Engineering and Design. On leaving University Peter worked for Marconi Elliott Avionics in Rochester on design of aircraft autopilots, 1973-74.

1974-75 was spent at Royal Air Force College Cranwell on Officer and Engineering training before arrival at RAF Marham as the Engineering Officer, 231 OCU (Canberra), 1975-76.

1976 saw promotion to OC Canberra Servicing Flight at Marham, 1976-

78. A move to RAF Shawbury followed as OC Mechanical Engineering Support Flight, 1978-80; a first Staff Posting to HQSTC as Canberra Engineering Authority, 1980-83, was followed by a move to RAF Odiham and helicopters as Senior Engineering Officer 240 OCU (Chinook and Puma), 1983-85; and still at Odiham as Senior Engineering Officer No. 7 Squadron (Chinook), 1985-87.

Posted to RAF Benson in 1987 to The Queen's Flight for a four year tour as Senior Engineering Officer, 1987-91; before becoming a student again at No.13 Joint Services Defence Course at Greenwich, 1991-92; then off to the MOD in London as RAF Engineer Branch Sponsor from 1992-94. A return to the helicopter world was made in 1994 with a move back to RAF Odiham as OC Engineering and Supply Wing (Chinook and Puma), 1994-96; before another staff appointment at HQSTC Role Office looking after VC10/Tristar/Hercules/BAe 146/BAe 125 aircraft, 1996-98.

Back to the Ministry of Defence, 1998-99, as a member of the Joint Helicopter Command Study team before moving in 1999 to HQ LAND DACOS J4/J6 Joint Helicopter Command as Senior Engineering Staff Officer 16 Air Assault Brigade and All Battlefield Helicopters.

Peter remembers well his tour as Senior Engineering Officer on The Queen's Flight, highlights of which include: Getting the first two BAe 146s into regular Flight service, the fitment of IRCM equipment to the BAe 146s and the Andover; the retirement of the last Andover; Travelling on a goodly number of route trainers, route proving and Royal Flights. The comradeship of all, particularly the groundcrew, during his time on the Flight.

Finally, the best of all, the appointment to be a Lieutenant in the Royal Victorian Order and the subsequent Investiture. Peter has a piece of paper that appears to indicate that during his time as SEngO a total of 11,128 flying hours, 13,290 flights and 4,666 Royal/VIP Flights were carried out. An excellent piece of history.

Chief Technician Andrew (Andy) John Bashford, RVM
Eng Tech A, The Queen's Flight, 1979–1993

Andy Bashford was born on 22nd July 1950 and attended Reigate Priory Boys School. Prior to joining the Royal Air Force in January 1972 Andy had been employed as a motor mechanic for the Wadham Stringer Group.

Following recruit training at Swinderby, his technical training as A-Mech-A was carried out at St. Athan before his posting to No. 242 OCU, RAF Thorney Island with Hercules aircraft and Andover Mk.1 (Black Cat XS599, XS600 & XS644) and Andover Mk.2 (XS791 & XS794) from 1972 to 1975.

More technical training at St. Athan (A-Fitt-A) and a posting to RAF Abingdon on Aircraft Production Squadron (Jaguar Majors) followed until he was selected for The Queen's Flight in 1979. Andy was appointed to be a Crew Chief on the Andover aircraft from 1984 until 1987 with XS790 being his special responsibility. He was appointed to be the Airframe Trade Manager in 1991. Andy served as a Crew Chief on both the Andover and BAe 146, as both SNCO and as a civilian. He logged some 339 Royal Flights with 1022.05 flying hours as a serviceman, which increased to 439 Royal Flights and 1105.50 flying hours when his BAe 146 totals as a civilian are added on.

Amongst Andy's 'magic moments' on the Flight he has listed: His first Andover tour to Botswana with Kitty4 crew. Receiving a route knowledge course from K4Nav, which served him well as a crew chief in the years that followed. The visit to Lobatsee and the darts night at the Lion Brewery in Gaberone and he won't forget the experience of operating in the build-ups from Harare to Lilongwe.

Visiting the Vatican whilst night-stopping Rome and managed to see the Pope by pure chance when he appeared in St. Paul's unannounced with only a few people around. Touring Australia with K3 crew in a BAe 146 in 1990. Great golf in Queensland and Western Australia; BAe 146 tour to Nigeria with K4 crew and the late HRH The Princess of Wales.

Crew Chiefing on XS790 with K2 crew during introduction of BAe 146, was hard and rewarding. We held the fort whilst the jets got their act together, and the most important book in the Air Pubs box onboard was 'The Daily Telegraph Book of British Golf Courses'

His Investiture Ceremony for the Royal Victorian Medal (Silver), that same chap who moulded my attitude towards being a crew chief was around again managing the situation to perfection, and being given a great farewell from The Queen's Flight in January 1994, with a fantastic Gizzit.

After leaving the Flight Andy served as Station Engineer, Cityjet Dublin International Airport; Senior BAe 146 Crew Chief, FRA Serco, RAF Northolt; Station Engineer, Jersey European Airways, Birmingham; Shift Supervisor for Monarch Airlines, Birmingham and Engineering Manager, British European Airways, Birmingham.

Group Captain Nigel E. L. Beresford, LVO, RAF
Officer Commanding: 26th November 1988 – 7th May 1992

Born 10th October 1948. Commissioned into the Royal Air Force in February 1968;

After completing pilot training was "creamed off" to return to Training Command as a basic flying instructor. Three years later joined the Strategic Transport Force flying Britannia and VC-10 aircraft as co-pilot, captain and flight instructor.

Nigel became a VIP pilot flying many Royal, Ministerial and Head of State Flights; No.46 Group Training Pilot, 1984; Air Force Staff College, 1987; Officer Commanding, The Queen's Flight, as Wing Commander; 1998-92;

In 1992, as a Group Captain, Nigel, was posted to the Air Warfare College, Air University, at Maxwell AFB, Alabama, USA, before being assigned to Air Mobility Command as the Divisional Chief of STANEVAL. On returning to the UK in 1996 he was posted to the Permanent Joint Headquarters at Northwood as SO1 SH/AT/AAR within the J3 Air Operations Division until appointed Group Captain AT/AAR Policy at HQ 2 Group which was formed on 1st April 2000 by the amalgamation of 38 Group and elements of 11/18 Group. Appointed LVO 1992.

Group Captain D.H.A. (David) Greenway, OBE
Deputy Captain, The Queen's Flight, 17th November 1989–22nd November 1991

" I was awarded a Cranwell Scholarship when I was a 15 year-old at St. Edward's School, Oxford, and was told by the Headmaster that I wouldn't like the Royal Air Force and they wouldn't like me.

I actually joined the RAF on a Direct Commission on 1st April 1957 and after Initial Training at RAF Kirton-in-Lindsey, I trained on Piston Provosts at Tern Hill, 1957, and Vampires at Swinderby, 1958, before graduating in December 1958 and joining Coastal Command.

After a spell at St. Mawgan, pre-MOTU, I went to Kinloss MOTU (Shackletons T4) in 1959, before returning to St. Mawgan and duties as a Co-Pilot with No. 206 Squadron flying Shackletons Mk.III in 1960.

On posting as a Captain on No. 38 Squadron, I flew Shackletons MR Mk.2 at Luqa, in Malta, 1963 before I became ADC to the AOC Malta, 1965 and Personal Staff Officer to him in his NATO hat as D C-in-C (Air) Headquarters Allied Forces Mediterranean in 1966;

Following Central Flying School, Little Rissington in 1967, I Instructed on the Varsity at Oakington in 1968 before going to Laarbruch as OC GD Flight in 1971; I was short-toured there to go to Lossiemouth as Flight Commander Operations on No.8 (AEW) Squadron, back on Shacks again (AEW Mk.2), 1973; and then went to Headquarters Strike Command as Air Defence (AEW) Staff Officer in 1975 before doing Staff College at Bracknell in 1977; A posting to Cyprus as Squadron Leader Plans and Group Flight Safety Officer followed before I was dragged back to go to MOD as Operational Requirements 60 (RAF), the desk responsible for trying to introduce Nimrod AEW into Service, 1980;

From 1982 to 1984 I commanded No.8 (AEW) Squadron (Shackletons AEW Mk.2), still at Lossiemouth, Awarded OBE; and then returned briefly to AEW Operations MOD, 1984, before being sent to the Supreme Headquarters Allied Powers Europe at Mons, I Belgium, 1986, to run SACEUR's Infrastructure Programme (with only about £2 Billion on my desk to spend each year)! In 1989 I was lucky enough to get the plum jobs of Station Commander RAF Benson and Deputy Captain of The Queen's Flight and appointed ADC to HM The Queen. My final tour was looking after Plans and Budgets in the Training Group at HQ RAF Support Command at Brampton, 1991, before I got too old for the RAF and was invited to leave in 1994. In all, it was 37 years of uninterrupted fun that I thoroughly enjoyed – mostly because of the people. We moved to Anna Valley near Andover in 1998.

I now run my own business, "Time to Remember", recording on CD the personal memoirs of anyone who can't stand the thought of writing it all down. It is great fun and we often howl with laughter. I think we owe it to our descendants to tell them what we have done with our lives and my hope is that my subjects will pass on their story to their successors. I am also a Director of Tidworth Gold Club Ltd, which is a grand way of saying that I am the Course Member. As a keen golfer, whilst at St. Mawgan I won the Coastal Command Golf Championship and whilst in Cyprus won the Cyprus Open Foursomes and was RAF Cyprus Golf Champion.

Group Captain M.V.P.H. (Mike) Harrington, CVO, BA, FBIM
Deputy Captain, The Queen's Flight, 19th May 1989 – 21st June 1991

Educated and trained at RAF Cranwell Mike began his flying career on the V Force flying Valiants and Vulcans. After qualifying as a QFI he returned to Cranwell instructing on Jet Provosts. He became Area Commander RAF Recruiting Organisation in Birmingham for the Midlands, then back to flying as Flight Commander (No. 83 Squadron) and Squadron Commander (101 Squadron) before attending RN Staff College Greenwich.

Staff appointments as Exercise Planning Officer HQNEAF Cyprus, Air Adviser to Defence Sales Organisation, HQSTC as Wing Commander Strike, SACEUR Representative to the Joint Strategic Target Planning Staff at Offutt AFB Nebraska USA followed before becoming Station Commander at RAF School of Recruit Training, RAF Swinderby then Military Adviser to the British High Commission in Singapore.

Whilst Deputy Captain of The Queen's Flight, from 1989-1991, Mike accompanied main Royal Tours to Central and South America (Princess Royal), India and Nepal (Princess Alexandra), Nigeria and Cameroons (Prince and Princess of Wales), Russia (Princess Royal), Hungary (Prince and Princess of Wales), Central and South Africa (Princess Royal), Poland (Duke of Gloucester) and Far East (Duke of Gloucester) carrying out 417 Royal Flight with a total of 4211 flying hours. His most memorable moments were accompanying HM The Queen and HRH The Duke of Edinburgh to Northern Ireland for his last flight with TQF and accompanying HM The Queen and HRH The Duke of Edinburgh on their tour of USA with a return to the UK on Concorde. Moment to forget was the diversion to Gatwick with the Princess of Wales with an engine fault at the start of the Royal Tour to Hungary and the subsequent adverse publicity.

Appointed CVO on leaving the Flight, Mike became Infrastructure Plans Officer on NATO (SACLANT) staffs at RAF Northwood for six years before retiring in 1997.

Squadron Leader Graham Laurie, MVO, RAF
Fixed Wing Pilot, The Queen's Flight 1981–1995
Later No. 32 (The Royal) Squadron 1995–2000

Graham was born on 15th December 1945 and educated at Rutlish School, Merton Park, London SW20. Joining the Royal Air Force in September 1964 and after Initial Officer Training at RAF South Cerney, he began his flying training with No.7 Flying Training School (FTS) (Jet Provost) at RAF Church Fenton in February 1965 and at No. 5 FTS at RAF Oakington (Varsity) in 1966. In September of that year at RAF Abingdon he completed a course at the Andover OCU before joining No.46 Squadron (Andover) in March 1967 at Abingdon and then overseas with No.84 Squadron (Andover) at RAF Sharjah in February 1969. Instructional duties followed with a course at the Central Flying School at RAF Little Rissington (Chipmunk) in April 1970 and the training the East Lowlands University Air Squadron pilots at RAF Turnhouse, near Edinburgh from November 1970 to 1973.

Overseas in April 1973 on a Loan Service Tour with the Sultan's Flight at Brunei flying the HS748 was followed in December 1875 by a tour at RAF Northolt with No. 32 Squadron (Andover) and in July 1977 to RAF Brize Norton and a flight checking tour with No.115 Squadron (Andover). April 1979 saw a move to No.38 Group Examining Unit at RAF Upavon as an Andover Pilot Examiner followed by a move to The Queen's Flight in June 1981 where he remained until the disbandment in March 1995. Graham moved to No.32 (The Royal) Squadron with the aircraft to RAF Northolt and continued to fly members of the Royal Family until his retirement in December 2000.

Graham continues with his own story:

"I joined the Royal Air Force straight from school and after basic and advanced training was posted to Abingdon to fly Andover aircraft. One co-pilot on our course was destined for The Queen's Flight (later he became my boss as OC The Queen's Flight – Wg Cdr Brian Synott). I flew the Mk 1 Andover – the one that kneels – rather than the Mk2, which was virtually a standard 748. After a tour as a co-pilot I was posted as an aircraft captain to Sharjah in the Middle East. Lots of tactical flying into sand and grass strips coupled with supply and parachute dropping.

After two years instructing on Chipmunk's at East Lowlands UAS in Edinburgh, I applied for a loan service post in Brunei. Much to my surprise I was selected and thus spent nearly 3 years in the Far East. Little did I realise how useful this tour on The Sultan's Flight would be in the future. Back to UK, again on VIP work with No 32 Sqn at Northolt, plenty of trips with senior Ministers and Service Chiefs but as yet no Royals.

Promoted to Squadron Leader in 1977 I was posted as Flight Commander Training on No 115 Sqn at Brize Norton, newly equipped with Andovers. My third role with the Andover, this one was calibration of landing aids. During this tour I visited almost all RAF flying stations in UK, Europe and the Middle East.

Following the calibration tour I was made the 38 Group Examining Unit Examiner for Andover and 125 aircraft. This was my first link with The Queen's Flight and after two years I was invited for interview for the post of Personal Pilot to HRH The Prince of Wales. The current incumbent, Squadron Leader Derek Lovett, who was to retire in the July, eventually extended by one day to fly TRH's The Prince and Princess of Wales on their honeymoon from Southampton to Gibraltar.

I took over the post on the royal couples return from honeymoon. Whilst fully 'catted' on the Andover Mk2 I still had so much to learn on the operation to 'The Queen's Flight Standard' and training officer Dave Rowe (Kitty 2) took me under his wing. For the co-pilots benefit, he gave me the same hard time as you! My first Royal came on 22 Jul 81 taking HRH The Duchess of Kent from Northolt to Leeds. What could be easier, the middle of the summer and an evening one way run! Well, do not assume, check, had by this time been drummed into me. I did an early met check and oh dear, the morning fog over Leeds had lifted into low cloud, enough to make the Leeds arrival, at least doubtful. Just to add to the pressure I had to get Linton on Ouse to stand by as diversion and the DC spoke to the Station Commander to explain he would not be using his car that evening, would he! In the event we landed at Leeds and my first Royal was over and lessons were certainly learnt, not least never trust the weather, and always check beforehand. It was something I never forgot and later I was known as the 'Positioning King' for the number of times I took a crew off the night before because of the possibility of bad weather the next morning. Needless to say invariably we woke to sunshine but at least we all got a good nights sleep with no worries of what the next day held for us. If you made the departure airfield, you could do no more but it would be exceedingly embarrassing not to make even the required start point!

On 9 Sep 81, I flew TRH The Prince and Princess of Wales for the first time bringing them down from Aberdeen to London and back the next day. Four days later I was away on my first 'tour', which was to the Cameroon's and Ivory Coast. The run out was to follow the well-trodden path down the west coast of Africa via Morocco, Las Palmas to Dakar in Senegal. Then it got interesting visiting places, previously only familiar for their stamps; Liberia or Monrovia as it is sometimes known. Nobody is allowed to board a TQF aircraft but try telling that to the airport security officer at Roberts Field, Monrovia, he just produced a gun and said 'I am coming on board'! He did and we treated him well, we shook his hand (the one without the gun in) and we all became friends. We did a little proving on the way out, followed by a quick visit to Lagos to deliver some fresh vegetables to the Embassy staff, who kindly organized a party (a lot safer than going downtown!). We picked up HRH The Duke of Kent in the main port of Douala, where he had arrived aboard a British Caledonian 707. We flew up to the capital Yaounde, having previously deposited our ground crew and baggage there, earlier in the day. After two days it was back to Douala where HRH boarded the Royal Yacht en route for the Ivory Coast. For us it was back to Yaounde to collect the ground crew etc. This was to become, if I had not already realised, a regular feature of operating the Andover in a worldwide role!

The Ivory Coast produced my first Royal to a 'strip', not small but natural surface; the local airline used Fokker F28 jets. After the day trip it was back to Abidjan before starting the homeward journey. We night stopped Roberts Field again, a fascinating stop at the old KLM Airport Hotel, which was used by the airlines in their pre war forays to Africa where passengers and crew, stayed together overnight (must have made for an expensive crew bar!)

By mid 1982 I was flying the more senior Royals and in May had my first trip with HM Queen Elizabeth The Queen Mother; little realising that in 2000 I would be flying her just after her 100th birthday. The following day I set off on a trip to the States with my new Navigator and mentor Brian Sowerby. Brian swapped from the Kitty 2 crew to join me to spread the experience level. I had never operated in the States so a small trainer was organised which included Nashville, Lexington (Blue Grass Country), New Orleans, Tampa, Chicago not to mention a 1 hour lunch stop at Memphis where we all jumped into a limo and dashed to see the home of Elvis, 'Gracelands'. Our return via Canada included the almost obligatory diversion from Gander to Stephenville. I was route checked from Goose Bay to Sondestrom before a night in Reykjavik and back to Benson. All this in just seven days, and people had told me it was a cushy number! In August 1982 I flew TRH The Prince and Princess of Wales from Kemble to Aberdeen; it was also the first flight for the young Prince William. To say there were quite a few 'Press' at Aberdeen was an understatement!

Later in August 1982 my crew after much labouring over the planning documents set off for a proving flight covering much of Africa and the Middle East. We were flying civil air to Jeddah before picking up an aircraft on its way back from the Far East. Our recce was for HRH The Princess Anne's first major tour with Save the Children Fund (SCF). The first day was Jeddah to Djibouti (a base for the French Foreign Legion) and whilst relaxing I had a phone call from Dougie Barr (TQF Adjutant) to basically say, 'Head south as quickly as possible you will be picking up a Royal to attend the funeral of the King of Swaziland'. Lesson 1 never leave all your planning on the aircraft! It was however initially going to be the same route as we had planned but after Mombassa we needed diplomatic clearance over Tanzania a day early plus all the other dip clears on the way down. Brian and I got together and tried to pre guess where the pick up would be. Harare or Johannesburg being the places served by BA, so we based it on Harare and very soon realised it was going to be tight either way. The BA 747 landed at Harare at 6.00 am and the earliest we could arrive was 4.00 pm the previous day, this always assuming no problems with the clearances! As we sat on the ground in Mombassa waiting for our Tanzanian clearance, the minutes ticked away, luckily it came through in the nick of time and at 5.55 pm we landed at Harare. My first sight of the beautiful Jacaranda and Bougainvilleas of Zimbabwe, but we had confirmation that we should fly direct to Matsapa in Swaziland, the next morning. HRH The Duke of Gloucester and party climbed off the 747 and straight on to the Andover; another seamless transition, if only they knew! In Swaziland, the crowds were immense and we watched the funeral in our air-conditioned hotel. The Deputy Captain had to sit through it live for six hours in the heat and all that after 12 hours flying!

Our problems increased when at the end of the funeral our party announced they wanted to visit the ruins at Fort Victoria on the Sunday afternoon, to fill in time prior to departure of their 747 from Harare later in the evening. Fort Victoria, no problem except it had no fuel listed and was closed on Sundays. Dear Mr Air Attaché please fix it for Kitty 4! He did and when we arrived we even saw some oil drums of fuel, yes it had to be hand pumped direct from drums. It was a good thing that the royal party were away for a few hours! We met up with some ex patriots who had been playing rugby and they gave us a hand and looked after us very well. We dropped our party at Harare and continued with the rest of our recce. It would only be 3 weeks before we were back doing the SCF Tour.

Needless to say there were still a few outstanding problems to resolve with the programme so we agreed to check a couple of other possible destinations in Zimbabwe on our way south. The Andover XS 789 left RAF Benson on Sunday 10th October, positioning to Johannesburg. Normally tour programmes were settled weeks before departure, but the nature of SCF work, necessitates a more flexible response. The trips to Victoria Falls and Lake Kariba (Binga) were confirmed but we would need to prove a strip called 'Aberdeen 2', situated in the Inyanga National Park. The Air Attaché explained that there was still some 'political' doubt about a royal visit to this area (the home of the 5th Brigade), however our proving flight had been approved by the Ministry of Defence and the requested fire cover had been put into the strip. Full details of the episode of Aberdeen 2 were covered in Chapter 10, Overseas Tours.

My first full year on The Queen's Flight and nearly 400 hours and over 100 Royal Flights, life was never dull!

Back in UK another first on 4 Mar 83 when Prince William flew from Glasgow to Aberdeen on his first solo trip, in the company of Nanny Barnes. Later that month I completed 5000 hours on type and qualified for another cake, organised by Brian Sowerby (and he is still organizing us today!). May 83 saw a quick SCF tour to Pakistan and my first glimpse of the Khyber Pass; on this trip we carried the Director General of SCF with us on the positioning out to Pakistan. John Cumber (later Sir John) was a lovely man and he insisted on becoming a member of the crew. He was everywhere chatting to ground crew and handling agents; it was only later we realised it was always in their local tongue. We later ascertained his father had been in the Indian Army and he had been brought up overseas. Brian Sowerby completed another milestone on reaching Karachi (I think it was 10,000 hours day flying) but the crew decided it was our turn to surprise him. The stewards saw the Beverage Manager at the Intercontinental Hotel and asked for a cake with the words 'Well done Nav'. Something went a little wrong in the translation. The next morning we got our iced cake with the following inscription 'With the words Well done Nav'!

In early 1984 there was another African Reccé, this time to Botswana, we were away for 22 days. In mid March we picked up HRH The Prince of Wales in Dar es Salam, visiting Tanzania, Zambia, Zimbabwe and Botswana. We finally flew the Prince from Maun in the Okavango to Lusaka, before returning to Maun to pick up the ground crew who during this tour had flown on Botswana Airlines F 27's and had even done one journey by coach (only a TQF ground crew could offer seats to a group of British Caledonian hostesses and organise them a lift back to Lusaka in a Zambian Air Force Yak 40!).

In July 1984 I did the first of two trips to Papua New Guinea (the furthest afield I got with TQF). This was a tour again with HRH The Prince of Wales and we had to do the proving a few days before the arrival of the Royal Party by VC10. On the way out I had a co pilot (Bob Taylor) and the incoming OC TQF (Wg Cdr Mike Schofield). Mike was along to see the Andover at work, although he was looking forward to the arrival of the BAe 146 in 1986. I say looking forward to it, particularly after I gave him a simulated engine failure, climbing out of Momote on Easter Island. Some minutes after the failure and a lot of 'huffing and puffing' we reached 1000ft! Mike had come from the somewhat overpowered Hercules and I think he was put off the Andover for life – at least he never came and pinched any legs off me again!

In October 1984 I flew President Mitterand of France to Exeter to link up with one of our Wessex. The passenger duly transferred and the Wessex started – or rather didn't! Out jumped the crew chief with the trusted 'rubber hammer'; he dropped the cowling and gave the offending item (I think it was always the flow converter), a gentle tap, well actually quite a bash! Whatever he did worked and off they went to the Devon coast. We scoured the papers the next day but what had gone on failed to be spotted by the photographers gathered on the airport perimeter!

The young Prince Henry travelled with us for the first time on 2 May 1985. His brother joined us for the trip to Venice to meet up with TRH The Prince and Princess of Wales who were on a State Visit to Italy. The boys were whisked away to board the Royal Yacht. We did the pick up a few days later from Olbia in Sicily. Prince William flew home in a VC10. This was the first time the family had been split, based on the 'line of the throne' not travelling together.

In July 1985 I flew HRH The Princess Anne from Kinloss to Edinburgh, the 1000th Royal Flight completed by Brian Sowerby (I was still a new boy with just 424!).

Towards the end of 1985, Royal Tours were coming thick and fast. I completed yet another African prover for SCF but left the aircraft in Nairobi, where Geoff Williams took over to go on a tour with HRH The Duke of Edinburgh. We had spent 18 days visiting, Sudan, Kenya, Tanzania, Zanzibar, Mozambique and Zambia. After flying home by VC10 we had less than two weeks to put the Royal Tour together before we were Africa bound again. The Royal pick up was in Dar es Salam but somehow we managed to prep the aircraft in Mombasa, something to do with aircraft schedules and spares I expect (nothing to do with the Bamburi Beach Hotel!). It was a fascinating trip including 4 strips. The one at Lake Manyara on the edge of the Ngorogoro Crater will live in my memory for its shear beauty for many a year. The lake seemed full of flamingos and thus looked pink! The strip went right to the lakeside on a 500ft escarpment. We had arranged for a British pilot to take his Cherokee in as ATC but for the return flight to Dar, HRH was running late so he had to take off, as he had no night rating. My safety cover was the pilot listening to us in the cruise! Mozambique was still war torn and SCF were working particularly well. At Inhambane HRH was presented with a pair of Doves. It was thought by the local council that these would be flown back to UK. I was given strict instructions by the Deputy Captain that these birds would not, repeat not be on the return journey to Maputo! With half the crew supplying distraction the birds were given their freedom. Alas, some bright spark spotted them and we nearly got a replacement pair! We explained they were obviously very frightened and HRH being such an animal lover would prefer to know 'her' doves were enjoying life in the wild – it worked, just!

In Zambia we visited the 'Copper Belt' but not before we had ventured to Mwinilunga near the Zaire border. HRH was to visit a Mission School at Sakeji and I still hear from them today. The kids all came to see the aircraft on the reccé but were heavily involved on the big day. We stayed at the airfield and Steve Giles (Steward) entertained the kids with his 'Magic Show'. He was to do another two performances that evening when we visited the Chingola Flying Club. The members not only organised on a party but put the crew up in their homes.

Onward to the Sudan where we were to spend two nights at Nyala at the Government Rest House. We had seen it on the reccé and without doubt I can say it was the worst accommodation I stayed in during my 15 years with TQF! We had this time, come prepared. We brought our own food, toilet paper and toilet seats! The request had been made after the reccé, so two spare Andover toilet seats were packed, one marked 'Officers'and the other 'Enlisted S--t'. We opened these as soon as we arrived, to find the 'lads' one even had a lambs wool cover, as used for Wessex pilot seat covers. As to the officers, it too was covered but with a DIY product that comes in Coarse, Medium and Fine and is used for rubbing down, Needless to say George Henderson and his men back in the 'top shop' had made sure it was coarse!!! We made the best of our stay and to be fair to the Sudanese they had also cleaned the place up and provided a cook; we ate a little of his food but only a very little. On the second day as we landed at the strip at Zalingei we noticed the security was provided by two soldiers on horseback! We dropped HRH at Khartoum to come home by BA Tri-Star and we returned quickly, via the inevitable and well-earned night stop in Nice. We reached Benson 1 month to the day from our departure. The story of this tour formed a chapter of the book to celebrate 50 years of Royal Flying published in 1986.

1986 was to be a year of change with the introduction of the BAe 146 but prior to the two new aircraft arriving I completed 500 Royal Flights on a trip from Norwich to Edinburgh with HRH The Prince of Wales and flew HM The Queen, as aircraft captain for the first time from London (Heathrow) to Norwich.

My BAe 146 flying training was carried out over a period of six days with Peter Hopwood, one of the BAe Training Pilots. Peter continued to fly with us on the route phase and by the end of the month I was 'route checked'. With just over 50 hours on type Geoff Williams (who had been on the first course) and I set off for Hong Kong and China; talk about a steep learning curve! Three days after returning to UK I was off again, this time over the Atlantic as far as Chicago and back. We returned in early September with The Prince of Wales. Geoff Williams and I continued to fly both types whilst Mike Schofield and Dave Gale concentrated on the 146 and Dave Rowe – UK 2 Air – as the crew became known, just flew the Andover.

In October HRH Princess Alexandra visited Lexington, Kentucky to present The Queen Elizabeth Cup at Keeneland Racecourse. We later flew to Washington, where HRH left us for a holiday. Lexington was superb, particularly for someone interested in horses. Kerri Davis, from the police department, was a superb host. He organised us to go racing at Keeneland where we met an owner, bet on her horse and won! I vowed then to return with my wife for our Silver Wedding and I made it to the day in 1993.

1987 saw TRH The Prince and Princess of Wales visiting Portugal and later Spain. In October my crew positioned to Hong Kong in a 707 of British Airtours for a recce of Thailand, Laos and Burma. Both these countries proved fascinating and we found the local people so welcoming. In mid November we set off for Seoul where we were to pick up HRH The Princess Royal for her SCF sponsored trip. We routed via Hong Kong to Singapore where HRH was, on behalf of the Foreign Office, opening the Singapore Mass Transit Railway. After Bangkok our next three destinations were Sakon Nakhon (a little village in Thailand close to the Laos border), Vientiane (Capital of Laos) and Rangoon (Capital of Burma). We were given a surprising amount of freedom in all three places and were soon to realise how strong the belief in Buddhism was in the area. I took time to visit the Commonwealth War Cemetery in Rangoon and I think it houses amongst the thousands of graves twelve VC's. It was certainly a moving experience wandering alone through these graves on a hot Saturday afternoon. We raced home through India leaving HRH to return by civil air from Bahrain.

My first use of the 146 'Coffin Fit' came on a sad day in March 1988, when three days after dropping HRH The Prince of Wales and his party in Zurich for their skiing holiday, we returned in sombre mood to bring him back after the avalanche that so nearly took his life. The body of his equerry Lt Hugh Lindsay was flown to Northolt, where his Regiment met us and moved the coffin with full military honours. Little did I know at that time that I would be doing another trip in 1997!

In July 1988 we flew another recce for a trip with HRH The Duke of Gloucester later in the year to Turkey and Pakistan. When we look at the two itineraries, there was little in common. On the recce we went to Eastern Turkey to Gazientep but the Turkish Government was not happy for a Royal Visit to that area. We were taking around businessmen, representing the British Consultancy Board (BCB); we had a similar problem in Pakistan with Bahawalpur, where the previous year the President of Pakistan's aircraft crashed, killing all on board, in the 'case of the exploding mangos' as it was known. The actual started with a middle of the night arrival at Ankara International. That was fine but in the latter part of the descent the flaps failed to extend, so there we were at a high altitude airfield, at night and flapless! All went well with the landing and the engineers soon put the problem down to the grease used in the flap tracks. Alas we were not the first of the BAe 146 operators to have this teething problem.

The CTQF tells a story of a trip with TRH The Prince and Princess of Wales to Paris. It was a State visit and the 146 needed to get the household and the baggage back to UK and then return for the Royal Party. The day did not start well when we were diverted by bad weather to London (Heathrow). That was fine but then the Air Traffic Control Computer failed and bedlam became the order of the day! Basically there were aircraft stranded in the air because nothing was moving on the ground. We were due to position back to Paris but had little priority at that stage. We just kept quiet and I assured CTQF that we would get away in time for the Paris pick up. Alas things did not improve but the magic name of TQF came good and we were given special permission to depart. From then on the day went smoothly!

In April 1989 I flew another SCF recce, this time to Ethiopia. The itinerary included Jijiga, a natural surface strip 8000ft high in the East of the country near the Somali border. We used a Mission Fellowship Cessna to have a look first and went back in the afternoon with the 146. It was rough but the aircraft performed well. The party were going off to a refugee camp 4 hours away but we decided to go back to Addis Ababa. Alas the tour did not take place for a few years, as there was a coup some weeks after we left.

My 1000th Royal was a summer holiday trip from Kemble to Aberdeen with HRH The Princess of Wales and Princes William and Henry. I was later presented with the mounted 'Pax Map' duly inscribed.

In September 1989 'Hurricane Hugo' hit the Caribbean and left a path of devastation. A number of the islands were badly hit and Her Majesty asked HRH Princes Alexandra to visit. We got four days notice, which concentrated the planning minds. We routed out via the Azores, Newfoundland and night stopped Bermuda, before going on to Antigua. There we had to strip out the aircraft, to get it as light as possible for the landing in Montserrat the following morning. HRH wanted to have a look round the island prior to landing. Looking at the Capital, Plymouth, it became obvious that over 70% of the buildings had been destroyed. After parking at what was left of the small terminal we spent the day wandering around what obviously had been a beautiful island (it has of course since been ravaged twice by volcanic eruptions in 1995 and 1997). After a night on Anguilla, which was to me, what I had always imagined the Caribbean to be, we moved on to the British Virgin Islands, We landed at Beef Island and dropped off some of the supplies we had brought with us. We got a lift into town via some of the wind-ravaged villages. You soon realised that the damage was worse because so many of the buildings are built with plywood and just nailed together. The advantage, if there is one, is that they are easier and cheaper to replace; alas it is such a trauma to the occupants. On the return journey we spent a night in Bermuda and Iceland, waking to find the morning papers full of stories about HRH's daughter. It was obvious that the media would be covering our arrival at Heathrow in some force.

In late 1989 I flew the Prime Minister, Margaret Thatcher for the first time, on a trip to Strasbourg. Over the next 12 months we flew the PM a number of times culminating a trip to Paris in November 1990. Having dropped her on 18 Nov we returned on the evening of 20th (the night of the long knives). We were told to stay at the aircraft until the result of the vote was known in case she wished to return to UK. Finding out the result was easy, we listened to BBC World Service on HF. Getting a decision out of the Embassy was not so easy, in the end we phone patched via Portishead Radio into the Embassy to be told we could stand down until the morning. On my birthday in 1990 I had the pleasure of flying the new Prime Minister, The Rt Hon John Major. We flew back to Heathrow from Rome, we had both attended the same school, a fact that was picked up by his Private Secretary and an article appeared in the 'Peterborough' column of the Daily Telegraph during the next week.

Just before the end of the year my crew positioned by British Airways to Cairo, ready to fly HRH The Prince of Wales to the Gulf, to meet British troops stationed there since Iraq moved into Kuwait. We visited Jubail and Bahrain, Dahran and Riyadh before going back to Cairo. The other crew then flew the party and my crew, back to Marham and we finally reached Benson on Christmas Eve

1991 started with me delivering our third BAe 146 (ZE 702) and on 28 Jan Dave Rowe and I flew, HRH The Prince of Wales, on the last Andover Royal Flight from Newcastle to Greenham Common in XS 790. The service the Andover provided to The Queen's Flight since its introduction in the 60's was immense and it was sad to see it go. The aircraft was taken over by RAe Bedford, before moving to Farnborough and later Boscombe Down where it is today, as a radio trials installation platform.

We spent a great deal of time flying members of the Royal Family to destinations meeting troops and families of those in the Gulf. My crew took the Defence Secretary and a number of senior media editors out to attend the signing of the Iraqi surrender. In April it was back to 'tours' with TRH The Prince and Princess of Wales visiting Brazil. We completed our reccé a few days ahead of the Royal. The tour started in the capital Brasilia; BAe were pushing to get a Brazilian 'start up' airline off the ground, so a BAe 146 demonstrator was painted in Air Brazil colours and used throughout the tour to carry officials and the press. This aircraft, coupled with our presence was expected to accelerate the order process.

The crew's introduction to Brazil had not gone smoothly, whilst checking the airfields to be used we night stopped Rio de Janeiro/Santos Dumont, the small city centre airfield near the famous cable car ride featured in the James Bond movie. The defence attaché briefed us thoroughly on the high levels of street crime. We were to go out in groups, spread money in all available places, including socks. Do not take out service identification cards or cameras and above all keep your eyes peeled for groups of teenage or younger children. We set of for the restaurant, which was some 400 yards from the hotel. His description came graphically to mind as we were 'bounced' by a group of 12 to 14 year old youngsters. Malcolm Brecht and Bob Shields were both knocked to the ground along with the defence attaché. The remainder of the crew followed the briefing and started making as much noise as possible (not difficult for a TQF crew!). The net result was a few dollars lost from Malcolm's slashed pocket but the DA lost his wallet. Despite his briefing he also lost his diplomatic ID card and more importantly the money he was to use to entertain us. It was a slightly sombre crew that ate a superb meal that evening!

The tour itself was a great success; after the initial visit to Carajas in the north we returned via Brasilia to Rio. The Royal party had separate programmes so we took His Royal Highness to Vitoria and the following day the Princess to Cataratas where she visited the Iguacio Falls (filmed in 'The Mission'). This was one of those sights that are never forgotten. So alas was the return journey. A fine forecast for a simple return to Rio in the late afternoon. Just before top of descent it started to rain. The next moment we were in the middle of the worst storm ~ I have ever known. The turbulence, lightening and hail were horrendous. Four or five aircraft were caught in it. Santos Dumont was closed as Bob Shields our Nav tried to find a safer area. The aircraft was difficult to control but eventually we heard that the International airport had reopened, so we diverted and landed safely some 20 minutes after the start of the bad weather. The Deputy Captain had apparently played a blinder, going into the Royal cabin on his knees advising the party how best to deal with the turbulence – I wish he had come to the cockpit and told us as well!! The next morning we departed the International and routed via Brasilia to Belem on the Amazon, where the royal couple were to meet up again on the Royal Yacht.

In September I visited Papua New Guinea for the second time. HRH The Duke of York was to open and attend the South Pacific Games. The pick up was in Hong Kong and we routed via Mactan (Philippines), Biak (Indonesia) to Port Moresby. It was again a quick visit to the airfields to be used along with a Captain from Air New Guinea, as again BAe were keen to sell the BAe 146. We visited

Goroka in the highlands area and saw the famous 'Mud Men'. Needless to say we had four or five mud helmets by the time we returned, including one for HRH.

Life was nothing but hectic at this time, as five days after our return the crew were off again, this time to Pakistan with HRH The Princess of Wales. The selling campaign for the BAe 146 continued in Pakistan. The northern airfields, among them Chitral, were currently served by Pakistan Airways Fokker Friendships. During our reccé we were asked to fly among others the Director of Civil Aviation and Chief Executive of PIA. Chitral is probably my favourite destination of all time; it sits in a valley at an elevation of 5,000ft with the valley sides at 16,000ft but just 25 miles away is Mt Tirich Mir at over 25,000ft. Spectacular is not the word and not surprisingly the airfield is one way in, one way out. The major advantage of the BAe 146 over the F27 was that it could overshoot from the runway threshold and out climb the terrain down wind and thus turn in the valley. We demonstrated this feature before our return to Islamabad. The sale never materialised as the service was subsidised by the Government and they did not want a private operator to take it on. The Princess was delayed visiting Chitral but we were able to land by mid afternoon and departed just before darkness fell. It was a memorable trip for all concerned. 1991 had been a busy year with over 500 hrs flown and 170 Royal Flights; the 146's were being worked hard and were responding very well.

The hectic lifestyle continued and in May 1992 my crew flew a tour to Egypt with HRH The Princess of Wales, without a Commodore! On the morning we were to depart Cairo for Luxor another BAe 146 of the Flight came through Cairo to refuel on it's way back to UK and just after we landed at Luxor HRH The Duke of Edinburgh landed the third BAe 146, to refuel on his way to Madagascar.

Despite the fact that we were so busy, the Captain was having more and more problems justifying the mere existence of The Queen's Flight. It was obvious that there was a move to disband or reduce the size of the organisation. This was to rumble for three more years but the manoeuvring of our enemies was already in full swing.

In August we flew all four members of the Wales family to Preveza, so they could join their yacht for a summer holiday. This was the last time they all flew together and this trip had been driven by 'secrecy from the press' and bad publicity, for wasting two aircraft.

In November the incoming State Visit was from The Sultan of Brunei. Having flown on Sultan's Flight in Brunei in the mid 70's I was very pleased that my crew were to fly him on this visit. We flew from Benson to Cranwell and then back to Northolt. During the flight I was able to check up on the two co pilots I had trained, only to find one was now Chief of the Air Staff and the other Chief of Defence Staff – and I had been a Squadron Leader since 1977!

Whilst on a trip from Valley to Farnborough with HRH The Prince of Wales, in Dec 92 I was advised by his Personal Protection Officer that there would be announcement in the House of Commons that afternoon about the marriage of TRH The Prince and Princess of Wales. It was particularly sad for my crew who had flown them both so many times.

Early 1993 saw a reccé to Mexico for a future trip by HRH The Prince of Wales. The tour took place in March and among our passengers was Jonathan Dimbleby who was making a documentary on The Prince of Wales. The trip started in New York; the Prince arrived on Concorde in a snowstorm and we were de-iced after HRH boarded but it was still 30 minutes later before we took off. Many aircraft that de-iced before their passengers boarded were returning to the ramp. We also visited Houston where we took the opportunity of visiting the headquarters of 'Uvair' who helped organise handling for us and fuel, particularly in Mexico. Mexico was fascinating I have never seen so many VW 'Beetles'; every Taxi was a green one! We also flew to Guadalajara but alas there was not time to go to the football stadium to see the famous goalpost, made famous by the Gordon Banks save in the World Cup!

1993 also saw a marked increase in Ministerial flying; this was obviously a rearguard action to show a more varied utilisation to the public, of the aircraft. In October HRH The Prince of Wales flew direct from Northolt to Istanbul; on landing he was involved with the handover of the first BAe 146 to Turkish Airlines.

We flew HRH The Duchess of Kent to the Ivory Coast in Feb 94 for the funeral of the King at Yamoussoukro. I was glad it was 'Kitty 4' crew that flew the task. As virtually every other aircraft was using the call sign '01'. The whole event was held up as the weather was poor and without radar, only one aircraft could land every 15 minutes. President Mitterand was arriving in Concorde, which was held on the ground, in Paris, until a slot could be guaranteed for landing. The opening up of the former Russian States also saw HRH The Prince of Wales visit St Petersburg.

For me 1994 was an 'Annus Horribilis' after the landing incident at Islay with HRH The Prince of Wales. The support from members and past members of The Queen's Flight was very encouraging. After initially being told to continue flying I was grounded for a short while but a month later I was cleared for Royal Flying but with the stipulation I could not supervise Royal pilots. The Prince of Wales decided not to fly and thus my crew continued to fly him to engagements.

The government Pocock Report was issued in draft form and suggested two or three 125's should move from Northolt and at the same time some of the elements of The Queen's Flight should be civilianised. Alas MOD did not like this and suggested yet more savings could be made; amalgamating the two units at Northolt. This was the option that was accepted and thus we realised that the end of the road was nigh. There was much talk of amalgamation but it soon became clear that disbandment was the order of the day. The aircraft, aircrew and a few operations staff plus a handful of engineers were to move to Northolt on 1 April 1995.

In between all the farewell Royal Visits from virtually every member of the Royal Family my crew managed two final tours. Another visit to Mozambique coupled this time with South Africa for Save The Children Fund with HRH The Princess Royal in Nov 1994. This was to be my first visit to Capetown and Pretoria and a return to Quelimane and Maputo. Whilst in Quelimane we gave a local school, The Queen's Flight soccer strip and by the time we left it was already in use!

The final tour was to Egypt and Morocco with HRH The Prince of Wales including visits to St Catherine's in Sinai and in Morocco, the infamous Fez (where the hats come from!). My last day on the Flight was a trip Cologne to Birmingham with the Foreign Secretary, before delivering the aircraft to Northolt.

Perhaps I may just share a little of Day 1 on No 32. (The Royal) Squadron with you – my first trip on the new Squadron was to position for a Royal flight with HRH The Duke of York. Where did we depart for? Why Benson, of course, there was a little justice left in this world on 1 Apr 1995!"

Group Captain G.H. (Hugh) Rolfe, CVO, CBE
Deputy Captain: 21st June 1991 – 31st March 1995

"I Joined the Service straight from school finishing my education at RAF Cranwell, graduating in 1962. I specialised in Maritime Operations flying Shackletons on No's 204 and 210 Squadrons from RAF Ballykelly in Northern Ireland, then No. 206 Squadron at RAF Kinloss.

I later returned to command No. 206 Squadron then re-equipped with Nimrods in the late 70's. The remainder of my flying was dedicated to training, starting as a QFI with Cambridge University Air Squadron (UAS), then in command of Queen's UAS in Belfast.

The last flying appointment was as Station Commander of RAF Linton on Ouse in charge of No.1 Flying Training School. I did not escape staff appointments and served on three occasions in the Ministry of Defence in London.

Being a French speaker, I attended the French Staff College in Paris for one year. Later served three years in Algiers as the Defence Attaché with the British Embassy. I was appointed Deputy Chief of the British Mission to the Soviet Forces in East Germany. This gave me a front seat to witness the collapse of the Iron Curtain. Appointed as Deputy Captain of The Queen's Flight in June 1991, which would have been a perfect ending to my service in the Royal Air Force, had it not been for the sad demise of The Queen's Flight and the considerable turbulence and reorganisation involved with the move to RAF Northolt.

Since leaving the service in December 1995, I have been living in West Sussex where my wife and I look after a small farm for my elder son who works in London. Needless to say, looking after sheep, horses and chickens and tending the land is a completely new way of life, but we find it every bit as enjoyable and challenging as life before retirement from the Royal Air Force".

Squadron Leader Richard (Dick) H. Stanton, MVO, MRAeS, MRIN, RAF (Ret'd)
Navigator, The Queen's Flight, 29th September 1980 to 31st March 1995

Dick Stanton was born on 6th January 1945 and was educated at Michaelhouse College, Natal in South Africa. He joined the Royal Air Force on 20th September 1965 and after Navigator training saw service with No. 50 Squadron, No. 114 Squadron, and No. 53 Squadron before attending a Staff Navigator Course and a posting to No. 6 Flying Training School as a navigation instructor. A posting to No. 32 Squadron followed before he joined The Queen's Flight on September 1980.

As normal with the navigators on the Flight, Richard moved around the crews and flew initially with Kitty 2, then Kitty 4 and finally with Kitty 1. His last three years was as the Adjutant of the Flight.

He well remembers his crew flying TRH's The Prince and Princess of Wales and TRH's The Duke and Duchess of York on the first stage of their honeymoons. Another day, not to be remembered, when he was in sole charge of TQF on the day the BAe146 with HRH The Prince of Wales on board crashed at Islay and the final act when Dick turned out the lights in D hangar and handed over the hangar to the station in October 1995.

Dick served on The Queen's Flight Association Committee from inauguration until May 2000, as Chairman from 1995 until 2000, and all members are most grateful to him for his eighteen years of service to the Association.

Retiring from the Royal Air Force on 14th March 1996, Dick took up employment as Agent and Secretary to the Rt. Hon. Michael Heseltine, MP for Henley from May 1996 to April 1997. He took up the post of Adjutant to the Oxford University Air Squadron in August 1997 where he is still serving as a Squadron Leader in the RAF Reserve.

Wing Commander N. (Neil) Thurston, LVO, RAF
Officer Commanding: 8th May 1992 – 31st March 1995

Born 25th September 1947 and educated at Waterloo Grammar School, Liverpool, Neil joined the Royal Air Force in April 1968.

His initial and flying training took until 1970 when he was posted to Bomber Command as a Vulcan Co-Pilot from 1971-73. He was appointed a Vulcan Captain in 1973 and flew as such until 1977 when he was posted to the Central Flying School to become an instructor.

Posted to Liverpool University Air Squadron as a QFI and later Chief Flying Instructor from 1977-80 he then became a Staff Officer at HQ RAF Support Command (responsible for all Light Aircraft in the RAF inventory) until 1983.

A change of role to transport flying saw Neil graduate from a VC-10 Co-Pilot, to Captain, Line Training Captain, VIP Captain, and Flight Commander in the Strategic Transport Role, from 1983 to 1989.

A course at the RAF Advanced Staff College followed in 1990 before once again becoming a Staff Officer, this time at HQ RAF Strike Command (Member of contingency planning team during Gulf War) until 1991. Neil was appointed Officer Commanding, The Queen's Flight in 1991 and the last one before the disbandment in 1995. He was appointed to be a Lieutenant in the Royal Victorian Order in 1995 (LVO).

A move to be Wing Commander Training Policy, HQ RAF Personnel and Training Command 1995-96 was followed by an offer of redundancy and Neil retired from the Royal Air Force in 1996 to pursue a career in Civil Aviation.

His career to date in Civil Aviation:

Debonair Airways Ltd: June 1996 to October 1999: June 1996 joined as Line Captain, Aug 1996 Line Training Captain, November 1996 Fleet Manager (BWAAOC), March 1997 Chief Pilot, October 1997 Head of Flight Operations/Chief Pilot (Debonair AOC), November 1998 TRE/IRE BAe 146, May 1999 Chief Pilot Boeing 737. As Head of Flight Ops/Chief Pilot he was nominated AOC Post-holder and, as such, he was responsible to the COO for the overall control and administration of Flight Operations, Ground Operations and Cabin Safety. His roles also included the recruitment and selection of all pilots and their training in both the simulator and on the Line. He was also responsible for the Flight Operations budget. During his tenure, Debonair achieved a JAR Ops AOC and the airline expanded from 5 aircraft/30 crews to 13 aircraft/65 crews. As Chief Pilot Boeing 737, he was the Project manager for the introduction of a new type to the airline.

Easyjet Airways: February 2000 – to date: February 2000, Joined as Line Captain and in August 2000 became Line Training Captain.

Group Captain A.M. (Marcus) Wills, CVO, OBE, ADC

Deputy Captain: 1ˢᵗ February 1994 – 31ˢᵗ March 1995
(see previous entry February 1985 to October 1987 in Chapter Five)

Whilst at the Ministry of Defence the lure of The Queen's Flight became too much and Marcus returned to Benson in 1994 – taking early retirement to become a Civil Servant, although still wearing uniform, to help in the sad task of disbanding The Queen's Flight and the move of aircraft and crews to No. 32 (The Royal) Squadron.

He remained at Northolt, as Deputy Senior Air Equerry, doing essentially the same job of coordinating Royal Flights and liaison with the Households, until being made redundant himself in 1996 on the formation of the Royal Travel Office!

Overall he flew on 897 Royal Flights with 23 different members of British and Foreign Royal Families, in 14 different types including Concorde and an airship! He was appointed an OBE in 1982 and a CVO in 1988.

Since that time, Marcus has been Director of Communications and Corporate Services at the Chartered Institute of Building in Ascot, an international organisation serving the interests of some 40,000 construction managers in 90 countries worldwide – again "something totally different".

Group Captain A.N. (Adam) Wise, LVO, MBE, ADC

Deputy Captain, The Queen's Flight, 22ⁿᵈ November 1991 – 10ᵗʰ December 1993

Adam Wise joined the RAF in 1963 and was commissioned as a pilot from the RAF College, Cranwell in 1965; He qualified as an Andover Transport Pilot in 1967 and began his long association with The Queen's Flight by telling 'Mouse' Fielden that he preferred an operational tour in Aden to being as co-pilot at Benson. After tours in the Middle East with No.21 and No. 152 Squadrons; and UK with No. 46 Squadron; Adam was ADC to the last Commander of the Far East Air Force, 1970-71; an exchange officer with the Luftwaffe flying Transalls; 1972-75 (after which he was appointed to be a MBE for services to Anglo-German relations; 1976); an Officer Trainer 1975-78, and flying instructor as OC University of Wales Air Squadron 1078-80; before being headhunted to be appointed Service Equerry to HM The Queen in 1980-83

Appointed LVO 1983; In 1983 he began to combine the posts of commanding the London University Air Squadron, 1983-1986; with being Private Secretary to TRH The Princes Andrew and Edward 1983-87; belated staff education at the Joint Service Defence College was followed by a tour at Cranwell managing the University Air Squadrons 1989-91.

Promoted to Group Captain and the almost inevitable appointment to command RAF Benson landed him as the last Deputy Captain of The Queen's Flight cum Station Commander; 1991-93.

Thereafter he learned Spanish to go with his German and became the Military and Air Attaché in Madrid, 1994-97; He left the RAF in 1998 and currently works for the Officers' Association, helping ex-officers of all 3 services to establish new careers in civil life. In all, he had 9 years in direct Royal service and 13 years wearing gold 'dinglie-danglies' from one shoulder or the other. He lives in Hampshire and London, is married to Jilly – a former Lady Clerk at Buckingham Palace – and has two children.

Appendix 1:   Royal Aircraft 1919-1995

Dates	Serial No.	Type	Unit	Remarks
1919	C4451	Avro 504J		Flying Instruction for Prince Albert
28 Apr – 28 Oct 28	J8430	Bristol Fighter F2b	24 Sqdn	First aircraft officially built for Royal Engagements
28 Jun 1930	J9095	Westland Wapiti 1A	24 Sqdn	Built for use by The Prince of Wales
28 June 1930	J9096	Westland Wapiti 1A	24 Sqdn	Built for use by The Prince of Wales
5 Sep 29 – 4 Feb 33	G-AALG	de Havilland DH60M Gipsy Moth		Owned by The Prince of Wales. Sold to Miss Jean Batten
1930	K1115	Fairey 111F	24 Sqdn	
16 Jul 30 – 18 Jul 30	G-ABCW	de Havilland DG60M Gipsy Moth		Owned by The Prince of Wales. Damaged in accident 18/7/30. Sold to Madras Flying Club as VT-AEC in April 1933
1930	J9772	Hawker Tomtit	24 Sqdn	The Prince of Wales visit to Dover
1930	G-AALL	Hawker Tomtit	24 Sqdn	On loan by Hawker for the Kings Cup Air Race
28 Jul 30 – 19 Jan 31	G-ABBS	de Havilland DH80A Puss Moth		Owned by The Prince of Wales
22 Aug 30 – 12 Jul 33	G-ABDB	de Havilland DH60 Gipsy Moth		Owned by The Duke of Gloucester. Part exchanged for G-ACGG.
18 Dec 30 – Aug 31	G-ABFV	de Havilland DH80A Puss Moth		Owned by The Prince of Wales. Shipped to Brazil for 1931 tour.
11 Jul 31 – 22 Sep 31	G-ABEG	Westland Wessex		Hired by The Prince of Wales for his holiday in France.
14 Jul 31 – 19 Dec 32	G-ABNN	de Havilland DH80A Puss Moth		Owned by The Prince of Wales. Exchanged for G-ACDD.
16 Sep 31 – 24 May 33	G-ABRR	de Havilland DH80A Puss Moth		Owned by The Prince of Wales. Part exchanged for G-ACGG.
July 1932	G-ABWW	Comper Swift (130HP Gipsy Major)		2nd King's Cup 9 Jul 1932. Tonbridge ATC Sqdn 1943.
19 Dec 32 – 17 Mar 33	G-ACDD	de Havilland DH83 Fox Moth		Owned by The Prince of Wales. Sold to Belgium as OO-ENC to Air Travel (NZ) as ZK-AEK in 1935 and to Fiji as VQ-FAT in 1957. It survived until 1960.
5 Apr 33 – Jun 33	G-ABXS	De Havilland DH83 Fox Moth		Owned by The Prince of Wales. Part exchanged for G-ACGG. Sold to Australia
15 May 33 – Mar 35	G-ACCC	Vickers Viastra X		Owned and specially built for The Prince of Wales
12 Jun 33 – 5 Feb 35	G-ACGG	De Havilland DH84 Dragon		Owned by The Prince of Wales. Sold to R. Shuttleworth Esq. RAAF 1941.
27 Apr 35 – 13 Mar 36	G-ACTT	De Havilland DH89 Dragon Rapide		Owned by The Prince of Wales. Sold to Olley Air Services. Originally allotted to Anglo-Persian Oil Co. Ltd.
8 Jun 35 – 8 May 37	G-ADDD	De Havilland DH89 Dragon Rapide		Owned by The Prince of Wales. Sold to Western Airways Ltd.
7 May 37 – 30 Oct 39	G-AEXX	Airspeed Envoy	The King's Flight	First Royal aircraft to be publicly financed. Reallocated to No.24 Sqdn as L7270. To Sweden as SE-ASN in Jun 46, subsequently scrapped.
9 Aug 39 – 22 Jun 42	N7263	Lockheed Hudson (Long Range)	The King's Flight	Reallocated to No.161 Sqdn.
1 Jan 40 – 19 Apr 42	K6120	Avro Tutor	The King's Flight	Crashed en-route to Silloth. 19 April 42
12 Feb 40 – 4 Mar 40	N7364	Lockheed Hudson	24 Sqdn	Loaned to The King's Flight. Reallocated to PDU Heston. Destroyed by enemy action at St. Luc, France, 29 May 1941.

Dates	Serial No.	Type	Unit	Remarks
15 Mar 40 – 25 May 42	P5634	Percival Q6	The King's Flight	Used by C-in-C Bomber Command. Reallocated to Halton.
7 Sep 40 – 14 Feb 41	G-AGCC	De Havilland DH95 Flamingo	The King's Flight	Reallocated to No.24 Sqdn as R2766
6 Jun 45 – Dec 45	KN386	Douglas Dakota IV	24 Sqdn	Reverted to general VIP work
15 Jul 46 – 11 Nov 46	RL951	De Havilland Dominie	The King's Flight	Written off in forced landing at Mount Farm, Near Benson.
11 Aug 46 – Jul 48	VL245	Vickers Viking C2	The King's Flight	Groundcrew aircraft. Crashed at Aberdeen 12 Sep 47.
4 Oct 46 – 6 Feb 47	VL226	Vickers Viking C1A		On loan returned to Vickers. The first Viking used for Royal Flights.
27 Dec 46 – 6 Feb 47	VL227	Vickers Viking C1A		On loan returned to Vickers. Originally G-AIKN. The second Viking.
12 Jan 47 – 30 Apr 58	VL246	Vickers Viking C2	The King's Flight	The King's aeroplane. Sold to Tradair.
Jan 47 – 29 Apr 58	VL247	Vickers Viking C2	The King's Flight	The Queen's aeroplane. Sold to Tradair.
Jan 47 – Nov 53	VL248	Vickers Viking C2	The King's Flight	Workshop aircraft. Sold in Mexico.
6 Aug 47 – 30 Sep 47	KL110	Sikorsky Hoverfly 1	?	On loan from Royal Navy for mail delivery to Balmoral. Returned to Brize Norton. Initially delivered to Canada, Was one of a series of 45, KK969 to KL113.
8 Aug 47 – 16 Aug 47	KL106	Sikorsky Hoverfly 1	?	On loan from RN for mail delivery to Balmoral. Abandoned at Aberdeen after engine failure.
25 Aug 47 – 30 Sep 47	KK973	Sikorsky Hoverfly 1	?	On loan from RN for mail delivery at Balmoral. Returned to Feltham.
10 Jan 48 – 24 Feb 48	MW140	Avro York	?	Built as VIP aircraft for Duke of Gloucester as Governor of Australia. On loan for flight to Ceylon. Returned to Bassingbourn, One of 200 Avro 685 York C1's of which MW100-102 were the VIP's.
5 Jul 48 – Oct 48	KL110	Sikorsky Hoverfly 1	?	On loan from RN for mail delivery at Balmoral.
6 Jul 48 – 30 Apr 58	VL233	Vickers Viking C2	The King's Flight	Sold to Tradair
10 Jul 48 – Aug 48	KK987	Sikorsky Hoverfly 1	?	On loan from RN for mail delivery at Balmoral
21 Jul 48 – 5 Apr 57	VL232	Vickers Viking C2	The King's Flight	Sold to British Eagle.
29 Jul 48 – Oct 48	KL104	Sikorsky Hoverfly 1	?	On loan from RN for mail delivery at Balmoral.
29 Oct 52 – 18 Apr 53	WP861	de Havilland Chipmunk T10	?	Prince Philip's flying instruction at White Waltham.
10 Dec 52 – 15 Feb 53	WP912	De Havilland Chipmunk T10	?	Prince Philip's flying instruction at White Waltham.
10 Feb 53 – 9 May 53	FX459	North American Harvard	?	Prince Philip's instruction at White Waltham.
17 Feb 53 – 27 Nov 53	KF729	North American Harvard	?	Prince Philip's instruction at White Waltham.
21 Apr 53 – 17 Jun 53	V4204	Airspeed Oxford Mk.1	?	Prince Philip's instructional and communications flying.
9 Jun 53 – 25 Oct 60	VP961	de Havilland Devon	The Queen's Flight	Originally for Prince Philip's instructional and communications flying. Joined The Queen's Flight Jul 55. Reallocated to 27 MU Shawbury. In Jul 84 sold by RAF and re-registered G-ALFM.
15 Jun 54 – 21 Jul 54	221	Boulton Paul Balliol	?	Prince Philip's flying training at White Waltham.
28 Aug 54 – 23 Apr 55	WF848	de Havilland Chipmunk T10	?	Prince Philip's flying training at White Waltham.

Dates	Serial No.	Type	Unit	Remarks
1 Sep 54 – 9 Aug 58	XF261	Westland Dragonfly HC4	CFS(H)	On loan to The Queen's Flight. Returned to South Cerney.
3 Jan 55 – 27 Jan 55	460	Gloster Meteor	?	Prince Philip's flying instruction.
17 Jan 55 – 12 Apr 55	G-AMTS	de Havilland Heron		On loan from de Havilland for Prince Philip's use.
8 Apr 55 – 16 Apr 55	WV678	Percival Provost	?	Prince Philip's instruction at White Waltham.
18 May 55 – 17 Sep 64	XH375	de Havilland Heron C3	The Queen's Flight	Prince Philip's personal aeroplane. Sold to Hawker Siddeley in 1968.
31 May 56 – 7 Jun 56	XJ432	Westland Whirlwind HC2	?	On loan to The Queen's Flight.
16 Apr 58 – 12 Jan 65	XM295	de Havilland Heron C4	The Queen's Flight	Reallocated to 27 MU Shawbury, sold to Hawker Siddeley in 1968.
16 Apr 58 – 5 Jul 68	XM296	de Havilland Heron C4	The Queen's Flight	Reallocated to Leconfield
24 Jul 58 – Dec 59	XL111	Westland Whirlwind HAR4	?	On loan to The Queen's Flight.
1 Oct 59 – 25 May 64	XN126	Westland Whirlwind HCC8	The Queen's Flight	Returned to Westlands, Weston-Super-Mare, for conversion to HAR10.
5 Nov 59 – 25 May 64	XN127	Westland Whirlwind HCC8	The Queen's Flight	Returned to Westlands, Weston-Super-Mare, for conversion to HAR10.
20 Sep 60 – 12 Jun 64	XP903	De Havilland Chipmunk T10	The Queen's Flight	For use by Prince Philip. Subsequently used for instructional flying for The Duke of Kent, Prince Michael and Prince Richard.
13 Jan 61 – Mar 61	KN452	Douglas Dakota	?	On loan to The Queen's Flight for State Visit to Nepal.
13 Jan 61 – Mar 61	KN645	Douglas Dakota	?	On loan to The Queen's Flight for State Visit to Nepal.
16 Jun 61 – 17 Jun 68	XR391	De Havilland Heron C4	The Queen's Flight	Reallocated to 27 MU Shawbury.
26 Mar 64 – 7 Dec 67	XR487	Westland Whirlwind HCC12	The Queen's Flight	Destroyed in fatal accident.
31 Mar 64 – 2 Jul 64	G-ARAY	Hawker Siddeley HS748		On loan from Hawker Siddeley for crew training.
6 May 64 – 23 Jul 69	XR486	Westland Whirlwind HCC12	The Queen's Flight	Reallocated to No.32 Sqdn.
10 Jul 54 – 31 Jan 91	XS790	Hawker Siddeley Andover CC2	The Queen's Flight	Reallocated to RAE Bedford.
7 Aug 64 – 20 Jun 86	XS789	Hawker Siddeley Andover CC2	The Queen's Flight	Reallocated to No. 32 Squadron.
1 May 65 – 7 May 65	XS794	Hawker Siddeley Andover CC2	Met Comms Sqdn	On loan to The Queen's Flight.
26 Jun 67 – 24 Jul 67	XS794	Hawker Siddeley Andover CC2	Met Comms Sqdn.	On loan to The Queen's Flight.
27 Jun 67 – 12 Jul 67	XT672	Westland Wessex HC2	72 Sqdn.	On loan to The Queen's Flight.
12 Dec 67 – 1 Oct 86	XS793	Hawker Siddeley Andover CC2	The Queen's Flight	Reallocated to No.32 Squadron.
31 Jan 68 – Jul 69	XP299	Westland Whirlwind HAR10	The Queen's Flight	Reallocated from No.230 Sqdn.
27 Jun 68 – 28 Jun 68	XT672	Westland Wessex HC2	72 Sqdn.	On loan to The Queen's Flight.
Jul 68 – Aug 70	WP903	De Havilland Chipmunk T10	The Queen's Flight	Flying instruction for The Prince of Wales. Now with the Culdrose Gliding Club.
10 Dec 68 – 5 Aug 69	XV726	Westland Wessex HC2	The Queen's Flight	Allotted for crew training. Reallocated to No.72 Sqdn.
25 Jun 69 – 31 Mar 95	XV732	Westland Wessex HCC4	The Queen's Flight	Reallocated to No. 32 (The Royal) Squadron.
27 Jun 69 – 16 Sept 71	XV770	Beagle Basset CC1	The Queen's Flight	Flying instruction for The Prince of Wales. Reallocated to No. 32 Sqdn.
11 Jul 69 – 31 Mar 95	XV733	Westland Wessex HCC4	The Queen's Flight	Reallocated to No.32 (The Royal) Squadron.
17 Apr 70 – 20 Apr 70	XV725	Westland Wessex HC2	72 Sqdn.	On loan to The Queen's Flight.
28 Jan 71 – 4 Feb 71	XS794	Hawker Siddeley Andover CC"	Met Comms Sqdn	On loan to The Queen's Flight.
8 Mar 71 – 20 Aug 71	XW323	BAC Jet provost T5	Cranwell	Flying instruction for The Prince of Wales.
29 Mar 79 – 13 April 79	XP904	De Havilland Chipmunk T10	RN Grading Flight	Detached for flying instruction for Prince Andrew.
21 Jul 80 – 25 Jul 80	XN151	Sedbergh Glider	ACCGS Newton	Detached for gliding instruction for Prince Edward.
9 Apr 80 – 15 Apr 80	G-ASYD	BAe 111-475	British Aerospace	Evaluation by Prince Philip

Dates	Serial No.	Type	Unit	Remarks
14 Jun 83 – 11 Jun 84	ZD696	BAe 146 CC Mk1	BAe 146 Evaluation Flight	
16 Sep 83 – 29 Mar 85	ZD695	BAe 146 CC Mk1	BAe 146 Evaluation Flight	
10 Sep 84 – 11 Sep 84	G-BGCO	Piper Seminole	British Aerospace	Flying instruction for The Duke of Kent
13 May 85 – 17 May 85	G-BGCO	Piper Seminole	British Aerospace	Flying instruction for The Duke of Kent.
23 Apr 86 – 31 Mar 95	ZE700	BAe 146 CC Mk2	The Queen's Flight	Allocated to No.32 (The Royal) Squadron.
9 Jul 86 – 31 Mar 95	ZE701	BAe 146 CC Mk2	The Queen's Flight	Allocated to No.32 (The Royal) Squadron.
30 Sep 86 – 27 Sep 87	G-BLVL	Piper Warrior	CSE Kidlington	PPL for The Duchess of York.
9 Sep 87 – 18 Dec 87	G-DOFY	Bell Jet Ranger	Air Hanson	Helicopter endorsement to PPL of The Duchess of York.
1 Sep 89 – 24 Nov 89	XS793	Hawker Siddeley Andover CC2	60 Sqdn	On loan to The Queen's Flight
14 Jan 91 – 31 Mar 95	ZE702	BAE 146 CC Mk2	The Queen's Flight	Allocated to No.32 (The Royal) Squadron

Appendix 2:   Significant Dates in the History of Royal Flying 1917-1995

Jul	1917	HRH The Prince of Wales taken for a flight in France. First flight by a member of the Royal Family.
Mar	1918	HRH Prince Albert taken for his first flight at RN Air Station Sleaford (Cranwell).
July	1919	HRH Prince Albert received his pilot's wings on 31st July 1919. Two Avro 504J aircraft had been allocated from the Air Council Communications Squadron for his flying instruction.
May	1928	Bristol Fighter J8340 allotted to No.24 Squadron for "Special Duties".
		First official air journey by a member of the Royal Family. (HRH The Prince of Wales)
June	1928	Westland Wapitis allotted to No.24 Squadron for Royal and VIP flights.
Sep	1929	HRH The Prince of Wales obtains his own aeroplane (Gipsy Moth G-AALG)
Nov	1929	Flight Lieutenant E.H. Fielden appointed personal pilot to HRH The Prince of Wales.
	1930	Wapitis replaced by Fairey 111F's
	1930	First Royal entries in the King's Cup Air Race. Prince George (later to become The Duke of Kent) a DH Hawk Moth G-AAUZ and The Prince of Wales a Hawker Tomtit (G-AALL).
	1931	HRH The Prince of Wales' private aircraft moved to Hendon.
Apr	1931	HRH The Prince of Wales flew on to the deck of HMS Eagle in a Fairey 111F off the coast of Rio de Janeiro during a tour of South America.
	1932	Edward Fielden flew a Comper Swift G-ABWW, entered by HRH The Prince of Wales to second place in the King's Cup Air Race.
May	1933	Vickers Viastra X, G-ACCC, the first aircraft specially ordered and built for a member of the Royal Family, delivered to Hendon.
Jun	1933	DH84 Dragon arrives at Hendon.
Apr	1935	Dragon and Viastra replaced by DH89 Dragon Rapides.
Jan	1936	HM King Edward VIII flew to the Accession Council in London from Bircham Newton in Rapide G-ADDD. The first occasion that a British Monarch had taken to the air.
Apr	1936	Air Ministry agrees to finance Royal aircraft and their support.
June	**1936**	**Formation of The King's Flight at Hendon with Wing Commander Fielden as Captain.**
Dec	1936	HM King Edward VIII abdicated in favour of HRH The Duke of York. The new King retained Wing Commander Fielden as Captain of The King's Flight.
May	1937	Airspeed Envoy joins The King's Flight.
Aug	1939	Introduction of Hudson (Long Range).
Sep	1939	The King's Flight moves from Hendon to Benson.
Sep	1940	DH95 Flamingo delivered to Benson.
Feb	**1942**	**The King's Flight absorbed by No.161 Squadron.**
May	**1946**	**The King's Flight reformed under Air Commodore Fielden at Benson.**
July	1946	Dominie written off in an accident.
Aug	1946	First special Viking delivered to Benson.
Aug	1947	First use of helicopters (for mail delivery).
Sep	1947	Viking VL245 crashed at Aberdeen.
Oct	1951	First crossing of the Atlantic by air by a member of the Royal Family.
	1952	Suggestion that The King's Flight disbands in favour of BEA, BOAC and RAF.
May	1952	Prince Philip starts instructional flying.
Aug	**1952**	**The King's Flight renamed The Queen's Flight.**

Mar	1953	First Royal helicopter flight.
	1953	Beginning of discussions on re-equipment with Viscounts.
Dec	1953	Agreement for certain Government Ministers and Service Chiefs of Staff to fly in aircraft of The Queen's Flight
	1955	Prince Philip takes helicopter flying course: Heron C3 arrives.
Jul	1955	Prince Philip's Devon and Heron reallocated to Benson.
Oct	1955	Draft Standard of Preparation for Whirlwind Mk.2's issued.
Apr	1956	Order placed for two Heron C4's.
Sep	1956	Dragonfly used for first mail delivery to HM Yacht Britannia.
Sep	1956	First visit by a Reigning Monarch to The Queen's Flight
Feb	1957	Draft Standard of Preparation for Whirlwind Mk.8's issued.
Apr	1958	Last Viking special flight; delivery of Heron CC4's.
Nov	1958	Tour of Ethiopia, British Somaliland and Aden by TRH The Duke and Duchess of Gloucester in Herons.
Oct	1959	First Whirlwind HCC8 arrives at Benson.
	1960	Aircraft painted fluorescent red overall.
Feb	1961	Dakotas used for State Visit to Nepal.
Dec	1961	Most ever hours flown in one year (2,678.50 hours).
Jan	1962	Air Commodore Fielden retires and becomes Senior Air Equerry.
Mar	1962	Air Commodore Mitchell appointed Captain of The Queen's Flight.
Mar	1964	Whirlwind HCC8's replaced by Gnome-engined Mk.12's; HS748 pilot training commences.
Jul	1964	First Andover delivered to Benson.
Aug	1964	Air Commodore Blount appointed Captain of The Queen's Flight.
Feb	1965	Both Andovers used for State Visit to Ethiopia and the Sudan, one aircraft on a tour of Saudi Arabia, India, Nepal, Singapore and Borneo with HRH The Duke of Edinburgh.
Mar	1965	HRH Princess Margaret toured Uganda in an Andover followed in November by a tour of the USA.
Jan	1966	Andover XS790 tour of Far East with TRH The Duke and Duchess of Gloucester
Mar	1966	Andover XS789 tour of Canada and USA with HRH The Duke of Edinburgh.
Sep	1966	HM Queen Elizabeth The Queen Mother made the first Royal helicopter flight onto an aircraft carrier at sea flying in Whirlwind XR986.
	1967	Royal Tours to Canada by HM The Queen and to the Pacific for the Coronation of The King of Tonga by TRH The Duke and Duchess of Kent.
Dec	1967	Fatal accident to Whirlwind HCC12, XR487.
Feb	1968	Air Commodore Winskill appointed Captain of The Queen's Flight.
Jun	1968	Last Heron Royal Flight.
Jul	1968	Chipmunk WP903 allocated for The Prince of Wales' flying instruction.
Dec	1968	Wessex Mk.2 delivered for crew training.
	1968	Andover tours for the State Visit to Brazil and Chile, and to Australia and Mexico.
Jun	1969	Whirlwinds replaced by Wessex HCC4's; delivery of Basset for Royal training.
	1969	Andover tours for the State Visit to Austria and visits by other members of the Royal Family to Australia, the Pacific, Canada, USA, Ethiopia, Singapore, Cambodia, Thailand, Iran, Swaziland and Malagasy.
Oct	1969	HRH The Princess Anne became the first member of the Royal Family to fly in a Queen's Flight helicopter to an oil rig.
	1970	The Andovers visited the USA, Canada, Mexico, Nepal, Yugoslavia, Iran, Canada and East Africa on Royal Tours

Mar	1971	HRH The Prince of Wales completes Basset training scheme. Awarded RAF Wings at RAF College, Cranwell on 20th August.
Apr	1971	Visit to The Queen's Flight by HM The Queen, Prince Philip, The Prince of Wales and Prince Andrew.
	1971	BAC 111 considered as Andover replacement.
Feb	1972	Andovers flew for the State Visit to Thailand and Malaysia by HM The Queen.
Mar	1972	HRH The Duke of Edinburgh flew in an Andover to Kenya.
May	1972	Death of The Duke of Windsor, founder of The King's Flight.
Sep	1972	Basset transferred to No.32 Squadron Northolt.
Apr	1973	Chief Technician Johnson retires after 19 years service. Longest ever service on the Flight.
		Megadata systems installed. The Queen's Flight independent of No.38 Group for operational communications.
Oct/Nov 1973		Longest period of operation away from base. 75 days.
1973/1974		Oil crisis. Reduction in operations.
Feb	1974	HM The Queen and HRH The Duke of Edinburgh flew in an Andover during a visit to Papua New Guinea, Solomon Islands, Indonesia. Later in the year the Andovers were used for tours of Canada and the USA whilst HRH Princess Alexandra flew to Poland and Berlin.
	1975	Andovers flew on Royal Tours of USA, Canada, Holland, Saudi Arabia, Morocco, Caribbean, Central American republics, Poland and to Spain.
Oct	1975	HM The Queen Mother – first Royal Helicopter flight onto aircraft carrier at sea.
Aug	1976	The last mail run to HMY Britannia.
Oct	1976	Most ever Andover hours flown in one month (237.15 hours)
		Wessex and Andover interior trim refitted.
Nov	1976	All three Andovers were involved in the State Visit to Luxembourg by HM The Queen.
Feb	1977	The Andovers had a very busy year starting with HM The Queen's Silver Jubilee Tour of Fiji and Papua New Guinea then Royal Visits to Afghanistan, Oman, Ghana, Ivory Coast, Nigeria, Canada and Jamaica.
July	1977	Two Andovers and One Wessex carried members of the Royal Family to Finningley for The Queen's Review of the Royal Air Force.
Aug	1977	The Queen's first flight in a helicopter.
	1978	BAC 111 specification revised.
Apr	1979	HRH The Prince Andrew's Royal Naval Pilot Grading.
Jan	1980	Air Commodore Archie Winskill awarded knighthood.
Jul	1980	HRH The Prince Edward Gliding Proficiency Certificate.
		First helicopter operation in France.
Sep	1980	First Royal inauguration of oil rig – HRH The Duke of Gloucester.
	1980	The Andovers visited the USA, Canada, Thailand, India and Nepal carrying members of the Royal Family on tours.
Feb	1981	HRH The Prince of Wales was guest of honour at a Dinner with The Queen's Flight.
Jun	1981	Fourteen Royal Flights in one day.
	1981	Between September and December the Andovers had their busiest period yet visiting Swaziland, West Africa, India and Nepal, Philippines, Indonesia, Malaysia, Burma and Thailand with members of the Royal Family. Earlier in the year visits had been made to United Arab Republics, Egypt and the Gulf.
Jan	1982	Air Commodore Sir Archie Winskill retires; Air Vice-Marshal Severne appointed Captain.
Mar	1982	Prince Andrew's Wessex 4 training.
May	1982	The Queen's Flight Association Inaugural Dinner.

Jun	1982	First Royal helicopter flight from British to foreign soil.
Jul	1982	HRH The Prince of Wales landed on SS Canberra.
Aug	1982	Andover basic servicing periodicity changed to calendar basis.
		HRH The Prince William's first flight.
Dec	1982	The BAe 146 is chosen to replace the Andover, subject to successful evaluation by the RAF.
Jan	1983	HRH Princess Alexandra visited the Flight.
Feb	1983	HRH The Duke of Edinburgh flies the Westland W30.
Mar	1983	HRH The Prince William's first flight as principal passenger.
Mar	1983	Wessex helicopters complete 10,000 hours on The Queen's Flight.
May	1983	Andover XS189 and XS790 each complete 10,000 hours.
Jun	1983	HRH The Prince of Wales becomes Patron of The Queen's Flight Association.
Jul	1983	Most ever Wessex hours flown in one month (135.05 hours).
Nov	1983	HM The Queen views the BAe 146 at Marham.
Dec	1983	BAe 146 confirmed for The Queen's Flight.
	1983	The Andovers visited Saudi Arabia, Jordan, Pakistan, Zambia, Zimbabwe, Turkey, Egypt and Canada on Royal Visits.
Apr	1984	Visit to The Queen's Flight by HM The Queen and The Duke of Edinburgh.
Jun	1984	HM The Queen flies in a helicopter in France.
Oct	1984	HRH The Prince William's first helicopter flight.
	1984	The busiest year to date with several records broken. Andovers flew 15 tours and 855.25 hours to the far corners of the earth. Total Andover hours 1837.50 beating the previous record. The Wessex flying 858.50 hours. The combined aircraft total hours flown, 2696.10 hours, was the highest ever with the combined number of Royal, Special and VVIP Flights being 784.
Jan	1985	Andover highest January total since their introduction (118.10).
		Andover XS793 achieved 10,000 hours.
Mar	1985	HRH The Prince Henry's first flight in an Andover
		Helicopters highest March total since 1978 (85.45)
		HRH The Princess Anne visited the Flight.
Apr	1985	HRH The Prince Edward undertook flying training on the Andover for the first time.
May	1985	New Helicopter Support Vehicle first task.
		Helicopter highest May hours and flights (123.30 hours/233 flights)
Jul	1985	Andover XS790 celebrated its 21st Birthday.
		Helicopter highest number of flights in a single month (240)
Sep	1985	A record September for helicopter hours and flights (128.55 hours/224 flights)
Nov	1985	A Jet Plan terminal installed in the operations room in readiness for the BAe 146.
		HRH The Princess of Wales paid an informal visit to The Queen's Flight.
	1985	The combined number of Royal, Special and VVIP Flights at 893 surpassed the previous best by 14%.
Feb	1986	The Deckwriter Jet Plan terminal replaced by IBM personal computer in Operations.
Mar	1986	Operations connected directly to the RAFAN system.
Apr	1986	BAE 146 CC Mk2 ZE700 handed over to The Captain at a ceremony at Hatfield.
May	1986	HM Queen Elizabeth The Queen Mother visited the Flight.
Jun	1986	The Flight held a Reception at St. James's Palace to celebrate the 50th Anniversary of the formation of The King's Flight.
		Andover XS789 reallocated to No.32 Squadron, RAF Northolt.

Jul	1986	BAe 146 CC Mk.2 ZE701 delivered to the Flight.
		First Royal Flight in BAe 146.
Sep	1986	First Royal Tour in the BAe 146 – ZE 701
Oct	1986	HRH The Duchess of York commences flying training in Piper Warrior G-BLVL.
		First Royal Tour of China in ZE 701.
		Andover XS 793 reallocated to No.32 Squadron, RAF Northolt.
Nov	1986	HRH The Duchess of York flies solo.
Jan	1987	The first category II ILS approach carried out on a Royal Flight by one of the BAe 146 aircraft, flying
		HRH The Duchess of Gloucester into Manchester Airport.
		HRH The Duchess of York gains her PPL, the first lady member of the Royal Family to do so.
Mar	1987	HRH The Duchess of Gloucester pays an informal visit to the Flight and officially opens The Queen's Flight Museum.
Jun	1987	Squadron Leader Derek James becomes the first member of the Flight to achieve 1,500 Royal Flights.
Dec	1987	HRH The Duchess of York obtains a helicopter endorsement to her PPL.
Feb	1988	HRH The Princess Royal was flown into Entebbe Airport in ZE701 to become the first member of the Royal Family to visit Uganda since 1965.
Mar	1988	The first night deck landing by a TQF helicopter when HRH The Duke of York was flown in XV732 to join the Royal Fleet Auxiliary Engadine off Start Point.
Apr	1988	BAe 146, ZE701, became the first jet aircraft to land at Dounray for a visit by The Prince of Wales.
		The busiest April for the Wessex since their introduction to the Flight. (98.45 hours and 178 flights).
May	1988	The Queen's Flight becomes affiliated to The Guild of Air Pilots and Air Navigator's.
Jul	1988	A particularly busy month with a total of 149 Royal, Special and VIP Flights.
Aug	1988	Princess Beatrice of York made her first flight with The Queen's Flight in ZE700 from RAF Northolt to RAF Kinloss.
Oct	1988	HM The Queen, accompanied by HRH The Duke of Edinburgh, was flown in ZE700 to Madrid, the first Royal Visit to Spain by a British Monarch.
Nov	1988	Air Vice-Marshal J de M Severne awarded knighthood.
		Highest ever November hours and flights for the Wessex (89.10 hours and 148 flights).
Jan	1989	Air Commodore The Hon T.C. Elworthy, CBE succeeded Air Vice-Marshal Sir John Severne, KCVO, OBE, AFC as Captain of The Queen's Flight.
Apr	1989	The busiest April for the BAe 146, flying a total of 99 hours and 20 minutes.
June	1989	The busiest June for the Wessex, beating the previous June highest in 1967 of 130 hours and 5 minutes by 1 hour and 15 minutes.
Jul	1989	Andover XS790 twenty-five years old.
		Kitty 3 in ZE700 flew from RAF Turnhouse to RAF Benson in 40 minutes at a groundspeed of 518 knots.
Aug	1989	Work services commenced on the floor of The Queen's Flight hangar, which required strengthening for the BAe 146 aircraft.
Sep	1989	The busiest September for the BAe 146 flying a total of 133 hours and 5 minutes.
Oct	1989	It was announced that a third BAe 146 is to be purchased for The Queen's Flight, to be delivered in a years time.
		The aircraft and equipment were moved back into The Queen's Flight hangar on completion of the work services.
Nov	1989	The Prime Minister, The Rt.Hon. Margaret Thatcher MP, flew for the first time in a BAe 146 of The Queen's Flight.

		The busiest November for the BAe 146, flying a total of 44 Royal, Special and VIP flights.
Mar	1990	HRH The Duke of Edinburgh paid an informal visit to the Flight, meeting Flight members on the hangar floor.
		HRH The Princess Royal was flown in ZE700 to Moscow for the first official visit by the Royal Family to Russia for many years.
Jun	1990	Nine Wessex tasks were cancelled due to HRH The Prince of Wales having an accident whilst playing polo.
Oct	1990	HRH The Princess Royal was flown in ZE700 to Bulgaria, the first visit to that country by an aircraft of The Queen's Flight.
Nov	1990	The Rt.Hon. Mrs Margaret Thatcher, MP, was flown in ZE700 on her last flight as Prime Minister.
Dec	1990	Visit to The Queen's Flight by HM The Queen accompanied by The Duke of Edinburgh. The log book of ZE702 was handed to The Queen by the Chairman of British Aerospace, together with a silver model of the BAe 146 aircraft.
		HRH The Prince of Wales was flown in ZE701 to visit the British troops stationed in the Gulf.
Jan	1991	HM The Queen flies in a helicopter in England for the first time.
		BAE 146 ZE702 first used for Royal Flying.
		Andover, XS790 leaves The Queen's Flight.
Feb	1991	Visit to The Queen's Flight by HRH The Princess Margaret.
		Squadron Leader Derek James becomes the first member of The Queen's Flight to achieve 2,000 Royal Flights.
Mar	1991	HRH The Duke of Edinburgh flown in ZE702 on a tour of the Falkland Islands and South America.
Apr	1991	TRH The Prince and Princess of Wales flown in ZE701 during a tour to Brazil.
		ZE702 first RAF aircraft to land at Tehran for many years.
May	1991	HM The Queen and HRH The Duke of Edinburgh flown in ZE 700 during the Royal Tour to The United States of America.
Jun	1991	HM The Queen flown in Wessex XV733 during a tour to Northern Ireland.
Sep	1991	BAE 146 crews carried out Royal Tours to Papua New Guinea, South America and Pakistan.
Oct	1991	HM The Queen and HRH The Duke of Edinburgh flown in BAe 146 ZE700 during the Royal Tour in Southern Africa.
		HRH The Duke of Edinburgh flown in BAe 146 ZE702 on a tour of the Far East.
Jan	1992	TRH The Duke and Duchess of Gloucester flown on a tour of Egypt.
Feb	1992	HRH The Prince of Wales flown by Wessex onto HMS Invincible.
		HRH The Princess Royal flown onto HMS Ark Royal.
Mar	1992	World tour by HRH The Duke of Edinburgh ends, having completed the first circumnavigation by BAe 146 on a Royal Tour. 21 countries visited and 104 hours flown on the task.
Apr	1992	HRH The Prince Edward flown on a tour of the Caribbean.
May	1992	HRH The Princess Alexandra visited The Queen's Flight.
		HRH The Duchess of Gloucester flown to the Channel Islands by Wessex.
		HRH The Princess of Wales flown on a tour of Egypt.
		HRH The Princess Royal flown on a tour of Scandinavia.
Jun	1992	HRH The Duke of York flown onto HMS Ark Royal by Wessex.
		Two BAe 146 aircraft fly in support of the State Visit to France by HM The Queen.
		HRH The Prince Edward flown to Northern France by Wessex.
Jul	1992	HRH The Duke of Edinburgh flown on a tour of Canada.
		The Foreign Secretary flown on a tour of the Balkans.
Sep	1992	HRH The Princess Royal flown on a tour of India.

Oct	1992	Two BAE 146 aircraft used in support of HM The Queen's State Visit to Germany.
		HRH The Prince Edward was flown on a tour of the Pacific. The tour took 24 days to complete and 85 hours were flown on the task.
Nov	1992	HRH The Duke of Edinburgh flown on a visit to Argentina.
		HRH The Princess Royal flown onto HMS Invincible.
Dec	1992	Informal visit to The Queen's Flight by HRH The Duke of Edinburgh.
Jan	1993	Air Commodore The Hon Timothy Elworthy retired from the Royal Air Force but remained as Captain of The Queen's Flight.
Feb	1993	HRH The Prince of Wales flown on a visit to the USA and Mexico.
		The Government Efficiency Team visited the Flight.
Mar	1993	HRH The Duke of Edinburgh flown to the Caribbean and then back to the UK from Florida.
Apr	1993	HRH The Prince of Wales flown by Wessex to the Orkney and Shetland Islands.
May	1993	HM The Queen flown to Hungary for a State Visit.
		HRH The Duke of Kent flown to the Baltic States.
		HRH The Prince of Wales flown to Poland.
Jun	1993	HM The Queen flown by Wessex during a Royal Visit to Northern Ireland.
Jul	1993	HRH The Princess Royal flown on a tour to Russia, Mongolia, Kazakhstan and Uzbekistan.
		HRH The Duchess of Kent flown on a tour to East Africa.
Aug	1993	Both Wessex grounded from 16th August to 16th September following a fatal accident involving a SAR helicopter.
Sep	1993	HRH The Prince Edward flown during a tour to Southern Africa.
		The BAe 146 visited Kiev and Odessa for the first time.
Oct	1993	HRH The Duke of Edinburgh flown to the USA and Canada.
		HM The Queen flown during a visit to Cyprus.
Nov	1993	HRH The Prince Edward flown on a tour of West Africa.
Feb	1994	HRH The Duchess of Kent flown to The Ivory Coast.
		HM The Queen flown during a tour to The Caribbean.
		HRH The Princess Royal flown to Ethiopia, Eritrea, Vietnam and Hong Kong.
Mar	1994	HM The Queen flown during second part of the Caribbean tour.
		HRH The Duke of Edinburgh flown from The Bahamas to the USA and Canada.
Apr	1994	HRH The Duke of Edinburgh flown to Bermuda and Trinidad.
May	1994	HRH The Prince of Wales flown to Milan and St. Petersburg.
Jun	**1994**	**Announcement in House of Commons that The Queen's Flight is to disband on 1st April 1995 and move to RAF Northolt to join No.32 Squadron.**
		Wessex completes 25 years service on The Queen's Flight.
		Both Wessex helicopters heavily involved in "D" Day celebrations in both England and France.
		BAe 146 ZE700 burst two tyres and went off the runway at Islay.
Aug	1994	BAe 146 ZE700 recovered to RAF Benson for repairs by civilian contractor.
Oct	1994	HM The Queen flown on State Visit to Russia.
		HRH The Duke of Edinburgh flown to Mauritius.
Nov	1994	HRH The Duke of Edinburgh flown on a tour to India and Pakistan.
		HRH The Princess Royal flown on a tour to South Africa and Mozambique.
		Visit to The Queen's Flight by TRH The Duke and Duchess of Gloucester.
Jan	1995	HRH The Prince of Wales paid a farewell visit to The Queen's Flight.

Feb	1995	HRH The Princess Royal paid a farewell visit to The Queen's Flight.
		HM The Queen and HRH The Duke of Edinburgh visited The Queen's Flight.
		TRH The Duke and Duchess of Kent visited The Queen's Flight.
Mar	1995	HRH Princess Alexandra visited The Queen's Flight.
		HRH The Princess Royal flown on a tour to Bangladesh and Sri Lanka.
		HM The Queen and HRH The Duke of Edinburgh were flown by Wessex during a visit to Northern Ireland.
		HRH The Prince of Wales flown on a tour to Egypt, Malta, Morocco and Spain.
Mar	1955	HRH The Duke of Edinburgh flown on a tour to Madagascar and South Africa.
		HM Queen Elizabeth The Queen Mother held a reception for members of The Queen's Flight at Windsor Royal Lodge.
		HRH The Prince Edward visited The Queen's Flight.
		HRH The Duke of York visited The Queen's Flight.

31st March 1995   **HRH The Princess Margaret paid a visit to The Queen's Flight and HRH's Helicopter Flight from Royal Air Force Benson to Windsor Royal Lodge was the last Royal Flight flown by The Queen's Flight.**

1st April 1995   **The aircraft were handed over to the civilian contractor in their usual immaculate condition.**

Appendix 3: The King's Flight and The Queen's Flight Senior Executives

Senior Air Equerry to HM The Queen

Air Vice-Marshal Sir Edward Fielden, GCVO, CB, DFC, AFC.	(D)	01 Jan 62 – 31 Dec 69

Captains

Air Commodore Sir Edward Fielden, KCVO, CB, DFC, AFC	(D)	21 Jul 36 – 31 Dec 61
Air Commodore A D Mitchell, CVO, DFC, AFC		21 Mar 62 – 01 Aug 64
Air Commodore J H L Blount, DFC	(D)	02 Aug 64 – 07 Dec 67
Air Commodore Sir Archie Winskill, KCVO, CBE, DFC, AE, MRAeS		15 Feb 68 – 27 Jan 82
Air Vice-Marshal Sir John Severne, KCVO, OBE, AFC		27 Jan 82 – 13 Jan 89
Air Commodore The Hon T C Elworthy, CBE		14 Jan 89 – 31 Mar 95

Deputy Captains

Group Captain A D Mitchell, DFC AFC		06 Nov 56 – 07 Oct 59
Group Captain T N Stack, AFC	(D)	13 Jul 59 – 25 Nov 62
Group Captain J Wallace, DSO, LVO, DFC, AFC	(D)	25 Apr 60 – 05 Aug 63
Group Captain P W D Heal, AFC		11 Jun 62 – 28 Feb 63
Group Captain P E Vaughan-Fowler, DSO, DFC, AFC	(D)	11 Feb 63 – 29 Dec 66
Group Captain J L Gilbert, AFC		17 Jan 66 – 30 Jan 68
Group Captain A R Gordon-Cumming		28 Dec 66 – 17 Oct 69
Group Captain B A Primavesi		11 Mar 68 – 13 Aug 71
Group Captain R C F Peirse		13 Oct 69 – 01 Feb 72
Group Captain M A D'Arcy	(D)	05 Aug 71 – 08 Jul 74
Group Captain B D'Iongh		02 Feb 72 – 16 Mar 73
Group Captain D L Edmonds, AFC*, ADC		16 Mar 73 – 31 Mar 78
Group Captain J D Spottiswood, AFC, ADC		07 Jul 74 – 05 Dec 76
Group Captain R A Miller, OBE, ADC, MRAeS, MBIM		06 Dec 76 – 30 Nov 78
Group Captain K J Goodwin, CBE, AFC, ADC		01 Dec 78 – 01 Dec 79
Group Captain D St J Homer, LVO, ADC		07 May 78 – 09 Jan 81
Group Captain A Mumford, OBE. ADC		12 Dec 79 – 14 Jan 83
Group Captain J F B Jones, ADC	(D)	09 Jan 81 – 19 May 89
Group Captain R B Duckett, AFC, ADC		14 Jan 83 – 22 Feb 85
Group Captain A M Wills, OBE, ADC		23 Feb 85 – 30 Oct 87
Group Captain P G Pinney, LVO ADC		31 Oct 87 – 17 Nov 89
Group Captain M V P H Harrington, ADC, BA, FBIM		19 May 89 – 21 Jun 91
Group Captain D H A Greenway, OBE, ADC		17 Nov 89 – 22 Nov 91
Group Captain G H Rolfe, CBE, ADC		21 Jun 91 – 31 Mar 95
Group Captain A N Wise, LVO, MBE, ADC		22 Nov 91 – 10 Dec 93
Group Captain A M Wills, CVO, OBE, ADC		01 Feb 84 – 31 Mar 95

Officer Commanding The King's Flight

Wing Commander E W Tacon, DSO, DFC, AFC		01 May 46 – 31 Dec 49
Wing Commander R C E Scott, AFC	(D)	01 Jan 50 – 31 Jul 52

Officer Commanding The Queen's Flight

Wing Commander R C E Scott, AFC	(D)	01 Aug 52 – 28 Feb 53
Wing Commander J E Grindon, DSO, AFC		01 Mar 53 – 09 Sep 56
Wing Commander D F Hyland-Smith, DFC, AFC	(D)	10 Sep 56 – 31 Dec 58
Wing Commander H G Currell, DFC, AFC	(D)	01 Jan 59 – 30 Jun 59
Wing Commander R G Wakeford, OBE, AFC		01 Jul 59 – 01 Jan 61
Wing Commander D L Attlee		02 Jan 61 – 21 Jul 63
Wing Commander A W Ringer, AFC		22 Jul 63 – 4 Feb 68
Wing Commander M J Rayson		05 Feb 68 – 19 May 70
Wing Commander D M Divers, LVO		20 May 70 – 31 Oct 72
Wing Commander D W Parsons		01 Nov 72 – 30 Nov 75
Wing Commander S Hitchens		21 Nov 75 – 06 Dec 79
Wing Commander E T I King		07 Dec 79 – 17 Dec 82
Wing Commander B P Synott		11 Dec 82 – 11 Oct 84
Wing Commander M L Schofield		18 Oct 84 – 25 Nov 88
Wing Commander N E L Beresford		26 Nov 88 – 07 May 92
Wing Commander N Thurston		08 May 92 – 31 Mar 95

Senior Engineering Officers

Flight Lieutenant G A Pearson	(D)	01 May 46 – 01 Jun 48
Flight Lieutenant W T Bussey, BEM		01 Jun 48 – 01 Jun 50
Flight Lieutenant E W Lamb		01 Jun 50 – 01 Jun 52
Squadron Leader J E Loxton		01 Jun 52 – 12 Jan 56
Squadron Leader W T Bussey, LVO, BEM		21 Nov 55 – 8 May 61
Squadron Leader E W Lamb, MVO		24 Apr 61 – 16 Mar 63
Squadron Leader E E Lake		28 Jan 63 – 10 Sep 66
Squadron Leader A Lloyd		10 Sep 66 – 18 Sep 67
Squadron Leader M W Hermon	(D)	09 Sep 67 – 7 Dec 67
Squadron Leader J Marshall		18 Dec 67 – 12 Oct 70
Squadron Leader M C Darby		26 Oct 70 – 15 Mar 73
Squadron Leader J W Mair		18 Dec 72 – 26 Apr 76
Squadron Leader M G Bartlett		08 Mar 76 – 24 Mar 80
Squadron Leader C M Gerig, MVO		10 Mar 80 – 14 Oct 83
Squadron Leader R C T Bent		15 Oct 83 – 04 Feb 87
Squadron Leader P B Akehurst, LVO (promoted Wg. Cdr. 01 Jan 90)		05 Feb 87 – 8 Jul 91
Squadron Leader D A Whittaker		08 Jul 91 – 20 Feb 95

Appendix 4: Personnel Carrying Out 500, 1000, 1500 & 2000 Royal Flights

Key: P Pilot   N Navigator   H Helicopter   FW Fixed Wing C Crew Chief   AS Air Steward S Security

No:	Name	Key	Key	Dates Served	No.Flts.
01	Squadron Leader R M Kerr, LVO AFC	P	H	22 Feb 1960 – 01 July 1976	500
02	Squadron Leader R M Lee, MVO DFC	N	H	16 Feb 1959 – 10 Oct 1966 05 Jan 1968 – 31 Jan 1978	1000
03	Squadron Leader R E Mitchie, LVO MBE	N	FW	03 July 61 – 31 July 1973	500
04	Squadron Leader H G Sealey, LVO	N	FW	09 Apr 62 – 08 May 1976	500
05	Squadron Leader T A Jackson, MVO AFC	P	FW	02 Jan 61 – 15 May 1972	500
06	Squadron Leader P G Fearn, LVO	N	FW	31 Oct 58 – 09 August 1972	500
07	Squadron Leader J. Millar, MVO AFC	P	H	07 July 1969 – 09 Aug 1977	500
08	Sergeant R H Harris, RVM	C	FW	01 Jun 1971 – 14 Sep 1977	500
09	Squadron Leader D J James, MVO	N	H	18 Feb 1975 – 27 Feb 1993	2000
10	Squadron Leader G H Williams	P	FW	01 Aug 1973 – 31 Mar 1995	2000
11	Squadron Leader D. Lovett, LVO	P	FW	01 Mar 1972 – 01 Sep 1981	500
12	Squadron Leader W B Sowerby, MVO	N	FW	03 Jan 1972 – 11 Nov 1985	1000
13	Squadron Leader M J Hawes, LVO	N	FW	23 July 1973 – 18 Oct 1992	1000
14	Squadron Leader D Hurley, LVO AFC	P	H	15 Dec 1975 – 30 Nov 1988	1000
15	Squadron Leader M I S Anderson, MVO	N	FW	01 Dec 1975 – 23 Apr 1992	1500
16	Squadron Leader B J Crawford, MVO	N	H	26 July 1977 – 13 Mar 1992	1500
17	Chf. Tech. A Hogan, RVM	C	H	24 Apr 1976 – 17 August 1987	500
18	Squadron Leader D J Rowe, LVO	P	FW	01 Apr 1975 – 12 Mar 1992	1500
19	Flight Lieutenant A R Bennett, MVO	N	H	04 Sep 1978 – 20 May 1985	500
20	WO K Broddle, MVO	S	-	03 Mar 1975 – 15 Jun 1985	500
21	FS J B Buck, RVM	S	-	01 Apr 1981 – 01 Jan 1988	500
22	Squadron Leader G H Laurie, MVO	P	FW	01 Jun 1981 – 31 Mar 1995	1500
23	Squadron Leader R H Stanton, MVO	N	FW	21 Sep 1980 – 31 Mar 1995	1000
24	MALM P R Stokes, RVM	AS	FW	12 Sep 1983 – 01 Mar 1989	500
25	Sergeant T J Griffiths	AS	FW	02 Jun 1982 – 24 Apr 1989	500
26	Chf. Tech. T M Fry	C	FW	02 May 1978 – 05 Apr 1988	500
27	Sergeant S J Giles	AS	FW	15 Jun 1983 – 25 Mar 1991 09 May 1994 – 31 Mar 1995	1000
28	Squadron Leader D L Mooney, MVO	N	H	25 Mar 1985 – 21 Dec 1990	500
29	Chf. Tech. A R Bird, RVM	C	H	03 Dec 1979 – 31 Mar 1995	500
30	Squadron Leader R F King	P	H	21 Apr 1986 – 31 Mar 1995	1000
31	Squadron Leader A H Guttridge, MBE	N	FW	02 Sep 1985 – 31 Mar 1995	1000
32	Sergeant S D Collins	AS	FW	03 Nov 1986 – 10 July 1991	500
33	Lt. Cdr. C W Pittaway, MVO. RN.	P	H	08 Jun 1987 – 04 Oct 1991	500
34	Flight Lieutenant R P Austin	P	FW	28 Sep 1987 – 06 Jan 1992	500
35	Squadron Leader T E Duggan	P	H	05 July 1988 – 31 Mar 1995	500
36	Chf. Tech. P Woods	C	H	30 Jun 1086 – 06 Jan 1992	500
37	Sergeant A House	AS	FW	20 Feb 1989 – 09 Feb 1994	500
38	FS J N Maggs	S	FW	01 Sep 1987 – 01 Sep 1993	500
39	Squadron Leader R M Shields, MVO	N	FW	06 Dec 1982 – 31 Mar 1995	1000
40	Squadron Leader J D Marshall	P	FW	29 Mar 1974 – 28 Nov 1976 20 Aug 1990 – 31 Mar 1995	500
41	Sergeant M D Millward	C	FW	01 Mar 1984 – 22 Jun 1994	500
42	Sergeant N P McGlynn	AS	FW	04 Feb 1991 – 31 Mar 1995	500
43	Sergeant D E Wright	AS	FW	03 Sep 1990 – 31 Mar 1995	500
44	Chf. Tech. R Lawtey	C	FW	02 Sep 1985 – 31 Mar 1995	500
45	Flight Lieutenant N P K Tredray	N	H	03 Sep 1990 – 31 Mar 1995	500